How Not to Kill Yourself

How Not to Kill Yourself

A PORTRAIT OF THE SUICIDAL MIND

CLANCY MARTIN

Pantheon Books

NEW YORK

Grateful acknowledgment is made to the following for permission to reprint
previously published material:

HarperCollins Publishers: Excerpt from "Suicide Note" from *The Complete Poems*
by Anne Sexton. Copyright © 1981 by Linda Gray Sexton and Loring
Conant, Jr., executors of the will of Anne Sexton. Foreword copyright © 1981
by Maxine Kumin. Reprinted by permission of HarperCollins Publishers.

Harvard University Press: Excerpt from *The Poems of Emily Dickinson*,
edited by Thomas H. Johnson, Cambridge, Mass.: The Belknap Press of Harvard
University Press. Copyright © 1951, 1955 by the President and
Fellows of Harvard College. Copyright © renewed 1979, 1983 by the
President and Fellows of Harvard College. Copyright © 1914, 1918, 1919, 1924,
1929, 1930, 1932, 1935, 1937, 1942 by Martha Dickinson Bianchi.
Copyright © 1952, 1957, 1958, 1963, 1965 by Mary L. Hampson.
Used by permission. All rights reserved.

Portions of this work originally appeared, in slightly different form, in the following
publications: Chapters 4 and 5 in *Harper's Magazine;* Chapter 8
and a portion of Chapters 1 and 10 in *Highline/The Huffington Post* and in *Epic;*
and Chapter 9 in *The Believer.*

Library of Congress Cataloging-in-Publication Data
Name: Martin, Clancy W., author.
Title: How not to kill yourself : a portrait of the suicidal mind / Clancy Martin.
Description: New York : Pantheon Books, 2023. Includes index.
Identifiers: LCCN 2022036118 (print). LCCN 2022036119 (ebook).
ISBN 9780593317051 (hardcover). ISBN 9780593317068 (ebook).
Subjects: LCSH: Suicide—Psychological aspects. Suicide—Prevention.
Classification: LCC HV6545 .M275 2023 (print) | LCC HV6545 (ebook) | DDC
362.28—dc23/eng/20220805
LC record available at https://lccn.loc.gov/2022036118
LC ebook record available at https://lccn.loc.gov/2022036119

www.pantheonbooks.com

Jacket photographs by Kent Rogowski
Jacket design by Kelly Blair

Printed in the United States of America
First Edition
2 4 6 8 9 7 5 3 1

For Amie and my children

That is what chills your spine when you read an account of a suicide: not the frail corpse hanging from the window bars but what happened inside that heart immediately before.

—SIMONE DE BEAUVOIR

When I'm alone, I realize I'm with the person who tried to kill me.

—JOHN MULANEY

Contents

PART III

THE LONG ROAD BACK

A Note to the Reader

I wrote this book especially for the people like me—many of whom I have come to know over the past thirty years—who have attempted suicide and failed, and who still struggle with the desire to kill themselves. I also hope to speak to people who have suicidal thoughts or may be considering an attempt, and to the many people whose lives have been drastically changed because of the self-inflicted death of a loved one. I hope that anyone who in some way orbits the dark sun of suicide may be helped, a bit, by reading about my own attempts, my failures and successes, to live with that gravitational pull.

That said, if you're in serious crisis right now, if you're reading this and thinking of doing it, please turn to Appendix I, "Tools for Crisis," where I list some resources that can immediately help. If you're having a bad time but feel like you can read something a bit longer, please page through the interviews in Appendix II, "In Case of Emergency: Interviews on Staying Alive," and perhaps also Chapter 11, "A Good Death?" where I discuss some of my own strategies for surviving rough times. Naturally, my aspiration is that you will read the whole book and that it will encourage you to keep on going, even when things feel hopeless.

Preface

The last time I tried to kill myself was in my basement with a dog leash. As usual, I didn't write a note. I carried down a green leather and wood chair from my office while my dog watched from the stairs. She's afraid of the basement. I took the heavy blue canvas leash, looped it over a beam, made a noose by snaking the leash through the handle, latched it, and checked it for strength. I stood on the green chair and put the noose around my neck. Then I kicked the chair away like the gentle old institutionalized suicide Brooks Hatlen does toward the end of *The Shawshank Redemption*. I hung there, kicking. But I wasn't dying, I was just in terrible pain. Hanging yourself really hurts. I had forgotten that, though I'd tried it before, because I'd recently spent some time reading about people hanging themselves, and it sounded so easy. Other people manage to do it from a doorknob sitting down. I started to panic, I resisted the panic, I panicked some more, and in a moment that I can't exactly recall, I lifted myself up and got out of the leash. I dropped to the floor and lay there on the dusty concrete for a while. I still haven't moved that chair back upstairs. It's too spooky, and I don't want it in our house.

Later that day I spoke to my wife on the phone—she was away on a trip—and she asked me what was wrong with my voice.

"I have a sore throat."

"Make yourself some ginger and honey tea," she said. "It sounds like you're coming down with something."

"Uh-huh," I said.

My throat hurt for another week, and several of my students asked me what I had done to my neck. The bruising was flagrant. I told them "Oh, it looks worse than it is," and avoided the question.

I probably could have told them the truth. But it's one thing to write about suicide and your suicide attempts and have those readily available to your students on the internet—students do google their professors—and quite another to look a student in the eye, with the black and blue evidence on display, and say, "Oh, I tried to hang myself a couple of days ago." Even if there were no professional consequences (and I suspect there may have been), I'd worry about laying that kind of weight on the minds of young people, and also about the possibility that it might encourage one of them who might already be suffering from depression or having suicidal thoughts to make a bad choice.

I've lived nearly all my life with two incompatible ideas in my head: *I wish I were dead* and *I'm glad my suicides failed.* I've never once thought, *If only I'd successfully killed myself, I would have been spared all this living I've done.* And yet when I'm feeling like my life has been a complete waste, my first thought is *Okay then, go kill yourself now.* Or rather, I tend to think along very concrete lines, such as *I'd better just hang myself, because I don't have any poison, and if I order some, I'll have lost my nerve by the time it gets here. And it's important that I do this right now, while my thinking is clear.* (Which shows you how confused I actually am.) In that moment when I am so convinced that killing myself is the right thing to do, I am as certain that I am finally admitting the truth to myself as one feels one knows, irrefutably, when very angry: now, at last, I can finally say what I actually always wanted and needed to say. Later, when calm, it's clear this angry certainty did not necessarily reflect the truth at all.

Of course, I'm not always struggling with suicidal thoughts. As I write this sentence in the winter of 2022, for example, I don't want to take my own life, and I'm grateful that I'm here. But in a way, gratitude misses the point. You can be grateful for something and still not be up to the task.

And if and when the thought should return—*Yes, do it, kill yourself,* or simply, *Come on now, it's time, you're too tired, end it all, get it over with*—I'll still be glad that I was previously unsuccessful, because all those failed attempts predate good things that have happened since then, including most important, the births of my children.

I realize how bizarre it sounds to be simultaneously thinking that I have to finally kill myself while also knowing it was lucky that my previous attempts had failed. If my prior lack of success allowed me to go on living and create and experience good things as a result, shouldn't that logic hold true moving forward? Can't I learn that giving in to this impulse is a mistake? Maybe I am learning, slowly. But in the moment I'm gripped by the desire to die, I don't believe more good things are coming down the road. More to the point, regardless of what the future may offer, I'm convinced my still being here will only make matters worse.

Holding two incompatible thoughts in one's head in this way is not so unusual, really: we often call it cognitive dissonance; it's the essence of self-deception; and it is an example of one of the many varieties of deep irrationality that make human beings the extremely interesting creatures we are. "Do I contradict myself? / Very well then, I contradict myself / (I am large, I contain multitudes)." Walt Whitman's famous observation applies not only to life-affirming thoughts but to self-destructive ones as well.

Being divorced with children is an easy example of how this kind of thinking works. I regret my two divorces and feel a great deal of shame about them. If I could, I would go back and correct my mistakes and be a better husband. But at the same time, I am grateful to have been married to all three of my partners, and especially for the children who came from those marriages. If I hadn't divorced my first wife and subsequently remarried, I wouldn't have my daughters Margaret and Portia. And if I hadn't divorced my second wife, I wouldn't be married to my wonderful wife Amie or be father to Ratna and Kali. Amie and my five children are my main reason for living. Often they feel like my only good reason.

Today I'm glad I am alive. I am thankful that, try as I might, I've never succeeded in killing myself. And that's one of the reasons I wrote this book: I believe that for the vast majority of people, suicide is a bad choice.

I deeply understand the desire to kill oneself. Not merely wanting to die but wanting actively to take my own life is among my earliest memories. And while the impulse ebbs and flows, there have been few days in my life, and definitely no weeks, when I haven't been overwhelmed by existence and thought about ending it. Multiple times I have tried to kill myself and failed. (I'm a comical figure in the history of suicide, a perennial fuckup who seems to always get lucky and keep on going.)

I'm not alone in this. I have lots of friends who have daily suicidal ideation, and who have attempted to kill themselves, many more than once. This is another reason I wrote this book. There are certain secrets about killing oneself that are only known to those of us *symparanekromenoi* for whom the thought of suicide is familiar, especially to those of us who have tried to kill ourselves and failed, perhaps repeatedly. Anne Sexton tells a few of these secrets in her famous poem "Suicide Note":

> *I could admit*
> *That I am only a coward*
> *Crying me me me*
> *And not mention the little gnats, the moths,*
> *Forced by circumstance*
> *To suck on the electric bulb.*

What is Sexton confiding here? First, that yes, there is some truth to what people say, that the suicide is a coward and that, more important, she considers herself a coward, and she wishes she were one of these brave hearts who could carry on marching despite the pain and discouragement and countless obstacles of life. She also confesses the connection between her cowardice, her suicide, and her vanity, with the "me me me," when every suicide knows that she will be reproached for being selfish, because the life we have does not belong to us alone but also consists of our obligations to others. "Me me me" is a terrible and humiliating thing to say, think, or feel, yet there it is, a voice that is loud in the experience of living for everyone—who hasn't fearfully or defiantly thought, *Well, if I don't look out for me, who will?*—and is screaming in your ear when you are deciding to end your life. The "me me me" makes the act possible—how could I kill myself if I were really only thinking about you?—and is also the thing we are trying to escape once and for all. Finally Sexton is also insisting that—and I will have more to say about this—it's not just cowardice and selfishness but also what Freud (following Schopenhauer) called the death drive, the very basic and primitive need to "suck on the electric bulb."

Sexton, who took her own life one month shy of her forty-sixth birthday, reveals a great deal about the desire to die in her poetry, and certainly her work should be recommended to anyone who wrestles with the desire to die. But her poems should probably be read only by someone who is feeling pretty steady on her feet, suicide-wise, because in the honesty and despair of Sexton's writing, there is also a kind of romanticization of suicide that is dangerous for a vulnerable person to encounter. If one of my students shared with me that they'd been struggling with thoughts of self-harm and asked if there were any books I could recommend, I have a few different ones I might (there is also quite a bit more I would want to talk about with this student, naturally), but one writer I would absolutely not steer them toward is Anne Sexton. Nor would I suggest Édouard Levé, David Foster Wallace, or Nelly Arcan: these writers, as we'll discuss later, knew about suicide, wrote about it in intimate detail, and ultimately killed themselves.

I'm always relieved and grateful when people bravely come to talk to me about suicide. It's a tough topic, a taboo one even today, and most people are reluctant to discuss it. Alcohol and drug addiction used to be this way and in some ways still are (thus the *anonymous* aspect of AA and NA). Depression and other forms of mental illness used to be this way and in some ways still are (thus the justified celebration, for example, when world champion gymnast Simone Biles talked openly about her struggles with mental illness). It wasn't so long ago that admitting to being gay was also taboo, strange though that may seem to us now (and, depending upon your cultural context, perhaps still is). A close friend's son recently took his own life, and even I have trouble talking to her about it despite having spent thirteen years reading and writing about suicide, and the last few years writing this book.

But suicide is all around us, and we must talk about it. And the truth is we all know something about suicide, if we are willing to be honest with ourselves. I used to tell my students that if we had a switch on our bellies that we could flip to end our lives, no one would make it to age eighteen. That's why it's particularly important for me to be as honest with you as I can about my own desire and attempts to kill myself. If I'm bullshitting you, you'll smell it. Because *of course* on some level it must be easier not to live. It doesn't help matters that the most negative emotions are also the most sure of themselves. Happiness and security are notoriously tentative and fragile states. But anger, depression, fear: what could feel more certain? (Yet this is of course mistaken: emotions, like thoughts, come and go.) Life is just so fucking hard so much of the time. Many of us have moments of panic. And we all get tired.

Which brings me to the main reason I wrote this book: to sincerely and accurately convey what it's like to want to kill yourself, sometimes on a daily basis, yet to go on living, and to show my own particular good reasons for doing so. Since I began talking and writing about this subject more than a decade ago, I've had numerous interactions with people who identified with my darkest feelings of self-loathing and despair and told me that hearing my story helped them.

Realizing that you are not alone with these feelings does something important. You start to understand that you're not a broken person, you're not the one fuckup in a world of smooth successes. Knowing others feel this way—and realizing it's okay to feel that way—helps us to understand that maybe there's nothing wrong with us. It's often the very thought that there's something wrong with us that threatens to push us off the edge.

There is a group called Suicide Anonymous, and I encourage anyone who is reading this and feeling suicidal to attend one of their meetings. (They have Zoom sessions.) Similarly, suicide help lines and, more recently, online chats are available. But in my personal experience this kind of assistance isn't as compelling as one might hope. I myself don't want to call an anonymous help line—particularly since they're not as anonymous as they'd like you to think, which is part of the problem, because they can and will send the cops to your house if they think there is cause. (I'm only speaking for myself, here: suicide help lines save lives every day, and they are an indispensable resource in our collective attempts to help people who are in danger.)

I also don't want to chat with a stranger or group of relative strangers about my desire to kill myself while the urge is actually pressing. What I can do, and have done, is read something that will either help the impulse to pass on that particular day or, better yet, help me to pause and even start to rethink the appeal of killing myself. I don't expect my suicidal thoughts to ever go away, though I'm happy to report that they may be diminishing. But I do believe that my attitude toward those thoughts can change, that they can feel both less appealing and less insistent—and indeed my attitude toward suicide has changed, in part through writing about it, but mostly through my exchanges with other people who are or have been suicidal.

Suppose a friend comes to you and says, "I've bought a gun, I've decided to shoot myself in the head later today." (The friend is not suffering from some incurable disease and seems otherwise like her ordinary self.) Is there any situation in which you would agree that that's a good idea?

Of course not. When someone else is thinking this way, the fact that suicide is a bad idea is clear and obvious. And yet when we ourselves are thinking in this way, we're somehow incapable of seeing the conspicuous truth that suicide is not the best solution to our problems. Ken Baldwin survived a suicide attempt by leaping off the Golden Gate Bridge, then later famously remarked that, immediately after leaping, "I realized that everything in my life that I'd thought was unfixable was totally fixable—except for having just jumped." Or as Joel Rose said of his friend Anthony Bourdain, not long after he died, "I've always had, since it happened, this overwhelming feeling that he committed himself to this, the act of taking his own life, and then said, 'Oh fuck, what have I done?'"

It's my hope as well that this frank accounting of a chronically suicidal person may help those who have or have had such a person in their lives to be gentler both with that person and with themselves. When we think and talk about suicide, we should try to do so tenderly.

The first person I knew who killed himself was my stepbrother Paul, who jumped off a building when I was six years old. When I asked my mom about Paul's suicide, she sent me this text:

> The year was 1974, I of course remember the day, Paul seemed happy, kind of at peace, he had an appointment with his psychiatrist that morning, he did not make it, jumped from the top of that office building.

Paul was twenty-one when he died and had been living with us in my childhood home. He was a 1970s hippie, spending a lot of time traveling between Vancouver and Calgary, where we lived, and he made us, his younger brothers and sisters (eight of us kids were living in the house at that time), bracelets and necklaces out of beautiful multicolored glass beads. Selling jewelry on the street was how he made his traveling money when he wasn't at home.

Since then I've known many people who killed themselves—as most of us do, once we reach a certain age—and I know what it's like to beat yourself up because you didn't somehow manage to prevent their deaths. And while I believe there are things we can do and say to help someone we care for who may be struggling with the urge to kill themselves—another reason I wrote this book—I don't think blaming yourself after the fact is one of those things, so I'm hoping insights into suicidal ideation may help people to avoid that.

My own relationship with my desire to kill myself can be divided into roughly three phases. I hasten to add that I don't think there are strict dividing lines between these three phases of my life or stages of suicidal thinking: they blend into each other in various ways, and sometimes fifty-four-year-old Clancy's fantasy of ending his life doesn't seem very far removed at all from the seven-year-old's.

When I was a child and a young man, I believed that killing myself would eliminate "me" as I was. I think of this as the "Suicidally Inclined" stage of my life. I oscillated between being "half in love with easeful Death," as Keats put it, and feeling desperation somehow to change my life and the failure I believed myself to be. To my mind, for much of this time, if suicide would not simply end my life, it would transform my existence so radically that I would no longer recognizably be the me I knew and suffered from. (I would go to heaven, say, or perhaps be reborn as someone else.) This phase came to a close with my first divorce, a radical career change, and the death of my dad—likely by suicide, though I don't know for sure (more on this later).

Then there were the suicide attempts I made once I was in the depths of my addiction to alcohol, with all my secret drinking and quitting booze and relapsing into hitting the bar every day again, and also the vicious depression that accompanied my battle with the bottle, which was especially bad the first three years of my sobriety. I think of this as the "Crisis" stage of my suicidal life. The theme and dominant psychological experience of these years was escape. Certainly, alcohol was part of that escape. But what provides a more absolute guarantee of escape than suicide? I survived this stage in my life through sheer dumb luck. It not surprisingly ended with my second divorce and a dramatic change in my way of living.

Then there are the two suicide attempts I've made since that time, one of which I described at the opening of this prologue, and which to my mind are quite akin to the relapses suffered by an addict. I think of this, somewhat tongue in cheek, as the "Recovery" stage of my suicidal life. Suicide now seems attractive to me in moments of despair. This despair comes with exhaustion, a feeling that I can't go on, a psychological surrender to my own worst instincts. When I run out of energy, I fall back into old ways of thinking. "Relapse is part of recovery" is one of

AA's trusted maxims, and I have found this to be true of drinking, of suicide, and also of much less obviously self-destructive behaviors, such as losing my temper or overspending.

This last period of my life, which is about a decade old as of this writing, has been increasingly characterized by a shift of my priorities away from professional success and what I used to think of as "having fun" to the attempt to be a good partner, father, and friend. I've also finally developed an educated respect for the physiology of good mental health: in my own case, remembering to pay close attention to such simple things as the food I eat, the physical exercise I do, the time I spend outside in the sunshine, and the sleep I get. The stage I'm in now has also been characterized by the dawning suspicion that suicide might not change much for me, mentally speaking (that is, I increasingly believe that a version of my mind will persist after the death of my body), though it would likely make things much worse for me and would profoundly hurt the people I love. Violence, especially violence done in anger, fear, and despair, seems always to make things worse for everyone it touches.

Accordingly, I've divided the book into three sections, which correspond to these three periods in my life. The first section addresses how we become suicidal. The second shows what a person in crisis looks like. And the third addresses how we might potentially move beyond the need to kill ourselves. In each of these sections, I discuss my own personal experience, sometimes the experience of other suicidal people, and some philosophical arguments that are well suited to or reflective of the thinking that I was experiencing at that time. I also look at the work of several writers who died by suicide. These writers provide some of the keenest insights we have into the mind of a suicidal person because they left a record of their own thinking in their books, stories, and journals.

Telling my story has helped me to develop a thesis about suicidal thinking more generally. I believe that the drive to self-annihilation is one that we all share. It expresses itself in many different ways: in attempts to escape yourself and avoid your problems, by overwork or Instagram scrolling or buying things or staying in expensive hotels; obviously, in addiction and related extreme behaviors; and in the thought, desire, or attempt to kill oneself. The drive to self-annihilation—the death drive—might be as primitive and fundamental to our psychology as the sex drive. We are all very happy to admit to and even celebrate, brag about, or fiercely defend our sex drives; but the death drive— that's a very different matter. As complicated as sex is, on a fundamental level we largely feel good about it and aren't embarrassed to admit we want it. But death? If only we could make the claim that yes, it's part of life. After all, living is dying, and every day you're one step closer. It's inevitable, and we have to come to terms with it. It's as natural to us as sex.

But just as there are justifiable and unjustifiable thoughts and actions when it comes to sex, so too with death. As Nietzsche observed, a thought comes when *it* will, not when *I* will. Nevertheless we have the ability to influence, cultivate, and train our thoughts. And obviously they don't all turn into things we say, thank goodness, and even more happily they don't all become things we do. You can have a thought and chase it away; you can have a thought and simply watch it come and go; you can have a thought and cling to it and encourage related thoughts.

You can get addicted to the thought of suicide, just as surely as you can get addicted to the thought that drinking a glass or two of Beaujolais will make everything seem a little easier, just as you can get addicted to sexual thoughts or thoughts about buying stuff or the importance of status or likes on an Instagram feed. I have come to understand that I am addicted to the thought of suicide and that lately I am what we might call a recovering suicide addict. As with all addiction, the question of nature or nurture will always be complex and difficult to resolve. Was I born an alcoholic, or did I become one through a series of bad choices? Were suicidal thoughts thrust upon me, or did I have them and then somehow come to nurture or rely on them and thus encourage their growth into action? Some people believe that suicide, like alcohol use disorder (what we used to call alcoholism), is a physical disease. Others think that killing oneself, like drug and alcohol addiction, is the consequence of bad choices and a weak will—in short, a kind of moral failure. Still others, like me, believe that a predisposition to certain thoughts combined with free will tie us into the knots of addiction, and the free cultivation of new ways of thinking may help us untangle ourselves, or even to cut the knot entirely.

The first job is to understand what the bad patterns of thought are and how they came to be. For me, being too dogmatic about my beliefs has often led to feelings of helplessness and anguish. When the world refuses to conform to the way I insist it ought to be, or more often, when I fail to live up to some standard I've set for myself, I freak out and go into fight-or-flight thinking, which in my experience is the seed around which the crystal of a suicide attempt can form. So in these past few years, I've been trying to be less sure of myself, less confident about what I think I know. I want to have a more supple, a less rigid personality.

As best I am able, I will tell you my story about suicide, my suicide attempts, and especially the details of my suicidal thinking. I believe that in the end it's a fundamentally life-affirming story. My fifth child was born on December 17, 2021, during the omicron stage of the Covid-19 pandemic—as I write these words, she's a few days more than a month old—and I don't remember ever feeling less inclined to kill myself than I do this morning. Right now the thought of hanging myself from one of the cedar beams in our garage seems almost ridiculous. But I also know it won't always seem that way—as with depression, these thoughts and feelings do return, unexpectedly, unpredictably, and aggressively—and I hope that when they do, I can notice them and let them go. As I like to tell people who come to me in crisis, if it ever gets so bad that I simply can't take it anymore, I can always just kill myself tomorrow.

PART I

SUICIDAL TENDENCIES

"Isn't there someone kind enough to come
and strangle me in my sleep?"

— RYŪNOSOKE AKUTAGAWA

The Suicidal Mind

"You know what's funny? Your jail anklet saved your life. They should put that in an advertisement. They should get a testimonial from you. If it weren't for that anklet, you'd be dead right now."

I came to in a hospital bed with a sore head. I reached into my hair and felt the staples in my scalp. A handsome young dark-haired doctor with a bushy moustache and brightly lit, amused eyes was standing at the side of my bed conversing cheerfully with me. I didn't know how long he'd been talking or if I had been talking back. I seemed to be joining the conversation midstream. But that might have been his manner: perhaps he simply launched into conversation with his patients and let them catch up when they were ready. I was very thirsty, and still nervously fingering those metal staples, I reached with my free hand for the large plastic cup of water on the bedside table. Then I realized that I was handcuffed to the bed.

"Here, let me get it for you." He tucked the bottle between the bed rail and the pillow and bent the plastic straw into my mouth. I drank the water and then spat out the straw. My throat was burning.

"Did I have an operation?" I asked.

"No, you were very lucky. Two minor procedures." He reached over to gesture at my head, where my staples and my fingers were. "You must have fallen at some point. Your head was bleeding. Quite a nasty cut. You have a mild concussion. You'll probably be experiencing some dizziness and nausea."

This was my second concussion in less than a year. Seven months before, I'd fallen down some stairs while drunk and had staples on the other side of my head. I couldn't remember either accident. I remembered taking all the Valium and getting the knife, climbing into the clawfoot bathtub, and keeping my leg hanging out, bent at the knee. I remembered having trouble juggling a glass of wine, the knife, and my phone. I remembered being at Davey's Uptown Rambler's Club before coming home and resolving to kill myself that night. But I didn't remember how I got back from the bar.

"My throat hurts more than my head. My voice," I said. "I sound awful. I don't feel sick."

"We had to pump your stomach, but basically you're fine. I'm sorry we have to shackle you. They will transfer you to the psychiatric ward tomorrow, and then this security won't be necessary. You ruined your fancy anklet." He laughed. He was a very likable doctor. "It seems to have short-circuited. But not before it sent off its alarm. Modern technology."

I wanted to explain about the anklet, that it wasn't a court-ordered thing, it was something I was trying on my own to keep myself sober, but I realized that any extra details from me would sound defensive and anyway were superfluous.

Some years later a good friend, a famous scholar of ancient languages, would tell me, "You know lots of people think that a suicide attempt is just a cry for help. A way to get attention. I know that's not true, because when I woke up in the hospital and realized I was still alive, I was gutted." That was how I felt: depressed, very disappointed and even more disgusted with myself. Not sad that I'd tried suicide again but miserable that I'd once again failed.

"Next time, don't get in the bath. Better yet, don't have a next time, would you? We'd like to keep you around. And if you want to kill yourself, don't use pills. Nobody dies from overdosing on pills anymore." Bizarrely, he discoursed for a minute or two on how best to kill oneself. "There's even a book you can buy that tells you how."

I knew the book he meant. It's called *Final Exit*. I don't recommend it.

"But you know, you were very lucky, and most people wise up after one attempt. So maybe this can be your get-out-of-jail-free card. That's how I'd approach it. You take care. Try to behave yourself. Things will get better."

He grabbed my foot, shook it gently, even affectionately, shrugged, and left the room.

I thought, *Well, that was actually kind of nice.* It was a much more pleasant encounter than you'd expect with a doctor after you'd attempted suicide. That guy ought to be training others on how to deal with people in my situation.

I had an IV in my arm. There was a phone by the bed, but I couldn't reach it, because it was on the handcuffed side. I had a nurse alert button by my hand, but I didn't want to beep a nurse to help me make a phone call.

"Three weeks ago I was in bed at home with my girlfriend," I said out loud, theatrically, to the empty hospital room. "Three weeks ago everything was normal."

But that wasn't the truth. My life had been abnormal for a long time.

They woke me up in the middle of the night to transfer me to Research Psychiatric. It was quiet in the ward: everyone was asleep. In 2009, 2010, and 2011, the three worst years of my adulthood, I had extraordinarily vivid dreams, and I loved to dream, because I often dreamed of my daughters and other good things that were no longer real in my waking everyday life. At this point, I was separated from my wife, who wasn't allowing me to see our children. I was kicked out of the house and living in a grubby little apartment that a friend described as "the kind of place where you expected Charles Bukowski to die." I was avoiding my colleagues who knew I was falling apart when they saw me and tended to regard me with pity or anger. One of them even said to me quite bluntly, "You look like shit, and you haven't been doing your job."

This particular suicide attempt was in the winter of 2011.

"Can't we go in the morning?" I asked the paramedics, who were taking me to the psychiatric hospital.

They took the handcuffs off my wrist but stood next to me as I got out of bed.

"We don't decide when you get transferred. Your ambulance is here. You're going to the mental health ward."

"Why an ambulance?" I asked, downstairs at the doors. "Can't we just take a car?"

The fact was it was within walking distance. Less than two blocks. It's all on the same hospital campus.

"It's a liability thing. You'll get a bill for it. You're not going to try to run on us, right?" the EMT said. I was in my hospital robe and slippers, shivering. It was very cold outside, where the ambulance was waiting. They wrapped a padded-vinyl silver blanket around me. I was hot immediately.

The field beyond the parking lot was covered in snow. The stars were bright. I thought, *That's what I'd like to be.* As far away and as indifferent as the night sky.

"Run where?"

"You can sit up here with us," the other EMT said. "It's not strictly according to regulations, but what the hell."

It was a bench seat, and I sat in the middle, between the driver and his partner.

"It's like *Bringing Out the Dead*," I said. "Did you guys ever see that movie?"

"Unh-unh," the driver said. He had a beard and looked about twenty years old.

The other one said, "I think I saw it."

"If you saw it, you'd remember," I said. "It's about an ambulance driver."

"Nicolas Cage. And he sees ghosts, right?" the driver said.

"That's it. You did see it." I paused for a second. We were pulling up to the psychiatric building. "You guys ever see any ghosts?"

I believe in ghosts, and I think suicidal people can see into the world of ghosts in a way that sturdier folks cannot. The great writer and sometime suicide attempter Yiyun Li observes, "I have always believed that, between living and dying, from being to being no longer, there are secrets understood by those nearer death." And the Canadian physician and addiction expert Gabor Maté describes alcoholics like me as living "in the realm of hungry ghosts," people who have become ghosts while still alive. For my part, I think you can almost see when a deeply addicted person, who is killing himself with his drug of choice, is making the transition into the ghost lands. Chronic suicide attempters also tend to have that shadow across them.

"Not Scorsese's best," the driver said, ignoring or avoiding my question. "I always thought *GoodFellas* was his real masterpiece."

"Or *Raging Bull*," I said. "That's one of the saddest movies ever made." I was thinking about my father, who had briefly been a professional boxer and who—like the boxer the movie is based on, Jake LaMotta—had a tragic, doomed quality to his later years.

"I've seen a couple of ghosts," the guy on my right said. "People see them. It's a real thing. My aunt once had a ghost ask if it could kiss her. A female ghost."

"No one wants to hear that BS," the driver said briskly, interrupting his buddy. "We're here. At the *psychiatric* hospital," he said, giving the ghost guy a pointed look.

At Research Psychiatric Hospital, in a tiny claustrophobic office just off the main waiting room—it was, I'd guess, four or five in the morning—a slender, pale thirty-something intake nurse asked me the standard questions: "Are you feeling suicidal right now? Are you having suicidal thoughts?"

I don't know why, but I was honest with her. Maybe I was still high from the Benadryl they'd given me at the hospital to keep me calm, or maybe I was at the end of my rope.

"Well. Glad you ask. If you leave me alone in here, I will slash my wrists with your scissors. I will hang myself with the blinds. I will electrocute myself with a fucking fork. Yes. What do you think?"

"If you're feeling violent . . . are you threatening me? Are you thinking of attacking me?" She picked up the phone. Her hands were thick, strong-looking, and her fingernails were cut short and impeccably clean. She had a no-nonsense expression and an all-American appearance, with glossy, nicely brushed brown hair. She was young and looked like she could have been one of my students. I regretted what I had said. She was just doing her job.

"No, I'm not feeling violent. I apologize. I'm not having suicidal thoughts."

I had momentarily forgotten to lie about what I was thinking. That's the cardinal rule of intensive psychiatric care, like the "deny, deny, deny" rule for adulterers. With psychiatrists, "lie, lie, lie" is the only way to survive, the only hope of ever getting out of there.

"I just want to sleep. I'm freezing. Are you cold? It's freezing in here."

I had the too-hot silver blanket from the EMTs, but it was cold in her office, and I was in the mood to complain. I was still in the hospital robe. I'd lost the slippers and was barefoot.

"I'm sorry about the temperature, sir, but I would appreciate it if you would try to use civil language with me. What have they done with your clothes?"

"I need some socks. I don't have any clothes. They found me in a bathtub."

"Oh, I see." This did not dismay or even surprise her. In fact, it seemed to reassure her, as if now we were making some progress. She typed it into her computer. "Well, there's a bed opening in the morning in the annex. I think you'll have to wait for a few hours here. We'll finish your paperwork, and you're welcome to take a nap in the waiting room if you like. I'll find you a real blanket. You should have someone bring you some clothes."

"Can I make a phone call? I'm sure I can have someone come right away. That would be really helpful, actually."

A white office phone sat on her desk. Her cell phone was beside it. "No. No, I'm afraid not."

Unlike when you're arrested, when they whisk you off to the madhouse, you have no guaranteed right to a phone call.

"Okay. I guess I'll wait in the waiting room."

She went to get me another blanket and locked the door behind me. She took her cellphone with her, and when I tried to dial an outside line on her desk phone, I couldn't get through. It requested a security code. I sat back down in my chair. Then I heard her at the door. She came into the room with an irritated, suspicious look.

"There's a camera right there," she said, pointing to the corner above her desk.

She handed me a red cotton blanket and some blue cotton slippers that looked as if another patient had left them behind. They were too fuzzy to be institutional slippers.

"You're going to have to wait in here."

I watched her close the door behind her and sit at her desk. I immediately regretted not having made a run for it when they were putting me in the ambulance. Those guys had been bigger than me and no doubt faster, but I could have found a place to hide. Dejected, I put the red blanket around my chest like a towel under the silver blanket so that I'd be more comfortable. And then, on impulse, I stood abruptly and tried the door. It was locked.

I startled her. She started to rise from her desk. "Do you need to go to the restroom?"

"Yes," I said. "Please."

Okay, this was my chance. As we left, we passed a few chairs in the little waiting room. A security guard was talking to a nurse or orderly who sat at a desk behind a counter with a sliding glass front, like in a doctor's office. The door out had a big metal push bar. It was a frozen Kansas City winter night outside, but if I were free, I would find opportunities. Something would present itself.

This was how I thought at that time. Everything was one second to the next. I truly couldn't conceive of tomorrow. Things just happened, and they were either good or bad, and I wanted to get away from the bad things and stumble into the good things. Or if there were no good things to discover, I wanted to commit suicide to get away altogether. It was kind of like the opposite of what William Blake and Søren Kierkegaard might have been talking about when they wrote about the bliss of immediacy in mystical experience. I had a kind of immediacy of despair, I suppose. Or I just couldn't bear to think more than a few minutes ahead, because I knew what was coming.

I twisted away from her and ran for the door.

She said, "Sir," and the security guard turned. But I was too quick for them. He didn't have time to get up.

I'd made it! Bang! Hit the metal bar! Dropped my blankets.

The door was locked. I pushed against it again with my whole body. For a moment, imagining liberty, I rested my forehead on the cold glass. Then I turned around, shrugged, and tried to pretend it was their fault. I picked my blankets back up.

I didn't think of it at the time, but this sudden wild attempt to escape from an unacceptable situation, only to be foiled, embarrassingly and ridiculously, at the moment of exit, had become the theme of my life.

"Why did you do that?"

"I'm sorry," I said, knowing I had betrayed her trust. Plus, I was stealing her slippers.

"Do you still need to use the restroom?"

She didn't say anything else about it. I expected some kind of formal reprimand or even a punishment or restraints. But she acted as if it hadn't happened. I supposed people must try to escape more often than you'd think.

"Yes, I need to use the bathroom," I said. I went to a door with a men/women/wheelchair sign on it and saw there was no lock. They had everything figured out. There was no air duct you might climb into like in a movie, just a sturdy-looking fluorescent light panel in the ceiling, and nothing I could use to take my life.

I sat on the toilet and cried. Then I stopped and looked in the mirror. They had a normal mirror, not a stainless steel one like you find in many institutional settings, and it was the one thing you might use to kill yourself with. I could smash it and slash my throat with a sliver of glass. If I'd been a different person, I could perhaps have used a shard to menace someone into an escape. But all my fight was exhausted by my useless dash for the door. I was defeated. And anyway, I doubted I could break the mirror if I tried.

In the mirror, in my great self-pity, I looked like I was about twelve years old. I wiped the tears off my face and for a moment relaxed the armor of irony about my ridiculous situation. I let myself feel very, very sorry for myself. My eyes were large and red, my face was pink from the cold, and I wanted my mom. My hair was freshly washed from my stitches, and my bangs were tousled and boyish. I was momentarily inspired and reassured by the childishness of my own desperation.

I thought, *What if it is the most cowardly, the softest—but hey, maybe also the gentlest, the most sensitive—yes, the weakest who kill themselves? Like a necessary genetic culling.* Then I thought, *But what if there is one kind even more faint-hearted and craven than those—the ones like me, who keep trying to kill themselves, but can't?*

About an hour later they finished my check-in, and I was lying on my bed in my windowless room, in the psychiatric ward I knew quite well. I was more or less ready for the routine to begin. I had been here before. I would be here again. Every time I tried to commit suicide in Kansas City, Missouri, if 911 got involved, as it generally did, this was where I wound up.

I'll finish this story later, when I'll discuss other suicide attempts in the second phase of my life, which were mostly wrapped up with my alcohol abuse. Before we get there, I want to talk about why people kill themselves, and examine my earlier suicidal thinking and attempts, to show how complicated and pervasive the desire to kill oneself can be.

In *The Sorrows of Young Werther* Goethe wrote, on the subject of suicide, "We can only discuss something honorably in so far as we sympathize with it." I want to discuss suicide in an honorable way.

In our contemporary culture, we have a fundamentally dishonorable relationship with suicide and, thus, how we talk about it. This isn't surprising. We've had a dishonorable relationship with suicide for centuries. At least since Saint Augustine came out against it in the fifth century (motivated in part by early Christian groups who believed that one could get into heaven more quickly by killing oneself while still sinless), an enormous variety of social and legal condemnations of suicide have dominated Western culture. Suicide was only very recently decriminalized in the United States, and it's still a crime in many countries. Moreover, any death by suicide reported in the news will skirt the fact of how the person died for reasons of privacy and public safety, which adds to our collective feeling that there's something shameful about this kind of death.

When we learn that someone died by suicide, we feel quite differently than when we learn of someone's death by old age, accident, or disease. It's typical to experience a whole range of complicated moral emotions and to start assigning blame: to the suicide herself, but also to friends and family, maybe to social conditions, or to poor mental health treatment, or to drug addiction or a host of other causes. A dear friend of mine committed suicide recently, alone in a hotel room, and many of our mutual friends were eager to blame his death on an accidental overdose of heroin, which apparently would have been a preferable cause of death to his deliberately taking his own life.

The truth is, Goethe got it exactly right: we don't speak of suicide honorably, because at some level we don't really sympathize with the person who kills herself. As the contemporary philosopher Shelly Kagan, among many others, has pointed out, even today "suicide is looked upon with . . . a mixture of disdain, fear and disapproval." Perhaps because we all experience suffering in some way and are free to take our own lives, yet choose to go on living, we judge others who've given up on life.

But I want to try here to speak honorably, respectfully, and sympathetically of people who have killed themselves or tried to kill themselves, including myself. That means coming to understand the choices I made when I attempted to kill myself, which means thinking through some very uncomfortable ideas, such as despair, terror, self-loathing, and death, and also being willing to ask myself some unpleasant questions.

To really sympathize with a person who has or has tried to kill herself isn't easy. We may be grieving, or angry, or frustrated, or worried about our own responsibility for her decision. And the person who has made the attempt and survived may also be having these feelings, with respect both to herself and to her loved ones. What if we find it particularly difficult to sympathize with ourselves? Which of course we do. What if we can see ourselves only as dishonorable? Which is part of why we tried to kill ourselves in the first place. And what about that person, as John Mulaney jokes, who tried to murder me? Can I really sympathize with him, can I speak of him honorably? I tend not to sympathize with my own past decisions to kill myself, particularly not the times I tried to do so after my children were born.

A friend of mine, a great translator in India, had attempted suicide when she was in her late teens. She told me that when she woke in the hospital, she looked at her parents, and her first thought was fear. She was afraid of what they would say to her and how they felt. All she saw in their eyes, when they saw she had recovered consciousness, was reproach.

Let's begin with the most frightening and upsetting instance of suicide: when a child tries to take her own life. I think we can all sympathize with such a case and do our best to understand it.

You might think that the desire to kill yourself arises only once you have a reasonably sophisticated idea about life and death and your own relationship with those things. For years, it was dogma among psychiatrists that young children did not attempt suicide. But the truth is that for many people, including me, the desire to end their own life is among their earliest memories.

Some years ago, in the spring semester of 2013, a student of mine told me and our class the story of his first suicide attempt as a child. We were holding my nineteenth-century philosophy class outside that day, in front of the stately gray-slate fine arts building. It's a pretty building, more than a hundred years old. My students tend to be smarter, more intimate, and more involved if I get them outside. Something about sitting in the grass in the open air makes it easier to think in original ways. The students aren't distracted by their computers and phones.

Recently Kansas City had seen a strange double-suicide—a father and daughter had leaped, hand-in-hand, off the Bond Bridge into the Missouri River. Since we'd been talking about Schopenhauer's pessimism and had read his famous essay "On Suicide," I used this event as an occasion to get us all talking openly about our thoughts on killing oneself.

Mary, who was normally quiet but was one of my smartest students, said, "I'm pretty sure our generation thinks a lot more about suicide than previous generations."

Other students nodded. I asked her why she supposed this might be the case.

"I think for us life actually is absurd. Everything for our generation looks so pointless. Because of climate change, we don't even know if we will have normal lives. We don't know if we're going to get jobs. My parents felt like the world was just getting better, but we all know that it's just getting worse. I mean, it feels like, what's the point?"

I asked how many of them agreed, and more than half raised their hands. Upsettingly to me, Schopenhauer's dark view of existence appealed to them. They expected their lives to get harder rather than easier, and they sincerely felt a bit hopeless about it. Their remarks had a kind of collective apocalyptic conviction. Although I tried to reassure them that things might be better than they seemed, it occurred to me that their outlook had changed from even my own somewhat disenchanted generation (I am an early Gen X-er): they seemed to have a deep belief that life was both meaningless and getting worse, whereas when I was their age, we seemed to have a basic confidence that life was worthwhile and that we had cause to hope for the future.

A certain existential angst often characterizes a philosophy classroom, which is particularly true in my "19th Century" class (Schopenhauer, Kierkegaard, Nietzsche, Freud, Dickinson), but in this instance I worried that my students were expressing a sincere change in the way their generation viewed not just their lives but their expectations for the future. If you're convinced in your heart that things are only going to get worse, it's going to impact how you adapt to the world around you.

Another student, Sam, raised his hand.

Sam was a philosophy major whose first class with me was "Intro to Philosophy"; then he took my existentialism course. I wrote one of his recommendation letters for law school. He also house-sat for me a couple of times: he's half a student and half a friend. He is now a successful civil rights attorney.

"I think it's more individual," he said. "For me, it's about whether you're a depressed person. I've tried to kill myself a few times," he admitted.

The fact that it was a sunny spring day made it easier to talk about suicide, although generally speaking college-age students are surprisingly willing to be candid about their suicide attempts.

"The first time I was three or four years old." Sam had his legs crossed, and he was playing with the grass as he spoke. Some students were watching him closely, others were looking away, but everyone was listening to him. "We had a floor-to-ceiling window on the landing of the stairs in our apartment building that must have been badly installed or something. Anyway, I always wanted to kill myself, and then I rode my tricycle right through that window and fell three stories."

"The window was open?" I asked.

"No, it wasn't a window that opens. It was just, like, cheap glass, and I rode right through it. I was in the hospital for a couple of weeks. I had a bunch of broken bones, and I was in a coma for a while. My right arm is still kinda weird from it." He held out his arm—the forearm looked like it connected to the upper arm at a slightly odd angle, with a twist. "When I woke up at first I thought I was in heaven. Then I told my mom I'd done it on purpose. From the earliest I can remember, I wanted to die. It's always been like that for me."

"We need to get you a poodle," I said, trying to lighten the mood a bit. "Schopenhauer's poodles are probably what kept him from killing himself. Maybe that's the reason I have two poodles now."

We'd been making poodle jokes for a couple of weeks, as you do when you're teaching Schopenhauer. Schopenhauer, whose father committed suicide by drowning himself in a canal, didn't like much of anyone other than his dogs, all of which he named Atman (Sanskrit for, roughly, "breath," "self," or "universal self") and nicknamed Butz (German for "puddle" or "little thing").

"I have a dog, a golden retriever," Sam said. "He definitely helps."

"Have you had many other attempts?" I asked. "If you don't mind the question?"

"Yeah, I have," he said. But I could see he didn't want to say any more, so I told my class about my first suicide attempt, which happened when I was six.

"In one of my earliest memories," I told them, "I remember both thinking how interesting the color of the carpet was, I seem to remember rubbing it with my hand, and also feeling inconsolably sad, and panicky—I think I was wanting my mother, and she was gone somewhere—and wishing that I were dead. I don't know how old I was at this time, but I think I was very young, two or three."

How could a two-year-old wish he were dead? It's a reasonable question. One answer comes from the Tibetan Buddhist lama Dzongsar Jamyang Khyentse Rinpoche, who wrote that suicide is simply a pattern we are repeating from past lives. "Suicide is a habit we pick up very quickly and is extremely difficult to break. It's a little like being addicted to alcohol and incapable of saying no to a drink. Habit plays a huge role in defining future rebirths. Once you have formed the habit of ending your life when things get tough, you will resort to suicide more and more quickly in your future lives."

To me, this is one plausible explanation for cases like mine and Sam's, people who seem to have had thoughts of suicide before we even had very clear idea of what life and death are. (Of course, as Khyentse Rinpoche himself points out, if you think that consciousness ends at death, or if you don't believe in reincarnation, this explanation will not make sense to you.)

"As a child," I told the class, "I developed a fascination with running in front of a car or a bus. This is a curious, obsessive thought I think many people share." I looked up at my students, and several of them nodded. "One day after school, in first grade, I jumped in front of a bus. I don't know if I would call it a suicide attempt, because in some ways it was spur of the moment. In the past when I've tried to catalog my suicide attempts, I've never included this one. What I think of as my first 'real' suicide attempt—whatever that means—was when I was sixteen, and I was definitely determined to end my life. At age six, as I did it, I'm not sure I was thinking, *Okay, I'm killing myself.* Though it's hard to say. I had definitely been thinking about suicide."

Maybe it was impulsive. Now that psychiatrists are increasingly acknowledging that children do attempt suicide, they tell us that most suicide attempts by children are impulsive. But thinking back on it now, little six-year-old Clancy Martin did a bit of planning.

"To go home, I had to take a right out of the school into our neighborhood. If I went to the left, there was Sifton Boulevard, a very busy street that we weren't allowed to cross without an adult. I went left that day, thinking I was going to jump in front of a bus, and I waited behind a tree while watching for it. I remember being very nervous and feeling sure that I was going to get in trouble for being on the Sifton side of the school.

"Then I saw a bus coming. I was scared. I remember thinking that things would be so much better if I were dead. My brothers and sisters would miss me, my mom would miss me, and the kids at school would be sorry that I was dead. Even Bruce DeVaart would think, *Wow, he killed himself. I can't believe I was so mean to him.*" Bruce DeVaart was our chief elementary school bully and my big nemesis back then. (We later became friends.) Once he made my friend Chris Carter and me eat yellow snow.

My students looked faintly shocked, and a few looked confused.

"And when it got close, I closed my eyes and ran into the street. Horns were blaring. I don't know if the bus actually hit me, but I fell over onto my back. There was a commotion of adults, and I was on the curb. They took me into the school, and I was totally fine. They let me walk home with my sister Teryn and my little brother Pat. When my mother asked me about it, I pretended it was all an accident, and I got a lecture about staying away from Sifton and looking both ways before crossing the street."

Pretending that it was an accident is a standard move for many failed suicide attempts, child or adult, especially first attempts.

"I never told anyone about it, until years later I told my older brother Darren, during an Ecstasy and coke jag—which, by the way, you should never do." My students laughed. "And I guess maybe I should just say that this was my first official suicide attempt."

I glanced at Sam and something passed between us, a look that said, *You still feel this way, don't you? After all these years.* Both of us knew that our childhood suicidal death wish had not gone away.

The great twentieth-century psychologist Alfred Adler, in his essay "Suicide," wrote that the kind of child who would be predisposed toward suicidal behavior later in life (and who might well already be thinking about it) would have

> a tendency to collapse under psychological pain when confronted with difficult life situations . . . in addition to increased ambition, vanity, and consciousness of their value for others. Fantasies of sickness or death . . . went parallel with this firm belief in their high values for others. . . . Among the early childhood expressions of the suicide, one also finds the deepest grieving over often negligible matters, strong wishes to become sick or to die when a humiliation is experienced . . . and an attitude towards others as if it were their duty to fulfill his every wish.

I have to admit that this description sounds a lot like young Clancy and maybe not only the young version. My alcoholism, my divorces, my narcissism, and my exaggeration of the importance of my own needs and goals, which led to my many failures as a parent—Adler predicted it all.

My earliest memories of wanting to kill myself included imagining myself at my own funeral, watching the teary aftermath.

My mom would cry. My brothers, stepsisters, and stepbrothers would all be devastated. My stepdad would finally understand how miserable he'd made my life. As I grew older, I viewed my own death differently: I wanted to die not to see how others would react but because at last my unhappiness would be over. One might say I started with the "You'll miss me when I'm gone" version of suicide and wound up with the "I can't take the smell of me any longer" version.

After that first attempt, a decade passed before I tried to kill myself again. I still wanted to die but was afraid to do it. I was very unhappy and felt sure that I wouldn't be if I were dead, and I knew I could do it if I just resolved to. As a kid and a teenager, suicide was one more thing I was failing at, along with not having a girlfriend and not being popular. I sincerely believed that ending my life would be the best thing for me, but I felt overmastered by the challenge of actually doing it. More to the point, I was scared. I was afraid of the pain involved. I was afraid of failing and getting in trouble. And that made the desire to do it psychologically heavier. My awareness of my own inadequacy and cowardice seemed to require a resolution.

My parents divorced when I was five, and my mother married a man with seven children. That made ten of us kids in the house including my two brothers and me. It was a volatile combination, and one of my early memories of that new, violent family was attending my stepbrother Paul's funeral after his suicide.

My stepsister Lisa also tried to kill herself. It was about three years after my mother and my stepfather married. I visited her in the psychiatric wing of Foothills Hospital in Calgary, Alberta. I was eight, and she was fifteen. My mom and the psychiatrist had said it was okay for us to be alone together. We talked in the gray-green light of a small scary room with a thick, wire-meshed window.

"I wasn't trying to kill myself, Clancy," she lied. "I was just trying to get out of there."

Her wrists were bandaged, and she was on an IV. Her spleen had burst as she fell from the third-story window of the home for troubled teens where she had been staying, and they had removed it a couple of days before.

"This was just, like, a joke," she said, showing me the bandages on her arms. "I thought if they thought I was trying to kill myself, they would let me go home." Then she pulled down the sheet and showed me the bandage where she'd had her surgery. I was nervous because she was too exposed. "But then they were going to transfer me here, because they said it was a suicide attempt, and I hate this place so much, so I tried to climb out the window, and I fell."

It was not my first visit to Foothills. The year before, eight or nine of us had come several times for family therapy. My mother and stepfather were there, along with my brothers Darren and Pat and my stepbrothers and stepsisters Lisa, Teryn, Drew, Jeff, and Kevin. Paul was dead, as you know, and my other stepbrother, Blair Jr., had moved away to Vancouver.

Two psychologists met with us in the big vinyl-tiled hospital conference room, which looked to me a bit like the lunch room at my school. At one point, one of them asked, "Can you think of ways people could cooperate with each other? Are there particular things people do or don't do?"

And for the first and only time at that therapy session, I raised my hand. I said, "Kevin doesn't bring his coffee cup up."

"What?" the psychologist asked.

Kevin was staring at me now. His eyes were a beautiful icy blue—much later I learned that he was an unusually good-looking kid—and his lips were pulled into a tight, angry smile. I would have been six or seven, so Kevin would have been sixteen or seventeen.

"Go ahead," the psychologist said. "A coffee cup?"

"Yeah, well . . ." I looked around the circle of chairs and noticed that no one in my family other than the psychologist wanted me to talk.

"Say what you're going to say, Clancy," Kevin said.

"Well, Mom always asks him to bring his coffee cup up from downstairs, from his bedroom in the basement, and he never does."

My little brother Pat looked at me like *Why the hell are you talking? Why are you rocking the boat?* and reached for the cup of apple juice they had given us when we came in.

"That's not—" my mom started.

"No, this is helpful," the one psychologist said.

"From the mouths of babes," the other psychologist said, and I wished I hadn't said anything. I knew I had betrayed Kevin, and that I would pay for it later, when we were home. It was a daily thing. Kevin's bedroom was in the basement. In the morning, he would come up to get his coffee, then go back down the stairs. (Not long after this, Jeff would chase Kevin around the house with a hatchet, then hurl himself down those same basement stairs to chop his big brother in the back of the head.) Then Mom would say, "Bring your coffee cup back up." But, as I said, "he never brings his coffee cup back up."

Now that I have five children of my own and my children have two stepmoms (my second wife is stepmom to my eldest daughter, and my third wife is stepmom to three of my daughters), I understand the silent, unhappy power struggles that erupt between stepchildren and stepparents. I blame my mother for her inability to make peace in our home. Rationally I don't condemn her, she was overwhelmed, but in my heart I know I have some strange anger about it, because I felt that she had some duty to keep me safer than she was able to do. I feel guilty because I know she treated us better than she treated them, and disappointed in her that she couldn't love them more. But I also think, *My God, how did she manage it? How did she survive raising three children of her own and seven children of someone else's, spread from ages five to nineteen, in a small three-bedroom, two-story wooden rental house?* A friend said to me recently, "You know, your mom, she was a real optimist." But that's the opposite of my mom. She's one of the most consistently pessimistic people I know. It was her pessimism that kept her in that situation. She felt sure things could get even worse.

But back to Lisa's hospital room in Foothills' psychiatric wing. She had been running away from home and refusing to go to school, and pretending to go to school but then going off to do whatever fifteen-year-old girls skipping school in Calgary did at that time. My parents had tried various punishments: in one of my worst and most vivid memories from childhood, my stepfather dragged her upstairs by her hair. Lisa screamed and fought him, kicking her feet as he pulled her up. He had a plunger in his other hand, which he used to beat her with once he got her to the bedroom she shared with Teryn. My parents eventually gave up on her and sent her to foster care. (She didn't stay there—she ran away and started living on the street.) My mother often said that one of the biggest regrets of her life was the way they handled Lisa. "Your stepdad was a good person," she told me, "But maybe he wasn't really meant to be a father." Later in life I came to care for him very much, but as a child I feared and mistrusted him.

"I really wasn't trying to kill myself," Lisa told me again. "Please tell them that. Otherwise they'll try to keep me here. I can't stand it in here." She started crying. I didn't know what to do, but I was sitting on the side of her bed, and she put her head in my lap while she cried, which she had never done before.

I felt she needed my care, that I could do something to help her, but I didn't know what it was. She was seven years older, and like my brother Darren, she was a hero to me. When my father moved away to Florida, Darren became his surrogate, and then when Darren was sent away to military school, Lisa replaced him. At that time, my mother and Lisa were at the center of my emotional life and gave me what little sense of security I had in the unstable world of our messy, unhappy family.

I stroked her hair. I didn't know what else to do. She had brushed my hair when we were all first living together, when my mom and stepdad first married. It was something that she and a friend of hers had liked to do, listen to albums in her room and brush my hair. At that time, I guess she would have been twelve or thirteen. She had a Donnie Osmond album she liked to play.

After a few minutes, they knocked on the door, and I had to leave. She was still crying. On the way out of the hospital, I had the idea that I could lessen her suffering by inflicting some pain on myself. So I rubbed my fingers as hard as I could along the walls of the hospital as my mom and Pat and I walked out. There must have been some brick once we got outside, though I only remember this slightly rough tile, and some edges that hurt. But I do remember taking pride in how much it stung, and I was also proud that, by the time we got to the car, all my fingers were bleeding.

My mom said, "Clancy! What happened? Did you fall? How did this happen?"

I couldn't tell her what I had done, of course, and I also remember feeling ridiculous about it, as if I already understood I was being dramatic and self-aggrandizing. But it also meant something to me.

I could chronicle in more detail the many other miserable and abusive events of my childhood, but they are not the focus of our investigation. Yes, it is probably for this reason—the usual dysfunctional family reason—that both my brothers have talked to me about committing suicide. My older brother Darren seems to have it on a default setting, as I do (though happily, he has never made an attempt, so far as I know). When we were in the jewelry business together, Darren and I would sit around joking about killing ourselves, or in darker moods coming down off cocaine, we would commiserate about how much we needed to kill ourselves, then make each other promise not to do it.

It can be helpful to remember that suicide seems to run in families. These families may well be dysfunctional, like my own, but strong evidence suggests that genetic factors also contribute to the likelihood of a suicide attempt. Maybe if you believe you have a genetic predisposition—or even if you can simply blame the self-destructive feeling you're presently suffering on the mistakes of your parents—it's easier to resist the view that the desire to kill yourself is well motivated.

Probably the greatest philosopher of the twentieth century, Ludwig Wittgenstein, had an interesting family. Three of his four brothers committed suicide, and Wittgenstein himself constantly battled the desire to kill himself. The Wittgensteins were brilliant, hugely wealthy, powerful members of Viennese society: superficially speaking, they ought to have had every reason to live. But that's not the way suicide or even the ordinary difficulty of life works. We don't know exactly why we are miserable, no matter what our circumstances may be, and that worsens the problem. You think, *I ought to be happy. I have every reason to be happy. And yet I am filled with self-hatred, unhappiness, and self-pity.* Meanwhile, people around the world are dealing with the miseries of extreme suffering—hunger, debilitating disease, poverty, the unexpected deaths of loved ones—and yet still wake up and make breakfast for their families. It's more proof that I don't deserve to live.

Whenever I try to talk to my mother about suicide, she changes the subject. Emotions frighten her, and she believes that talking about things makes them more dangerous. When I was thirteen or fourteen, I asked my father about my suicidal fantasies, and he explained that suicides went to "the astral hells." He was a New Age guru and believed in reincarnation and many different planes of existence. "Don't do it, son," he told me calmly. "You don't die. You just wake up some place much worse. But please tell me if you're feeling that way. Are you feeling that way now?" I knew to lie to him, naturally: he was my dad. Thinking about it now, I realize that he was quite literally right about suicide for me. Every time I've tried it, I've woken up someplace worse.

My father had not been making an argument, of course. He had just been putting forth an opinion, one that he believed with absolute conviction: that life does not end with death, and that certain rules govern how we are to die. If we break those rules, he thought, there were ghastly consequences.

We find this standard argument against some forms of suicide in almost every religious tradition. These traditions commonly make exceptions to these consequences for particular kinds of "virtuous" suicides, such as martyrdom in the Abrahamic tradition, suicide for honor in the Confucian tradition, or suicide in a heroic battle in many Indigenous American religions. (Many religious traditions also suggest exceptions for euthanasia.) But generally these traditions consider suicide a bad idea because it will result in a highly undesirable afterlife.

My father's view was motivated by his own religious convictions: he was a kind of Vedantist who believed consciousness was eternal. Similarly, religions don't tend to have *arguments* that support the "don't kill yourself because you're immortal" view. They simply assert that there is an afterlife and that suicide will result in a nasty one. That said, it's easy enough to construct such an argument. If we grant that we don't really know whether there's an afterlife, then we don't really know whether killing ourselves will make things better, the same, or worse. We're just gambling that it will make things better. The person who commits suicide may suppose that she knows what happens when you die, but she doesn't. If upon dying we go someplace better, or we vanish entirely, as when deeply anesthetized, then someone who is deeply unhappy and who expects life only to worsen may reasonably choose to kill herself.

But we don't know what's going to happen—we're simply hoping, and what we are hoping for varies considerably from person to person. It's not irrational to make certain gambles, and whenever we gamble, we are making a prediction about the unknown. The suicide's gamble is that if there is another life, it can't be as bad as this one, and anyway maybe there is no life after death. As Schopenhauer wrote, "As soon as the terrors of life reach the point at which they outweigh the terrors of death, a man will put an end to his life."

But the suicidal person should at least acknowledge that she or he is merely betting on an unknown. She may also want to admit to herself—as I try to remember—that lots of wise people from the past have insisted that there is an afterlife, and that our currently popular materialistic view that consciousness ends at death is an unusual one in the history of human thinking on the subject. Furthermore, speaking from my own perspective, if I'm seriously thinking about killing myself, am I confident that my own judgment is the best?

If you don't know whether there's life after death, and a violent death inflicted by your own hand might result in a much worse situation than your present one, it's a hell of a risk to take. As Hamlet famously observes:

To die: to sleep;
no more; and by a sleep to say we end
the heart-ache and the thousand natural shocks
that flesh is heir to, 'tis a consummation
devoutly to be wish'd. To die, to sleep;
To sleep: perchance to dream: ay, there's the rub:
For in that sleep of death what dreams may come
Must give us pause: there's the respect that makes calamity of so long
   life.

Hamlet had more reason than most of us to worry that suicide wouldn't solve his problems: we sometimes forget that the suicidal young man had already seen his father's ghost and been warned about the afterlife. *Hamlet* is both a suicide story and a ghost story.

My friend Jim Lowrey is a lifelong Buddhist practitioner and author of a terrific book, *Taming Untameable Beings*, about the great twentieth-century Tibetan Buddhist philosopher Chögyam Trungpa Rinpoche (you'll come across several Rinpoches in this book, it's an honorific). He and I were recently emailing about the question of what happens to the suicide when she dies, and he reminded me of the story, told in his book, of Tom, a friend of Jim's, also a serious Buddhist practitioner, who took his own life.

At Tom's funeral, Trungpa Rinpoche turned to one of his students, who was suffering terribly over the loss, and told him not to worry and it wasn't a big deal because we don't really die. "At the same time," he said, "it's not going to be easy for him. If you commit suicide, you will have problems in the bardo. Because of that act of aggression, [he] could be stuck in limbo for a long time." At another point during the funeral, Trungpa Rinpoche remarked to a different student, "Just about now, Tom is discovering that he didn't get out of anything." He said this because if there is an afterlife, suicide is strictly speaking impossible, since the mind that you are trying to eliminate is by its nature indestructible. As Lowery wrote, "Rinpoche said that the failure of suicide is that you are trying to make the world go away, and that doesn't happen. What does happen is that you lose your ability to influence the world. When you commit suicide and cut off your body, you're using your creative power to destroy creativity, and this limits your ability to work with your problems, and so it's really not a good idea."

This argument that life may well continue after death may not stop someone who is in such pain that they're desperate to escape. We often leap out of the frying pan into the fire just because we can't take the frying pan any longer. But it may give some people pause, as it sometimes does me. And a pause can be enough: the dreadful moment of self-destructive resolution passes, and we manage to go on with our day.

My own first stay in a psychiatric hospital was after a suicide attempt when I was sixteen and still living in Calgary. After my girlfriend dumped me for a basketball player at a different high school and broke my heart, a psychiatrist had prescribed Librium for anxiety. To complicate matters, I was living with the girl and her family at the time. I had lied and told them my own parents had thrown me out so that I could stay with them and keep an eye on her, and they had kindly if unwisely taken me in. It was creepy behavior, admittedly, but that did not occur to my wildly jealous teenage mind. One night, after sitting outside the window of her room in the basement and listening to her have sex with the new boyfriend, I went back into the house, got my Librium and a bottle of rye that I had bought from a chef at the country club where I worked (I was planning on drinking it that weekend with two friends of mine), went to a snow-covered playground not far from the ex-girlfriend's home, and swallowed all the pills with about half the twenty-sixer of whiskey. I had read that freezing to death was briefly painful and then surprisingly blissful, and that was my plan. I also thought deliberately leaving a naked, frozen corpse as a witness of my devotion and her betrayal would show my girlfriend how much I'd loved her (now it sounds to me about as compelling as cutting off your ear for a gift).

I took off my clothes and lay down in the snow. The snow turned from white to blue to green to pink. At first I shivered and desperately wanted to get up, then got so cold that I literally couldn't bear it any longer. Then, quite suddenly, I felt almost overwhelmed by a blanket of warmth and gratitude. I passed out. I should have frozen, but a passerby found me, and I woke up in the hospital and spent a couple of days in the psychiatric wing.

There I learned that other people frequently fantasized about suicide, and a fellow patient shared with me the crucial fact that we wouldn't be released until we learned to say that we no longer felt like hurting ourselves.

I understood the desire to inflict pain on oneself: as a kid, I did engage in some self-harming behaviors, such as the finger-lacerating after visiting Lisa I mentioned previously, as well as some similar incidents. But I'd never really been motivated by the desire to hurt myself. All my life I've feared and avoided physical suffering. It's mental suffering that I wasn't able to avoid—as indeed none of us can—and that was what motivated my suicide attempts. Precisely what I was hoping to prevent when I thought about my own death was worse pain. Self-harm? No thank you. Self-extinguish? Now you've got my attention.

Perhaps you are finding this level of self-pity, as I often do, unbearable. I tend to think of self-pity as the flip side of self-aggrandizement. As Sexton observed in her poem "On Suicide," if I'm thinking "me me me" all the time, whether I'm up or down, it's the focus on myself that's the problem. I can forgive this in myself as a child, but as an adult, isn't it reasonable to expect that maybe I could stop thinking about myself so much and start thinking about other people a little more?

At one point I was going through a bad time in my second marriage and was worried that I was heading toward another divorce. I wrote to my friend and mentor the writer Diane Williams about it, then added, "But don't listen to me, I'm just feeling sorry for myself." She wrote back immediately, "Never say you're just feeling sorry for yourself. Feel sorry for yourself! Feel more sorry for yourself!" This was some of the best advice I've ever been given, because it gave me permission to accept the feelings I was actually having rather than reproach myself and (ineffectively) try to bury or hide from those feelings. Diane was basically saying, *Yes, it really sucks to be human, so don't be afraid to admit that. Feel sorry for yourself, feel sorry for all of us!* That is a big step toward a more generous and a more honorable way of thinking about our human situation in general and the situation of the suicide in particular.

The Buddhist lama Dilgo Khyentse Rinpoche was probably the greatest Tibetan Buddhist teacher of the twentieth century. He gives similar advice when talking about the practice of opening one's mind to the world. The experience may at first be frightening or painful, he says, but one should welcome that fear or pain, because that is how we learn to experience the world as it truly is. As Audre Lorde bravely remarked in one of her notebooks, when she knew she was facing death, "I am listening to what fear teaches."

Speaking of what fear teaches: not very long ago, at the end of 2020, I found myself in a very rough phase. I was so depressed that I was barely able to write. But I also suspected that writing was helping me to manage the thought of suicide—writing has often helped me when struggling with depression, and if I go too long without writing, it even causes depression. So I believed it was important to try to keep writing as best I could. I also tried to apply some simple strategies I've learned that help me to avoid killing myself.

Here is a sample from my journal at that time:

> When the complete pointlessness of the whole thing hits me, at 3:17 on a Sunday afternoon, and my stomach feels sick and I can hear a gurgling like pipes half-filled with water, then it really feels like, please let me out.
>
> Get through today. Day after day after day. It's too much. I can't fucking do it.

> Also plagued by uncomfortable impulsive self-destructive thoughts. Pouring hot French fry oil over my head. Cutting off my fingers or genitals with a knife

or pruning shears. Stabbing myself in the eyes with a pen.

It's the will to fight. That's what I need, and don't have. When you don't have the will to fight, it's very hard to want to live. But the will to fight is the opposite of hopelessness. I am hopeless.

Hopelessness can come from an apocalyptic way of thinking. MP [my mother-in-law] recently wrote to me, during an argument with my wife, "Please don't take this out to the end of the world." The hastiness, the impatience, the panic and claustrophobia that make you want to take things to the end of the world. Psychologists call this "catastrophizing." Try to stop catastrophizing. For the Greeks, this usually means the death or destruction of the hero.

   Do I feel like I'm in trouble? In danger? Do I feel genuinely suicidal right now, today, this moment, for the last few hours, for the last few weeks?
   Yes.
   Am I willing to tell anyone about it?
   No.
   Why not?
   I am afraid of the consequences.
   Are those consequences worse than the consequences of me killing myself?
   No.
   What am I trying to do?
   I am trying to do nothing. I am trying to remember that I don't always feel this way and I won't always feel that way.

I include this excerpt here because it's important to remind myself that managing depression and suicidal thinking is an ongoing process, and because I suspect other people will know these feelings. And yet at the same time I imagine someone reading these words, and thinking to herself, *My God, will this guy never stop complaining?* And this mode of self-accusation, worsened through the eyes of an unknown other, is characteristic of suicidal thinking. The psychiatrist and suicide expert Nathan Kline beautifully summarized the psychological state: "He has failed in his own eyes the test of will and spirit. He blames himself for his weakness, and he assumes that others blame him, too."

That particular spell of depression was at its worst for a few weeks. The whole thing lasted perhaps two months. These days I am always careful to increase my physical exercise when I am depressed, and some vigorous bike riding helped one day, but some mornings it seemed only to have made things worse. I was conducting interviews with experts on suicide at that time, and it was difficult to approach those Zoom calls.

Sometimes the pain of depression causes me to panic, and when I am panicking, it's hard not to react. Panic provokes this primitive fight-or-flight response. Suicide is the most extreme form of flight and also a murderous passion to fight. All too often I feel like one of those autodestructive Métamatic sculptures by Jean Tinguely, designed to batter itself to pieces in front of a confused and dismayed audience, that falls apart into screws, springs, and bolts as it scrambles and jerks across the floor, and ultimately fails even to achieve its own demise. Or I find myself fantasizing about going to buy a gun. Find a peaceful field where I can park the car, with maybe a river to watch. Goodbye, cruel world.

What to do? On my work desk, I keep a black-and-white picture of Dzongsar Jamyang Khyentse Rinpoche. He is smiling very widely, and it looks like the photographer has caught him in midlaughter. The picture always reminds me of a recommendation by Dilgo Khyentse Rinpoche (who was Dzongsar Jamyang Khyentse Rinpoche's main teacher): that one should try to see the humor in difficult situations. I find that if I can even just smile at my own struggle to see the humor in my situation, it helps a little bit. Smiling is like taking a breath. It's something that I am feeling, something simple and real and positive.

In December 2020 Dzongsar Jamyang Khyentse Rinpoche (hereafter, Khyentse Rinpoche) was giving a talk in Taipei on vipassana meditation—the style of mindfulness meditation that involves observing your thoughts and emotions as they are, without judging or dwelling on them—and one of the students remarked, in the course of a question, "Sometimes I feel terrible, as if I'm stuck in a prison. It's like being locked in a coffin sinking into the sea." The question seemed to describe the student's experience generally, not her experience while meditating.

Khyentse Rinpoche replied:

> Practically, you should just observe that. Really. Don't do anything. Even if there's a formula to counter this, some sort of solution, don't use it. Just observe that. I know for beginners this may not satisfy you. . . . Everything has to be fixed right away. . . . But really, even that low feeling. Just watch. Please bank on this. It really is the most economical. It has no side effects at all. And there will be a lot of discovery. In about two months you will want that low feeling. You will become like a fisherman who is fishing in a river where there are not many fish. You will want that low feeling, so that you can catch it and feel gratified.

It can be very difficult to do this when you are in acute pain or despair. But again, the key is *not to* do something. So if I'm depressed, I could try telling myself, *All you have to do—your entire task—is not to do anything. Be depressed. It hurts. And that's okay.*

David Foster Wallace made a similar observation in one of his notebooks. Wallace suspected that everyone suffered from "a deeper type of pain that is always there, if only in an ambient, low-level way," and added that "most of us spend nearly all our time and energy trying to distract ourselves from feeling [that pain], or at least from feeling [it] directly or with our full attention."

Wallace and Khyentse Rinpoche agree that running away from the pain or hiding from it exacerbates the problem rather than solves it. Which makes me wonder: What if I tried a more creative approach to my own pain other than my usual panicky, jerk-your-finger-out-of-the-fire reflex? What might that mean?

I don't want to tell you just yet everything that I now try to do—that's the last chapter of the book—but the short version is: I leave my finger in the fire. I am slowly learning that trying to control how I feel is a lot like trying to control how the people around me feel: utterly useless and counterproductive. I have to liberate myself from the idea that I have control. I also have to learn how to let myself feel pain.

Dr. Sunita Puri, a palliative care physician who has helped thousands of people die and helped their loved ones to accept that death, writes, "I have learned to look when I want to look away. I have chosen to stay when I want to run out of the room and cry. The prelude to compassion is the willingness to see."

And that willingness to see is everything. I've been wanting to run out of the room and cry since I was four years old. But I've learned that I can choose to stay and see who I really am.

2

Is There a Death Drive?

When discussing someone's death by their own hand, it's quite common to hear, "We'll never know why she did it." It's a popular myth that we simply cannot know why a person would kill themselves.

When we talk or write about suicide generally or about some particular person's death by suicide, we tend to focus on the immediate act, the day and manner of the suicide. We always want to know why someone (or anyone) died in this way, but we tend to shy away from psychological explanations. We do this in part out of respect for the dead, in part because we all know that the human heart is profoundly mysterious, in part because many contemporary thinkers about suicide insist that suicide is an impulsive act (after all, about nine out of ten suicide attempters do not repeat the attempt), and in part because we think we kind of already understand that person who took her own life. Probably most people have dallied with the thought of suicide or even uttered the words "I just want to die" and meant what they said as they said it, yet they don't make an attempt. For that reason, again, we may tend to feel that while we get why someone might do it, we also accept that we can never truly understand their motivation. That's just how it is when you feel you can't go on anymore.

But the truth is that the act of killing oneself is the culmination of a process of thinking, and that thinking continues after a failed attempt (especially for repeat attempters). Focusing on the day or the trigger or the act of suicide is a bit like someone telling you that sex is all about the orgasm: this person doesn't understand sex or the sexuality of our culture and also is probably not much fun in bed. This is why, especially with someone like myself who's attempted and failed at suicide repeatedly, it's important for us to try to understand the thinking of the suicidal person. Why do people try to kill themselves at all? What brings them to this point? And for failed suicides, how does their thinking about suicide change as they come to understand their own attempt? Why is one suicide attempt the best predictor of an eventual death by suicide? Could it be that some people are just cursed with the desire to kill themselves?

I made one of my particularly clumsy attempts at suicide when I was seventeen years old. My best friend Tom Bradford and I had been out on a long drive just to talk. Tom was at the wheel. The highway was dark, and in the headlights of his Mustang SVO, the snow was sliding across the road in sideways serpentine patterns the way it does on cold, moonless winter nights. We were almost an hour northwest of Calgary, Alberta, my hometown, riding parallel to the Rocky Mountains. We had two six-packs of Kokanee in the back seat, and each of us had a beer. It was January or February 1985.

We'd had two or three beers each. We weren't drunk at all. Tom had wanted to talk about a problem he was having with his girlfriend at the time, and I hoped he wanted my advice. I had just moved back into my parents' house. (Prior to that, I'd been sleeping in the office of the gas station where I worked and before that at my ex-girlfriend's parents' house.) I'd dropped out of high school again and had no plans for the future. Also, my ex-girlfriend kept taking me back and then changing her mind and dumping me again. I was living in that day-to-day way that you do when things are all fucked up and you don't know how to change them. I tended to oscillate between long stretches of mild depression and brief moments of exhilaration.

I had tried and failed to kill myself about a year before (the naked-in-the-snow attempt). I hadn't tried since, but I was really wanting to die.

I wanted to listen to Tom's worries but was really sinking deeper into my own. At some point in the conversation, I told him, "You know, I just don't want to go on living. I want to jump out of the car right now."

He said, "Yeah, I know what you mean," and kind of laughed. He thought I was sympathizing with his situation. He was also embarrassed for me, the way you are, especially as a teenager, when someone says something they aren't supposed to say. "I do sometimes feel that way," he said. "But we don't really mean it. We don't really want to die. It's just sometimes life sucks."

Tom didn't know that I had tried to kill myself before, or that the desire to die was a daily thing with me. He was my best friend, but I'd never confessed this desire to anyone other than my older brother and my father.

I don't know why exactly I couldn't tell anyone how much I wanted to kill myself. I was deeply ashamed of the fact that, as I saw it, I didn't have the courage to live. Also, they might ask me why, and then I'd have to say: *My girlfriend doesn't love me anymore. I'm unpopular. Girls don't like me. I have bad skin. I'm from a poor family, I'm lazy, I'll never amount to anything. I've always felt that way. I can't do this like everyone else can.* And once I started talking, who knew what I might say next?

Then I thought to myself, *Yes, fuck it, I do mean it,* and I unbuckled my seat belt, opened the door to the car, and tried to jump out. Tom grabbed me, braked as hard as he could in the snow, and pulled over onto the side of the highway.

Was I confident that leaping out of the car at that moment would kill me? Hard to know. I hoped it would. But maybe this was a classic case of either way I won: if it succeeded, I was out, I was done. If I failed, suddenly I'd managed to say through my suicide attempt all the things I was otherwise incapable of articulating.

Tom was angry. Red-faced, he shouted, "Jesus Christ, you could have killed us both!" Then—and this was the kind of friend he was (he's a very successful psychiatrist now)—he calmed down and tried to have a serious talk with me about what had just happened. I tried to play it off, apologizing and telling him that I was just joking. I told him I was safe, that I was just being an idiot.

Tom drove us back toward Calgary at about thirty-five miles per hour, one eye always on me. Sounding like a cop, he said, "Keep your hands where I can see them, Clance. Keep them on your knees."

A friend and student of mine who attempted suicide a few years ago told me, "I wasn't depressed, I wasn't feeling impulsive. Maybe I was too tired to keep going. Anyway, I just thought death was preferable to living." Perhaps it is that simple: sometimes you want to die rather than live.

Put that way, it sounds a bit weird to say I want to live. I take living for granted. I'm not separate from my life, after all: I am my life. There's no "me" independent of my life. It's what I know, what I'm always doing, and I don't have a desire for it because it's something I already have.

But often I do want to die. And many people, like me, are acutely conscious of what the Buddhist philosopher Thích Nhất Hạnh called "a desire for nonexistence." Not existing is what you *want*.

In fact, for the Buddha, that desire for nonexistence was one of the three fundamental forms of suffering that constitute life. (The other two are the suffering that comes from the desire for physical and emotional pleasure, along with the disappointment and pain that accompany that desire; and the suffering that comes from the desire for life itself, which is always slipping through our fingers.)

People attempt in many ways to annihilate the self, at least on a temporary basis—the heavy use of alcohol and other drugs is one of the most obvious. But many people who want self-annihilation, like me, make the assumption that *dying* is the surest way to get what they want.

By contrast, the vast majority of thinkers who discuss our relationship with death, and even most writers who address the subject of suicide, take it for granted that human beings have a fundamental aversion to the thought of dying. It sounds plausible: after all, most of us don't want to think about death, neither our own nor that of those we love. Death terrifies us. It does seem a bit weird, then, to imagine that the desire for self-annihilation might be a common aspect of human psychological experience.

Rousseau's masterpiece *Julie*, for example, contains a dialogue on the ethics of suicide wherein even its defender insists that "we have all received from nature an enormous horror of death, and this horror conceals from our eyes the miseries of the human condition. One long endures a painful and doleful life before resigning oneself to relinquishing it; but once the weariness of living overcomes the horror of dying, then life is obviously a great evil, and one cannot too soon be freed from it."

Rousseau's observation about our great fear of death is the standard line among many, many writers on the subject of the end of life, and it does make me wonder a bit about my own constitution, and that of other suicidal people I know and have known. Because I don't think about death in that "great fear" way, and I've never known any other suicidal person to speak of death with that kind of horror. In fact, it tends to be just the opposite: we suicidal types have a tendency—one that is misled—to suppose that death would be a relief.

The desire to die can be as straightforward as our desire to live, or to have sex, or to eat. As the contemporary writer Yiyun Li wrote, "One's wish to die can be as blind and intuitive as one's will to live, yet the latter is never questioned." And the philosopher and Holocaust survivor Jean Amery, who attempted suicide in 1974 before dying by deliberate overdose in 1978, wrote that he "didn't hate death but anxiously longed for it."

The Buddha's idea that the desire for self-annihilation is fundamental to human psychology is actually not foreign to us at all. The so called "death drives" or *Todestriebe* are a crucial part of Freud's psychoanalytic theory. Freud introduced the idea in *Beyond the Pleasure Principle* (1920), following a 1912 paper by Sabrina Spielrein, and while he was under the influence of Schopenhauer's drive psychology, which owed a great debt to Buddhist psychology. In Freud's theory, we have drives both to life

(Eros) and to death (Thanatos). The former underlies such life-affirming activities as sex and creativity; the latter explains those human actions and habits that seem hostile to life, such as obsessive and compulsive behaviors, aggression, murder, all kinds of neuroses and psychoses, and naturally, suicide. In an explicit nod to Buddhism, Freud also refers to the "nirvana principle," the tendency of the mind to seek the elimination of all tension, a state possible, according to Freud, only in death. Thus the nirvana principle is simply an extreme form of the death drive.

To the suicidal person, this all makes perfect sense. She suffers from unbearable tension, she knows that the continuation of life will be only the prolonging and perhaps worsening of that tension, and she seeks its elimination in death. Her fondest, wildest hope is that it will indeed prove to be nirvana.

But the will to die is more complicated than that, because even the suicidal person is still contending with the will to live. "I made my first suicide attempt at the age of fourteen," the Canadian novelist Nelly Arcan wrote in her novel *Exit*, which she finished a few weeks before she killed herself. "They called it a cry for help. A warning signal. They believed, and they were perhaps right, that I didn't want to die. Who knows? I still don't know, even today, if it's possible for someone unambiguously to want to die, if it's possible to truly have only that as your goal in life, to take the exit once and for all and disappear forever. For real. For keeps."

Some years ago, immediately following one of my suicide attempts, an irritated friend told me, "If you were really serious about killing yourself, you'd be dead by now." After I told another friend about a recent attempt to slit my own throat, he asked me, "Well, but what kind of a knife did you use?" And it's true that one of the most annoying (and devastating, really) questions a person can ask a repeat attempter like me is "Why haven't you succeeded in killing yourself?"

It's a fair question, if not particularly polite. We attempters know what people are implying when they ask that, and one response I could give is that, like most things, suicide is harder than it looks. Another is that, as with most things, the majority of successful suicides practice before they succeed. In her fantastic memoir *Negroland*, Margo Jefferson attacks the old myth that Black women aren't allowed to kill themselves, "Practice, practice, practice. Like playing scales, taking a barre. Do your daily suicide warm-ups." It may take several failures, and you'll have to deal with the consequences of those failures before you find the nerve to guarantee that you do not fail. And yet another reply I might offer is that, as Freud insists, even if we are aware of the death drive, we also have at the same time the drive for life.

That challenge—*after all these attempts, why aren't I dead yet?*—stays with me. Is it possible that I don't really want to die? Of course. You can want both things. On many days I did want both things: to die, so I didn't have to live this life anymore, so that I could stop struggling, stop suffering, stop failing, stop disappointing—in an instant, all my problems, gone; and to live, because to die meant—who knew what it meant? These days I try never to forget that at a minimum, it means a lot of suffering for a lot of people I loved and would be leaving behind, people who did not deserve the suffering I was inflicting on them.

Anyone who has attempted suicide is intimate with this ambivalence. In ordinary talk about suicide, we like to make the distinction between "a genuine suicide attempt" and "a cry for help." So, for example, if someone shoots herself with a gun or leaps off a tall building and yet survives, none of us would say, "Oh, that was just a cry for help. She didn't mean to kill herself." But if someone swallowed an entire bottle of aspirin and wound up getting his stomach pumped, we might console ourselves or reproach the suicide by insisting, "It wasn't really a suicide attempt. It was a cry for help."

Here we are particularly judging what we think of as the dramatic or even theatrical aspect of suicide, especially a failed attempt. We have a tendency to suspect the failed suicide of putting on a show, of trying to get attention for himself, of playing at someone who is in complete despair rather than actually being in despair. We will discuss this dramatic aspect of suicide more than once in these pages, but here I want briefly to say, both to the person who is feeling suicidal or has attempted suicide and to the person who may be feeling judgmental: what's wrong with it being dramatic? We are dramatic in so many aspects of our lives, we are constantly playing at roles, we are actors (and often very amateur actors) in many things we do. That a suicide attempt was theatrical neither morally impugns it nor changes the fact that the person who attempted was expressing the wish to die and might have done so. A depressed person too often has a feeling both of playing the part and of being depressed, and the inability to sort out which is which is part of the depression. Similarly with the suicide: she may not know how much of her attempt was "sincere" and how much was "show," and that does not make her feel better about the attempt and its failure but worse. *Was it a lie, or was I trying to die?* It's not a pleasant question to be asking oneself.

The French phrase *cri de coeur* or "cry from the heart" means "an urgent and strongly felt request for help from someone in a very bad situation," and it is often used to describe a suicide attempt, just as in English we characterize a failed suicide, often with a faintly derogatory or judgmental tone, as "a cry for help." "Oh my God, he tried to kill himself?" "Yes. But I don't know if it was a real attempt or just a cry for help."

An advantage of trying to kill yourself while you still expect to live is that you may at least hope that afterward people will be a bit gentler with you, and perhaps also more forgiving of whatever the suicide attempt may have exposed. If you want to tell your wife that you've been drinking in secret, to take an example from my own life, you might half-heartedly hang yourself, so that when the whole truth comes out, she's nervous about getting too angry with you: *I'd better not yell at him about the drinking, I don't want him to try to kill himself again.*

But even trying to kill oneself in such a way as to all but guarantee that one doesn't die from the attempt often still results in death. And the best predictor of death by suicide is a previous suicide attempt. So it's important to insist that even the most fainthearted suicide attempt should still always be viewed as a warning and often as a plea by someone who doesn't know a better way to tell the world or her loved ones how desperate she truly is.

This is why I prefer *cri de coeur* over "cry for help": it's gentler, and it comes closer to the truth of the failed suicide's situation. She is making a cry from the heart. She doesn't know whether it will be heard, but the heart is in pain, and it is shrieking.

That the person who attempts suicide isn't often perfectly clear on whether she wishes to live or to die is part of the wisdom of the Buddha's and Freud's thinking about this question. If we really do have a desire for self-annihilation along with other competing desires, then a suicide attempt will tend to be a muddled business, motivationally speaking. For the suicidally inclined person, vacillation about whether one wants to live or die is the norm rather than the exception.

And before we go assuming that all suicide attempts, successful or not, contain an element of indecision, we should remind ourselves how difficult suicide actually is. It seems easy until you try it. This was why Mahatma Gandhi, who attempted suicide in his youth by taking *dathura* (jimson weed) seeds with a friend, tended not to worry too much when someone came to him and reported thoughts of suicide: it's both psychologically and practically challenging. Or as the great American humorist Dorothy Parker wrote:

> Razors pain you
> Rivers are damp
> Acids stain you
> And drugs cause cramp.
> Guns aren't lawful
> Ropes tend to give
> Gas smells awful
> Might as well live.

Parker's case is an interesting one: she thought through all the ways and found none of them attractive, yet she tried suicide at least five times before finally dying of a heart attack.

It's not just people like me who try to kill themselves by overdosing, cutting their wrists, or hanging and do not succeed. People use what seem like guaranteed methods of ending their life and fail all the time. The suicide expert Kees Van Heeringen dedicated his book *The Neuroscience of Suicidal Behavior* to "All the

Valeries," because of a "bright young girl named Valerie" he met when he was a young psychiatrist, who "stayed at the rehabilitation department of the university hospital because she lost both her legs after having jumped from a bridge a few weeks earlier." In December 1979, Elvita Adams, at age twenty-nine, in poverty and despair, leaped from the observation deck of the Empire State Building, eighty-six floors above the street below—and was blown back by a gust of wind onto a two-and-a-half-foot ledge on the eighty-fifth floor. She was pulled through the window by a security guard and taken to Bellevue, with a fractured pelvis. In fact, once you start looking, you find that an astonishing number of people have been improbably blown back up from leaps off cliffs and miraculously survived falls from terrific heights. The universe likes to play such jokes on suicidal people.

The most common "foolproof" method is to shoot yourself. The writer Sarah Davys, who tried to kill herself twice and wrote a memoir about her attempts, notes with characteristic irony that shooting is "the best method of all," quickly adding that, "Few of us can obtain a pistol easily, and a gun may merely lead to nasty accidents." (Davys was writing in England in the 1960s. These days, unfortunately, almost all Americans can obtain a pistol easily.)

The first person I knew who committed suicide by shooting himself was my friend Graham from Mr. Wickson's IB Physics in the tenth grade. (My friend Tom with the Mustang SVO was in that class, too.) Graham was a tall, quiet, good-looking kid, with gentle features and soft, shoulder-length brown hair. Like me, he wore glasses. He was taller than me, and we tended to compete with each other, especially about topics in thermal energy, which we both loved. At one point we worked together on that drop-an-egg-off-the-top-of-the-high-school project that they love to assign in tenth-grade science classes. Our egg broke.

One day Mr. Wickson came into class and told us that Graham had died the day before. He couldn't very well let it go at that because we had seen Graham in class that day, and so he had to explain that it was a suicide. We learned later that Graham had put his father's shotgun into his mouth and pulled the trigger. We were all surprised that he had had access to a shotgun, and we wondered if his father, who was a university professor, could possibly be a hunter.

Killing oneself with a gun has always seemed particularly scary to me, not just because of the violence of the act but because the physical consequences of surviving such an attempt can be so grisly. On April 16, 2020, in the early days of California's lockdown, Drew Robinson, a twenty-eight-year-old, shot himself in the right temple. The bullet went only far enough to crush that part of his skull and destroy his right eye. Twenty hours after shooting himself, he recovered consciousness on the living room floor of his apartment and called 911. After a year of physical and psychological therapy, he reports feeling lucky to be alive.

A lot of people go online to talk about methods of killing themselves and to discuss their fears about the process. A common fear is the one I mentioned about using a gun: that one might fail and wind up mutilated instead. This also points to the ambivalence we've been discussing, that someone would want to destroy but not disfigure himself. Even in the wish to commit suicide, there is still self-cherishing. In some ways, the wish to kill yourself is an expression of self-cherishing, because you don't want to have to suffer. A failed suicide attempt tends to increase your suffering, especially if the failed attempt results in some kind of terrible physical mutilation. If one can avoid acute physical pain in the act of killing oneself, one quite reasonably wants to do so. Pain is scary, and the kind of pain we associate with death is especially so, in part because we don't know how painful it will be or how long the pain will last.

Some teenager is only half in love with an easeful death but makes his noose too well and dies. Some other person saves up barbiturates for a year, arrives at the dreadful day, takes an overdose big enough to kill ten people, vomits while unconscious, and lives. You may want to change your mind, as you make your attempt, and what luck! You live. You may think, *No, I'm not ready*, and suddenly try to reverse course, yet you wind up dead. You might desperately desire death, but again you survive, seemingly unkillable; and then you might also know in the depth of your heart that now you must go, and at last you get your way and they find your corpse. The truth is, for most people who are suicidal, these four possibilities or combinations permeate each other.

Clinical psychologist Edwin S. Shneidman, a founder of the field of suicidology, wrote "One curious paradox in suicide is that individuals *do* leave clues—perhaps as part of their deepest ambivalence between the need to stop the pain and the concomitant wish for intervention and rescue." Part of wanting to be lost may be hoping to be found; part of the need to abandon oneself may be a longing for rescue.

In February 2009, according to my older brother Darren, I tried to take my life by charging into busy traffic on an icy street in Calgary, Alberta. I'd gone to visit him a few weeks after I'd gotten out of a stay at the psychiatric hospital following an earlier attempt. He managed to get into the street and pull me out, among honking and swearing drivers, without harm. As I recall, I'm pretty sure I wasn't attempting suicide—I was just addled on a bunch of psychiatric medications and was trying to cross the street. I may have felt a certain carefree cavalierness about whether I dodged the cars successfully—kind of like when you realize, while asleep, that you're dreaming, and now you can do whatever you please. But I don't recall resolving to throw myself in front of a moving vehicle with my brother watching.

When I insisted on that with my brother, he shook his head with obvious fear in his eyes. He was pale and trembling. I'd never seen him so upset.

"Clance, you've got to stop trying to kill yourself," he said. "We're going to get through this. Don't do that to me. I can't handle that kind of guilt."

"I won't do it to you, Darren, I promise," I said. "I really wasn't—"

"Let's just drop it," he said.

It's also entirely possible that I was trying to commit suicide without admitting it to myself. We do things without admitting them to ourselves all the time—this is the essence of self-deception.

In lots of cases, people seem to attempt suicide without

exactly knowing they were doing so. The twentieth-century poet and critic A. Alvarez, one of Sylvia Plath's closest friends, attempted to kill himself during a blackout. (I also tried to do that. I was dragged from the Seine by a waiter in Paris after leaping off a bridge—I don't remember much of what led up to the jump, but perfectly recall the aftermath.) Alvarez didn't know that he'd tried to kill himself—at least, part of his brain didn't know—until he woke up in the hospital and was informed by the doctor. He knew he'd been thinking of doing it and had even taken steps toward it, like saving up a large enough dose of barbiturates, but he had no recollection of making the attempt itself. So allowing for the complex weirdness of the brain and the fundamental unknowability of ourselves, our beliefs, and our motivations, maybe I did mean to kill myself on that icy day with Darren without actually knowing that I intended to. Maybe it was like a kind of muscle memory attack on my own life. Perhaps part of my brain was operating without the knowledge of another set of neural systems.

In *The Wire*, there is a scene where Marlo Stanfield executes his mentor Proposition Joe. Joe is sitting at his table and knows what's coming. As his sidekick Chris slowly raises the gun behind Joe's head, Marlo tells Prop Joe, "Close your eyes. It won't hurt none. There, there now. Joe, relax. Breathe easy." Then Marlo nods, and Chris fires. Pliny the Elder (AD 23–79) distinguished between violent and nonviolent means of killing oneself and thought the latter might be justifiable for those "weary of life," while the former should be avoided. It may not be the horror of death, or even the horror of pain that discourages some of us, but the horror of violence. As I watched Marlo execute Prop Joe, I thought, *Well, that's an awfully nice way to go. It might have been violent for Marlo and Chris, but for Prop Joe it was just, turning out the lights.*

Let's talk a bit more about guns. I never keep a gun around, and I ask anyone who comes to me to talk about suicide whether she or he has access to one. If I have one crucially important piece of advice to offer in this book, among all its many practical recommendations about living as, or with, a suicidal person, it's this: absolutely do not keep a gun in the house. If you have one, get rid of it immediately. Slightly more than fifty percent of people who die by suicide in the United States kill themselves with a gun, and the reason more men die by suicide than women, despite the fact that women attempt suicide about three times as often as men, is that men are far more likely to use guns. (As of 2020, in the United States, out of 100 deaths by suicide, about 70 were men and 30 were women—the suicide rate for women has been slowly increasing for the past few years—and in 2020 there were about three female attempts for every one male attempt.) The states that have the lowest percentage of gun ownership and strictest gun laws, like California and New York, also have the lowest rates of death by suicide. By contrast, in states with high gun ownership rates, like Utah, 85 percent of firearm-related deaths are suicides.

If you're panicking and you own a gun, in short, you can make an irremediable misjudgment.

When I was in my late twenties, I always had a gun nearby. I didn't even have to go to the store to buy the guns I tried to shoot myself with. My first and second guns, and the last gun I ever owned—a dark gray second-generation Glock 17, with a square barrel like all Glocks have, and checkering and serration on the pistol grip—were all brought to me by a retired FBI agent who was a client of mine.

This was in the 1990s, when I was in the jewelry business in Texas with my two brothers. After graduating from college, I went to graduate school in philosophy at the University of Texas at Austin, to study Kierkegaard. My girlfriend Alicia and I were married, and then we went on a fellowship to Copenhagen so that she could write a master's thesis on Hans Christian Andersen and I could write my dissertation on Kierkegaard's concept of irony. Before we knew it, during that very nice year, Alicia was pregnant with our daughter Zelly, and we started to worry about money. At the same time my older brother Darren, who owned a small jewelry store in Arlington, Texas, wanted to buy out his partner and asked me to help him write a business plan to find an investor. We raised several million dollars, and Darren asked me to join him in the business. I had always adored my older brother but had never been able to spend the kind of time with him that

I wanted to—he lived with my dad when I was a kid, and he was living on his own by the time he was seventeen—so this opportunity, combined with the money, was irresistible to me. Repeating my pattern from high school, I dropped out of graduate school, and in 1994 we moved to Fort Worth. I wouldn't return to graduate school until 2000, and those intervening years would prove to be some of the unhappiest of my life.

But there I was, the co-owner of first one and then several jewelry stores of various sizes. At that time I traded jewelry for many illegal things, including the cocaine that I was using regularly (the jewelry business made it easily accessible), and for my guns, which had their serial numbers removed. "Not that you're going to need that," the retired FBI agent explained. "But it never hurts to have one that's clean. Plus you don't have a permit." This fellow was a Rolex collector or perhaps he resold them. Either way, all three of my guns were purchased as lots with guns for other people who worked at the store in a swap for a used Rolex.

I was reluctant to get my first gun, but it was a rite of passage. "You have to own a gun if you're going to be in the jewelry business," my older brother explained. "Because a lot of the time they just kill everybody, so they don't leave witnesses. If anyone ever pulls a gun in here, we start shooting." I don't think this was accurate information. And thank goodness, I never had to point my gun in anger or self-defense.

Before my first attempt to shoot myself, that gun sat in my right-hand desk drawer for a long time. I was afraid of it. This might seem strange: if I wasn't afraid of death, why was I afraid of a gun? But the gun didn't represent death to me. It represented violence. Also, it was too easy. The suicide switch I'd always dreamed of, I finally had it. No excuses anymore. The means to kill myself was literally ready to hand.

But for a long time, more than a year, I didn't try using the gun on myself. Then late one night, coming down off a long day of using cocaine, alone in the jewelry store, depressed and certain that my life was both unbearable and useless, I went back to the bathroom, sat on the toilet, flipped off the safety, put the gun in my mouth, and tried to shoot myself. I pointed the gun at my chest, thinking this might be less frightening, and at my temple, which I had read was unreliable, and then put the gun back in my mouth, trying to point it towards my brain. I turned it upside down in my mouth to get a better angle. I tried to pull the trigger, but I couldn't bring myself to do it. I kept on trying. Every minute sitting there was not about going on living but simply not being able to die. It was ridiculous: all you had to do was pull the trigger. I sat there for about half an hour. Then I put the gun back in my desk, and I didn't go back to the bathroom with my gun to try again for at least a year after that.

Maybe I couldn't do it because I knew it would work—unlike most of my other suicide attempts, when I might still have been able to think, somewhere in the self-deceptive layers of my mind, *Okay, I'm likely to die, but it's not guaranteed, I may yet live*. Or maybe I couldn't pull the trigger for some other reason. But it didn't get truly bad until a few years later, and I was on my third gun, the Glock. By this time I was having an affair. I no longer lived with my wife and baby daughter in Fort Worth but had an apartment in Dallas, and I was convinced that I was a completely worthless person, damaging everyone around me. I was sometimes up and sometimes down. It was at times a strangely happy period for me, especially in the early evenings, when I was usually half-drunk, and I was also finally writing again, which I'd stopped doing when I left graduate school. But in the mornings I almost always felt a crystalline clarity about my own utter uselessness, and so I would again resolve to end my life.

I got up at around five in the morning, to beat the traffic from Dallas to Arlington where our main store was, and to be the first one to arrive in the morning. I often put the top down on the convertible I drove, even on the highway, but this was Texas and I wore a suit every day, so with the heat, you could only do it at night or very early. Normally I would park my car in my usual spot outside the store and walk around to the other side of the Lincoln Square Shopping Center to where my coffee shop was, get a large latte, and then go sit at my desk. I'd open the safes, read part of a story in *The New Yorker*, *Harper's*, or *The Paris Review*—I had these and other magazines delivered to the office, they were lifelines for me—drink my coffee, and sometimes do a line or two of coke. Then I would take my Glock out of its right-hand drawer and go back to the "Executive Bathroom," which only the brothers were supposed to use. (Forgive us, we were young men, rubes really, with a sudden influx of cash, and really stupid about this kind of thing. And anyway, everybody used that bathroom.) I'd sit on the toilet or stand facing the mirror and try to shoot myself. I'd flip the safety off and put the barrel of the gun into my mouth. I will always remember the oily taste of the barrel and the clean machine smell of it that came up into my nostrils through my throat. We had a shower in there, and some-times I would go in the stall and stand or sit on the floor and try to do it, thinking there would be less mess for Darren when he came in. I hoped it would be Darren who found me and not Pat-rick, my little brother, because I thought Darren could handle it psychologically, but it might do some permanent damage to Pat.

This went on for almost two years. When you are trying to shoot yourself, in my experience, thousands of thoughts go through your mind, but you are fundamentally wrestling with three feelings: your misery and self-loathing, your fear of the violence of the act, and your need to insist *Aw fuck it*. It's that *Aw fuck it* that tightens your finger on the trigger and makes you wonder how hard you have to squeeze before it goes off. You squeeze a little, release a little, scare yourself, take the gun out of your mouth, put it on the sink, sometimes sit on the toilet or the floor and cry, stand up, try again. I'd look at myself in the mirror and think how ridiculous I was. It was so theatrical, so pathetic, so overwrought and predictable, shooting myself in the marble and bronze bathroom of my luxury jewelry store in my Armani suit and Zegna tie. It was too grotesque, too laughable. But I was so unhappy, I couldn't go on. And the long list of my failings was stretching out in front of me, and the day ahead, all those people I couldn't face one more time, our overspending and our overdrawn bank account, sitting with rich people per-suading them to buy diamonds and Swiss watches, stalling our vendors, mumbling excuses to my lover about how I'd be home late, yet again . . . *Aw fuck it. But no, don't do it.*

I eventually got rid of the gun, selling it back to the man from whom I had purchased it. But, interestingly, not because

I was only stalling until the day I pulled the trigger. I have my eldest daughter Zelly to thank for eliminating the gun. She was five years old at this time, and she was often in my office, and one afternoon I was sitting at my desk while she was playing next to me and I looked to my right and she had opened my desk drawer and had the Glock in her hand. It was still in the drawer, it was pointed away from her, and the safety was still on, but her little five-year-old hand was clutching the gun, and she was looking at it with interest. It still turns my stomach to think about it. I took the gun away from her, put it in one of our two enormous Tann safes, and called the FBI guy to say that I wanted to sell it.

That was the end of my gun-in-mouth phase. It seems silly to say that this may have been the closest I've ever come to dying by suicide: after all, I've woken up in the hospital following a suicide attempt on three separate occasions, and I've been interrupted by the police to be whisked off to the psychiatric hospital on at least two others. Other people have stopped me in midsuicide. And I've made secret attempts, by hanging, drowning, and other ways. In most and maybe all of those attempts, I believe, I was trying in earnest to kill myself. But that gun felt like the hand of death itself. Perhaps a bit paradoxically, attempting suicide was easier when I was less sure of the outcome—which actually made the likelihood of dying from suicide much higher. The fact that my skin was actually touching death when I had that trigger tightening under my finger might have revealed to me that I wasn't as ready to die as I supposed.

When I tried to do it in that bathroom with my pistol, I had the strange idea that it was shameful to close my eyes. Strange, in part, because I believed that it was profoundly cowardly for me to commit suicide—a belief I'm less sure about today—and yet I clung to this particular way of refusing to see myself as a weakling and kept my eyes open. Or maybe I wanted to force myself to watch what I was doing. Or maybe it was a combination of deep self-preservation and good luck, because if I had ever closed my eyes, I might have been able to pull the trigger. But as long as I insisted on standing in the bathroom in front of the mirror to observe myself as I did it, something about watching kept me from firing. I don't think it was the fear of death. It was not what I would be leaving behind for Darren to find when he arrived at our store an hour or so later.

Truly, again, I think it was just the raw violence of shooting myself that saved me. That fear of violence might make it a bit easier to understand those of us, like me, or like Yiyun Li and Jean Améry, for whom suicide is awfully hard, even though death is or at least often seems to be fundamentally attractive. Such people may tend to think, every time they get on a plane without any family members joining them, *Here, now, is one more chance to die without doing anything. Let the plane crash into the sea.* Would they even be willing to let all those strangers die with them? To be fair, having talked to other people who have made this wish, as I admit with shame that I often have myself, one irrationally hopes that the other passengers will somehow miraculously survive.

On this subject Freud wrote:

> Is it not for us to confess that in our civilized attitude towards death we are once more living psychologically beyond our means, and must reform and give truth its due? Would it not be better to give death the place in actuality and in our thoughts which properly belongs to it, and to yield a little more prominence to that unconscious attitude towards death which we have hitherto so carefully suppressed?

Which unconscious attitude toward death? That we all desire it, in very much the same way we desire sex or food or love or fame. Some of us desire it unconsciously; some of us semiconsciously; and some of us, like me, can't get the desire out of their heads. On this account, the suicidal person, and also the person who is often contending with suicidal ideation but not making a suicide attempt, is in her way giving death its due. She is not suppressing a part of her thinking that other people manage or subjugate more expertly.

. . .

"Pretty well everyone, I should imagine, has at one time or another envisaged the possibility of suicide," the English satirist Malcolm Muggeridge wrote in a 1970 essay about his own suicide attempt, "but as between the person who actually pulls it off and all the various degrees of attempting and failing, there is a wide chasm." Unfortunately, I'm not sure the chasm is quite as wide as Muggeridge imagines. As I've noted, the best predictor of death by suicide is a previous attempt, which means that all the various degrees of attempting and failing are often just one step away from succeeding. But the people I'm most interested in investigating are those in the chasm, those who are struggling with suicidal ideation or have attempted it already. After all, the people we can try to help are the people who are still here. And this includes survivors whose loved ones have killed themselves, and who now think about suicide in a terribly intimate way.

The modest thesis I'm developing here is that thinking about killing oneself and addictive thinking have a lot more in common than is normally recognized. They may even be different variations of the same fundamental kind of thinking. With this model—which, granted, may only characterize one kind of suicidal inclination—wanting to kill yourself is like an extreme version of the relief you find after drinking a few glasses of wine, and the pungent smell of yourself seems to drift off into the breeze. And in fact this theory is really just an elaboration of the Buddha's idea that the desire for self-annihilation is among our most basic forms of suffering, or Freud's idea that the desire for life and the desire for death are two sides of the same coin.

Consider the many people who never actually try to kill themselves but whose lives end prematurely as a result of their own actions, which were obviously motivated by a dominant need to escape themselves. Does it make sense to say that Amy Winehouse committed suicide? Or the poet Robert Lowell, whose extravagant all-consuming alcoholism seemed to lead directly to the heart attack that killed him in the taxi on the way to see his ex-wife, Elizabeth Hardwick? Or DMX, who like Lowell died of a heart attack but seemed to be obsessed with his own death throughout his career and, through his addiction to cocaine, seemed relentlessly to seek self-destruction? Or my favorite actor of the last twenty years, Philip Seymour Hoffman, who died of "acute mixed drug intoxication, including heroin, cocaine, benzodiazepines and amphetamine" in a secret apartment hidden down the street and around the corner from where he actually lived with his family?

Though I've certainly tried to drink myself to death in the past, in some sense I *want* to say no, these acts are not akin to more obvious attempts at suicide. Death by alcohol poisoning is not the same as lying down in a nice warm bath with a bellyful of whiskey, several hundred milligrams of Valium, and a sharp razor (another of my failed attempts). But then, thinking about it more, does it really make sense to say that Amy Winehouse *didn't* commit suicide? Like so many other members of the so-called 27 Club—Robert Johnson, Brian Jones, Jimi Hendrix, Jim Morrison, Janis Joplin, Basquiat, Kurt Cobain, it's a long list—she lived with self-destruction as the guiding principle and herself anticipated that she wouldn't live past twenty-seven. She was alive, but she was trying to die. So while I might argue that Amy Winehouse didn't commit suicide per se, she did deliberately kill herself. The tools were different, but the mission was the same. This is why, when considering suicide and related behaviors, people talk about categories like "deaths of despair": in some ways, it doesn't matter much whether it took a person three years of worsening heroin addiction or three days of ferocious drinking or three terrible minutes with a handgun to end his or her life. The goal is death. In that way, it's even more flagrantly suicidal than a game of Russian roulette.

"Between 1999 and 2017," Atul Gawande writes in *The New Yorker*, "more than six hundred thousand extra deaths—deaths in excess of the demographically predicted number—occurred just among people aged forty-five to fifty-four." The majority of these deaths were a consequence either of suicide or self-destructive "parasuicidal" behavior: the abuse of alcohol, drug addiction and overdose, extremely dangerous sexual behavior, or other unusually violent lifestyles, and of chronic suicide attempts, often of increasing violence or seriousness. (What is meant by the seriousness of an attempt is part of what we've been questioning in this chapter.) The psychiatrist and psychothera-pist Karl Menninger, a pioneer in contemporary thinking about suicide, characterized such self-destructive behaviors as "suicide by degrees."

Death by despair or *parasuicidal behavior*: these terms refer, gen-erally, to a person who doesn't attempt one specific act designed to end her life—such as hanging herself from a belt in the bath-room, for instance—but consistently and repeatedly engages in conduct that will likely hasten her death, sometimes by quite a lot. Many people would say that Amy Winehouse, while not an example of suicide, was an extreme parasuicidal type. A "para-suicidal event" is usually defined as a suicide attempt in which the desire is not death, but something close to it—yet another example of a *cri de coeur.*

My wife Amie is a big fan of Jeff Buckley (who isn't?). On the evening of May 27, 1997, Buckley went swimming fully clothed in Wolf River Harbor, just outside Memphis, Tennessee. As the story goes, he was singing Led Zeppelin's "Whole Lotta Love" as he swam out into the slackwater channel of the Mississippi River. A friend was on the bank watching Buckley swim; the next moment, he was gone. Buckley, who was thirty years old, had no alcohol or drugs in his system, and his death was ruled an acci-dent, which it may well have been.

"I know you think he killed himself," Amie said to me. To be fair, going swimming in a river fully clothed is a traditional way of killing oneself, found in many different cultures and dating back thousands of years. I didn't say this to her. "But to me," she continued, "he seems like one of those cases where he was kind of thinking about doing it, but hadn't made up his mind. Like, will I die as I do this? I don't know. I don't know if I want to or not."

We don't know. And as I've said, in the attempt to kill one-self, many suicides themselves may not know whether they really hope to die: *I can't make up my mind—I'll let the river decide.* To die without having to take responsibility for one's own death might free oneself from the moral guilt that comes with taking your own life, and is one of the reasons the Prop Joe death sounds so appealing to me.

Sometimes the desire for self-destruction and the expression of that desire seem to constitute both the rise and the fall of the parasuicide. Take the case of the famed cyclist Marco Pantani (1970–2004), also known as Il Pirata (The Pirate, because of his signature bandanna and earring) and Elefantino (Little Elephant—one can only speculate). Pantani was legendary for his ability to inflict pain on himself. He was notoriously aggressive in his style and is generally considered to have been the greatest climbing cyclist of all time. He rode the famously punishing 13.8-kilometer Alpe-d'Huez stage of the Tour de France in 36.40 minutes, the fastest ascent ever made, and he also holds the second and third fastest times, followed by Lance Armstrong at fourth and Jan Ullrich at fifth.

Although he won many notable races and prizes, including the Tour de France and the notoriously elusive Giro-Tour double, he never quite enjoyed the huge celebrity status of some comparable riders, and he was reportedly disappointed with his career. He faced accusations of doping and spent some time in a psychiatric hospital for addiction. He was still in his early thirties when he holed up in a hotel room and snorted cocaine until he died. Maybe parasuicides like Pantani both want to die and are convinced that suicide is wrong: *I'm not the suicidal type, yet, I will go on living in a way that more or less guarantees my premature death.*

Pantani, unlike Amy Winehouse, was unquestionably at a low point in his career when his life ended. But another reason cases like Pantani's are particularly interesting to me is that they illustrate the way suicidal thinking and behavior exist on a continuum. On the one hand, I know and have studied with people—some of them, like Khyentse Rinpoche, have been crucial to my own survival and the writing of this book—who are apparently so stable and gentle that they seem never to harm themselves or others, yet are able to understand and speak to those of us who do, even if they themselves have never made an attempt or even imagined making an attempt. On the other hand, I have read many, many cases of people whose lives were so full of rage and self-loathing that they killed other people before taking their own lives.

Between these two extremes are people like me, who are

much too close to the harming-self-and-others side of things, have wreaked havoc in the lives of their loved ones, tried to kill themselves and perhaps succeeded in doing so; others who lived kind and caring lives but perhaps could not bear themselves and so committed suicide; numerous parasuicidal cases who died much younger than necessary due to self-abuse; people like Amie who understand addiction from personal experience but never actively sought to destroy themselves; people who lead perfectly ordinary lives and have only passing addictions but went through a rough time and thought often of suicide, or even attempted it, before returning to a safer place in the world; and fortunate ones who have never attempted suicide nor had any addiction issues and have trouble, perhaps, even understanding what could cause a person to engage in self-destructive behavior. (I have talked to many people who profess to be completely mystified by the act of suicide.) And many of us do engage in bouts of self-destructive behavior during which, if our attention were called to the fact, we might recognize some secret longing for self-annihilation.

In the earliest work on suicide in English, *Life's Preservative Against Self-Killing,* published in 1637, the philosopher and theologian John Sym separates those who kill themselves "directly" by using some immediate means for the job, like hanging, and those who kill themselves "indirectly" with alcohol or some other self-destructive lifestyle. "An indirect self-murderer conceits the good that he aims at, by his course, to be and rest in the very means themselves that he uses, therein expecting the present enjoyment thereof before, and not after his death. The cogitations, and inflicting whereof he abhors, although he does prosecute with eager delight, the courses that do hasten and bring his death." Sym, who believed that suicide is a sin, argued that indirect self-murder might in some ways be more blameworthy, morally speaking, than direct self-murder, because the former involves self-deception. The indirect self-murderer "self-deceives himself with excuses and colorable pretenses, and so does wink (as it were) that he may not see the blow of death that he is giving himself, with his own hands," and doesn't necessarily proceed from the same degree of sorrow as the direct self-murderer. Sym was mistaken about the moral quality of these behaviors, on my way of thinking about suicide and para-suicide, but he did make an interesting point about how the two different types of would-be self-murderers proceed, and he was right to insist that they are two different expressions of the same fundamental motivation. I think Sym might have overestimated how much enjoyment the parasuicide takes in the act of self-destruction: for my part, the only real pleasure I ever took in trying to drink myself to death was the satisfaction of knowing I was destroying myself. I suspect the same is true for most addicts and other parasuicidal types.

Recently in an exercise class the instructor remarked, "Maybe consider the possibility that you can improve without hurting yourself." We were raised, many of us, thinking "no pain, no gain." The parasuicidal person seems similarly to believe that somehow or other, one wants, needs, or deserves to suffer, that one ought to inflict as much suffering as possible on oneself.

But surely that is exactly the wrong way to think. Even if life is full of suffering, as the Buddha insisted, it doesn't follow that we *ought* to be suffering. It might not be something that we can escape, but that doesn't mean we have to pursue it.

3

I Can Always Just Kill Myself Tomorrow

June 8, 2018, was a warm, windy summer morning in the village of Kayserberg. Guests at the Chambard Hotel and Spa breakfasted outside in the breeze. Kayserberg, a tourist town, home to five thousand people, is in the Alsace-Lorraine region of France, in the eastern foothills of the Vosges mountains, about an hour's drive from Germany and Switzerland. This part of France is one of the most picturesque places in the world, and the town is considered to be among the prettiest in all of France. They grow and make particularly good Pinot Gris in that part of Alsace-Lorraine, but are also known for riesling, sylvaner, Gewürztraminer, and pinot noir: Kayserberg is on the "Route du Vin," a celebrated wine route. Because of the intersection of French, German, and Swiss influences, the cuisine is also exceptional, offbeat, and prized. People tour this part of the world to relax, hike, admire the forests, rivers, lakes, and mountains, drink wine, and eat. The area has a number of Michelin-starred restaurants, usually in small, exquisite hotels and spas like the Chambard, the sorts of places that only locals and wealthy sorts know about.

That day Anthony Bourdain woke early, as he almost always did—"I'm a morning person," he said of himself, in part because when he was still in the restaurant business, he had to do his writing before the restaurant opened—and had a light breakfast of Alsatian cheese, cold cuts, fruit, bread, and jam with his friend

Eric Ripert at the Chambard, where they were both staying. He'd been in "a dark mood," Eric had told his mother, but the shooting of the latest episode of *Parts Unknown* was proceeding as usual. "He'd put everything into the shoots and then go back to his room to isolate," Eric later remarked.

On June 7, however, Bourdain didn't come down to have dinner at the Winstub, where he normally ate.

"Mr. Ripert thought it was strange," Maxine Voisin, a waiter at the hotel restaurant, remarked. "We thought it was strange. Mr. Bourdain knew the chef, Monsieur Nasti; he knew the kitchen. Maybe he went out and ate somewhere else."

Later that evening—in the midst, as best we can tell, of an argument with his sometime-partner Asia Argento, who was in Rome at the time—Anthony Bourdain went into the bathroom of his hotel room and hung himself with the cotton belt of his bathrobe.

When the news was announced that Bourdain was dead by his own hand, the world reacted with predictable astonishment. And why not? True, whenever someone wealthy or famous kills her- or himself, we are surprised, thinking naïvely that money or celebrity would solve anyone's problems. But Anthony Bourdain choosing to take his own life was especially shocking. He was a person who had it all: a loving family, including a child; good physical health; fame; romance; more than enough money, but not such wealth that it was burdensome; great success as an artist, in multiple fields (writer, chef, performer, producer); good looks, rugged elegance, and enormous charisma; and perhaps most important, joie de vivre—that effervescence of life that made him such a pleasure to read or to watch. He won ten Emmy Awards for his work in television; he even won a gold medal in jiu-jitsu two years before he died. Aristotle made a list of the many ordinary things one needs in order to have a virtuous, flourishing life: friends, property, money, family, health, education, artistic pursuits: Bourdain had them all.

He was a noble person in other ways, too, a good person. He was, according to people who knew him, exceptionally generous and kind. His longtime publisher and friend Daniel Halpern told me that Tony was unfailingly giving to his many fans and admirers. "He never said no to someone who asked something of him. It took forty-five minutes to get to the bar when you were with him because of all the selfies he'd take with people." Halpern continued, "He never took it for granted: his life, his success, none of it. . . . He loved his life. He looked like he had the ideal life." He seemed like a kind of Nietzschean *Übermensch*, capable of affirming both happiness and suffering, who literally wanted to eat life in all its complexity and richness. Here was a person who shouted yes! to life, and to our genuine delight (and perhaps reassurance), life shouted yes! right back at him.

He'd created his success with his own hard work and talent. He seemed an ordinary guy who through stick-to-it-iveness had gotten it all. He was beloved by an unusually broad array of people across many walks of life, presumably in part because he made us believe in ourselves. He had such an easy way with people, and he didn't seem to care whether they were rich or poor, famous or humble, talented and disciplined, celebrities or ordinary folks—he liked and apparently respected people just because they were fellow human beings. And yet this particular human being, robust, in love, at the height of his career, at the age of sixty-one (looking, one might add, like a much younger man)—an age when we might expect a certain wisdom to be dawning alongside the brilliance of his youth—dies alone, one of 794,000 people who killed themselves that year. He wasn't suffering from chronic depression, and he wasn't in psychiatric treatment.

Cases like Amy Winehouse and Pantani, such clearly self-destructive types, may be too convenient as examples for this hypothesis that we all harbor the desire for death. You might think, reading about my life, that a person like me is bound to suppose we're all self-destructive. *This guy's broken.* And if a person's life looks like a Kurt Cobain burst of firecrackers or a Jeffrey Epstein clear downward slide, then we're not surprised to see it end in death.

But what about those suicides who seem to have it all? People who are abundantly full of life, then abruptly, mysteriously,

throw their lives away? Doesn't that force us toward a different way of thinking about suicide, something more akin to a
momentary urge or misguided passion? If someone like Anthony
Bourdain wasn't safe from suicidal impulses, who is?

It's true, many suicides are impulsive, but the impulse may
have been a long time in the making. In Bourdain's case, the
immediate cause (the source of "the impulse") was probably an
unhappy event in his love life. In the vast, ancient literature on
suicide, heartbreak is one of the most commonly cited causes.
"It may have been because of what was going on in his relationship," Halpern told me in conversation, quickly adding, "It was
a momentary act of desperation. If the moment had passed, he
might have been all right."

Argento herself said of the possible connection between
their relationship and his death, "People say I murdered him.
They say I killed him. . . . I understand that the world needs to
find a reason. I would like to find a reason, too. I don't have it."

In a way, Argento is gesturing toward the truth of Bourdain's
suicide. Yes, things had taken a bad turn in their relationship,
but people break up and hurt each other all the time, and no
one dies as a consequence. The timing of Bourdain's suicide was
tied to heartbreak, but the psychological gears that provided for
the possibility of the act had been turning for years. He once
remarked that he was not the sort of person who should ever
own a home, that he was someone who always ought to rent. As
soon as I read that, I thought, *Oh yes, I recognize you, I know exactly
what you mean.* It reminded me of the great writer Stefan Zweig,
who killed himself along with his wife Lotte in a suicide pact: "A
friend once remarked that, no matter where you met Zweig, his
manner suggested a half-packed suitcase in the next room."

While Bourdain's suicide was surely preventable, as I believe
almost all of them are, he likely had lived with the thought of it
for a long time. He often compared himself to the fictional salesman and suicide Willy Loman, but it's hard to see much similarity between the two unless he believed his life would end in the
way it did. His friend Fred Morin said, "He had just a weird
darkness, you know? I don't think he was afraid. I think he had a

metaphorical cyanide pill, under his tongue, at the ready, all his life, since he was very young."

Bourdain's often extravagant use of drugs and alcohol is commonly found among people who eventually die of suicide. And though it was not part of his public persona, many of his friends described his ongoing struggle with anxiety and depression, and he often said he didn't expect to live beyond fifty-seven, the age his father died. He remarked in his best-selling memoir *Kitchen Confidential* that because of his heroin use, he never really should have survived his twenties. Even if he wasn't yet suicidal at that time, he was clearly parasuicidal.

Bourdain's age was probably also a factor in his death. One tends to think that the older you get, the better your skills at living, at rolling with the punches. And in fact people's resilience does seem to improve with age. That said, as men age, they grow steadily more likely to kill themselves. For an American man, Bourdain was approaching the time of life at the highest risk for suicide. According to data from a 2015 study, men over 65 were the most likely to die of suicide (27.67 suicides per 100,000), closely followed by men aged 40 to 64 (27.10 suicides per 100,000), with the number dropping fairly significantly with men aged 20 to 39 (23.41 per 100,000), and happily much lower yet with boys aged 15 to 19 (13.81 per 100,000). Generally speaking in the United States, according to recent comprehensive data from the American Foundation for Suicide Prevention, those at the highest risk for death by suicide are white middle-aged men.

It may sound like I'm saying that Bourdain was somehow fated to kill himself. Suppose I'm right that we all have a more or less conscious desire for self-annihilation. Does it mean that people who do in fact kill themselves are simply acting out a desire that had become overpowering?

That's not my view. I don't believe I'm fated to die by suicide, and every time I've attempted it, I've had reasons. People kill themselves for reasons, and largely those reasons aren't terribly surprising. The importance of our self-destructive drive, to my mind, is that it helps to explain why one chooses suicide as a response to life's problems rather than another solution. It also explains people like me, who can't get suicide out of their heads.

The idea that people kill themselves for specific reasons is important, because if we are killing ourselves on account of reasons, then perhaps we can also find reasons not to kill ourselves. This is also a good reason to study the lives and thinking of people who have died by suicide.

In his groundbreaking seventeenth-century text on depression, *The Anatomy of Melancholy*, Robert Burton displayed an ambivalence about suicide that many writers on the subject share: at times he sounds as though he thought people chose suicide as an escape from mental or physical suffering, but often he seems inclined toward the view that suicide is a direct consequence of mental illness, and so it doesn't make sense to say that a suicide decided to kill herself. Donald Antrim, a contemporary novelist who has attempted suicide and written brilliantly about it, agrees with this latter view: "I believe that suicide is a natural history, a disease process, not an act or a choice, a decision or a wish." He goes on to say, "It is a disease of the body and the brain, if you make that distinction, a disease that kills over time." Nelly Arcan, who hung herself promptly after completing her final novel, *Exit*, a meditation on suicide, wrote in her earlier novel *Folle* (*Madness*), "for some people like me, the question of which choice to make did not arise because they were simply guided by the voice of nothingness and, by way of response, we remained silent." We'll examine her work in more detail in Chapter 7.

When depression comes, it is not a choice or even usually the consequence of a series of choices. As one friend who has suffered from severe depression all his life put it, "Your weather just changes." Or as Kevin Sampsell put it in an essay in *Salon* about his own depression and near suicide, "It was almost like something had physically happened to me—like I had been in a car accident or suffered a concussion from falling down the stairs—and my chemicals had been jarred somehow." That is what it feels like when depression hits you: you don't know where it came from or why it arrived, it's just *bam!* misery, and sometimes terror. And when a famous and accomplished person such as Kate Spade commits suicide, at age fifty-five, with a thirteen-year-old daughter, wealthy and successful, in the prime of life—someone who, like Anthony Bourdain, had "every reason to be happy," so we suppose—we do look for severe mental suffering as an explanation. As *The New York Times* reported in Spade's obituary, "Andy Spade, her husband, later said that Ms. Spade had sought treatment for depression, adding that it had been severe at times."

Calvin Trillin wrote *Remembering Denny* as an attempt to understand the suicide of his friend Denny Hansen, who had been the most gifted, accomplished, and happiest of his buddies at Yale. He was known for "his California presence." This fellow was expected to be a senator or even president: he was a Rhodes scholar, was twice profiled in *Life* magazine, and was known for his "million-dollar smile"(as Trillin's father described him). And yet, as Trillin remarked when he saw a picture of his friend at his funeral, by age fifty-five he "didn't look as if he had any smiles in him." Another friend of Denny's wrote of his death, "A future president was not meant to be found lying on the floor of a locked garage in Rehoboth Beach, with the ignition of his Honda turned on and the gas pedal held down by a book and a frying pan." Even in youth, Trillin finds at the end of his investigation, "Denny had black moods that were unexplained and perhaps inexplicable."

But when we are considering mental suffering, we don't have the same confidence about the justification for suicide that we have when someone is facing physical suffering. When I was discussing the idea for this book with a friend, I mentioned that I had been shaken by the suicide of Robin Williams. "Oh, me too," she said. "But I felt a bit better when I learned why he actually did it. [His] was a terminal disease thing." (As it turns out, his case is much more complicated than most people suppose.) The point is that our emotional responses to these cases smuggle in a hidden *real* and a hidden *merely*. He was *really* suffering from a terrible disease; he wasn't *merely* suffering from personal struggles or depression.

It's perfectly natural to want to excuse a suicide or to make apologies for it or to tell ourselves that the person somehow "didn't really mean it" or was "forced into it" by physical pain or psychological disturbance beyond her or his control. But that's another way of saying that anyone who kills her- or himself who *didn't have* these compelling external causes should be held accountable, should be judged. It reminds me of the scene from *The Long Goodbye* when the drunk, self-destructive writer Roger Wade asks the tough private eye Philip Marlowe, "Do you ever think about suicide?" And Marlowe replies, with just a hint of moral disdain, "Me? I don't believe in it."

Some of this is age-old Judeo-Christian moral baggage having to do with the notion that the human soul is drawn toward vice and has to resist it to discover virtue. With physical pain and a terminal illness, resisting makes no sense, but with mental pain, we can win the struggle. Some of it is probably our awareness of the fact that any of us could choose to take our own lives if we wished, yet we do not. (Whether this is cause for discreetly patting ourselves on the back and judging others is another question.) Some of it is probably the fact that we've all experienced physical pain, and so can sympathize with wanting to avoid unbearable physical suffering, but many of us may not have experienced moderate or severe depression and/or suicidal ideation, so we just don't have the same natural understanding. Some of it is probably also an ongoing prejudice against mental illness: it's only quite recently that the medical community has recognized depression and other sorts of psychiatric maladies at all. If we get to the point where we can treat depression the way we treat diabetes or, better, polio—if we could vaccinate mild-to-acute depression right out of existence—would that solve the problem of suicide? Or are sadness, anxiety, melancholy, loneliness, and despair, as the Buddha, Christ, Saint Teresa of Ávila, Kierkegaard, Rilke, Lorde, and so many others have thought, fundamental to the human condition and crucial opportunities for spiritual growth?

We are also unwise to bind our concepts and analysis of depression and suicide too closely together. People who kill themselves are often depressed when they do so, but it doesn't follow that depression and suicide operate according to the same rules. The depressive may see suicide (mistakenly or not) as the best solution to her despair without it being the only solution or the natural culmination of her psychological condition. Happily, most depressed people don't choose to kill themselves. And unhappily, many people kill themselves for reasons other than depression.

As we saw in the last chapter, when thinking about the range of cases from the chronically suicidal to the parasuicide, it makes sense to allow that those cases exist along a spectrum that runs from free will to, as Antrim calls it, "natural history." The continuum is similar to the spectrum we see with addiction. Maybe I was doomed by my biology to be an alcoholic; maybe my biology similarly condemned me to attempt suicide. But it feels to me like my will was active in both cases, that I made lots of choices going down the road to hell, so to speak; just as, the last time I went down into the basement to hang myself, I felt like, yes, there were other things I could have done right then, like use this leash to take the dog for a walk rather than wrap it around a beam in the ceiling and then my neck. But this was what I was choosing to do right then. Even if the urge to kill oneself is a disease for some people, as it may be for Antrim, we can take steps to mitigate the disease, just as a diabetic can learn to live with diabetes.

Holocaust survivor Jean Améry, who eventually died by suicide, wrote about this curious interplay of free will and the heavy external and internal factors that might cause someone to take their own life. Some people, he noted, "have already developed for themselves a constitution that is suicidal." This phrasing captures just the spectrum of free will and determinism I have in mind: developing for oneself a suicidal (or addictive) constitution. That is, just as choices become habits, which then make the act of choice less noticeable or even unnecessary, so the forming of a character—a constitution, a way of being—expresses the choices we make as well as the many elements of our lives, both internal and external, that are not strictly in our control.

That said, on Améry's account, when we kill ourselves, we act both freely and with self-liberation in our minds. For this reason, many suicides can be prevented if the person who is momentarily choosing to kill herself is diverted from her intention, or if the immediate means of her death are denied her. When fences are built to prevent people from leaping from bridges, suicide rates go down; when they give gas a smell so that you can't breathe it without knowing what you are breathing, or phase out coal stoves (thus making suicide by carbon monoxide poisoning from charcoal more difficult), suicides go down; when you ban certain pesticides and herbicides—a method popular in Asia and South Asia, where deadly poisons are easier to come by—suicides go down; when you make guns less accessible, suicides go down. Some people may simply be destined to take their own lives, but I believe those cases are unusual and that most deaths by suicide are in fact avoidable. Then again, I may be committed to this view only because I don't want to see myself as a victim of fate or believe that I am inevitably determined to die by my own hand.

What I do believe—and this may be part of what motivates Antrim's observation—is that survivors of loved ones who died by suicide should try not to blame themselves for what happened. We all have to grieve in our own ways, and self-accusation and recrimination are doubtless an important part of the grieving process for many people. Blaming yourself and being angry at the person who died are natural responses, even if there was nothing we could have done differently, and even if that person saw no other solution to his or her dilemma. If the chain of cause and effect led to the death of someone we love, then of course we will wish we had managed to slip some other cause into that series to prompt a different effect.

Most of the time we probably can't (and in some cases, maybe shouldn't) prevent someone else's death if that person genuinely wants to die. A follower of the Russian mystic Rasputin came to him in terrible grief because a loved one had committed suicide and she had been unable to stop it. He told her, "Who are you, to think that you could stop another from suicide? Our Lord and Savior Jesus Christ was incapable of preventing one of his own apostles from killing himself," referring to Judas. In fact, the people who blame themselves after a suicide may very well be the ones who helped the suicide delay for as long as she or he did.

Speaking from my own experience, no one else should have said or done anything differently to prevent my attempts. Yes, people may make matters worse or better. Yes, people kill themselves during arguments or as a result of heartbreak. But one can take alternative actions that don't involve death. You don't choose to murder the person you're arguing with. As a suicidal person, I am in a struggle with myself. It is me that I want to eliminate.

Emily Dickinson wrote:

> *Me from Myself—to banish—*
> *Had I Art—*
> *Impregnable my Fortress*
> *Unto All Heart—*
> *But since Myself—assault Me—*
> *How have I peace*
> *Except by subjugating*
> *Consciousness?*
> *And since We're mutual Monarch*
> *How this be*
> *Except by Abdication—*
> *Me—of Me?*

For anyone who has lost a loved one to suicide, I hope this may help you to understand that their untimely death was not your fault. I don't know if suicide is inevitable for some people, but I strongly believe that the person who has spent a lot of time thinking about suicide and attempts it more than once and finally succeeds—or who dies on the first attempt—is fundamentally alone in waging a battle. This is why suicide notes are not full of anger or accusation but are almost always apologies.

What are (some of) the reasons people take their own lives? In his landmark work *Les Suicides*, one of the definitive studies of the subject, Jean Baechler divides the motives for suicide into four groups: escapist, aggressive, oblative, and ludic. The meaning of the first two categories is obvious. By "oblative," he means suicides that are justified by seeking a higher goal, like saving the life of another, but also striving for an ideal, such as killing one-self to prove one's love or to protest a war. By "ludic," he means suicides that may be related to game-playing (think of Russian roulette) or an ordeal one willingly suffers in order to prove one's merit (like religious martyrdom).

Here I am mostly discussing escapist cases of suicide, because these are the cases I understand. For me, even thinking of suicide (and especially a suicide attempt) is a bit like having a drink: it's taking a break from Clancy. *Please, somehow, get me away from me.* That said, the escapist and aggressive reasons for suicide often blend together (this development of Freud's view was popular among twentieth-century psychoanalysts like Menninger): that is, part of what I may be trying to escape when I try to kill myself is my frustrated aggression toward someone else. Six-year-old me trying to kill myself, for example, was surely angry at my mother about our new family; at my father about leaving us and moving so far away; at my older brother for running off to the United States to live with our dad and abandoning me; and at my new stepfather, who in many unfair ways I blamed for all my unhappiness and that of the people I loved. I couldn't directly attack any of my family. But I could, in my six-year-old heart, by committing suicide, make them pay for what they had done to me.

Sometimes the why of a person committing suicide is more or less obvious. In his 1937 essay "Suicide" Alfred Adler argued, "There are certain situations from which the normal person regards suicide as the only way out . . . situations which are too distressing and unalterable, such as torment without any pros-pect for relief, inhumanly cruel attacks, fear of discovery of dis-graceful or criminal actions, suffering of incurable and extremely painful diseases, etc. Surprisingly enough, the number of suicides actually committed for such reasons is not great." Adler goes on to offer some other motives, contending that, in his extensive experience as a psychologist, "among the so-called causes for suicide, disregarding the cases of the psychologically ill, loss of money and unpayable debts take the first place. . . . Disappointed and unhappy love follow in frequency."

Similarly, more than a century ago, among the Navajo Indigenous Americans, the four common causes of suicide were said to be "brooding over incurable illness; sexual jealousy and marital problems; the desire to avoid jail or other serious punishment for an offense; and the death of a relative." These reasons are familiar to us: sickness, a broken heart, shame, grief.

When the French existentialist philosopher and novelist Albert Camus discussed the "why" of killing oneself in his essay "The Myth of Sisyphus"—probably his most widely taught and read essay, and certainly the best-known essay on suicide—he wrote that "what sets off the crisis is almost always unverifiable. Newspapers often speak of 'personal sorrows' or of 'incurable illness.' These explanations are plausible. But one would have to know whether a friend of the desperate man had not that very day addressed him indifferently. He is the guilty one."

Which is to say, yes, people kill themselves for reasons, but those reasons are only what bring them to the brink of suicide; what finally drives a person over the edge, what makes him decide "today is the day, I can't take this any longer," may be the most trivial thing. Camus gets this exactly right: because things are going badly, a person who might otherwise never take her own life starts feeling increasingly suicidal, and then as she gets more and more despondent, one final slight is enough to make her say *enough*.

The truth is that for many people, and perhaps even for everyone at some point or other, it takes a tremendous effort just to go from one day to the next. Charles Bukowski once remarked that the mere thought of having to get out of bed every morning and tie your shoelaces and brush your teeth was more than enough to drive any reasonable person to the brink of suicide. The repetitive drudgery of everyday life that seems to take us nowhere can be oppressive and very discouraging. And even when it's not, sometimes the thought of what one has to confront in the day ahead—reproach, failure, fear, bitterness, anger, disappointing the ones who depend on you—is more than you feel like you can handle.

Our hold on reality may be more fragile than we like to suppose. In one episode of *Parts Unknown*, Anthony Bourdain remarked, "I will find myself in an airport, for instance, and I'll order an airport hamburger. It's an insignificant thing, it's a small thing, it's a hamburger, but it's not a good one. Suddenly I look at that hamburger and I find myself in a spiral of depression that can last for days."

On June 9, 2020, the screenwriter and journalist Jasmine Waters, popularly known as Jas Fly or Jas Waters, died by hanging herself in her home in Los Angeles County, California. She was a celebrated writer on the popular television show *This Is Us*. She was also one of the first Black women to break through the many barriers to artistic and financial success as a writer in Hollywood.

In the *Miami Times* obituary, the staff reporter asks the natural question, "But how can this be? Jas was a beautiful Black woman, who was also successful in Hollywood with accolades from her peers and notable stars. It seems like she had everything going for her. So, what happened?"

Jas Waters's death received more attention than usual in the media because of what is sometimes called "the suicide paradox" of Black women in America: while no one denies that, as a socioeconomic group, Black women have (and for centuries have had) among the most challenging circumstances, nevertheless "out of four primary subgroups in the United States—white males, black males, white females, and black females—the final group, black females, has and always has had the lowest rates of suicide." In her memoir *Negroland*, Margo Jefferson—who wrote brilliantly of her own struggle with the desire to kill herself—noted that "one white female privilege had been withheld from the girls of Negroland . . . they had been denied the privilege of freely yielding to depression." Not until Ntozake Shange wrote *For Colored Girls Who Have Considered Suicide / When the Rainbow Is Enuf*, Jefferson continued, could Black women "consider—toy with, ponder, contemplate—suicide."

When I spoke with Jefferson about the relative rarity of suicide among Black women and about her own struggles with depression and suicidal ideation, she reminded me that for Black women, survival has always been understood both as an obligation and as a victory. "Survival was the triumph," she said, which included "the survivors of suicidal longing." To be a Black woman in America, she added, was to be taught, "In every way I must rise above." This makes the willingness of women of color like Jasmine Waters and Margo Jefferson—and recently, prominent voices like Simone Biles and Naomi Osaka—to speak openly about their psychological struggles all the more remarkable.

Which is not to say that the suicide of Jasmine Waters was a good thing—of course not. Perhaps the fact that she felt she had *the right* to kill herself was a good thing, even if there were other, better solutions to her dilemma. As best we can tell, she took her life because she was in unbearable psychological pain. The taboo against depression and suicide among Black women also interestingly complicates the question of how such taboos may protect entire populations while at the same time increase the suffering of the individual. On the one hand, Black women in general may not commit suicide because it's verboten, while on the other, an individual Black woman may find her torment increased because her desire for self-extinction violates a perceived norm or duty. Throughout the history of depression generally and suicide in particular, taboo has been used for the purposes of discouraging both honesty about the experience and its expression in action.

Waters had attempted suicide at least once before, at the age of twenty-one, by consuming an entire bottle of Tylenol. She had been diagnosed with depression when she was nineteen, and she seems to have wrestled with it throughout her adult life. The isolation and lack of routine created by the coronavirus seemed to exacerbate her depression and anxiety—as it has done with so many—and in the months immediately preceding her death, it played out in her Twitter feed:

"Creative strangulation."—March 30, 2020, at 6:12 p.m.

"Spent the last hour doing yard work instead of spiraling. That's it. That's today's victory."—April 15, 2020, at 4:59 p.m.

"What did you learn in our time away? I've been think-ing about my rolling series of answers a lot. But if I could pin one down long enough to share it would be this: as someone that's had my greatest fears hung above my bed for me to wake and then go to sleep daily."—April 16, 2020, at 12:54 p.m.

"Wonder what my next life will be like."—April 20, 2020, at 7:04 p.m.

"I'm in hell."—April 22, 2020, at 4:36 p.m.

"I'm tired of sheltering in place with my anxiety. Most days is nearly debilitating. Hence, the cooking simply for the calm it brings. So if you are struggling just to keep the fear of the unknown in check, know that you're not alone. I'm with you."—April 24, 2020, at 10:12 p.m.

"Some shit just changes you."—May 8, 2020, at 12:05 a.m.

About a month after this last tweet, she took her life.

She knew she was struggling, and she knew she wasn't alone in her struggle. Although many of her tweets might be used as evidence of what was to come, just as many show that she was taking her condition seriously and trying to help others like her-self who might be suffering.

In August 2014, in an early example of both her own struggle and her recognition of the suffering of others, Waters wrote a long Tumblr post about Robin Williams's suicide:

FOR ANYONE THAT NEEDS IT . . .

Robin's death hit me in a way I never expected. . . . I was first diagnosed with depression at 19. I'd stumbled through a pretty rocky childhood, and eventually two years later, it all caught up with me one night when I just didn't think I could stomach another day of intense sadness. I swallowed a bottle of Tylenol PM. Now, did

I want to die? Not really. But that was the only way I could break through this overwhelmingly thick barrier of hopelessness that stood between myself and everyone else. Having your stomach pumped is enough to scar you for life. Trust me on this. More importantly, that and the look of genuine fear in my father's eyes were enough to make me want to learn how to live with depression. It is a disease. It is not an emotion. And it's something that with lots of time, self-work and consistent effort, anyone can overcome. I am living proof. People with depression often hide in plain sight. In the worst of times, we go about our lives with canned responses, doing just enough to not ring any alarms because when you're in the thick of it, the answer to everything is, "what's the point?"

But, you. That's the point. You.

These days depression is a part of my life much like dieting. It's an exercise in discipline. Once every four or five months I'll have one really tough day where it'll feel like my entire life is going to hell. It's in those moments where I evoke the emergency response part of myself that's ready to remind me that I'm not having a bad life, just a bad day. Then I wait it out. Or if I can't, I call someone. More than anything I've learned there is no shame in simply saying, "I need some help" or "I'm having a tough time" or "I just need to hear a friendly voice." I'm human. And thankfully, so is everyone else.

I say all of this because as I reflect on Robin and the brilliant catalogue of laughs and lessons he left us, I can't help but wish he'd remembered that he wasn't having a bad life. Just one last bad day. And maybe we can all use this as Robin's final gift to us, a heart-breaking reminder that there is no shame in simply picking up the phone, sending a text, a tweet, a status update or simply walking outside and saying, "I'm having a tough time." Maybe that can be the lesson amidst our confusion and grief . . . for anyone who needs it. O Captain! My Captain! Thank you.

"Now, did I want to die? Not really." This part of the long and loving eulogy for Robin Williams will haunt anyone who has tried to commit suicide and failed, or who has thought about it a great deal but hasn't made an attempt, or who has known someone who attempted it and about whom they still worry. Because Jas Waters didn't really want to die, yet suicide wound up ending her life.

Jas Waters told us the story of her depression and eventual suicide mostly on Tumblr and Twitter. But the use of social media itself may have had a role in her death. Social media can do a lot of good. People struggling with depression share posts for people struggling with depression, especially, aimed at people aged ten to twenty-four, whose suicide rate skyrocketed even before the coronavirus pandemic and now has escalated even higher. When I look at their social media postings, I am grateful that they are sharing their stories. We should be thinking about ways to use social media to help people struggling with depression and the desire to die.

But Jas Waters's experience also teaches us something about social media's impact on mental health. The medium may give us the illusion of communication with other people without actually providing any of the benefits of traditional human interaction. What if you are speaking out on social media, asking for help, as Waters clearly was, and no one speaks back, really?

In an interview before she died, Jas Waters said of social media, "It's an absolute panic room, and that's not good for anyone. It doesn't actually solve anything, because there's very little conversation actually being had." Not only are we not helping each other by trying to communicate in this way, but we may actually be harming each other, because the use of social media seems to correlate roughly with one's degree of loneliness, particularly among young people.

Another obvious problem with social media is the fact that much of what we see and read there tends to convince us that other people's lives are better than our own. Many recent studies have documented this, but we are all familiar with the twinge of envy that comes from seeing someone else's obviously perfect vacation or obviously gorgeous home or obviously flawless body. (In the literature on the subject this is called "compare and despair.") Seeing these images over and over again—even if one similarly curates an unreal online image of one's own life—exaggerates our natural tendencies toward self-doubt and self-accusation. Even if I only suspect that I'm not okay and that other people are definitely okay (and even much better than okay), half an hour of Instagram swiping will convince me my suspicions are well-justified.

There's also the old familiar problem of popularity. When we don't get enough likes, we doubt our own likability. When we see how many likes other people get, we feel further diminished. When we don't have enough friends, we become convinced we are unlikable. When we see the parties that our friends are invited to that we weren't, when we admire the happy circle of beautiful loved ones they have that we don't, when we count up our own birthday well-wishers versus those of the people we know . . . well, it goes on and on. Social media may actually generate self-loathing, and we're still figuring out how to handle it. And this is without even going into the many cases of suicide among young people that are directly attributable to bullying online.

Last year I interviewed Dese'Rae L. Stage, a suicide survivor and contemporary expert on suicide, whose website LiveThroughThis.org and podcast Suicide-n-Stuff.com I heartily recommend. Toward the end of the interview, when Dese'Rae and I were talking about staying in touch, she said, "Well, we're both on social media, right?" That normally would have been followed by "Let's become Facebook friends or get on each other's Instagram" or whatever it happened to be. But as I explained to Dese'Rae, I'm not on social media, simply because I found that Facebook made me depressed, and Instagram wasted too much of my time.

I haven't had a suicide attempt that was tied to social media, but when I realized that social media was harming rather than helping my mental health, I got off those sites entirely. Not surprisingly, a teacher I admire, when asked why suicides were increasing among young people in the Himalayas, explained that it related to smartphones and likes on their various social media accounts.

In short, without overstating the obvious, if a person finds that the use of social media is making her or him feel sad or anxious or depressed, it's probably a good idea to stop using it. For my own part, I already have so many sources of self-loathing, so many lists I can compile of why I'm not measuring up, and how I've disappointed the people I love, and how I've not achieved what I might have and how I've failed to be a good person that I don't want to add more—especially one that seems to be a fundamentally misleading source of information.

Self-loathing, the sources of self-loathing, and the dangers of self-loathing were strong catalysts behind my prior suicide attempts, so for me, staying away from social media is a matter of survival. In fact, for many people I've spoken with about suicide, both inside and outside of psychiatric hospitals, their feeling of self-loathing was a principal cause behind their attempt. In the eighteenth century, Madame de Staël described the desire for suicide as "the mortification which sometimes afflicts those who believe themselves useless upon earth." It is certainly the motivation for suicide I understand best.

And while I don't always understand the sources of my self-loathing, I have learned to avoid those things that tend to increase it. My hope is that I can come to better understand these triggers, so that they become less threatening to me. That's one thing I'm attempting to do in these pages: to examine my life during some of my most desperate moments to see if some of those sources of self-loathing can be exorcised. This is something we suicidal people need to do. Anthony Bourdain clearly grappled with it effectively enough to fool others, if not himself. As his friend David Simon observed,

> I never got a sense of any level of self-loathing [in Bourdain] that I took seriously. I have all kinds of memories of beautiful and comically delivered self-loathing, and, "I'm so full of shit, but nobody will catch me now," laughing at himself sort of stuff, that I'd be lying now if I said I'm hearing it with a different ear because of his suicide. I don't think so. It was delivered in such a way that it seemed like the very wit of mental health.

Bourdain tried to exorcise his self-loathing with humor. Acknowledging, and being willing to laugh about, and laugh with others about the ways you hate yourself surely must help. But it's a struggle, a lifetime's work, and it doesn't always give us the result we want. Sometimes self-loathing wins.

Could someone have helped Jas Waters or Anthony Bourdain? What if anything can we say to the person who wants to kill himself or herself? How do we talk a jumper off the ledge?

To quote again from *The Sorrows of Young Werther*, "It is in vain that a man of sound mind and cool temper understands the condition of such a wretched being, in vain he counsels him. He can no more communicate his own wisdom to him than a healthy man can instill his strength into the invalid, by whose bedside he is seated."

I believe this is importantly false. I agree that there is some truth here: a person who tries to calmly persuade a suicidal friend, in a desperate moment, that her life has meaning will likely fail and is going about the task in the wrong way. "Look on the bright side" arguments will not work at such a time. But there are ways to talk to a suicidal person that can help him or her, ways of moving that person from a catastrophic mindset into a less panicky place. There are also techniques we can use on ourselves. I discuss one of my own tried-and-true arguments or techniques at the end of this chapter, and I try to provide them throughout the book as well.

It's different if a person reaches out for help or, in a slightly less resolute state of mind, sends an email, surfs the web, or reaches for a book. Many of the emails I've received over the years from people considering killing themselves have begun with some variation on "I was googling least painful methods of suicide when I came across your writing." But trying to get through to a person who isn't asking for your help and who is in crisis—or more difficult still, recognizing that you are yourself in crisis and you have to talk yourself through it—that's a real challenge.

I've asked numerous people what they might say to someone

on the brink of killing herself, and even the experts tend to be at a loss for words—not because they haven't considered the question over and over again, but because at those times words might not be terribly adequate. And yet words are often all we have to work with.

When we ask "Why did she do it?" at best we're hoping to find answers for ourselves or others about how we might avoid a similar fate. At the very least, we're taking suicide out of the realm of the taboo, so that we can begin to make some progress on the subject collectively, rather than leave it in the frightening and often disorienting echo chambers of our own minds. And the fact that we attempt suicide for reasons, as I have been arguing, really does matter, because it shows that suicide is not inevitable. But asking "Why did she do it?" about a person who died of suicide is quite different from asking "Why do you want to do it?" of someone who is suicidal.

The first step toward better understanding and preventing a suicide attempt may be admitting that "Why do you want to do it?" or "Why did you try to do it?" are usually not the most helpful questions to ask a suicidal person. Even people who have spent their lives studying suicide and their own suicidal tendencies may not quite understand why they tried to kill themselves. In a masterful analysis of her own suicide attempts, the Princeton professor and novelist Yiyun Li wrote, "There are many ways to answer the question. Not everyone would ask, but some would if true curiosity—a genuine desire to understand—were allowed in place of good manners. I would, too. In fact, I still do ask myself: What made you think suicide was an appropriate, even the only, option?"

Almost every expert on suicide agrees on one thing: that if possible, you should get the suicidal person to talk about whatever is going on by asking direct, specific, and fearless questions. If a person will tell you what's going on with her when she's about to kill herself, she is more likely to find the emotional space not to act on the desire. This is not about solving the problem that the person may find herself in. It's not about identifying reasons for the suicide attempt. (That can even be unhelpful, as people tend to dig in with their reasons.) It's just a technique for creating some room, for helping a person to see that in fact she is not locked in a coffin sinking into the sea. Also, in my own experience, if you can coax someone on the brink to go outside and breathe some fresh air and walk around a bit, it's very beneficial. Get them talking, and get them walking. Talking dissipates the terrifying loneliness they experience at that moment, and they start to feel they can make it through the next few minutes, maybe even the next hour, the next day. And once they're walking, something magical happens: it reminds them of the beauty of the world, and panic's claustrophobic grip seems to loosen its hold.

So much of the fear of those final minutes before you actually try to kill yourself comes from a feeling that the world is closing in on you. But when you're walking, it's hard to feel that way. Even a short walk will give you a much-needed endorphin boost. And if you're walking outside, the secrecy that accompanies most suicide attempts—and secrecy is a weird part of their appeal, like the secrecy of masturbation or illicit drug use—is no longer possible. People commit suicide in public all the time, but significantly less often than they kill themselves in private.

Many people frequently consider suicide but don't attempt it, yet they see it as a temptation. Such "passive suicidal ideation" is increasingly acknowledged and discussed in the larger conversation about suicide. (It's long been a part of the psychiatric literature on the subject, and whether it's a likely indicator of a future suicide attempt continues to be highly controversial.) One of my dearest friends recently sent me an excellent article by Anna Borges, "I Am Not Always Very Attached to Being Alive," on passive suicidal ideation, adding in the email, "I didn't know this was a thing, though I have felt this way many times."

It's statistically proven that successful suicides, especially when widely publicized, will increase other suicide attempts and the overall rate of suicide. In guidelines to reporters on how to talk about death by suicide, the American Foundation for Suicide Prevention explicitly warns, "Do not refer to suicide as a 'growing problem,' 'epidemic' or 'skyrocketing' as this has shown to cause contagion." This is particularly true when a famous person kills her- or himself. After Robin Williams took his own life, for one, researchers estimate that the suicide rate in the United States increased by 10 percent—a terrifying statistic when you consider that 42,773 people that we know of died by their own hand that year. That means that about 4,200 people who, statistically speaking, might otherwise not have killed themselves, died as a consequence of learning about Robin Williams's death.

What we today call "suicide contagion" (or "the Werther effect," because of the sudden spike of suicides after the publication of Goethe's Bildungsroman *The Sorrows of Young Werther*, which concludes with Werther's suicide) is widely documented but not well understood. A 2019 paper studied one "suicide cluster"—a group of copycat suicides—among teenagers in an affluent community, concluding that the suicide of one person, especially someone prominent and respected in the community, made suicide more acceptable to other members of the community. This makes intuitive sense: if Robin Williams or Anthony Bourdain, both of whom I admire, thinks it's okay to take his own life, then the idea is more likely to occur to me and seem more appealing when it does. Sadly, adolescents are particularly prone to suicide contagion. If a cool person commits suicide, suddenly it may seem like suicide is cool. In Chapter 7, while discussing the author Édouard Levé, I mention the suicide contagion that some thinkers tie to the myth of the macho suicide in the American West, personified by Ernest Hemingway, who killed himself with his shotgun in Ketchum, Idaho, on July 2, 1961, at the age of sixty-one. Hemingway was so famous and embodied such a powerful stereotype of a kind of American masculinity—boxer, hunter, ladies' man, outdoorsman—that his death by suicide, and the manner of his death (the gun), might have exerted (and may still exert) a contagious effect among the suicidally inclined.

The phenomenon of suicide contagion is undoubtedly influenced by the theatrical nature of suicide and its mindset. It *is* dramatic when someone kills herself, especially someone we know and admire. Why shouldn't I too be allowed that performance and receive all that attention? Even if the attention is in death, at least, finally, someone cared about me, someone noticed me, someone took the trouble to say: *Look, he mattered.*

In my own case, I want to insist that both the theatricality of suicide and the fact that a number of my heroes have died by suicide most certainly have contributed to particular attempts and my overall mindset. Probably my earliest encounter with a writer glorifying suicide—and so many writers have made suicide seem attractive or even glamorous—was a poem by Rudyard Kipling. Like many other six-year-olds, I loved Kipling's stories, and I read everything I could get my hands on. At some point, I came across the poem "The Young British Soldier" and I was especially fascinated by these lines from the last stanza, which I immediately learned by heart: "When you're wounded and left on Afghanistan's plains, / And the women come out to cut up what remains, / Jest roll to your rifle and blow out your brains / An' go to your Gawd like a soldier."

Today, as the father of a four-year-old, I'm horrified to think of six- or seven-year-old Clancy going through his days repeating this poem to himself and cherishing it in his heart. The truth is, at that time I was already obsessed with suicide, and even wrote a lot of childish poetry about killing myself, which prompted a parent-teacher conference after my teacher found one of them in my desk, melodramatically and embarrassingly called "Sweet Suey, Suicide." I told them some lie about writing poems for fun, and though this fact astonishes me now, neither my mom nor my teacher brought it up again.

While news of popular people killing themselves may make suicide contagious, and writing by our heroes about suicide may make it seem more legitimate or even appealing, discussion of suicide itself, especially among people seeking to understand the act, reduces its prevalence. As Meghan Markel succinctly put it in remarks about her own struggle, "I was ashamed to have to admit it to Harry. I knew that if I didn't say it, I would do it. I just didn't want to be alive anymore." Talking about it helped her avoid trying it. The NBA star Kevin Love, who has struggled with thoughts of suicide for years, similarly insists that talking about his close brushes with an attempt—include googling ways to kill himself—is one of the best techniques for dealing with his thinking. "You don't get to turn it on or turn it off," he says. "Nothing haunts us like the things we don't say, so me keeping it in is actually more harmful." The same is true for people who attempt suicide and live to tell the tale: discussion of the attempt reduces the risk of subsequent tries as well as the prevalence of suicide in the community.

In other words, if we kill ourselves, people may be more inclined to copy us. The ripple effects among family members are particularly devastating and well documented. But the happy statistical fact is that talking about suicidal thoughts, actual attempts, and the whole painful and embarrassing business tends to discourage the act.

April Foreman of the American Association of Suicidology warns, "We don't really know [the impact of] having more casual conversation about suicide. . . . Stigma is lower than it's ever been and suicide rates are as high as they were during the Great Depression. If reducing stigma alone saves lives, the suicide rate should be going down." But with all due respect to Foreman, this doesn't track: reducing the stigma may be saving lives and reducing suicide, but the suicide rate is nevertheless increasing due to a host of other factors.

The perceived need for keeping one's suicidal impulses secret is understandable; even as I write this, I generally keep these thoughts secret from my own loved ones and even my psychiatrist. But the secrecy definitely exacerbates my thoughts. My shame increases; my fear and worry about them amplifies; the vertiginous feeling of them threatening to take me into an accelerating downward spiral heightens. So why do I keep them secret? I fear burdening others; I fear intensified psychiatric care, including hospitalization; I fear the practical consequences of expressing such thoughts. In short, I fear the ongoing social stigma, which includes the reactions of my own loved ones: *I thought you were getting past all that. . . . You've been doing so much better! . . . When was the last time you tried? . . . Do you think you're in danger now?* Et cetera.

But writing about my thoughts of suicide has been helping me, and I am told, it helps others who have read my previous writing about them. If nothing else, it's good to know that other people out there are dealing with this way of thinking and still managing to live their lives. As Anna Borges wrote, "Speaking freely need not solely carry the weight of prevention. It can simply be about the comfort of social connectedness and knowing you're not alone. . . . I might want to die forever. . . . In the meantime, I need to talk about the treading [water]." If I can't talk about it, at least I can write about it. And if my writing appears somewhere on the Web, people might respond. Then suddenly we're emailing about it, and helping others also helps me.

Margaret ("Peggy") Battin, a professor at the University of Utah, is the world's leading philosopher on suicide and related end-of-life decisions. In an interview, she told me about her long-term membership in the American Association of Suicidology (Suicidology.org), the principal U.S. organization dedicated to preventing suicide (or the "zero suicide" goal—as distinguished from medical aid in dying, commonly referred to as euthanasia).

Battin told me that about fifty years ago, when the American Association of Suicidology was founded by Edwin S. Shneidman (whose work has been indispensable to my own), many people associated with the organization had had personal experiences with suicide, but it absolutely wasn't discussed. This wasn't because they feared "triggering" more attempts, but simply because there was a strong social stigma against suicide, and the person who had tried and failed risked humiliation.

It *is* humiliating to have tried and failed, especially, like me, to have tried and failed multiple times. I consider my own case to be a bit comical—in fact, I would consider it utterly ridiculous if I hadn't met and talked to so many other people who have also tried multiple times, and learned about and known people who have tried multiple times and ultimately did die by their own hand. While the best predictor for a future death by suicide is a previous attempt, the next-best predictor is ongoing mental health difficulties, especially hopelessness, depression, substance abuse problems, and psychosis. These problems are commonly shrouded in silence and can only be dealt with once we start talking about them. You won't overcome them just by talking about them, but until you do, you won't get the help you need. And as anyone who has benefited from cognitive-behavioral therapy or an AA meeting will tell you, talking about your problems may be much more helpful than you realize.

And while we may never learn "why" someone desires to kill

herself, or why someone dies by suicide, talking about the *possible* reasons is more important than finding an answer. In 1989 William Styron wrote of his own depression and suicidality, "I shall never learn what 'caused' my depression, as no one will ever learn about their own. To be able to do so will likely forever prove to be an impossibility, so complex are the intermingled factors of abnormal chemistry, behavior, and genetics. Plainly, multiple components are involved—perhaps three or four, most probably more, in fathomless permutations. That is why the greatest fallacy about suicide lies in the belief that there is a single immediate answer—or perhaps combined answers—as to why the deed was done."

Similarly, in James Hillman's *Suicide and the Soul* (1973), one of the best books written on suicide, the great American psychologist briefly reviews the "immensely muddled terminology" on the subject, the result of the misguided if natural attempt to create "a taxonomy of suicides." Hillman argues that while we certainly can make progress in understanding suicide—including our own suicidal thinking—focusing too much on finding a one-size-fits-all explanation will inevitably lead us astray. He also thinks that trying to sort the suicidally inclined into different types is just making the same mistake in a more complicated way. People have used an enormous variety of means to commit suicide, from eating poisonous spiders or broken glass to leaping into volcanoes to entering lions' cages; suicide *en masse* and ritualized suicide; suicide as a way of avenging oneself on the dead or in imitation of the martyrs; and so on. In considering the mystery of suicide, Hillman wrote that "suicide is one of the human possibilities. Death can be chosen . . . each death is meaningful and somehow understandable, beyond the classification."

That's what I'm looking for in my own life, and in the lives of the people I've known and read about who have attempted suicide or died by it. Can we learn the meanings of these particular kinds of deaths and attempts to die? Styron was right: We won't solve the mystery of why we commit suicide. But talking to each other about it will help those who are feeling suicidal. And we can make some progress toward understanding suicidal thinking.

. . .

People often ask me for an effective method of talking someone "off the ledge," and I always point to one argument in particular, a version of what the Stoics called "the door is always open."

A funny story illustrates the argument well. Back in 2006, on a Kansas highway, I rear-ended a car in bumper-to-bumper, five-mile-an-hour traffic. I didn't damage the other car, but apparently panicking over the possibility that the people I had hit would call the police and I would be arrested for driving under the influence, I quite reasonably drove off the highway onto the embankment, bursting two of the tires on my own car, then tried to make my getaway (missing the front and rear wheels on the passenger side of my Infiniti G20) on a nearby frontage road. Mercifully, I soon wound up in a ditch, and no one was harmed. I then tried running away on foot. The police finally caught me.

"I've got a video of pretty much the whole thing on a CCTV camera," my lawyer told me. "It's actually hilarious. You want to watch it? Might be therapeutic."

"Uh, no," I said. "So we got the deferred adjudication?"

"Yeah, it's exactly what we were hoping for. No criminal charges, nothing like that. You lose your license for a while. And you have to do three days in prison. But it's a minimum-security place down near Olathe. It's no big deal, there will be lots of other people there just like you. It's really pretty comfortable. You'll do some group therapy, AA, that sort of thing."

He was right—it wasn't that bad. But what made the experience fundamentally different from the other times I've been in jail or locked up in a psychiatric ward was one simple thing: I was free to leave. They actually show you the door you can exit, and when you check into the prison, they tell you, "You can leave anytime. Be aware that as soon as you do—and we have cameras and alarms, so we'll know when you do—that a warrant will be issued for your arrest. But no one is going to stop you, and no one from this facility is going to chase you down. Some people make it all the way home. Some people get picked up on the highway. I'm not saying it's a good idea," the intake administrator informed me with a smile. "But you're free to do it."

I was never even tempted to leave while I was there, but the terrible, mind-crushing, almost unbearable claustrophobia that I suffer when constrained to stay in a jail or a psychiatric hospital was utterly gone. Because I was free to leave, I felt like I was choosing to be there. And that tiny attitudinal difference—which in some practical sense was no difference at all; the consequences would have been so dire if I had left that I would have been crazy to leave—was absolutely crucial.

And this is the key intuition behind the Stoics' "the door is always open" argument in defense of the right to kill yourself. The first explicit mention of this argument in the Western philosophical literature is in one of Plato's dialogues about the death of Socrates, *Phaedo*. There one of Socrates's students, Cebes, asks Socrates why suicide is unlawful, and Socrates replies, "There is a doctrine whispered in secret that man is a prisoner who has no right to open the door and run away: this is a great mystery which I do not quite understand." Cebes then mounts an argument (which we will discuss in greater detail in Chapter 6) that human life really belongs to the gods, from whom it derives and in whose greater judgment we should trust. Notably, Plato attributes the argument to Socrates's student and not to Socrates.

For the Stoic, the ability to commit suicide is the most fundamental and all but irrevocable expression of our freedom. Seneca put his short version of the "door is always open" argument this way: "A wise man will live as long as he ought, not as long as he can." Life, thus, is not the highest value. Other values may well matter more. So when life comes into conflict with those other higher values, one should simply step through the open door of death.

The Scottish philosopher David Hume, too, made this his strongest argument in defense of the right to kill oneself. The possibility of committing suicide, he claimed, liberates us "from all danger of misery." That is to say, as long as we know we can kill ourselves, we know we have an escape from all pain. Things can only get so bad, because if they do get so bad, we have a legitimate solution to the problem. I like Hume's version of the "door is always open" argument because he implicitly adds the psychological observation that most of us actually do think about killing ourselves from time to time, and maybe we all do. It's not simply that the door is always open but also that we notice the door is open and even consider entering. Hume is saying, *Look, everyone feels that way sometimes, and you are always free to do it: the only way to close the door is by actually walking through it.* Waiting may not be easy. But all we need is a moment of pause. The sheer claustrophobia of the thought of suicide, the pressure of its walls coming ever closer in on us—which is itself part of the panic that leads to an attempt—is suddenly less intense when we realize: okay, it doesn't have to be today.

A friend and fellow philosopher wrote to me recently, "I have not spent a week of my life without thinking of how much better it would all be if I could just end it. Even in the happiest of times. Sometimes I find instant relief just by indulging a quick suicidal ideation." I wrote back to say how healthy I thought this way of thinking was, for someone who understands herself to be suicidally inclined. We have the habit of thinking that thoughts and words tend to manifest as actions, but just the opposite can be the case. Letting yourself have the thoughts and the words can be precisely what relieves you of the need for the action.

Ultimately, we might be better off deferring adjudication on the great question of life or death. Suicide is indeed a human possibility, but, and somewhat paradoxically, for that very reason, we don't have to choose it. After all, you can always kill yourself tomorrow. Take a breath, get some space: tomorrow isn't here yet. And maybe you'll find you can get through today.

4

They Fuck You Up / Your Mum and Dad

(PART I)

All of my suicidal thinking might be traced back to my father's abuse of my mother. My older brother Darren remembers him striking her with a rolled-up newspaper, the way people used to hit dogs, years ago. They subsequently divorced, and he relocated to Florida, which back in 1972, was a long way from Calgary. I missed my father desperately. And when, eventually, I was fully reunited with him, on a drive we took together all the way across the United States, he had a terrifying mental breakdown that was the real beginning of his end. Eight and a half years later he'd die alone in a psychiatric hospital for homeless people.

The death of my father was a great turning point in my life. Afterward a new understanding of suicide, depression, and hopelessness opened up to me. I didn't know it at the time, but at such moments everything suddenly enters a new phase, life becomes quite different than before, and an unfamiliar perspective emerges. I don't think my first divorce would have been possible without the death of my father, and without my first divorce, I don't think I would have ever become addicted to alcohol in the truly debilitating way I did, which in turn means I would never have learned what it was like to be deprived of my children, and whole unfamiliar realms of self-loathing and dread would not have been revealed to me. These discoveries in turn led to what

I now think of as the beginning of my possible recovery from my addiction to suicide.

But the real heart of the story is that road trip we took together in the summer of 1988. You can't understand my suicidality without knowing a little bit about my father, and my own knowledge of my dad underwent a great transformation on that three-month-long drive, which is why I need to tell you this story now. His demise and my complicity in his death began then.

I had just turned twenty-one, and he had just turned forty-eight. I was planning on selling encyclopedias door to door that summer—college kids still did that in the 1980s. He asked me what I thought I would earn, and I told him (eight grand), and he said he'd pay me that much to drive across the country with him (I never saw the money) so that he could form a partnership with his old friend Ken Keyes. Keyes had a New Age spiritual wellness and teaching center, the Ken Keyes Institute, in Coos Bay, Oregon: he'd written a best-seller in 1974, *The Handbook to Higher Consciousness*, which my dad credited with saving his life after he went bankrupt in Miami and was plagued by thoughts of suicide. My dad had traveled to California to study with Ken and had been a student and friend of his ever since. He also made frequent pilgrimages to India to study with the famous Indian holy man and education reformer Sri Sathya Sai Baba. (Years later, no doubt for this very reason, I would make my own annual pilgrimages to India.) In the 1970s my father had himself been a New Age guru and therapist (he specialized in sex therapy but did every kind of counseling), and he hoped he and Ken could create a ministry together.

We started our journey in Palm Beach, Florida, in a brand-new gold Honda Accord. We were traveling from the southeastern tip of the country to the northwestern edge. And we were doing it the long way, driving across the bottom of the country to visit my big brother in Texas, then up the coast of California, so that my dad could visit his New Age haunts from his California days in the 1970s, including the Esalen Institute and Paramahansa Yogananda's Self-Realization Fellowship Center in Los Angeles.

I should add, before I tell the story of this trip, that watching my father's mental illness take hold of him, then learning later of his premature death as a result of his condition and the homelessness that resulted from it, made complete and utter failure real to me in a way that it previously hadn't been. Most people, when fretting about their life and how badly they might screw it up, worry about losing it all and winding up on the street. Few probably take it to the apocalyptic perspective where they imagine dying alone in a mental hospital. But for me that end feels entirely real, because I watched it happen to my dad—and as I will explain, in some ways I helped cause it. So (as I think about it now, and it didn't occur to me until I wrote this book), *of course* as an adult suicide has often seemed preferable to me when I feared my life was going off the rails. I had seen my father suffer much worse things.

Deep in the first part of the trip, past Texas high in the Arizona desert, we were driving along a narrow broken off-road under the huge June sun. I was at the wheel. Up ahead, I could see the bodies of men and women, perhaps alive, perhaps dead, in clothes, on their backs and bellies, blocking our path.

"There are people lying across the road, Dad."

He opened his eyes reluctantly from his nap or meditation. "Pull over, son," he said. "Keep it running. I don't think you've got us lost. But we're out in the boonies, that's for damn sure."

I stopped the Honda, and we got out. The heat was unbelievable. The silent two-story Sonoran cacti watched us. Was this retreat or commune that my father insisted on visiting a Jim Jones affair, I wondered, and would we be the ones to discover a Kool-Aid self-massacre in the sand? I was grateful that no children appeared among the victims. As we approached, I saw that the men and women were made of papier-mâché but dressed in real clothes. They had been painted to look like individuals. Several had glasses in crude black rings around their eyes.

"It's an exercise," my father said. "A purification ritual. Funny. I should have known immediately. My telepathy is off today. For a minute there, I worried they'd closed down the center."

"Should we move the bodies out of the way?" I asked.

"No, son. Stellar alignment. Or it may be a challenge specifically for you. For all we know, my higher self put these bodies here. I don't know why you're scared of this place."

It was creeping me out, this center deep in the desert that he insisted upon visiting without telling me the whole truth of why, and I was convinced some horrible surprise awaited us.

"It's just a treatment for my diabetic neuropathy," he explained. "You won't even be permitted to come in the doors. We have to work on your fears on this trip."

My social anxiety and my overall tendency to worry (what he called my fears) were a favorite subject of my father's and one of the things I most disliked talking about.

At this point, it's helpful to mention that my father believed himself to be completely sane—indeed, perhaps the only sane person he'd ever known, with the exception of some great spiritual leaders he'd met in the United States and India. But he had more than once been diagnosed as a schizophrenic and had, according to my mother, been suffering from worsening schizophrenia ever since she'd met him, when they were both sixteen. He claimed to have "mystical visions"; other people would call them hallucinations. On this trip I discovered that he was taking lithium—"for mood swings, son," he told me, "just because I get down from time to time. It's a salt, like a supplement."

On this trip, for the first time in my life, I considered the possibility that my father was suffering from a mental illness. Before, I had believed with all my heart that his oddities—like his visions—were expressions of his advanced spiritual state. If I ever worried at all, I reminded myself of my hero William Blake's wife, who was asked what it was like living with the great mystic. She replied, "I get very little of Mr. Blake's time. He spends most of it in paradise." For me, that was my dad.

I met my first wife, Alicia, on this trip. She was a cocktail waitress working at a Bennigan's, in a town outside Fort Worth. I told my dad, when she brought his club soda and my beer to the table, "That's the girl I would ask out if I had the balls to ask any girl out on a date." When she came back, he told her what I'd said, and not long after the end of our trip, I decided to transfer to Baylor, where she went to school. My father had that effect on the universe. I often felt he was inventing it as he went along.

About thirty years after this ill-fated journey, I was telling one of my students in India about it. We were sitting on the grass in the quadrangle at Ashoka University near Sonipat, in Haryana. She said, "Wait, I want to read you something." She was in a Jack Kerouac phase and pulled *On the Road* out of her backpack—and read aloud to me the famous passage from the opening: "It really had something to do with my father's death and my awful feeling that everything was dead."

I smiled at her and said, "That's the very line I used to introduce the piece I wrote about him and this trip back in 2011."

She might well have read my essay—it had been published in a glossy magazine—and been humoring me. But I had the feeling that my father was reaching out through her to say: *Yes, son, you were right, I'm dead because of that trip. And your inability to escape from suicide is one consequence of my death. These two things are still circling around and around like the vultures they are, so Clance, please be careful.*

Even before he died, I often had a feeling that my dad was watching over me and trying to shape things for the better in modest or even splendid ways. Especially since his death, I've often suspected that the good things in my life are a consequence of his extravagant pleading on my behalf with the otherwise strict and unyielding forces of the cosmos.

When I was four years old, my dad gave me an orange plastic Fisher-Price record player as a goodbye present. The divorce was coming soon, and I guess he knew he'd be leaving the country because he also gave me a 45 of John Denver's "Leaving on a Jet Plane." This kind of melodramatic gesture was typical of my father. When I reflect on it now, it seems to me like such a preposterous, self-aggrandizing and almost cruel gift, especially considering how I felt when I left my own adult homes because of divorce, first in 1996 when my eldest daughter Zelly was two, then in 2011 when Margaret and Portia were seven and five. But it meant so much to me at the time. It was a physical representation of my father that I clung to for several years afterward, and I still love the song.

I sat cross-legged on the blue carpet of my bedroom in our old house—the house that he had built "for your mother," with a sunken den for himself and a wall-size brick fireplace and bedrooms for all three of us boys—and played the record over and over again, thinking about him flying down to Florida, a place that I associated only with orange juice, which we didn't often buy. My two-year-old brother and I were both apple juice drinkers, like most Canadians.

Later, when my brothers and I visited him in Miami, he would embarrass us by crying as we stepped off the jet bridge. He hugged us by size: first Dindy, his nickname for my brother Darren, the oldest by seven years; then me, Clance or CW; then Garbage Can, his nickname for my brother Pat, who had been a very good eater as a baby. Sometimes he hugged me and Pat at the same time, both of us pressed against his hairy face, the strong good masculine smell of his Yves Saint Laurent cologne mixed with the vanilla pipe smoke that gathered in his beard. He was deeply tanned back then, in his early years as a successful commercial and office-warehouse-space real estate developer in Florida. His hair was short and neatly brushed across his forehead, and he wore madras shirts and khaki pants. He always wore a pair of pale calfskin Gucci loafers with that red and green flag across the top. He rotated several pairs of them, along with a pair of dark brown Gucci ankle boots that had a zipper up the side.

When we went on our long drives at night, he often brought along—"in case of emergency"—a blue blazer with the family crest emblazoned in gold on the right breast, which he hung on the inside hook of the car. I never questioned his insistence that we Martins, a wealthy but otherwise ordinary family from the hick town of Winnipeg, Canada, had a family crest. I was convinced that we were directly tied to nobility back in England. "In a blue blazer," he always told me, "a repp tie and gray flannels, you can meet the queen, son." I never had the courage to ask him what a repp tie was.

There was no question he wouldn't ask you about yourself, though you often didn't want to be asked, yet there were so many questions I never found the confidence to ask him. When, in college, he presented me with my own gold-crested blue blazer, my fraternity brothers were ruthless about it. One of them, who came from real money, said, "You could fry a waffle on that weave." I wore it only three or four times before losing it in a move from one girlfriend's trailer home to another girlfriend's trailer home.

"We should talk about the penis, son."

This was earlier in the trip. We were only a couple of states out of Florida, driving through Atlanta. I had the wheel again. We were bumper to bumper at sixty-five miles an hour, on our way to spend three nights in New Orleans—"it's time your old man took you to a real whorehouse, son," and I was nervous and excited about that—but we were also in a hurry to get to Arizona. He was keen to attend a two-day kriya yoga seminar in Phoenix on June 17. Following that, we would head for a New Age center far out in the desert that he was convinced could heal his "diabetic neuropathy": the center where I'd pulled over on the side of the road because of the papier-mâché bodies.

"Dad, we are not having this conversation."

"Cool your jets, CW. I'm not talking about the size of your cock."

My father had a series of jokes about the purported enormity of the Martin penis. "The Martin method" for peeing while driving was "you just unzip your pants and sling it out the window." Whenever he was in a men's room, before he started to pee—never at the urinal—he'd say, after the exaggerated sound of his fly unzipping, "Brrr, that water's cold." I can recall my father's penis floating in the water of a bathtub—I was seven or eight, we were in a motel—but I have no idea whether it was unusually large, or average-size, or small. It would not have made any difference to his insistence that he was spectacularly well-hung, or that it was a family trait.

"Let's talk about cock. It's nothing to be scared of, son. That's just what I say in my counseling sessions. Your cocksmanship."

Whatever he meant, I did not want to know. As a kid, I had

seen in his counseling office *The Joy of Sex* and also *The Joy of Gay Sex* and had peeped through the happy hippie pen-and-ink drawings, nervously. Throughout the 1970s and '80s—actually, until this trip—my father always offered counseling services. It was branded "spiritual counselling" or "new Age counselling" or "enlightened counselling." He saw it as a supplement to his New Age church, the Church of Living Love. The vanity plate on all his cars was GR8GURU.

I accelerated and moved into the fast lane in the hopes of distracting him.

"At your age it's perfectly natural to think that fucking is about nothing more than your cock."

I wished my father would stop saying that word. He kept red silk sheets folded neatly in a clear plastic bag in the trunk of the Honda, which he had already used—and had dry-cleaned—three or four times on our trip, with women he had met in restaurants and motel lobbies, and a cashier at a drug store in Tallahassee where he was buying his insulin. "Let me have the room for a few hours, son," he'd say, and hand me a twenty-dollar bill. I'd go find a tanning salon, or change it into quarters and call my girlfriend. It was that summer, I think, when I fell in love with cool, quiet, empty bars—a love I may never overcome.

"A woman finds only two kinds of pleasure from penetration by a man's penis, son. There are seventy-seven erogenous zones on the female body: eleven for each of the chakras. That's not to say that you can't use your cock in other ways. That's what I'm going to explain to you. This is not ordinary knowledge. I look at you and your girlfriend, and I see orange light shining from both of your sacral chakras. You're horny for each other, that's good. Do you masturbate together?"

If there is a bridge to drive off of . . . , I thought. Not seriously, though. As I say, this was early in the trip, things were still okay. By contrast, after Ken Keyes rejected his plan and we had to return home, I was thinking, as we drove the shortest route through Utah and Colorado to Texas and Florida, *I'll just turn the wheel hard, we'll plunge off the mountainside, and that will be it.* It would have been a relief for me and a favor to him. He'd failed at getting his new job, and it was suddenly abundantly obvious to me that I'd been lying to myself all this time about my dad's spirituality. He was just a crazy person, and that's why his life had been so unstable for so many years. (My view now is that both his spirituality and his insanity may have had their own particular legitimacy.) But as much as the idea of us dying together appealed to me in a variety of ways, I couldn't bear the idea of murdering my dad.

Now I understand that at that time his schizophrenia was getting very bad, he had likely stopped taking his lithium, and he was hallucinating frequently. But I was panicking and would have happily left him at one or another hotel in any major city. The problem was, without him, I had no money, and Darren wasn't willing to help me get away by buying me a plane ticket.

"Are you bringing her to climax with your tongue or just your fingers?"

A big truck was tailgating me and flashing its brights. Someone honked.

"I'm glad you're munching her bread. But you've got to start moving things up the spine. Your mother had the same problem, son. I remember when you were conceived on the swinging bench on the porch of our lake house. The point I'm making, son, is that even if a woman is born frigid, like your mother, with patience and learning you can show her that there are as many ways for her to come as there are for a man."

As painful and embarrassing as this speech was, I was also accustomed to it. This was how he had spoken about my mother since we were little kids.

"But it takes the active practice of your intelligence. You can't just climb on top of her and start bucking like a horse. I'm still working with your mother. We do it all astrally now, because of that jackass she married after me. One of these days I know she'll come back, so I'm happy to be giving her the lessons. Even though we're at a totally different place in our spirituo-sexual development."

I still have the letters he wrote to my mom from this time—she saved them for me—in which he detailed for her the sexual lessons he'd been giving her astrally, while she slept. He explained that her dreams—dreams that she'd never had, nor had told him she'd had—were actually an indispensable education that would save her from much suffering in her future lives.

Shortly before his seventeenth birthday, my father took a .30–06 Springfield hunting rifle from its rack in the trophy room of his parents' mansion and attempted to murder his mother. He fired three shots—she was standing at the top of the stairs, and he missed—then dropped the weapon and ran out the front door. It was prom night in Winnipeg, 1957, and he was arrested while dancing with the young woman who would become my mother.

"We were in the middle of a slow dance," she reminisced. "And three Mounties in their red uniforms came through the crowd and put cuffs on your father. He was grinning the whole time. So you see he was crazy even then. I know you think his mental illness was degenerative. But believe me when I say that he was already schizophrenic—or whatever it was he was—when he was a teenager."

These violent episodes were not uncommon for my father when he was young. My mother met him at Lake Winnipeg, where my grandparents had a summer house and my mother was working for the season as a motel maid. She was nineteen, he was eighteen. A few months later, drunk, he was locked out of the house in the city. He chopped his way in with an ax like Jack Nicholson—way before *The Shining*—to hunt for his mother, presumably for the purpose of chopping her to bits. She fled out the garage in the Lincoln. Another time, he waited until his parents were asleep and then set fire to the lake house, which burned to the ground. (His parents escaped.) I don't know why he was so violent toward his parents. I suspect it was related to their preference for his older brother Jimmy, which continued after Uncle Jimmy's death. I didn't learn about any of these events until after he died, and my mother could feel comfortable telling me.

I asked my mom why on earth she had married this lunatic. "Because I thought I could save him," she told me. "I thought his mother was making it all up."

Their marriage startled Winnipeg society because the Martins, for a new money family, were as aristocratic as anyone in

Manitoba could be, while my mom lived in a two-bedroom apartment with her sister and parents: a broken-down Irish drunk and a toughened Russian Jewess. According to my maternal grandmother—who told me this story on the trip I took with my dad and fiancée to Winnipeg to introduce her to my mother's side of the family—she killed my grandfather by bashing him on the back of the head with a hammer and pushing him down the basement stairs. My grandfather was an alcoholic and regularly beat my grandmother and their two children (my mom and her sister), and finally she'd just had enough.

My grandmother said, "Now Clancy, I like this girl you've decided to marry. And I want you to look me in the eye and promise me something."

"What is it, Grandma?" I shouted. (She could barely hear.)

"Promise me you're not going to cheat on that nice girl the way your son-of-a-bitch father cheated on my daughter."

I made and later broke that promise.

My father first went bankrupt—I don't know how often he declared bankruptcy in his life, especially if you include the business bankruptcies, but it's safe to say several times—when "that bastard Nixon declared the false oil crisis and everyone stopped taking their cars to the beach on vacation. I owned half of downtown Miami at the time. And suddenly everything was worth half what I'd paid for it. The banks were foreclosing, and my partner had disappeared with what capital we had, and I was sitting on the window ledge of my office, forty stories up, deciding whether to jump.

"Then one of my tenants came in—a lawyer, believe it or not—and handed me a copy of Ken Keyes's *The Handbook to Higher Consciousness*. I wouldn't be here today if it weren't for a damn attorney." He always laughed and shook his head at that part. "I moved to California to study with Ken. And that's when I met Tim Leary, Shirley MacLaine, the Esalen gang, Daya Mata, Ram Dass, that fraud Maharishi Mahesh Yogi, the whole gang. The first time I experienced cosmic consciousness, Tim Leary and I were sitting on a hillside in Carmel tripping on acid and watching the sun go down. We stayed there for two days and didn't drink a drop of water or have a thing to eat."

I still don't know whether these stories are true, confabulated, or some mixture of the two. I know that when we drove up the coast of California, we met many of his old friends, and they talked about these same times and people, and it certainly seemed as if everything he had told me about his adventures in California in the seventies was a fact. I wondered about certain things, like, if you're sitting on a hill tripping with Timothy Leary for two days, what about your insulin shots? It was one of those questions I should have asked but didn't dare.

"There it is, son. There's the rock where I first made love to Shirley MacLaine."

For the record, I do believe that my father was one of Shirley MacLaine's lovers. He made up many stories, but I don't think he ever lied about sex. It was too important to him. I believe it so much that I've read everything she's written, looking for him, and found no trace. But that's hardly surprising.

My father kept large white binders with gold embossed letters—1958–61, 1965–67, 1972–74—with all his medals, awards, press clippings, magazine mentions, and important invitations, pressed behind clear plastic sheeting. On long boring summer days before we took up the habit of playing tennis, my little brother Pat and I would flip through those binders and read about our father's many acclaims. He won medals for weight-lifting in the Commonwealth Games and had victories in just about any sporting competition you can think of. When he first moved to Florida, he'd owned the house right next door to John Lennon's on the island of Palm Beach. He had appeared on the cover of *Maclean's* magazine—the Canadian equivalent of *Time* or *Newsweek*—smiling on his motorcycle, one of "The New Millionaires."

That was the thing about my dad. Whenever I started to doubt his stories, I'd look in one of those enormous white albums, and I'd see, yes, my dad winning a road race through the mountains when he was sixteen, or a headline about his development company in Miami or a picture of him receiving vibhuti ash in his hands from Sai Baba. My mom verified as many of his stories as she disputed or refined. In Calgary at his old country club, the Glencoe Club (I got my first job there, as a busboy), I met other friends of his who would tell me even more glorious tales about Bill Martin. So though I often doubted what he told me, at the same time I revered him and mostly supposed that he was simply reporting the fantastic facts. Both my wife Alicia, who knew him, and my wife Amie, who didn't, insist that my father, while unstable, was mostly telling the truth.

In California, my father's schizophrenia, if that's what it was— our family has no other history of mental illness, other than my own—started getting down to business. He was genuinely disappointed at not getting the reception he'd wanted at the spiritual center in the Arizona desert. He had supposed he would receive a deep realignment of all his chakras, which would clean out all the negative energy he was experiencing and also help with his worsening diabetes. And when they refused him—they didn't even let us spend one night there—he felt it was a sign that he was doomed.

The weeks on the road weren't helping. I started to understand that my father needed routine and a better diet, he needed to sleep in his own bed. He conducted complicated, circular conversations about life on parallel planes and planets—or about my mother—with invisible passengers in the rear of the car, and he would get angry with me when I didn't respond to their questions. I had a bad feeling about Coos Bay. I wanted to switch to Interstate 5 to improve our time, but my father insisted on Route 1 and 101. "There's no point driving if you're going to be on one of those damn twelve-lane mega-highways. You may as well be in an airplane with wheels. Nothing to look at but the billboards and the strip centers."

In the fifth grade, my dad had said I could come live with him and my brother in Coronado, on San Diego Bay, where they had a house near the beach. I told my mother about the move— one of two times in my life that I've seen her cry—and bragged to my friends about living near Disney World and Hollywood. I sang "I Wish They All Could Be California Girls." My father drove up to Calgary, and we made our plans over dinner. The next morning I waited on the porch with my packed suitcase. He pulled up in his Lincoln and sat down next to me on the steps.

"Son, I've had a long talk with your mother," he told me, "and we think that this is where you need to be right now. It breaks my heart to say it, Clance." He was weeping.

This was not true. He had just correctly realized that he was in no position to take care of an eleven-year-old boy. My older brother Darren had been in and out of high school while living with my dad, and was himself about to leave California, move back to Calgary, and become a coke and marijuana dealer. He'd wind up in Spyhill Prison for dealing drugs not even a year after all this happened.

"I cried through B.C. and two states," Dad liked to tell me later. "I cried all the way back to San Diego." He was an easy crier, my old man.

We haven't gotten to the circumstances of my father's death yet, in 1997 when I was thirty years old, but bear with me a bit longer. One morning a few weeks after he died, his death certificate arrived in the mail. I still had a little money in the state of Florida, and I opened the large envelope eagerly, thinking it was a check or a bank statement. There it was on my desk, eighteen inches long and six inches wide, blue on both sides with a stripe—unmistakably flesh-colored, the size of a wrist and a narrow forearm—down its middle.

When I saw it, I immediately thought about his arms and my own. My father was undefeated as a flyweight amateur and had had a brief professional career. He fought two tough midcareer Canadian Irishmen like himself right in a row, but he was beaten so savagely in the first match that my mother didn't attend the second. He took an even worse beating in the next fight, then gave up boxing forever, except to train his sons. He had powerful biceps and the shoulders, chest, and neck of a bull bred for the ring, but his legs and his forearms were slender, almost as fine as a ballerina's, like my own. He taught me to box when I was five, six, seven, fighting on canvas slicked with oil so you couldn't throw too hard a punch. He emphasized keeping my wrists and punches straight, because of the risk of a break "with your tiny bones, son." In fact, I've broken both wrists more than once, and I have the crooked fingers of a "boxer's break" on my right hand.

His success as an amateur boxer and my failure to learn how to fight and live up to my idea of him, are parallel in my mind to the difference between his death and my suicide attempts. It's like he fought and fought and then finally lost, spectacularly, while I never really had the balls even to throw a good punch at someone else.

Before I went into a match, scrawny scared kid that I was, my dad would tell me, "Don't believe you're going to beat him, son. *Know* you're going to beat him." I've never been much of a fighter, and I pretty much always wound up with my ass on the mat. Later, in our many discussions about the astral universe, alternate futures, samadhi, past incarnations, the veil of maya, philosophy, and "metaphysics," his response to my growing skepticism was always a mildly puzzled but not condescending glance, and the simple affirmation: "Son, sometimes you know that you know that you know."

"You know that you know that you know": I was starting to understand that this was what had sustained my father, and that things fell apart for him as he gradually lost his faith. On that road trip with him, my own confidence was deeply shaken but not altogether gone. Then suddenly, when he died, it was my situation, too. When he was alive, I had someone to whom I was accountable, for whom I was a great promise—"Your name will be in lights, son," he used to tell me, with utter certainty. With him alive, I had a fundamental conviction, in a way that's hard to articulate, that the world was a good place designed for us to become better people. With him dead, I was losing my religion. Everything went up for grabs. I didn't know what to believe anymore. I didn't know who I was or what I was supposed to believe. Was it all a lie, this myth of being a Martin? Was the whole enlightenment-India-"existence has a purpose" thing complete bullshit? Had he made it all up?

None of us expects to hold a parent's death certificate in our hands, though many of us will. My father's contains many *unknowns*. "13b. COUNTY: Unknown. 13c. CITY, TOWN OR LOCATION: Unknown. 13d. STREET AND NUMBER:

Unknown. 13e. INSIDE CITY LIMITS (Yes or No): Unknown. 18. MOTHER'S NAME: Unknown." His father's name—John, the same first name as my father, though my dad always went by Bill or Billy—is listed, which was confusing: he must have told them my grandfather's name, but he couldn't remember my grandmother's? When I spoke with him in the hospital the last time, he was coherent, he could answer all my questions clearly, he was his regular infuriating self. He died on December 22, 1997, and the death certificate was signed on January 15, 1998. I asked the physician who signed the death certificate about the lapse of three weeks. "I don't know," he said. I asked an expert on end-of-life care how much time typically passes between death and the signing of the death certificate. He told me, "Minutes, at most hours, never days . . . unless there is suspicion of foul play."

Here there had definitely been foul play of some kind. I don't know whether it was by someone in the hospital or if my dad hung himself. When the doctor called on December 23—my eldest daughter's third birthday—I asked him what my father had died of, and he said "respiratory failure." My father had plenty of physical ailments, but he had never had any problems with his lungs. I'd talked to him just days before he died, and he'd sounded like he was physically in fine health. There was no cough, nothing reminiscent of a respiratory problem.

I demanded an autopsy, but they told me the location of the body was unknown. When my lawyer called, he was informed that the body had been found but had already been cremated. When a square brown cardboard package arrived from "A Cremation Alterantive [sic]," P.O. Box 55-7736, Miami, Florida, 33255-7736, I very much doubted that ashes in the plain heavy plastic bag, tied with a purple twist-tie, sitting in the box in my lap, were actually my dad's. I was afraid to lift the bag from the box, and indeed I never did.

I do not know where that box is now. During my second divorce, while I was gathering my clothes and possessions, I looked everywhere for them. They weren't in the closet where I'd always kept them or anywhere in the basement. Maybe we'd left them behind when we moved from our apartment to the new house: it had been a hasty chaotic move, near Christmas, in the cold Missouri winter, with two small children. But I don't know. I'd promised him I'd pour his ashes into the Ganges, "to release me from any remaining karma, son." Now if I had that bag in its box, I know what I'd do with it. I'd take it to Varanasi and pour it into the river at daybreak. But it's taken me the twenty-five years since his death to return to those old convictions, which have changed along the way, and I went through a long period of complete disorientation to get where I find myself today.

Darren recently suffered a series of strokes, and after one of them, my mother called to ask if I knew how my dad had died. I told her what it said on the death certificate, which was a relief for her, as it ruled out the likelihood that Darren was suffering from some similar medical problem. But she agreed with me that "respiratory failure" made no sense.

"For a long time I assumed he had been murdered by an angry nurse," I told her.

"It wouldn't be surprising," she said.

"Yeah, the way he treated nurses," I said. Over the years I had been with my father in many hospitals, and he almost always made outrageous demands and cruelly, even viciously, insulted the people trying to help him.

"But now the idea that he was murdered seems so obviously far-fetched," I continued. "He wanted so badly out of the hospital, and I'd told him no, I wouldn't get him out. I wouldn't send him money for a bus ticket so that the hospital could release him. So he found the only way out that he had. There was one way out, and he took it."

"You think . . . ?" She didn't finish the sentence.

"It was an underfunded hospital for homeless people, Mom. I don't think they kept a very close eye on them. Respiratory failure. I'm sure he hung himself. He killed himself because I didn't get him out of there."

But I don't know this to be true.

So now I'll tell the story of how he actually died—that is, what I do know. On December 17, 1997, my father telephoned from the state mental hospital in Miami. They had taken him there after finding him asleep in his Honda on the side of the highway. They impounded the car—he didn't have current insurance or a current license, and the vehicle had been repossessed, as he'd stopped making his payments months before. It's surprising they didn't take him to jail, but I expect he'd been off both his lithium and his insulin for weeks, and, given his likely overall physical and psychological condition and the impression that car must have made—he'd been living in it for half a year—I can see why the cops were compassionate. At this time my brothers weren't taking his calls.

"CW, they've locked me up in an Alzheimer's ward! It's a loony bin in here. They won't let me out unless I have a bus ticket showing I have somewhere to go. I need you to wire me fifty dollars, son. That will get me to Tallahassee. Let me give you the Western Union."

"Dad," I said. "Dad, I think you're in the right place for now." Only much later did it occur to me that those were nearly the exact same words that he had spoken to me, almost twenty years before, on the front porch of my mother's home in Calgary.

He pleaded, and the last thing he said before I hung up was "If you don't get me out, I'll die in here."

Like me, my father was melodramatic, and I'd heard this kind of thing from him before. It was the Christmas season, during that terrible time when I was in the jewelry business with my brothers. A customer was waiting at my desk, and others were outside. And I suppose I thought, *Well, in January we'll see if we can find a better place for him.* Only six months or so before, we had sent him to India, where he had always claimed he wanted to retire, with ten thousand dollars and the promise of a thousand dollars a month to sustain him. But within a few weeks, he got on a return flight to the United States and was back on the road. He drove to our store in Arlington, Texas, and we tried to set him up in a cheap apartment. That lasted seven or eight nights, and he was on the highway again, headed west.

On December 23, 1997, six days after my father called me from the hospital, Darren walked into my office to tell me the news. I didn't even quite understand what my brother was saying. An important client was at my desk, looking at an eight-carat black opal he planned to give his mistress, and a platinum-and-diamond tennis necklace I planned he'd give his wife. (The client didn't yet know that he would be buying gifts for both of them, but I did.)

"What?" I asked my brother, whose face was filling with tears.

My client quickly stood and stepped out of my office.

"He's dead, Clance. I just hung up the phone with the doctor. Dad's dead."

All three of us would admit to wishing for his death, toward the end. He'd come through town and stay with Darren for a few days, and we'd clean the trash from his car and clean his clothes, then he'd get back on the road. One time he sat on the floor of Darren's son's bedroom and fished dollar bills out of the giant glass jar Darren had been filling with change and small bills for his son for years. We never spoke about our wanting him to kill himself, but we'd ask one another, "Why doesn't he rob a bank? Or hold up liquor stores? Anything would be better than this." Over the years, several of his psychiatrists—both in and out of hospitals—had told me his mental illness was mild. My dad was something of a con man and was likely concerned with impressing the psychiatrist. But we brothers knew the truth about how far he had sunk. He could have spared us the pain of worrying about him, by overdosing himself with insulin or buying a gun and ending it neatly on the side of a road in Arizona or New Mexico somewhere, with the headlights staring up endlessly into the black desert night. But my father had a raw vitality that I've always lacked, and it sustained him for a long time.

In 2011 I visited the state hospital where he'd died fourteen years earlier. They wouldn't let me up to see his ward. That was the craziest year of my life—a year when I repeatedly tried to kill myself and wound up in my own psychiatric hospitals—and yet that didn't click for me until ten years later, these chthonic connections. But a kind old nurse who had been at the hospital for years walked me outside to show me the windows of the seventh floor—"that used to be the psychiatric floor, it was restricted, I never worked that floor myself or perhaps I could tell you more, I am sorry"—which are thirty feet above the tops of the sinewy, bent palm trees and almost at a level with the three roaring highways that intersect around the brown and pink hospital building.

These last few years I've thought of my dad often, because I spend a lot of my time worrying about my five children and how to be a better father. In this chapter he may sound like a terrible person to you, but in so many ways he was a great dad. We never doubted how much he loved us. When I was kicked out of high school for the umpteenth time and just wanted to hitchhike around Canada and the United States, he got me into college. He gave me the enduring conviction that what matters most about human life is the investigation of its meaning, which is why I became a philosophy professor, a job I love. For all his appalling failures as a husband to my mom, and his embarrassing and misguided elitism and snobbery, he taught his children that what really matters is the love of other human beings and a more spiritual life.

Only in the course of writing this book did I realize that the gun-in-mouth phase of my daily morning suicide attempts began shortly after his death. Bizarre though it is to confess, I had never put the two things together before. I didn't cry when my father died. I didn't cry over his death until many years later. I don't know if I was numb or if something else was going on with me. And I have no recollection of thinking about his death or my culpability in it when I was trying to kill myself with that Glock. Many people who love me have told me, "Look, you didn't kill him." (My mother, who is more honest, has more than once told me, "Yes, you should be ashamed that you let your own father die in there.") No, I didn't physically kill him, but by not sending him that money that day, which I could easily have done, I more or less guaranteed the outcome that he himself told me would follow.

So while trying to shoot myself with that pistol, I don't remember thinking, *Yeah, Dad's dead, now I'm going to do it.* In fact, the patent ridiculousness of that thought would surely have stopped me. But now I see that that was when I made up my mind to shoot myself. And the way his life ended, whether he killed himself or some sudden, mysterious respiratory disease swooped down and destroyed him almost overnight, alone, incarcerated, surrounded by other homeless people who'd lost their minds—my dad, the same man who'd taught me all that I believed in—well, I knew where I could wind up, how badly my own life could end. And I can see now, too, that the many times since that I have tried to kill myself, I feel that I have permission to do it, because my father is not alive to reproach me if I should fail, or to suffer that disappointment in me if I should succeed. If I'd made one trip to the psychiatric hospital that he knew about, he would not have tolerated a second—he would have just let me know that it simply wasn't allowed. For all my doubts about my father and my anger at him for the way he fell apart toward the end, putting responsibility for his life in our hands rather than his own, he was in a way my reason for living. Once he was gone, all bets were off.

PART II

ONE FOOT IN THE GRAVE

"Reflexions on suicide, & on my father, possess me. /
I drink too much."

—JOHN BERRYMAN, "ON SUICIDE"

5

Drinking Myself to Death

I was a week out of the hospital following a suicide attempt, twelve days since taking a drink. January 12, 2009. That winter night the snow was making halos in the streetlights, and three or four of us were outside smoking on the temple steps. I met Dave, who was probably 250 or 260 pounds. He looked like one of the big blue Tann safes we used to have in my jewelry store.

Dave's wife had thrown him out and gotten a restraining order against him. "Another man is sleeping in my bed," he said, "sitting on my couch, watching my TV, eating my Cheerios for breakfast."

Dave had all the complicated DUI (driving under the influence) arrest arrangements many AA people have or once had, and because he had been court-ordered into county jail on weekends, he'd been fired from his job. He lived at an Oxford House, the halfway house in Kansas City where I lived. (There are Oxford House Recovery Homes all over the country, named after the Oxford Group, a defunct 1920s evangelical movement where AA got its start.) But Dave and the manager of the house had had an argument a few nights earlier, so now he was out of there too. Dave told me his story quietly, without self-pity, anger, or even regret, as snowflakes melted on his brows and lashes.

Nietzsche wrote, "Memory says: 'I have done that.' Pride

replies: 'I cannot have done that,' and remains inexorable. Eventually, memory yields." Dave was all out of pride.

"I must forget the past as much as possible," counsels one of the prayers in AA's *Twenty-Four Hours a Day*, and you can see why one alcoholic might offer that self-deceiving advice to another.

I smoked a cigar with him, out there on the steps—I had a metal box of those baby-size Macanudos you can buy at the pharmacy. I'd offered him one, shyly, and was glad when he took it, if only for the extra ten minutes of his company. His calm, patient look in his eyes stood in direct contrast to the angry, devastated, and helpless expression I saw in the mirror, and I wanted to wrap his arm around me like a blanket. He seemed to have accepted a situation that both of us shared but that I was still desperately trying to escape.

"I got a bus to catch," he told me suddenly, and lumbered away into the dark.

Heavy drinkers and drug users are much more likely to kill themselves than people who don't have chronic substance abuse problems. A statistic that always startles me is that about 25 percent of all chronic alcohol and drug users kill themselves. Alcohol is involved in about a third of the suicides in the United States, and more than half of all suicides are committed by people with substance abuse problems. (It goes to 70 percent for adolescents.) The causal relationship between "drinking and drugging" (as we say in AA) and killing yourself is complicated—it could be that people prone to substance abuse are also prone to suicidal thinking, or vice versa, and suicidal thinking is certainly facilitated by substance dependence. It's clear that drinking alcohol, especially excessively, makes you more likely to commit suicide, especially while you are drinking. (The risk associated with drugs other than alcohol varies according to the drug.)

It's no secret that alcohol lowers one's inhibitions, including inhibitions about doing risky and violent things. Of my own adult suicide attempts, at least four took place either while I was drunk or in the immediate aftermath of a night of drunkenness, during the blistering misery of a half-drunk hangover. I've lost count of how often I've gone to the rooftop of a building or found a high open window when I was drunk. One time in Kansas City at around three in the morning, I even managed to scramble over a chain-link fence topped with barbed wire to climb to the top of an electricity tower. The air smelled of smoke from the Gates Barbecue Restaurant below. Nine years ago I "got sober" and have more or less stayed that way, but anytime the drinking continues past a couple of beers, my thoughts will usually turn to suicide with an urgency, anguish, and menace that are absent from my alcohol-free daydreams of self-destruction. For me, alcohol turns the volume knob of suicidal thinking from a two or three to a ten.

For my fellow suicidal drunks out there, I should say a bit more about addiction to alcohol. Alcohol use disorder is defined as "a pattern of alcohol use that involves problems controlling your drinking, being preoccupied with alcohol, continuing to use alcohol even when it causes problems, having to drink more to get the same effect, or having withdrawal symptoms when you rapidly decrease or stop drinking."

I've been writing about alcohol abuse for more than ten years now, and in my opinion it's a good thing that the terms *alcoholism* and *alcoholic* are going out of fashion. Psychiatrists who work on alcohol abuse increasingly recognize many different kinds and degrees of addiction to alcohol, and that one is not simply diagnosed as an "alcoholic" and then defined forever as a person who above all must abstain from the consumption of liquor. This "once an alcoholic, always an alcoholic" way of thinking—the phrase is an adage in AA—is in part what led the AA movement to define alcoholism as a disease that could be cured only through a combination of abstinence and a kind of moral therapy.

The on/off way of thinking about alcoholism is problematic for a variety of reasons (as I will explain in Chapter 11), but my basic complaint is simple. We tend to apply on/off thinking to alcoholism and other addictions in two ways. One is the "either you're an alcoholic or you're not": you're either born that way or you weren't. And the other is the "once an alcoholic, always an alcoholic" way: regardless of whether you were born that way, once you've turned yourself into an alcoholic, you can't undo it—"it's like turning a pickle back into a cucumber," as they say in rehab. Both ways of on/off thinking harm people in both directions. They harm problem drinkers or potential problem drinkers by enabling their thinking that "after all, I'm not an alcoholic, I just drink a little too much sometimes." And it harms the serious abusers by reinforcing the idea that they're doomed by their addiction. And both ways of thinking are misleading. Addiction to alcohol, like every bad habit, occurs on a vast and complex spectrum of misbehavior.

The term *alcoholic* also carries a heavy load of moral baggage. Whenever one says, "Oh, that guy? He's an alcoholic," or, "No, none for me, I'm an alcoholic," the atmosphere suddenly becomes charged with judgment, with a history of self-abuse and very likely the abuse of others, with suspicion and perhaps also a need for understanding or forgiveness. It's a very different statement from "Oh, her? Well, she's a diabetic."

Thinking about alcohol addiction as an on/off thing—you either are one or you're not—ignores the many subtleties and degrees of the use and abuse of alcohol: the occasional binge drinker; the three-drink-a-nighter who never suffers any real personal or physical damage from her drinking but gets nervous at the thought of not getting her glass of wine every evening; the former chronic drinker who "relapses" once or twice a year, gets drunk, then easily returns to a life of not drinking; the thirty-year-old who used to drink two or three times a week but now finds himself drinking earlier and earlier in the day, every day (this was me, once); the fifty-year-old who has given up and decided to drink himself to death, one six-pack at a time. These are all very different cases, and because alcohol is woven into most of the world's cultures in a way that no other drug presently is, almost every adult has some kind of relationship with it. So it's not surprising that there are so many different kinds of drinkers.

Furthermore—and this is probably the most important aspect of the debate, for people who worry about alcohol addiction—the *Am I an alcoholic?* question leads only to the strategy of absolute abstinence, which works for some but not for a majority of alcohol-dependent people, and away from the many good moderation and harm-reduction techniques that can help people with drinking problems get their lives back into a relatively orderly place. We do not yet have good comprehensive studies of the suicide rates of people who are newly abstinent, but that data would also be helpful in thinking about how to help alcohol abusers manage their addiction. Based entirely on my own experience and that of other recovering alcohol abusers, I suspect that suicide attempts are more common in the first year or two of abstinence, given the severe depression that often results from abrupt withdrawal. But as I say, this suspicion is merely anecdotal.

That said, I quit drinking through abstinence, and I will still tell people that I'm an alcoholic if the question is relevant. I will probably always self-identify as an alcoholic. It may be just a generational thing, a fact of my age, but it's the lingo I'm accustomed to. To me, it sounds a bit inaccurate and a bit dishonest to say that I "presently suffer from alcohol use disorder," especially since I don't drink anymore. Like every other addict, I know that if I start using again, I won't be able to have a normal relationship with my drug of choice, and so something is missing from the label alcohol *use* disorder, since my condition is permanent, and not a function of an ongoing relationship of use or abuse.

My father, who described himself as an alcoholic until his death, often used to say to me, "Son, the reason I don't drink is simple. If I take a single drink, within six months I'll either be dead or in prison." For me, it would take more than a single drink. But if I started regularly drinking again, I'd lose my wife and family in short order, and then it wouldn't be six months, it would be weeks before I was dead.

It's the spring of 2020, and we are in India's first lockdown. I'm sitting on the balcony of an apartment owned by a new friend in Bir, Himachal Pradesh, India, looking out at the Dauladhar range in the lower Himalayas. He was first my landlord and started to become my friend when I noticed that a large pillow under the wooden bench near his bed was embroidered with the Serenity Prayer. I asked him if he was "a friend of Bill's." (Bill

Wilson was the founder of AA, and asking if someone is a friend of Bill's is coded way of inquiring if he or she is a member of the program.) He said, perhaps a bit apologetically, "Oh, I'm a twelve-stepper." I told him I was, too, though I've never been very good at the steps, and we agreed to start having meetings up here in his apartment. His apartment was right next to ours, and neither of us could attend a real meeting, because we were on day three of India's twenty-one-day—or so we hoped—lockdown for the coronavirus.

I didn't tell my new friend that I hadn't been to a meeting in years, or that I had had a very complicated relationship with AA ever since publishing about it years ago. I have never described myself as a "twelve-stepper," and I will always think of AA as something more like how an attorney of mine once described bankruptcy: "Chapter 13 is like the emergency room, Clancy. It's really important when you need it, but you don't want to stay there any longer than absolutely necessary." I'm not an advocate of lifelong, active membership in AA, but it was very helpful to me at a crucial time, and if any of my children ever developed an addiction to alcohol or another drug—as I very much fear, given my own history and that of my family—I would take them to a meeting when they were ready.

Some years ago, I was at a party with the poet and memoirist Mary Karr, and when I briefly brought up the current state of AA and her recovery memoir, she looked at me coldly, said, "Nothing needs to be changed about Alcoholics Anonymous," and walked away. Here I am going to be pointing out some flaws I see in Alcoholics Anonymous, while also insisting that I don't think I would be a nondrinker now without it. In fairness to AA (and Mary Karr), the most recent large-scale study of various methods for treating alcohol abuse has concluded that "other treatments might result in about 15 percent to 25 percent of people who remain abstinent; whereas with AA, it's somewhere between 22 percent and 37 percent (specific findings vary by study)." So, as is often repeated at the end of AA meetings, "Keep coming back, it works if you work it."

Now, with this terrifying virus spreading around the world, I find it soothing to meet with my new friend every other day, read the Preamble and the Twelve Steps and the Twelve Traditions and a daily prayer, and talk about our struggles as two fathers, two husbands, two people on the descending rather than the ascending half of the arc of professional life, to think about our mistakes together and what we have tried to learn and accept. I don't think either of us was particularly worried about addiction. But we both have had our struggles, and so we can take this unexpected time to try to help each other a little. This kind of thing is rare, and it's possible through AA, and it's something to be grateful for.

Some people grow up Southern Baptist or Orthodox Jew. I was raised Alcoholics Anonymous. When I was not yet four, my mother left my father for his sponsor in AA. "He was my best friend," my father later told me, "and my sponsor, he was my only grip on reality, and he stole your mother away from me. A man can't sink any lower than that." My father's face was bruised and unshaven and sad. He limped to the table, and when he came in, Mom left the kitchen. "Sons, promise me you'll never take a drink," he said. I looked at my cup of apple juice with suspicion and pushed it away. Patrick stared at Dad from his high chair and sucked fiercely on his bottle. Funny, I became the drunk, and to this day Patrick has never so much as sipped a beer.

Not long after that, my dad, the former professional boxer and medaling weightlifter, was trying to break down our front door. Inside the house, Darren and my mother were piling up furniture on the other side of the door. As he and Mom pushed a bureau across the floor, my brother looked at me with scared and irritable eyes, like *Aren't you going to try to help?* A few minutes later the police cars arrived, and we all watched Dad through the bay window, in the red and blue light, tossing the cops like toys until he was submerged beneath their bodies and nightsticks.

My mom's marriage to my stepfather, Blair, added seven more kids to our family. Blair had been a brown-bag-in-the-gutter drunk in his day and then, post-recovery, ran a recovery home called 1835 House. It still operates today and "is known in recovery circles for the quality of its programs." Some weekend nights he held family readings—mandatory attendance, eight or ten kids in a circle, our own little meeting right there in the living room—and we listened to him recite passages from Carl Jung or William James's *The Varieties of Religious Experience*. (Jung and James were two of Bill W.'s greatest intellectual influences, along with Aldous Huxley, who introduced Bill W. to his life-long LSD habit.) We read the AA comics like "What Happened to Joe," featuring dark seedy alleyways, wild nights, and lurid, promiscuous women in torn dresses. Two or three times a week my mother and stepfather went off to "their" meeting—I hated those meetings, I was jealous of them. Often I'd hear the phone ring late at night, and Blair would answer and talk sometimes for hours to the struggling addict on the other end, being, as he always was, an excellent sponsor (except for the part, I suppose, when he had an affair with and subsequently married his spon-see's wife, my mom—an astonishing transgression, as my father never failed to remind me and my brothers). I have no doubt that he talked many, many people out of killing themselves. When he died, more than a hundred people, and half of Calgary's AA establishment, turned out for the funeral.

Shortly after his death, one of my stepsisters told me this story: "When I was in real trouble, my husband and I tried to borrow a thousand dollars from Dad, and he turned us down. I found out that back when we were kids, when we were suppos-edly so broke, he gave one of the alcoholics from 1835 House his credit card so the guy could go out to Vancouver to see his kids. He'd give some guy in his halfway house his credit card so that guy could visit his children, but he wouldn't lend his own child a grand when she needed it."

My mother insists this story isn't true, and I don't know. My mother, my siblings, and I all remember our years together in quite different ways. I know that my stepfather was a great men-tor to people in AA, and that I never knew him at all. Growing up, I never spoke more than a few words to him, and I saw him lose his temper with my stepsisters and stepbrothers in terrifying ways. He was a better sponsor than a father.

In my experience, the kind of personality division that my stepfather had—between one's ordinary, professional, or family self and one's AA self—is common in AA, and indeed it's talked about in meetings. People will say, "This is the only place where I can be honest," or "It's only in these rooms that I can truly be myself," or "No one knows me except the brothers and sisters in these meetings," or "I fake all day but I come here to be real." My father used to complain that AA was an addiction like every other addiction, and part of what he meant was that we still live in the bottle, still secretly drink, still lurk in the shadows, until we can integrate the honesty, care, and compassion that we find and develop in meetings into our ordinary lives. But it's not easy to do. When you are dealing with someone else who is in AA, you know that, mostly, you're both playing by the same set of rules of forgiveness and understanding. But as soon as you are dealing with someone from the outside world, a regular person—even one of your most intimate loved ones—those rules don't apply anymore, and if you try to apply them yourself, you may find someone devouring you.

Recently during an open AA Zoom meeting, someone was giving a very moving share about being abused by her alcoholic mother, which in turn led her to abuse her own children. One of the other attendees wrote, "Yeah, gotta say, you're a total fucking mess" on the screen for all of us to see, including the woman sharing. All us old-timers in the meeting could see the person who wrote this was a voyeur and not really in recovery. We did what we could to mitigate the situation. Such nasty voyeurism is a problem with the open online format—it never really occurs in an ordinary meeting. But the episode did illustrate what all of us in AA know: that you can expect and must give understanding within the church walls, but you can't expect it beyond them. And that kind of partitioned thinking can lead to all kinds of problems in how AA people like me, and my stepfather, try to incorporate what they've learned from AA into the real world.

My dad took me to my first AA meeting in Jupiter, Florida, when I was seventeen years old. It was an open meeting, so I didn't have to say, "My name is Clancy, and I'm an alcoholic," which I wanted to do. After seeing all the movies about AA and hearing the stories, I felt cheated that I wasn't fully included in the drama of the thing. My dad described AA as "a great institution, if you want to live in an institution"—a line he stole from Groucho Marx. He attended AA meetings off and on all his life. When my two brothers and I were visiting him for summer vacation in Florida, Arizona, or California, he'd often say, in the evening, "Okay boys, I'll be back in a couple of hours. I'm going to a meeting of the drunks' club."

Following a suicide attempt on December 31, 2008, I learned at an AA meeting how not to drink alcohol. (It wasn't my first AA meeting, but it was the first time an AA meeting actually worked for me.) Whenever I return to that temple, I usually run into people who knew me during my early devoted, broken, weepy Ativan-lithium-Lamictal-and-baclofen-riddled months, and then I look away with "meeting guilt," which lots of us also know. Certain old-timers quickly catch you before you can sneak out the door at the end. "It's good to see you, Clancy," they'll say meaningfully. A tension in their smile asks, *Where've you been? When's the last time you had a drink? Doing any service? Working the steps?*

With regular attendance, my friend Christina began to suspect that every meeting was somehow about her, "like God is speaking directly to me." Christina thought the whole meeting had been designed by an Unseen Power to reveal truths to her about herself. Anyone who has ever fallen in love knows the feeling she was describing. It's not narcissism run amok: it's the direct experience of the fact that our way of looking at the world is interwoven with everything we can think or imagine, and that as our way of looking at the world changes, all that we know begins to shift. This is considered a desirable early outcome of attending as many meetings as possible in the early months of recovery: the addict should start to feel that new aspects of her own personality are being continually revealed to her. As those doors open, new choices, new freedoms, and perhaps even opportunities for happiness may appear.

At the end of the meeting, we stand in a circle around the big old wooden conference table and join hands, usually say the Lord's Prayer (depending on who's leading the meeting), then shake each other's hands and remind each other to keep coming to meetings.

Was I an alcoholic? I often asked myself this question before accepting the truth about my addiction. Look online, and you'll find plenty of self-diagnostic tests. On all the usual fill-in-the-blanks, I always scored high (I'm good at standardized tests), but I remained unconvinced. I was raised by my stepfather and mother with the theory that "alcoholism is a disease" (AA does not officially endorse this as a medical theory, but it's a very popular view in groups), and it seemed to me that I was always choosing to drink, so I considered myself neither genetically afflicted nor chemically controlled. Just because the question "Are you an alcoholic?" makes you nervous doesn't mean you're hooked; flip side, the certainty that you're a heavy drinker or a "functional alcoholic" (as opposed to a "real alcoholic") won't get you off the hook with yourself, AA, or anybody else who might be observing your drinking with one eyebrow raised.

Once in a bar together, just after I turned twenty-one, Dad with his club soda and lime and me with a beer, I deliberately left a few fingers in the bottom of the glass. As we walked out, he turned to me and said, "You know, maybe you're not an alcoholic, son. I've never seen an alcoholic leave the last swallow in his glass." He was forgetting he'd often told me that "a sure sign of an alcoholic is that he always finishes his drink."

In one of the most thoughtful books about alcoholism, *Heavy Drinking* (1988), the philosopher Herbert Fingarette argued that the label *alcoholic* might harm the heavy drinker in a variety of ways, very much anticipating and perhaps even influencing our contemporary change to the label *alcohol use disorder*. In Fingarette's account, the label *alcoholic* can excuse behavior ("I can't help it, I'm an alcoholic, my life is unmanageable"). It may interfere with recovery ("I have to quit cold turkey: I'm addicted, I'm an alcoholic"). It has a social stigma ("Poor bastard. He's not just a real drinker, he's an alcoholic"). And it creates a self-fulfilling prophecy ("Because I am an alcoholic, my life will always be determined by the stalwart, morally praiseworthy denial or the disastrous, perverse acceptance of this drug"). Fingarette believed that with help, honesty, and the disciplined exercise of will (this last in particular is anathema to AA, which insists that we have become powerless before alcohol), we can recover and even continue to drink.

To its credit, AA insists that the alcoholic who cannot recover should not be blamed for her failure. But listen to Bill W.'s language:

> Rarely have we seen a person fail who has thoroughly followed our path. Those who do not recover are people who cannot or will not completely give themselves to this simple program, usually men and women who are constitutionally incapable of being honest with themselves. There are such unfortunates. They are not at fault; they seem to have been born that way. They are naturally incapable of grasping and developing a manner of living which demands rigorous honesty.

It is tempting here to bring out Bill W.'s old Ouija board and confront his raised spirit with his well-documented postsobriety years of infidelity to his wife and ask him more specifically what he intended by "rigorous honesty." Ad hominem attacks are not logical fallacies for this crowd: what's at stake is the kind of person you are. You must take fearless moral inventories, admit wrong, confront defects of character, and practice "these principles in all our affairs" (no pun intended).

The point I'm trying to make, with Fingarette, is that AA is deeply and perhaps very unhelpfully infused with a moral view of alcoholism. As one old-timer, Gary R., explained with great solemnity at the end of an Escalade meeting (so called because it took place in the most expensive zip code in Kansas City, where the parking lot of the magnificent church was full of expensive SUVs), "Look, folks. Before AA we were sinners. Simple as that. Ninety meetings in ninety days is a kind of baptism. We follow that up with daily confession and the complete submission of our will to a Higher Power. And as long as you're in the program, you're in grace. The grace of sobriety. It's not complicated. This is how it works."

Gary's is an extreme statement of the moral view, but while few alcoholics would describe "the alcoholic who still suffers" as a sinner, most understand themselves in just that way. "I was a sinner, but now I'm saved" is a centuries-old, proven-effective, hugely attractive attitude, and it's surely one of the reasons AA works better than any other program of recovery.

The problem with understanding alcohol abuse in this way relates directly to the old problem of how we understand the depressed person and the suicidal person. For centuries, depression and other forms of psychological suffering, as well as alcoholism—or the mental illness of dipsomania, as it was called—and suicide were all understood as expressions of moral failure at best, and as the presence of evil spirits or the devil at worst. In the popular discussions of addiction and mental illness, we still talk about overcoming our demons. For centuries, people who suffered from these conditions were imprisoned, were subjected to violent treatments that approximated the torture, and especially in the case of successful suicides, were generally refused burial in sacred ground. In fact, the bodies of successful suicides, because they were viewed as having committed the gravest sin against God, were disfigured in a variety of ways: dismembered, hung upside down at crossroads, beheaded, and so on. All this was done in the name of morality and spirituality, in defense of the idea that the suicidal person was morally blameworthy.

But this way of thinking is not just repellent to us as compassionate people, it's dangerous because even in the more sublimated forms that we encounter it today, it reinforces in the mind of the alcoholic, the depressed person, or the suicidal person, the idea that she or he is guilty, bad, even evil, someone who deserves to be cast out from good society. And that view is exactly the kind of thinking that leads you to drink yourself to death, or overdose alone in your apartment, or hang yourself with a sheet in a closet. It also reinforces the culture of silence that surrounds these feelings and increases an addict's or suicidal person's fear of reaching out for help.

What I'm saying here is well known, and we are, as a society, moving slowly beyond thinking in these terms. The reason I bring it up is that it is hard to overestimate the pervasiveness and insidiousness of viewing alcohol and other forms of addiction in this way. Unfortunately, in my experience, it is still very much a part of the AA way of thinking. Which is absolutely not to say that AA cannot be of great help to the struggling addict. Rather, I am saying that when we go to AA, we should keep this in mind and not fall into the trap of seeing ourselves or each other in this moralizing way.

I'll admit that I didn't like the tall, lean, wolfish Gary R. and his square dentist's spectacles. (He's not a dentist, but he ought to be.) He's an old-timer who acts like he ought to be running the whole group, if only AA would allow it. Once when I had been in the program for about five months, I was in the middle of telling a story, and he gave me the hand sign *T* for "time." Maybe I was running long, I don't know. Keeping your share to two minutes is a good general practice. But I've never seen anyone call time during a meeting like a referee.

To accept the moral view of alcoholism—the "I was a sinner" view (as a secret drinker for three years, I can tell you it felt like sin)—you have to accept that the alcoholic is free to refrain from drinking. In a paraphrase of (teetotaler) Immanuel Kant's famous observation, when we say, "You ought not drink," it implies, "You can in fact not drink." But AA, while holding the drinker responsible for her drinking, also insists that alcoholics have a chemical imbalance:

> We have an allergy to alcohol. The action of alcohol on chronic alcoholics is a manifestation of an allergy. We allergic types can never safely use alcohol in any form at all.

A sometime sponsor of mine, Greg M., gave me the surprisingly helpful formula he calls Peanuts: "Some people are allergic to peanuts, I'm allergic to booze. So just like some people don't eat peanuts, I don't drink alcohol."

But the dilemma is obvious: either I am the victim of my chemistry (whether it's a disease or an allergy doesn't matter), in which case I ought best to hope for a chemical solution to my problem; or I have made a series of bad choices about drinking and have slowly transformed myself into an addict. AA would like to have it both ways, conceiving alcoholism as a sort of manageable disease, like diabetes. (For AA, the failing pancreas is located in the soul.) And it occurs to me, as I write this, that it's interesting that I choose diabetes as my example of a manageable disease, since this was the disease that dominated my father's life (though he managed it with some difficulty), and I had an awkward, miserable physical intimacy with his diabetes, helping him inject himself from an early age and mostly managing his insulin shots for him when we were on our disastrous road trip to Coos Bay.

You see the problem vividly illustrated in the formulas different groups apply to recovery. For Fingarette (and many others in the recovery community), it's a matter of willpower: you drank your way into alcoholism, and by taking baby steps and moderating your drinking, you can drink your way back out again. Fingarette doesn't think you fall off the wagon or jump onto it: he thinks that every time you drink or don't drink, you are making a choice, and it's that ability to choose that must be emphasized to the addict. If you can erode your willpower through drinking too much, you can also rebuild your willpower by recognizing that you can choose whether to drink at all or how much. He insists that this will be a slow and careful process—but it's a process that depends on the importance of the will, rather than one that is somehow removed from the realm of choice.

By contrast, AA, Fingarette argues, invokes willpower while insisting on complete abstinence: to recover, the alcoholic must make the strenuous effort of working the steps (she must use her willpower) but is not allowed to apply that will to the question of her drinking (she must simply not drink at all). At best, Fingarette thinks, on AA's account, the will is divided: half of you wants the drink, the other half doesn't, and you have to consciously find clever ways to guarantee that the good angel wins.

My first psychiatrist, meanwhile, believed that alcoholism was an entirely physical phenomenon that could be cured with purely chemical means. If you found the right pills, you would no longer be an alcoholic. After our initial few sessions, he would do a ten-minute phone interview with me once a month—seventy-five dollars "a visit"—and then call the pharmacist. Soon my brain was so addled with drugs that I was falling asleep in my office and in meetings; a colleague commented on my "drooling"; and I descended into a depression that was qualitatively unlike any sadness I had ever experienced, even after my father's death or before any of my suicide attempts. I was still going to meetings, but even there—where, and this is perhaps the best thing about AA, there is always someone who has done just what you have done, suffered just what you have suffered, lied just as you have lied, despaired just as you are despairing—I couldn't see past the next five minutes, the thought of tomorrow was unendurable, and I knew that I either had to drink again or kill myself properly this time.

I'm talking to Owen D. about all this on the temple steps. It's warm out. Owen is a red-faced, smiling Irishman about my own age with a head of thick, curly hair who claims that Jolly Ranchers kept him sober: "I bet I ate a pound of those feckin' things a day. You shoulda seen me. I was fat as a Christmas goose." For me, it's ice cream late at night. Every alcoholic is a sugar junkie.

"It's not the cravings so much anymore." I'm almost ninety days in. "It's the depression. I really don't think I can take it. It's like I can't even move. I feel like my head is exploding. I want to tear my teeth out."

"It's the feckin' pink cloud, Clancy. For me it lasted thirty days, and then I crashed. I was walking on air, and then my second month was hell. But it started to ease up about week eight or nine."

The pink cloud is the initial high an alcoholic often feels in the early months of successfully quitting booze. I never had a pink cloud. In that way, my case resembled that of William Styron, who, interestingly, quit *against* his own will.

After forty years of alcohol abuse, Styron's body suddenly refused it: "I discovered that alcohol in minuscule amounts, even a mouthful of wine, caused me nausea, a desperate and unpleasant wooziness, a sinking sensation, and ultimately a distinct revulsion." *We should all be so lucky*, I thought when I first read this. But without alcohol to bandage Styron's mental pain, things immediately took a psychological turn for the worse, and he was plunged into the depression that would ultimately fuel his great memoir, *Darkness Visible*: "Alcohol played a perverse trick on me when we said farewell to each other: although . . . it is a major depressant, it had never truly depressed me during my drinking career, acting instead as a shield against anxiety. Suddenly vanished, the great ally which for so long had kept my demons at bay was no longer there . . . and I was emotionally naked, vulnerable as I had never been before. . . . I was in the first stage—premonitory, like a flicker of sheet lightning barely perceived—of depression's black tempest."

Some of you reading this have quit drinking. I don't know if this passage resonates with your experience, but it almost exactly describes mine. As a child and in my teens, I constantly battled anxiety and depression. By the time I was in college, I thought it had been mostly cured—but that was also when I started drinking regularly. And when I finally quit drinking, the depression I had to pass through was unlike any other I had ever experienced.

My childhood and teenage depression, while constant, rose and subsided depending on external circumstances. It was often so painful or oppressive that I felt my only escape was suicide. As a child, I'm not sure I distinguished between sadness, depression, anxiety, and suicidal thinking—they were all of a piece. And while these feelings didn't subside when I started drinking, they certainly became more manageable. Back in college, when I began drinking on a nearly daily basis, I often felt happy for long stretches at a time. The desire to kill myself was still always with me, but it was less pressing, less claustrophobic, and less urgent. When I was in the jewelry business, as I've said, things got harder, and the old depression and suicidal urges intensified; and then when my father died, it got a lot worse. I went through a long period of trying to kill myself, which abated only when

I started drinking more—in my thirties, with my father gone, I was free to become a roaring drunk—and that seemed to help for a time.

But when I quit drinking, like Styron, I suddenly had to deal not only with withdrawal from alcohol but also with all those psychological difficulties that my use of alcohol had been ameliorating. My own view-in-progress is that alcoholism is not a disease or an allergy or a condition; rather, it is a very effective and potentially addictive medication for a whole host of psychological and neurobiological problems. I suspect that my father was right when he used to say: "I was always a drunk, but it took me years to get good at it." That is, different people, according to their psychological history and their neurochemistry, tend to become addicted to alcohol with greater ease or celerity; others may have a relative resistance to (and/or less need of) the drug. To me, any religion that prohibits the use of alcohol is a bit like a religion that might emerge 150 years from now forbidding the use of benzodiazepines or SSRIs. The problem with alcohol is not so much that it is an addictive medication; rather, that unlike other addictive medications—to which people will also grow or not grow addicted at varying speeds and in unpredictable ways— its social function, its glamorization, and its accessibility obfuscate this reality. If you're prone to overdoing it, the fact that you're self-prescribing (and choosing your own dosage) doesn't help.

When I quit drinking, I lost the ability, for several years, to write fiction. This was devastating to me because I was at the beginning of my writing career, and writing stories, like drinking, almost always alleviated my feelings of anxiety and panic. If I was in a particularly foul, depressed, or sensitive mood, my wife Rebecca would tell me, "You need to write. Go write. Go write, right now," and it worked. I was surprised by this change because I had never written while drinking, though the bitter clarity of a hangover often helped me solve creative problems in my fiction, and I did much of my writing while hungover. It took about three years before my ability to write fiction started to return, and as it did, I noticed that my style had changed: my language was simpler, some might say cruder (one famous writer friend described it as "less writerly") and more direct. This makes sense to me, because my entire experience of the world now feels much rawer than it did when I could drink.

It's a quarter past eight, a freezing night, the streets black with ice. I'm about forty days sober, and can't find a meeting anywhere on the west side of Kansas City. I try two places listed on the Kansas City AA website, both about ten miles from my house, but no one's there, so I call my wife and ask her to get on the computer (by now I'm almost in tears), and she finds a meeting over on the east side. Kansas City has a scar up its middle called Troost Avenue. Due to blockbusting in the 1950s and '60s, the west side of the avenue is about 80 percent white, while the east side is roughly 90 percent African American, and has the reputation, among Brooksiders and the Overland Park set, of being a very dangerous place.

"Do you think it's safe to go over there this late?" It was approaching nine.

"You need to go," my wife said. "Just be careful."

"I guess it *is* an AA meeting," I said, meaning, if you can't be safe at an AA meeting, where can you be safe? Specious logic is convincing when it tells you what you want to hear.

I park next to a big new BMW in the crowded lot behind a church that has all its windows covered in bars, find the right door, and come in about ten minutes late. A prostitute is in the middle of her story of losing her kids to crack. A smiling, round, motherly type in a daisy-print purple dress crosses the room to bring me a cup of coffee.

The next speaker in the circle, Rob M., says, "You know, these meetings are a lot like being in a bar. You sit there with your buddies, the world's a long ways away. Ain't nobody gonna get you in here. That's what I always loved about a bar. Long as you're in the bar, you're safe. It's what's outside the bar waiting for you that's got you scared. 'Cause you can't stay in the bar forever. You got to get outside and get to business. These meetings here are the same way. You come in here, you're safe for a while, but then you got to get out there and get into motion. As long as you're here in a meeting room, you're still halfway in the bar."

"Tell it, brother," somebody else says. I'm feeling conspicuously out of place, but no one seems to be paying any attention to me, and I'm not sure I like that. Like most alcoholics, I prefer to be the center of attention. That's one reason drinking was fun—you're the hero of every story. I can see by the lineup and the clock that the circle will never come round to me. I don't know where the bathroom is, so I can't sidle out to put a sweet Ativan under my tongue. (That's a trick from rehab: they dissolve in a minute and hit your bloodstream faster that way.)

"I'm not saying don't come to as many meetings as you got to come to. I been sober more than twenty years, and you all know me, I still come most every day. I'm saying what counts is what you do after you leave the bar, after you leave the meeting. This meeting's just a bar without the cocktails, that's what I'm saying. And if I'm gonna sit in a bar, I wanna have me a bourbon on the rocks, you know what I'm saying?" Everybody laughs. "And with that I'll pass."

I look at Rob, and he's looking over at me and smiling. After a few minutes, he goes and gets the new pot of coffee—whoever empties the last one makes the next one—and makes his way around the room, topping people off and giving them refills. I choke mine down so that I can get another full cup. When he gets to me, he winks and fills me up. Then I realize I haven't been listening, several people have passed, and it's my turn to talk.

"I guess I first hit rock bottom when I stood in a corner of my ex-wife's guest bedroom and took a piss with my twelve-year-old daughter watching," I say. "She was crying, and she told me, 'Daddy, that's not a toilet.' The second time was when I punched my wife in the face." I want to explain that both times I was in a blackout and don't remember it, but that's unnecessary here and irrelevant anyway. "I saw her face the next day, the jawline, the cheekbone, the bottom lid of her eye. The makeup only made it more obvious. She tells me she almost said, 'Hit me again,' but then thought better of it."

A little laughter of recognition and acceptance from the group. I am choking up a bit. "Go on, now. Lay it out." "Keep going. It's all right, Clancy."

"I found them in a motel room the next day. I tried to quit. But I was white-knuckling it and started hiding bottles. I did that for three years before, a little more than a month ago, I tried to hang myself. That was rock bottom number three."

"Three times the charm. That's the truth." People are nodding: they've hit their spouses—men and women alike—they've tried to kill themselves, once, twice, more. No one is doubting me, judging me, or asking me questions. It is like the best bar ever, a bar without any obnoxious drunks who can't hold their liquor. Everybody here's a drunk, and none of us, despite years of practice and all our boasting, can hold our liquor.

"My wife cut me down in our bedroom closet and checked me into Research. Then I started the program. I don't even know if I'm past the third step yet." The third step—in my own opinion, the most important and difficult of all twelve—runs: "3. Made a decision to turn our will and our lives over to the care of God as we understood him." This step is crucial, because realizing you don't have the will to control yourself is profoundly different from choosing to release control of that will to another. Drinking is a way of releasing your will to a drug; attending AA meetings is a way of releasing your will to not-drinking. *Letting go*—a funny concept, like the Taoist idea of accomplishing things through not-willing—depends on the idea that somehow your will is the problem in the first place, that as long as you are fighting to not-drink, the booze will always win.

Think about having your heart broken. You can't let her go until you really stop trying to win her back—that is, until you stop making yourself *not* try to win her back. You don't forget her or what you did together; you forget that she is the focus of all your need. And quitting drinking really is like losing a lover. You hear it from Al-Anoners every week: "It was just like he was having an affair." You also hear, later, "Now I feel like he's married to his sponsor. I feel like I'm still second in line." As Rob said, the alcoholic remains an addict; his new drug is AA.

"And my wife quit the same day I did."

Mm-hmm, several people agree, nodding.

"If she hadn't, I wouldn't be here tonight. I'd still be drinking. And if I hadn't found this meeting tonight, I think I would have driven to a bar. I was that close. And I'll pass."

At the end of the meeting, we say the Lord's Prayer and the Serenity Prayer, and a few people come over to talk to me, ask where I usually go to meetings, and give me their phone number. Normally I hustle out of meetings because I hate the talking afterward. But I'm clearly a stranger here, and it seems rude to run out the door. I help fold up the chairs before I leave.

I called my mother the other day from a coffee shop, and her first words, before she even said hello, were "Where are you calling me from? It sounds awfully noisy in the background." She assumed I was in a bar.

Here is the alcoholic's karma, what I call the secret drinker's paradox: while you are "secretly" drinking, somebody always knows. It might be your handful of regular bartenders and your friends at the liquor store and the convenience store (in Missouri where I live you can buy vodka at a gas station), but usually it's a much larger group than you think. When you're sober, nobody knows except you. Even my ex-wife Rebecca once said, "Well, all I can do is assume he's not drinking," which is, of course, true. If you think about it too much, you want to run out and have a drink; therefore, you don't think about it.

Not-thinking about things is one of the secrets to recovery. From the AA "greatest hits" manual *Twenty-Four Hours a Day*: "The alcoholic is absolutely unable to stop drinking on the basis of self-knowledge." How this squares with rigorous honesty is a puzzle worth trying to piece together. The truth is it doesn't: "rigorous honesty" should be understood as trying slowly to become more truthful, which will not result in a thorough understanding of oneself but will help with achieving a more caring, open, and sympathetic attitude toward both oneself and others. And that attitude will result in a reduction of the pressures and anxieties that drive a person back toward booze.

I've been in jail more than once on account of my drinking,

but my favorite time was a weekend I did in Olathe, Kansas, as part of a DUI deferment. (The bad joke is, it's a drunk's de-fermentation.) The second day of the jailed retreat, the counselor asked us, "How many people here believe you got here because you are an alcoholic?" Of the twenty-five or so of us, I was the only one who raised his hand. I was honestly astonished. The other members of the group looked at me with surprise, dismay, or pity. It turned out, as we told our stories, that for most of the people there, "it was my first time driving drunk. I just had bad luck." I suspect they were worried that we were being recorded on camera and that somehow an admission of guilt might be used against us later in court. But after the session one of the younger women approached me and said, "So you really think you're an alcoholic? I'm so sorry, Clancy. That really sucks."

I don't mean to suggest that these people were all deceiving themselves, only that I believe—though I may be self-deceived—that I have become a more honest person since I quit drinking, and that the cleanliness of honesty is a big reason I don't go back to drinking when it seems tempting. "But then I'd have to tell my wife I had a glass of wine, and then . . ." No. It's easier to skip the burgundy and have an iced tea.

But the truth is, that's too easy and not quite honest. Yes, now that I don't drink anymore, I have one less cause for lying, and lying about my drinking was a very regular thing back when I drank and then drank secretly. But I always have reasons to lie. And when I have no reasons to lie, I have reasons to tell half-truths. And when I have no reasons to tell half-truths, I have reasons to keep a secret, or to fail to tell a truth that I know ought to be told, or to hide a truth from myself so as to be able to hide it from someone else with a clean conscience.

I cannot claim to be clean and sober when it comes to telling the truth. That part of recovery is a lifelong project. But it may be a project worth living for, like trying to be a good spouse to your partner, or a good parent to your children, or a good friend, or a good professor or writer. I may never be able to do any of these things as well as I would like, but one reason for not killing myself today is that trying to improve in these projects makes sense to me. Or rather, to kill myself now in the midst of the effort seems premature. I can imagine doing better today and still better tomorrow.

It is of the essence of hope to imagine that things can be better, and a particularly optimistic form of hope believes that one of those things could be you. If I were hopeless right now, I would believe that nothing was ever going to improve, and that even if things might incline toward the better rather than the worse, the one thing that would never go up rather than down would be me.

The great twentieth-century philosopher and theologian Dietrich Bonhoeffer, who died in a Nazi concentration camp, wrote about suicide, "A man who is on the brink of suicide no longer has ears for commands or prohibitions. . . . A man who is desperate cannot be saved by a law that appeals to his own strength; such a law will only drive him to even more hopeless despair. . . . A man who can no longer live is not helped by any command that he should live, but only by a new spirit." Which sounds an awful lot like letting go, like realizing that my own will can't do the work for me. I don't know that my projects of self-improvement will be of much help the next time the chips are down, but I still feel better off with them than without them.

One day when I was in the grip of that worst episode of depression, some months after quitting drinking, I was walking home from the university past the Nelson-Atkins Museum of Art. The Walter De Maria pond *One Sun / 34 Moons*, one of my favorite pieces of art, is installed behind the museum. My depression had been getting worse every day, and at this point it was so bad that I could no longer talk to anyone about it. My friends' complete inability to understand what I was suffering made it even worse. It was not only the worst pain I'd ever suffered in my life; it was of an entirely different order than any previous pain. I couldn't breathe. There was nothing I could do. Clearly my only escape was to kill myself, but I couldn't even muster the strength to do that. Then, passing that pond, I realized I could no longer walk. I stood there, not knowing what to do next. I couldn't move my feet. It sounds dramatic, I know, but it was true. I was in too much mental pain to move. Then I prayed. I said, "I don't know if there's anything out there. Dad, I don't know if you're out there." (This was ten years after my father had died.) "God, if you are out there, now is the time. If anyone can help me, anyone, now is the time. I'll do anything. Help me. Please help me." I would have fallen to my knees, but I couldn't kneel. I couldn't even cry. In that moment, I was beyond all that.

Then from who knows where, the clouds inside me parted, and the sun appeared. It was not much sun, just a few beams of sunlight. But suddenly I could walk again, and I started to cry.

And that was the real beginning of my recovery, which continues today, as I write this paragraph here on an apartment balcony in the foothills of the Himalayas, with the Dauladhar range on my left, where I can see the man who lives in the small apple-green concrete house next door praying, holding a smoking offering in his hands, in front of the small white household shrine that is next to the orange tree at the end of the yard.

The old rule for making an earnest attempt at recovery is "ninety meetings in ninety days." I've never been much good at following rules or finishing things, and that first time I got sober I didn't hit the mark. I've "gotten sober" a number of times now, and I've never managed ninety meetings in ninety days.

But at the beginning, those meetings were like a drink. Not like a drink used to be—not a bottle of Beaujolais on a sidewalk table with my wife laughing opposite me, the sun in her eyes and hair—but a long, deep, double swallow of Jägermeister from a pint or a quart I had hidden near the dumpster behind the apartment. At a noon meeting the other day, Christina D. talked about the alcoholic feeling of "hiding in meetings," as if she is attending too many meetings in a day. That's what I mean: meetings as a compulsive, dirty necessity. Meetings as an addiction one wants to conceal.

In Calgary, visiting Darren, I was about six weeks sober. In the desolate gray night snow, my cousin Anna drove me up and down the hills of the city looking for a meeting: we went to three or four forgotten, empty strip malls and church back doors before giving up. (Because no one officially runs AA in any particular city, some websites and hotlines are better than others.

AA is the world's largest functioning anarchy, and on the whole it performs astonishingly well.) When my cousin took me back to her home and made me tea, I panicked. I tried not to look at the walls, at the carpet, at the ceiling, at her. I had nowhere to look. *Help me, God, anybody*, I was thinking. I don't remember what we talked about. I kept going to the bathroom and sitting on the toilet with my head on my knees. I was fantasizing about walking to a highway and stepping in front of a truck or a bus, but I knew she wasn't going to let me out of her sight. The next morning I found a meeting at a breakfast place in a hotel downtown. The owner had to be in recovery, I figured. "My name is Clancy, and I'm an alcoholic," I said, and as I told my story, it was like three fingers of vodka straight to the amygdala.

It's time for me to say something that I haven't been straight about yet. The truth is, I've never been able to stay sober without the help of my wives. When I was married to my first wife, Alicia, she knew that my drinking was a problem, and she kept a close watch on it, and with her it never escalated. We didn't drink recreationally together, except on vacation or maybe a glass of wine over dinner two or three times a week. When we split up, I started dating another woman, I'll call her J., who loved to drink with me—until, after a couple of years, she started to see what my drinking was doing. Alicia would often say, and might still insist, "His drinking was all J.'s fault." It's true that when my first wife and I split up, I felt unleashed to drink as much as I wanted to, and my drinking skyrocketed at that time. I had my first real problems from alcohol then: I missed important meetings, had trouble getting to work, had a car crash while drunk, and used alcohol to contend with the feelings of insecurity, failure, and abandonment that came with my first divorce. I never drank when my daughter was with me (that came later), but the moment I returned her to her mother, I started drinking. Alcohol was the medicine I used to manage the pain of suspecting I was losing the love of my child. At that time, too, when I was feeling suicidal, alcohol could still cheer me up. I was suicidal mostly in the mornings then—those were the years with my gun in the jewelry store. Mornings were clear-eyed and desperate, but by the end of the day, by six o'clock, if I had time to walk across the parking lot in the mall to get a beer at Bennigan's, I felt happy.

I never drank in the office back then—I kept several bottles of very expensive scotch in the bureau behind my desk for important clients, but I never wanted it myself. In fact, I've never been much of an at-work drinker: I've always preferred the atmosphere of a bar, and even during my secret drinking days, when alcohol truly was just medicine that I felt I needed to survive the night, I was happiest drinking if I could find a spare half hour to slip into a bar without anyone—meaning, usually, my partner—noticing.

My second wife, Rebecca, also loved to drink with me at first, and she now considers herself to be a recovering alcoholic. Most of my story with AA comes from that second marriage. She insisted I quit drinking, and my years of secret drinking after that were the most miserable of my drinking career, culminating, as I've recounted, in a suicide attempt.

Surely as I went into that closet to hang myself, drunk from some champagne that she had put in the fridge for herself and a friend to celebrate New Year's Eve 2008, I knew that one of two outcomes would result: I would succeed, and then—so I thought—my problems would be over; or I would fail, and then she couldn't be too too mad at me for my secret drinking. The secret drinking would pale in comparison to the fact that I was so guilt-ridden about the secret drinking that I wanted to kill myself rather than face her.

If I am capable of being honest about the subject—this book is the attempt to be honest about it, but hopefully it also shows the difficulty of being honest about it, since it is also the case that we just don't know ourselves, our intentions and our desires and our beliefs, as well as we like to pretend, and we lie to ourselves even more often and with greater facility than we lie to others—I think I was all out of juice and just wanted to die and be done with it. The misery and self-contempt of that sustained secret addiction takes the will to life right out of you. It's not just escape, but the conviction that you do not deserve to live, that sends you into that closet to try to die.

Rebecca and the fear of returning to a life of lying to her kept me sober. But when we split up in 2011, I started drinking again, and really the worst year of my adult life began, from around January 2011 until February or March 2012, when alcoholism and suicide worked together like a wrestling tag team to keep me on the ropes or in the mental hospital for more than a year.

Then I met my third wife, Amie, and in the summer of 2012, we came to India, and I got sober again. Only then did I manage mostly to stay away from alcohol.

In the early years of our marriage, Amie was in grad school in Iowa City and I was in Kansas City, commuting back and forth, so we were often apart. I would sometimes fall off the wagon and wind up sitting on a sofa at home, hung over and desperate, smelling like the wine from the night before, thinking about a knife or a rope, or wondering how to overdose without any good overdose pills. And even today, though we spend stretches apart in India while I'm at Ashoka teaching and she's with our son somewhere far from New Delhi, and I could drink but do not want to, I wonder if I could stay sober if I didn't know I would be returning to her soon.

In short, though everyone in AA will tell you that the only sobriety worth having is the sobriety you have for yourself, I'm not sure I've ever had that, or have it now. My ability not to take a drink—even though I don't want one, I can say truly as I write this—still depends on my wife, my promise to her and her trust in me, as well as my fear of her anger and of losing her. And maybe that relates to the old AA idea of turning your will over to someone else—not to a Higher Power, in my case, but to my wife. Like, I don't have the will to stop drinking on my own, but she has enough will for me to stop drinking, and that does the job. In the end maybe it's not so much fear of my wife that stops me—as it would certainly not be fear of a Higher Power— but a trust that good things come with our marriage that would otherwise be impossible, and that my need of her is inextricably bound up with those good things. Similarly, in this way of thinking about it, I may well be turning over my will to my children, my job, and my friends, all these superficially external powers that are, in a deeper way, in fact constitutive of whatever self I am.

I hope and pray that I never have to find out that I'm wrong and that actually I could go it alone.

When I got my sixty-day coin and was asked to explain "how you did it"—a tradition at the opening of meetings, and an honor, a one-minute birthday speech—I said (having anticipated and mentally rehearsed this moment) that I had "learned how to listen." Complete BS, by the way: I still sat through every meeting waiting for my chance to talk, watching the clock, worrying that we'd run out of time before they got to *me*.

These days in a meeting, I really do prefer to listen. But the emotions I experience are confusing. When I listen to Frank R. talk about living in his own apartment for the first time in his life and driving across town to pick up his two-year-old son, I feel compassion and almost cry along with him. After the meeting, I talk to him about what it was like when I first left my wife, how I'd drop my daughter off at her mother's doorstep and then immediately go buy a six-pack, drink that on the highway, and be ready for another one by the time I was back home in Dallas, forty-five minutes away. But do I feel superiority or fear when Susan tells us about taking a drink two days ago, after a year of sobriety, and the pain of starting all over again? Can I sort my voyeurism, narcissism, and self-congratulation from my sympathy, anxiety, and fragility? Somehow, in that shadowy, crowded, claustrophobic room smelling of soured coffee and sweat, they all collapse into one another.

I quit my eight p.m. meetings because they attract the late-night, new-to-the-program set, and every night became about someone climbing back onto the wagon after falling off. "Relapse is part of recovery," the mantra goes, and it can be helpful: people will go back to booze, or their drug of choice, and they shouldn't believe that that means their case is hopeless. A dear friend of mine, Ronda K., relapsed and drank secretly, then recovered and relapsed again, over and over, for perhaps fifteen years, hiding it more and less successfully from her family for all that time, but she is sober now and has been for a decade or more. She takes Adderall and smokes an astonishing amount of weed, both prescribed by a psychiatrist, but she doesn't drink alcohol, and it was alcohol that was creating problems in her life. This is how complex these cases really are.

In my past eleven years of recovery, I have relapsed more than a dozen times (more on that in Chapter 9). One of my relapses lasted for almost a year, though every time I drank during that year I told myself quite sincerely that it was the last time. I don't take any psychiatric drugs or other mind-altering substance, though I would like to try ayahuasca one day, under the right circumstances. I fully expect that I will relapse again before I am dead, probably more than once, though I'd prefer not to, and maybe it finally just won't happen. It's been a long while now, and I really seem to have lost the desire to drink. I never want an alcoholic drink anymore, and the thought of one no longer appeals to me. But it may come back, and if the circumstances are wrong, I imagine it may happen.

But to return to my situation in 2009 and 2010. When you keep hearing "Relapse is part of recovery, relapse is part of recovery" every night from a different person, sometimes two or three, and then you leave the meeting and see the neon beer signs of the bar on the other side of Main Street, well, those lights get a little sparklier. Elbows on the bar, squeezed in, the bartender smiles; that smell of the bar, the smell of self-acceptance, joy, and fellowship. The warm-up to that first drink, letting it linger there for a moment, water beading on the glass, stirring the ice cubes with a red and white bar straw, and ah! the first swallow, and the honey-gingered sun glows at the back of the head, and now, three swallows later, you order your first real drink, the second one. The night is young and loving: as you hear in AA rooms: "With me one drink's too many and a million's not enough."

Why do so many people relapse, especially in the early years of recovery? Why do we go back to this drug that is no longer much fun and is so incredibly destructive to our mental well-being, our relationships, and our professional lives? Why are recovery rates for alcoholism—maybe 30 percent on the high side, with the help of AA—so low?

Here's AA founder Bill W. again, describing his own first couple of drinks at a party in 1917, at age twenty-two:

> Well, my self-consciousness was such that I simply had to take that drink. So I took it, and another, and then, lo, the miracle! That strange barrier that had existed between me and all men and women seemed to instantly go down. I felt that I belonged where I was, belonged to life; I belonged to the universe; I was a part of things at last. Oh, the magic of those first three or four drinks! I became the life of the party. I actually could please the guests; I could talk freely, volubly; I could talk well.

Lo, the miracle. I belonged. Heroin addicts talk about "chasing the dragon," trying to recover that feeling you got the first few times you smoked or injected the drug. For drunks like me, our dragon is that golden feeling of belonging; that temporary release from those deadly four words "I am not okay"; that escape from the oppressive smell of yourself, your "self-consciousness" as Bill W. puts it, with all your inadequacies, failures, and rejections. If you can get all that with just two glasses of wine or three beers or one and a half double margaritas on the rocks with salt, who wouldn't go back and give it one more try?

For better or worse, eventually, it stops working.

Back at an eight-o'-clocker, my third meeting of the day, I see my friend Christina again: her long brown hair, her narrow shoulders, and her easy smile; her eagerness to come check on me, to make sure I'm doing all right. Is Christina Thirteen-Stepping me? (That's when an old-timer preys on a new member for sex.) She sees my wedding ring, but hell, it's all broken homes and lost love here. Still, I don't think it's that. Christina doesn't know it, but she's right on the edge of being a "thumper," the AA version of the Bible kind. Most thumpers are crafty about not letting on that they're thumpers. You're not really supposed to be a thumper—the self-irony of the alcoholic is supposed to keep you from becoming a dogmatist, and almost every serious alcoholic has a healthy sense of self-irony, a survival technique from suffering years of what F. Scott Fitzgerald called "postmortems" of one's behavior the night before. The secret thumpers are the most dangerous ones.

It's the fall of 2009, I've been sober for about nine months. My new psychiatrist has me (shakily) on my feet, with an SSRI and a different anxiety medication (Valium), and I decide to give the Escalade meeting another try. I cringe when I see that Gary R. is there again. He doesn't even *look* like he belongs at the Escalade meeting: he doesn't look "white, rich, and proud of it." He looks like a street drunk, scrawny and scarred and angry. He's also a true thumper, the scary kind—he will get in your face—but I've also seen him cry at meetings. He's always the first to volunteer to be a temporary sponsor, and I expect he's helped dozens of people get and stay sober. But even without the "time" incident, Gary would have been my enemy. There's always been an antipathy between us, for reasons I don't think either of us could specify. If you've been in rehab or in a setting where you're somehow forced together, you know what I mean.

After the meeting, outside in the generous sunlight, he grabs me by the elbow. "You know, Clancy, everything you put ahead of your sobriety you're gonna lose."

It's a maxim. Just some of the things I put ahead of meetings: my wife and daughters; my teaching; my writing. These come before an AA meeting. But it's true, I could lose them all if I don't stay off the booze.

"You're right, Gary," I tell him. "But sometimes coming to a meeting helps you stay sober, and sometimes it doesn't."

He shakes his head. "You still don't get it, Clancy. Keep it simple, stupid. How long have you been sober now? Nine months?" He remembers. He's that kind of a guy, with the plus and the minus of that. "Well, call me anytime. You still got my number, right? Use it."

Although I've benefited from having a sponsor, I've never

called my sponsor or another alcoholic when I wanted a drink. I've answered calls and talked people down, but I'm not really a phone person. I did talk to Ben A. once on the phone when my depression was so bad I was about to jump off the roof of UMKC's Royall Hall. I had my feet over the edge and my hands positioned so that I could just give the gentlest shove. I was worried that I wasn't high enough, and that I'd just cripple myself and make everything so much worse. Then my phone rang. I thought, *Who would have the psychic acuity to call me just now?* It was a guy I liked from AA, and I thought, *Well, maybe this will be the last person I talk to in my life,* and that struck me as funny, and I laughed and answered the phone and told him the truth about where I was and what I was up to.

At a meeting in a little town north of Kansas City that I had been invited to by a real old-timer, I met a couple about my and my wife's age. But unlike with us, she was the drunk; he was the Al-Anon husband attending the open meeting. They both looked frightened, but they were frightened of different things. He feared what he didn't understand. She feared what she knew.

After the meeting I thanked him. "I never could've gotten sober without my wife, man. What you're doing is so important."

Then he wandered into a conversation with someone else, and I spoke with his wife. She had been sober for six weeks.

"It's just so hard to let go of all that," she said. "Sitting on the front porch in the late afternoon, on the swing, with a Jack and Coke. We've got four kids. After I get them to bed, we'd just go sit on the porch and talk." She wasn't worrying about "the alcoholic who still suffers"—she was envying her. I could smell the drink coming after her. I hoped I was wrong, naturally.

I told her, trying to help, "Listen to your psychiatrist. I know people tell you to just get clean. But my first year I took a handful of drugs, and I still take Valium and an antidepressant. It can make it so much easier."

She eyed me dubiously but hopefully. The alcoholic is, we may forget, an addict like any other addict. And addicts like to take things. We are seriously and chronically dissatisfied with

our ordinary brain chemistry. Why that is the case is the interesting question. Most of us have a tough enough time getting
through the day. Is the alcoholic just more impatient than other
people? More sensitive? Weaker? Why does alcohol take hold of
certain people and destroy their lives and let so many others be?

Bill W. believed that there were three possible solutions for
the alcoholic who was not helped by AA alone: (1) a mystical
experience, (2) LSD, or (3) niacin, or vitamin B3. He believed
this because in his own recovery he had been helped by a direct
experience of the presence of God, by ongoing experimenta-
tion with LSD, and by countering occasional urges for a drink
with high doses of niacin. Indeed, toward the end of his life, he
believed that he would be remembered not so much for the creation of AA as for the discovery of the B3 treatment for alcoholism, which has subsequently been shown to have some efficacy.
(And at the very end of his life, on his deathbed, Bill W. asked
for a drink. The people caring for him refused to give it to him.
As Morpheus said to Neo, "Fate, it seems, is not without a sense
of irony.")

Despite Bill W.'s beliefs, when I was a regular attendee at
meetings, no one ever talked about drugs except as part of the
problem. I've often heard people brag about not taking pain
medication after a surgery: "I knew if I took one Vicodin, two
weeks later I'd be back at the bar." Back in 2010, in the two hundred or so AA meetings I attended in that year, I'd never once
heard another alcoholic mention her or his psychiatrist.

I'm told it's changing now, and that's a very good thing. Here
in Bir, Himachal Pradesh, where I am writing these pages in
2020, at the meetings I have every other day with Sunil, we both
talk openly about our past psychiatrists and our problems with
the medications they prescribed us. But I've noticed that, despite
all our candor on every other matter, I am very scrupulous not
to ask if he is on any medication now, and I weirdly make a point
of letting him know that I no longer take anything. For his part,
he stays silent.

·   ·   ·

"This is how I did it." I'm getting my one-year coin. I've decided to tell the truth. "A year ago my wife found me dangling from a sheet I'd twisted into a rope in our closet. It wasn't a very good rope, and I was strangling slowly, but it wasn't painful. She got me down and checked me into the hospital—I cried the whole way there and begged her not to. They diagnosed me with depression and bipolar disorder and put me on Klonopin, Lamictal, lithium, and a drug I'd read can help alcoholics with cravings, a muscle relaxant called baclofen. Four days later they released me, and that night I crashed my car into a post getting to my first meeting, here." A little laugh. But people are nervous. I know they're hoping I get to the part about being really clean. My coin already feels a little less earned. "The Klonopin pitched me into a terrible depression, so I went on to Ativan, which was worse, and then Valium, 40 milligrams a day. I still take 15 milligrams of Valium every day but am trying to get down to 10."

It took me five years of sustained effort to get from 15 milligrams a day of Valium to zero (started early 2010, off in late 2015), and during that time I ran out more than once and had to endure the horrible, incredibly anxious, itchy-tickling feeling that burns through all the nerves in your body and especially the top of the spine when you are withdrawing from a benzodiazepine. When my second psychiatrist told me that her goal was to get me down to 5 milligrams of Valium a day and then switch me to Librium, I nodded politely and laughed uproariously inside, because I was sure I couldn't live without a serious daily dose of benzos. In the end I didn't take the Librium, because the Valium was easy to break into smaller and smaller doses. I spent a year going from 5 to 2.5 milligrams, and I could still feel the physical difference when I hadn't yet taken the pill. But she was right, and as much as AA, my eighty-year-old psychiatrist, Grace Ketterman, saved my life. I should add, as I hope I've stressed, that the majority of the credit goes to my ex-wife Rebecca and my present wife Amie: it all would have come to nothing if those two hadn't been willing to quit with me and wait as I went through the harrowing early months of sobriety, first in 2009 with Rebecca and then in 2012 with Amie.

"The Lamictal and the lithium made me feel like my head was full of static electricity so I stopped taking them, and for the first ninety days I came to lots of meetings. Eventually I stopped the baclofen when, at about six months, my cravings were manageable, but I was still very depressed, and my new psychiatrist put me on Celexa. Then about two weeks later, the clouds just lifted. For the first time since I quit drinking, I didn't want to kill myself. I could imagine a good future. Now I come to meetings when I need to, I see my psychiatrist, and I take my drugs. I'm sober, and I'm happy."

Embarrassed silence. Everyone was looking straight ahead or down. It was as though I had stood in that packed, low-ceilinged room and farted like a bugle. We proceeded with the meeting, and no one else spoke about pharmaceuticals or psychiatrists.

But after the meeting, outside—where the real action always was, before and after, smoking cigarettes—five or six younger members came up to me and thanked me. Everyone said the same thing: "I'm on"—fill in your drug, these days the fashion is Lamictal or Seroquel plus something else—"but I've always been afraid to talk about it. My sponsor doesn't even know."

I underestimated the last dose of acid I ever took, at a Grateful Dead concert in Orlando, Florida, in 1987, and had a terrifying trip. Sometimes, if it weren't for that, I'd be tempted to drop a couple of hits of purple microdot before a meeting and explain that, following Bill W., I was buttressing my sobriety with LSD. And indeed, these days the suggestion wouldn't be as controversial as it would have been even in 2009: lately hallucinogens, including acid, magic mushrooms, MDMA, and other psychedelic or psychoactive drugs, are being used in scientific studies all over the world to treat anxiety, depression, PTSD, and addiction and to assist with the fear of death. In Oregon the governor recently announced a Psilocybin Advisory Board.

You'd better not be flip when you've been sober for less than two years and a volunteer program run by people who really understand your addiction takes the time to cure you solely out of a desire to help. Moreover, in writing about my experiences in AA, I am breaking at least two important rules of the group that has helped me so much. One of them, "The Eleventh Tradition," runs: "Our public relation policy is based on attraction rather than promotion; we need always maintain personal anonymity at the level of press, radio and films." (We should add, these days, "and other forms of media.") I was once ostracized for a time from my regular group when in a newspaper interview I mentioned in passing that I attended AA meetings at a particular location. Most members of AA read this tradition as meaning that one simply cannot say anything publicly about AA, but that reading would make the group a cult. AA is strong enough to bear the light of day, to withstand a little self-criticism from the inside. So I'm not as worried about that one.

The more important principle I'm breaking is a saying that's often repeated before meetings: "What you say here, what you hear here, when you leave here, let it stay here." To that end, I've tried to quote directly from meetings as little as possible. But a bit of it is necessary, and I'm justifying it to myself because storytelling is essential to AA's therapeutic effects.

We all know about writers and booze. Richard Yates had no patience for AA ("Is just functioning living at all?"), but an awful lot of good writers have been or are in the program. Mary Karr, in her memoir of alcoholism and recovery—recovery with the help not only of AA but also a religious conversion—relates the story of how she met her future friend and sometime partner David Foster Wallace at one of her first AA meetings. Kurt Vonnegut's Billy Pilgrim kept the Serenity Prayer on his office wall. And you'll notice that AA has developed a lot of very catchy slogans over the years. This is no mere coincidence: even in its very earliest days, when Bill W. was writing the Big Book, advertising executives and former *New Yorker* editors were involved in its crafting. So it's not surprising that storytelling became so fundamental to the culture of AA.

What is more interesting is what it contributes to recovery. *It's just confession*, you might think, or *It's just free psychotherapy*. And that's partially right. But it's not just confession or psychotherapy when everyone in the room is doing it, and it turns out that listening to stories is just as important as—maybe more important than—telling them. Stories give you a chance to laugh at yourself and others. When you hear your own story repeated back at you, you understand that *Hey, I can forgive her for what she did, I can see that she's still a person worth knowing, a valuable person*, and then you might realize *Maybe I'm not as bad as I thought. Maybe others can also forgive me and still want me around.* When you learn to listen to other people, you may realize that you don't have to be the star of your own soap opera, you don't have to be the center of attention, that it can be okay to be the quiet guy in the corner who just pays careful attention to others. Also, in telling a story, or in listening to someone else tell a story, you have the opportunity to uncover more and more of the painful truth, things you didn't want to think about, fears you didn't want to admit, and again, watching someone else do this, you see their bravery and their merit.

Suicide and failed suicide come up often in meetings, and no one is surprised, no one is angry, no one asks: "But what about your kids?" We all know that the other people in the room understand the need to destroy yourself. We just want you to be able to tell one of your stories about why. I heard a share some years ago from a single dad who ate rat poison with a bottle of Seagram's gin, his two small kids asleep in his bed in his one-bedroom apartment. Everyone just nodded, a couple people held back tears.

He told this story, and we still respected and cared for him. Stories break through loneliness and self-loathing. And perhaps the worst thing about alcoholism—and one reason I tried to kill myself that night—is the conviction that you deserve your loneliness, that no one needs to be cast out more than you do.

"I've never met a stupid alcoholic," my father used to say, and there's something to that. Subtlety, nuance, and insight can often be found in AA meetings. It's not just that you feel camaraderie, it's also that you can see other people striving to understand you, really thinking their way into your problems and your life.

AA people like to say they can tell about the difference between AA and Al-Anon this way. "Stand in the hall between two meetings and listen. From inside the AA room all you hear is laughter; from inside the Al-Anon room all you hear is tears." It doesn't seem fair, I've often thought, but then it also presents two classic responses to the suffering of the human drama: comedy and tragedy.

When an earlier version of some of this material appeared in a national magazine in January 2010, the members of my home group were mostly supportive. Naturally it took some time for them to digest it. And for some of them, I had committed a real betrayal. I had made public what must stay private. A few days after the article came out, one member called me on the phone and asked me, "Where are you? Where are you right now?" I was in my office at UMKC. "Where's that?" he asked. I told him. This was a guy I knew and trusted completely. "Good. Because I'm coming up there with a baseball bat, and I'm gonna beat you to death."

I probably should have told my group, "Listen, I'm a writer, and I'm going to be writing about some of my experiences here, but I'll change names and I won't report any details of the stories other people have shared within meetings." That's what I should have done, but I didn't do that. About the article, my sponsor said, "Hey, I think anonymity is important for your recovery, and for that reason I don't think it was such a great idea. But I don't think you've hurt anyone else, and you might have even helped some people. I don't know if that's what you were trying to do." When I told him the story about the baseball bat, he laughed and said, "I hope in coming to AA, you didn't think you were coming to the place where all the sane people are." "Good point," I said, and laughed with him, but the truth was, I had kind of thought that.

Recently, I gave a talk in New Delhi about suicide and my suicide attempts, and afterward a famous Bengali poet who I very much admire made a comment. He said, "I understand what you have been going through and I will pray for you. But I must beg you never to give a talk like this in public again. I feel like I have been violated, and I feel like you have violated the minds of all these people here." He gestured around to the crowd. "People should not have such things in their minds."

I don't know if talking about my alcoholism or my suicide attempts is the right thing to do. Certainly, as I said to the Bengali poet, it is important that I give a trigger warning. I gave one with the title of this book, and I give one at the beginning of every talk I give. This is grisly stuff. Maybe such things should be written only anonymously. AA says in one of the Twelve Traditions, "Put principles above personalities." That is, don't make it about someone's individual suffering and recovery, especially not about that particular personality; instead, find what we have in common, what we all share.

But I suppose that in my attempts to think through this stuff, I can't truly place principles before personalities, because it's all so personal to me. I don't connect with the principles, I connect with the people. And whether it's AA or suicide, speaking for myself, those personal connections with real individual people are what has made possible my freedom from addicted and self-destructive thinking. Which is the main theme of my recovery, of this chapter, and in some ways, of this book.

Adrienne Rich wrote in *On Lies, Secrets, and Silence* (1979) that "the liar . . . leads an existence of great loneliness," and for me, lying, hiding, shame, secrecy, and loneliness have been at the heart of the problem. One thing I learned in the protected space of the meeting rooms of AA is that it isn't necessary to lie in order to be accepted. That if I had had the courage to try to tell the truth about what I was thinking and feeling, other people would have been eager to try to help me, and perhaps would also be helped.

Defending confessional literature these days may be superfluous. Probably the most serious accusation is that there is too much of it. And the truth is, we don't get out of our own heads. We seem condemned to forever misunderstand each other and perhaps also ourselves. But there are different degrees of intimacy, and the effort to be intimate with someone else about the scariest parts of one's inner life still seems meaningful.

When F. Scott Fitzgerald published his confessional memoir of his mental collapse, *The Crack-Up*, in 1936, Hemingway reportedly said to his former friend that he should "cut off your balls, if you still have any balls, and throw them into the sea."

That's a rather different complaint from the one the Bengali poet made to me: Hemingway thought that one should not say such things out of respect for oneself; the poet, out of respect for other people. They both have a point. But I also think that sometimes we ought to just let our masks down and say, *Hey, this is how I'm feeling, and if you're feeling the same way, maybe it will help you to know that you're not alone.*

When I was in Delhi during the early weeks of the coronavirus, getting our boarding passes for our flight to the mountains, the young SpiceJet employee behind the counter said to me, "Well, we're all afraid of losing our jobs. And if we do, what happens to us?"

I nodded, not knowing what to say.

Then she added, "But I guess we're all in it together."

It's the winter of 2010. I don't know it yet, but the worst year of my life is only a few months away.

I am in San Francisco, and I catch a ten o'clock AA meeting. It's easy to find an AA meeting almost any time of day in San Francisco. This one is a speaker meeting, where an honored member of the AA community (usually a local, but sometimes a well-known visitor) takes the full hour, and I listen to this twenty-year veteran tell his story of heroin and alcohol. He's one of those members I struggle to comprehend, someone who lost everything—family, career, home, even health—yet still cleaned up. He had no reason to go on, but not only did he go on, he recovered. As strong as the death drive is in any addict, sometimes the will to live wins. He didn't reclaim everything he'd lost, but he was still standing; in fact, after the meeting, he is very pleased to be standing in the cold San Francisco night with the smokers and the people heading out for coffee or ice cream.

I go into a restaurant to ask for directions back to my hotel. I stand at the bar. A woman a few seats down looks at me. She looks a bit like Salma Hayek with a softer chin, and I figure her date's in the bathroom.

"What's your drink?" she says.

"What?" The restaurant, a small, hip Italian place, maybe

twenty tables, is very noisy. I'd heard her, but I was surprised by the question.

"She asked what you're drinking," the bartender says in a thick accent. She is even more striking than Salma, I notice.

"Jägermeister," I say, and laugh. "That's my drink."

"Jäger? Isn't that for frat boys?" She laughs. I see then that she is drunk. "Do you even have Jäger here? I don't think they get a lot of orders for Jäger here."

The bartender nods.

"Pour him a Jäger."

"Excuse me, I was joking," I say. The bartender is already pouring the drink. Salma pats the chair beside her.

"Sit here, next to me," she says. The black shot of Jägermeister, purple at its edges, is poured tall and heavy in a rocks glass. Three fingers. A quarter pint. Two big graceful swallows, or one mighty gulp. I can drink a quarter pint in one gulp, if I hear the wrong door opening at the right moment. Two swallows is a perfect half pint, even though you try to stretch it to four.

I sit down. "Whatcha doin'?" she says. She leans close to me. I think, *The devil himself has come to San Francisco.* My wife is four hours away by plane; my hotel room, fifteen minutes on foot, five minutes by cab.

She makes as though to toast, and I lift the glass and clink with her wineglass. I think, *You'll drink this one, stand up, and leave. You'll be polite, you'll drink it, buy her another glass, and then go. You don't want it, and that makes it different. It's German NyQuil, that's all it is, it's cough syrup. You're not breaking any promises. You're not going to cheat on your wife.* I think about John Travolta in Mrs. Marsellus Wallace's bathroom in *Pulp Fiction.* One drink.

Then I put it down. The beautiful Italian bartender in her low-slung jeans gives me a strange smile that I still haven't figured out.

"That's bad luck," says Salma.

"Yeah, I know. I'm sorry," I say. "I've got to go. I don't drink."

She stares at me. "Then why'd you sit down?"

I pay for another glass of wine for her.

"The shot's on me," the bartender says.

"That's a deal," I tell the bartender. "I don't know," I tell

Salma. I have the absurd urge to kiss her on the cheek, but I don't, of course.

When I get outside, I realize I still don't know where my hotel is. I call my wife. I want to tell her the story immediately. She doesn't answer. She's asleep in bed with the kids. I'm very thirsty; I can admit that much. I think about taking half a Valium—I have one in my pocket, as I always do for a meeting at this time, because meetings often still made me want to take a drink—and then think, *No, I need a Diet Coke*. For maybe an hour I walk along the high, cold, bright, busy streets of San Francisco, until I find that hill with the red hanging lanterns of Chinatown, and from there I know my way back.

But I have no idea where I'm headed back to. That's the funny part.

6

Philosophical Suicide

In an interview with Robin Williams in 2010, Marc Maron introduced the subject of death. Maron said that Williams didn't seem like he was especially fascinated with the question of dying. Williams seems to agree with him and then goes into one of his brilliant, signature riffs:

"When I was drinking there was only one time . . . where I thought, 'Fuck life.' And . . . my conscious brain went like: 'Did you honestly just say Fuck life? You know you have a pretty good life as it is right now. Have you noticed the two houses?' 'Yes.' 'Have you noticed the girlfriend?' 'Yes.' 'Have you noticed that things are pretty good even though you're not working right now?' 'Yes.' 'Let's put the suicide over here and discuss it. . . . First of all, you don't have the balls to do it. . . . Have you thought about buying a gun?' 'No.' 'What were you going to do, cut your wrist with a Waterpik?' 'Maybe. . . .' 'Can I put that here in the What the fuck? category? Can I ask you what you're doing right now? You're sitting in a hotel room with a bottle of Jack Daniels. Is this maybe influencing your decision?' 'Possibly.' 'Okay. And who's that in the bed over there?' 'I don't know. . . . Who is this?' 'It's your conscience, asshole.'"

Williams wraps up the monologue by thanking Maron, saying that discussions of death are "very freeing."

Before we get into the discussion about suicide between Robin Williams and his conscience, and the ancient Egyptian dialogue on suicide that it reminds me of, I should say, for the sake of orientation, that I wrote this chapter for me. I suppose I've written all these chapters for me, to try to understand my own self-destructive urges in order better to live with them and perhaps even be liberated from them, but this chapter in particular is about suicide and my own professional life, you could say.

In 1999, after five long years, I left my brothers and the jewelry business we'd built together—they are both still in the business, though they both now run their own independent companies—and moved to Wilmington, North Carolina, with my girlfriend at the time, leaving my ex-wife and five-year-old daughter Zelly back in Texas. I had some savings, and I was trying to write a book about my time in the jewelry business. (This eventually became my first novel, *How to Sell*.) But the novel was going badly, my relationship with my girlfriend was going even worse, and I missed my daughter too much. And eventually my savings were going to run out. So I moved back to Texas to write a new dissertation with the philosopher who would become my great friend, mentor, and co-author, Robert C. Solomon.

I told Bob that I wanted to write a dissertation on either the philosophy of suicide or failure in the thought of Thorstein Veblen. These were two obsessions of mine at the time. He told me, wisely, that if I wrote either of those dissertations, I would never get a job in a philosophy department. I then proposed a dissertation on deception in the thought of Friedrich Nietzsche, which he also initially rejected, but then came to enthusiastically support. I wrote that dissertation and got a job as a philosophy professor at the University of Missouri in Kansas City, where I've happily and gratefully taught ever since.

But I didn't stop thinking about suicide and philosophy, and I became increasingly interested in philosophers' arguments against suicide and also, through history, philosophers' personal relationship with suicide. Suicide was not uncommon among ancient Greek and Roman philosophers—the biographer Diogenes Laertius humorously remarked that it was difficult to find a Roman philosopher who died a natural death. But it seems to have been rare among philosophers in the past thousand years or so. This is unexpected when one thinks about the frequency of suicide among writers, artists, mathematicians, and intellectuals generally. It's encouraging to me that almost none of the philosophers who wrote about suicide subsequently killed themselves. That could be pure coincidence, but careful reflection might also have revealed that suicide, generally speaking, isn't the best course of action.

The oldest known meditation on suicide is an Egyptian text from approximately four thousand years ago (c. 1937–1759 BC), a New Kingdom papyrus called "Dialogue of a Man with His Soul." Like Robin Williams in his improvised conversation with his conscience, the "me" of the Egyptian dialogue wants to die, while the interlocutor (the conscience for Robin Williams, the soul or *ba* for the unnamed Egyptian author) tries to talk the "me" out of it.

Williams doesn't give us an argument for why he ought to kill himself, just this one idea, "Fuck life," an idea that he seems to think outrageous, though he is clearly wrestling with it. The thought occurred to him back when he was still drinking alcohol, he says, mentioning a bottle of Jack Daniel's. He mentions in passing one argument in support of killing himself: "you're not working right now." It's certainly relevant that he's feeling professionally unfulfilled, perhaps unwanted.

But otherwise the arguments are all against the idea of killing himself. This is interesting, because he seems to take the desirability of killing himself for granted, but in the dialogue he is recreating a dark time. For that reason, I particularly like the dialogue, because it's just when we feel the way he was clearly feeling then—that killing oneself is the obvious and necessary thing to do—that we need these arguments.

Williams's conscience makes five arguments against suicide. First, he has "a good life" that includes "two houses": that is, he has material prosperity, more than he needs. Financially, he has reason to be grateful. Second, he has a girlfriend: he's not alone. He has love in his life. Third, he doesn't "have the balls" to do it: he's too scared of death and/or pain, as evidenced by the fact that he has never bought a gun, and he mocks himself, suggesting that he hasn't thought of any better way to kill himself than cutting his wrists with an electric tooth cleaner. Fourth, he's not in his right mind: his thinking is being distorted by alcohol, loneliness (he's in a hotel room), moral disorientation, and self-reproach (he has a stranger in his bed). Fifth and finally, his conscience argues that he should at least delay the decision—talk about it in therapy or in a podcast.

Williams does not re-create his own replies to his conscience's arguments, if he made any, though he acknowledges to Maron that his worldly success is not what keeps him alive. Maron says, "You've had all this stuff and . . . it doesn't matter," to which Williams replies: "Big time!"

In the end, as we know, the suicidal Williams, suffering from Lewy body dementia, won out over his conscience. On August 11, 2014, at the age of sixty-three, he hung himself in a spare bedroom of his home, while his wife was sleeping in the bedroom.

The ancient Egyptian dialogue on suicide works just the other way: the soul or conscience doesn't get to say much, and all the convincing arguments come from the text's weary author. Although the soul's portion of the text is a bit difficult to understand, the soul seems to make two simple claims: that suicide will guarantee a poor afterlife, and that the Egyptian author shouldn't focus on his troubles but rather "pursue the happy day and forget care!" The soul seems to recommend a blithe, fun-seeking, don't-take-yourself-so-seriously approach.

For better or worse, the Egyptian author is incapable of doing that, and he makes five arguments recommending suicide to himself. First, he says, pursuing a life of mere pleasure, as his soul has argued, would ruin his reputation. He would rather die with a good name than live ignobly. Second, the people of his own time are immoral, and he doesn't want to live among such people, or in such repugnant times. Third, he is unbearably lonely: "To whom can I speak today?" he repeatedly asks his soul. "I am laden with wretchedness / For lack of an intimate (friend)." Fourth, he looks forward to death: especially given how difficult life is, it sounds very pleasant to him. Life is a sickness, a confinement, a rainy day, a cloudy sky, a state of exile. He writes, in one particularly powerful part of the dialogue:

> *Death is in my sight today*
> *(Like) the recovery of a sick man,*
> *Like going out into the open after a confinement.*
> *Death is in my sight today*
> *Like the odor of myrrh*
> *Like sitting under an awning on a breezy day.*
> *Death is in my sight today*
> *Like the odor of lotus blossoms,*
> *Like sitting on the bank of drunkenness.*
> *Death is in my sight today*
> *Like the passing away of rain,*
> *Like the return of men to their houses from an expedition.*
> *Death is in my sight today*
> *Like the clearing of the sky,*
> *Like a man fowling thereby for what he knew not.*
> *Death is in my sight today*
> *Like the longing of a man to see his house (again),*
> *After he has spent many years held in captivity.*

Fifth and finally, he argues directly against his soul that, rather than suicide giving him a bad afterlife, the dead are among the gods and are either gods themselves ("he who is yonder / Will be a living god") or are good people, or at least better people than in life. "He who is yonder / Will be a man of wisdom." (This interestingly anticipates a remark by Socrates that while the average person should avoid death, the philosopher may seek it, and in death, for all we know, we may well have the chance to speak with great minds who died before us.) At the end of the dialogue, the soul seems to concede the argument to the author, allows him to take his life, and reassures him that whatever he decides, they will be together.

I wanted to open with these dialogues for two reasons. First, I like the fact that both texts reveal the kind of argument that people actually engage in with themselves when debating committing suicide. My own experience certainly mirrors this back-and-forth. And this is fortunate for anyone who believes, as I do, that under the vast majority of circumstances, suicide is something we should avoid. Because as long as an argument is taking place, we're still open to reason, we can still be persuaded. Even if we have resolved, we haven't yet acted.

In her memoir about her suicide attempts Yiyun Li controversially wrote that "one never kills oneself from knowledge or understanding, but always out of feelings." This is importantly true, especially of the kinds of suicides that are motivated by the urgent need to escape overwhelming mental suffering. But even if we endorse Li's account of why people kill themselves, we still have room for reasons *not* to kill ourselves. Maybe we can choose not to kill ourselves because of knowledge, because of understanding.

Although the great Scottish philosopher David Hume was surely right when he observed that "reason is and ought to be the slave of the passions," nevertheless reasons can and often do change our passions or the way we express them. I can have a passionate desire to die, yet talk myself out of it with reasons.

Like other philosophers, I love to argue. I have argued with myself going down the stairs into the basement with the tools for killing myself in my hands, and I've argued with myself with a rope around my neck, balancing awkwardly with one foot on each arm of a chair, and I've argued with myself with my Nikes dangling off the roof of a twenty-story hotel in Miami, and I've argued with myself behind the wheel of a car at night on a highway going as fast as the car will go, and so on. And although I've argued with myself and then tried suicide anyway, at many, many more times in my life the arguments worked, and I talked myself out of it. Similarly, I've used argument as a tool for talking students, friends, and acquaintances through a suicidal episode.

The second reason I have begun this chapter with the pairing of Robin Williams and our unknown Egyptian sufferer is that I am struck by how alike these two texts are. Their tone is incredibly similar despite the fact that our two philosophers are separated by four thousand years and radically different cultures and belief systems. Nonetheless we hear two people in despair, worrying about what might be the most fundamental question, or what Albert Camus called "the only serious philosophical question": is life worth living? Neither of them really answers the question, which is another intriguing similarity. The texts share the tension of uncertainty. The Egyptian author wants to believe that he should die but hasn't quite persuaded himself; Williams wants to believe that it makes no sense to say "Fuck life" but is still wondering why he hasn't bought a gun.

The Egyptian author might be more nakedly honest than Williams, not because he's more strongly inclined toward killing himself but because he is frank about his fear and loneliness. Williams skates pretty quickly over the desire to kill himself (perhaps because he's a celebrity appearing on a podcast and knows better than to be too open), but his dread appears darkly through the cracks of what he is and isn't saying. Maron notices this, repeating that the things Williams suggests ought to bolster his desire to live—the two houses, the girlfriend, the "pretty good life"—really don't matter. Even if we didn't know that four years later Williams would take his own life, a perceptive listener (like Maron) had cause to worry about him.

The biggest difference between these texts is that the Egyptian author straightforwardly romanticizes death, while Williams makes only an elliptical, somewhat mysterious remark about "discussions of death" being "very freeing." Free to what? Free to say things that otherwise we fear to say? Free to consider a more radical liberation? Free to see clearly why you ought to go on living, even though sometimes it's hard? Free to kill yourself?

The other great difference is that the Egyptian author, though seemingly inclined toward taking his own life, consistently mentions beautiful, compelling aspects of living as his examples of how death is in his sight: the passing of rain, the odor of lotus blossoms, the clearing of the sky, returning home. The most alluring things about life are offered as incitements to death, suggesting both how deeply he experiences life and how profound his ambivalence about leaving it must be.

Perhaps the most powerful argument in defense of the right

to commit suicide ties freedom and death closely together—the Stoics' "door is always open" argument that we discussed in Chapter 3. The idea is that as long as we recognize that we are always free to kill ourselves, as long as we are alive, our freedom can never be compromised. It's complicated, though, because as soon as you're dead, it's reasonable to ask: are you still free? Maybe not. Killing oneself could be the most fundamental rejection of freedom (depending on one's view about the existence and character of the afterlife). And suppose there is no afterlife: does it make sense to say that a basic exercise of one's freedom is the relinquishing of that freedom?

You may think, as Yiyun Li hints, and as I also sometimes tend to think, that when it comes to a question as serious and as passionate as suicide, philosophical arguments are of no use. Certainly if I were sitting alone in my home right now, in despair, with a bottle of barbiturates in my hand, I doubt that I would reach for a compendium of philosophers' arguments for and against suicide. Regardless of whether I had made up my mind at that moment, I doubt that the arguments that might sway me—and I do think I would still be bending to and fro in the winds of reason, however basic my reasons might be—would come from the history of philosophy. At that moment, my needs and my fears are likely quite primitive and direct—pain fighting against love, fear fighting against obligation—and I might not care if what I was doing was fundamentally irrational or even shameful. In fact, at that moment, the irrationality and shamefulness of my desire for suicide might even increase its appeal to me: *All the more reason to end my life if I am the kind of contemptible person who wants to kill himself!* So this desperate and paradoxical line of thinking goes.

But my discussion of philosophical thinking about suicide isn't really targeted at that guy in that moment. It aims at a slightly different person: the less frantic, more everyday me. That guy still thinks about suicide all the time—or at least, he has spent much of his life thinking about suicide frequently in the course of the average day, both rationally and irrationally. Sometimes I'm in such a state of despair or panic that reasons simply won't get through to me. But at other times, when I'm less frantic, I can be persuaded by sound thinking and argument. That guy, the guy who isn't freaking out, can think things through. And I want to raise a question in that guy's mind: Is suicide a good idea? Because for years—no, for decades—he has thought, somewhere very deep down, that committing suicide was probably a desirable thing to do. And that's the idea I'd like to change, because I think it can be changed.

To be clear, I wouldn't say I've changed my mind, even after writing this book. But I may have begun the process of changing my mind. In place of a long-held conviction that I would be better off dead, I am now able to question whether by actually living, I might do good that I couldn't do by dying. And also to consider whether I might cause more harm by killing myself than I could by staying alive. In fact, couldn't I solve many of my problems by living, whereas dying would do nothing but worsen them? And most fundamentally, isn't it possible that tomorrow might in fact be better than today? Like my recovery from alcohol addiction, this is an ongoing daily process. But it's a process that has at long last begun.

The great writer on depression Andrew Solomon puts the hope this way: "the more fully one comes to terms with the idea of rational suicide, the safer one will be from irrational suicide." Which is to say, once you understand that the choice to take one's own life should be based on reason and not on impulse, then you have a chance to think your way to the other side of that impulse. And perhaps those reasons will help dissuade the suicidal impulse from arising to begin with. It's an optimistic notion, but I believe there is truth to it.

Look, he thinks about lots of things, this wayward miscreant named Clancy, and as with everyone else, some of his thoughts are reprehensible. Ideas run through his mind that are nasty, contemptible, violent, even evil. But when he thinks those things—that is, when *I* think those things—he almost always dismisses them. He's not going to steal or run away from his responsibilities or act out whatever dark thought pops up—and many are darker than those—because, well, training, habit, education, and argument kick in. Beliefs about right and wrong kick in, and those beliefs determine or at least strongly influence further thought and action.

To some ears, this will sound obvious. But to me it came as a revelation. The discovery was in part a consequence of my slow, stumbling recovery from alcoholism. Like many other drunks, I have had the persistent thought that taking a drink is actually a good and pleasant idea, a happy idea. Even at this moment, if I consider, for example, sitting outside some café in New York or Rome with my wife on a cool afternoon, the coronavirus gone, a breeze blowing and the sun on our skin, people walking by, the smell of exhaust and coffee, I think, *Well, a glass of light red wine sounds very nice.*

But, do I? For years and years, I did think so. This was the thought to which I always returned to remind myself that I was an alcoholic. I even thought, *Well, maybe not now, but when I turn sixty (or seventy, or whenever), then I will be able to do that.* Lately, I have to confess, even a bit sheepishly, somewhat awkwardly—almost as though I've lost something good—that no, it doesn't sound good. It might sound nice for my wife to have a glass, but I want a coffee and a sparkling water. The truth is I just don't particularly want the wine anymore. Not even the thought of it.

Now, let me add immediately that if I were alone in Paris and a spring day slyly winked at me, I'm far from sure I wouldn't go down to the café hoping that a half-*pichet* of Beaujolais might revive all those old feelings of youth and vigor that I (kind of) remember from past days in that city: I very well might. But for the past few years, all the very good arguments against me drinking seem to have slowly done their work, or much of their work. My beliefs have been changing. Not entirely, maybe, but in a profound and liberating way. The conviction that I ought to drink or that I am owed a drink or that drinking could benefit me, at least sometimes, is gone.

I don't want to jinx myself, but I'm beginning to feel the same way about suicide. At least sometimes.

And still, if I imagine that death is complete escape from the troubles of the day in the way that sleep can sometimes be, for example, I can sigh and relax my shoulders and think, *Haven't I earned that much?* As Socrates famously says about death in *The Apology*, when confronting his own death sentence:

> Now if you suppose that there is no consciousness, but a sleep like the sleep of him who is undisturbed even by dreams, death will be an unspeakable gain. For if a person were to select the night in which his sleep was undisturbed even by dreams, and were to compare with this the other days and nights of his life, and then were to tell us how many days and nights he had passed in the course of his life better and more pleasantly than this one, I think that any man, I will not say a private man, but even the great king will not find many such days or nights, when compared with the others. Now if death be of such a nature, I say that to die is gain; for eternity is then only a single night.

But as Socrates also points out, we don't know what happens when we die, and so we have to consider whether living or dying is the right thing to do, and how we live or die, and if we are no longer to live but to die, then when.

Another layer to this is the difference between *wanting to kill myself* and *wanting to want to kill myself*. Philosophers sometimes call this the difference between first-order and second-order desires. A second-order desire is the feeling one has about a first-order desire. So the desire to eat a hamburger is a first-order desire, and the feeling that eating and wanting to eat hamburgers is a fine thing is a second-order desire. But lately, as you've been learning about the impact that the human consumption of beef has on the environment, and have seen a documentary or read an article about the terrible suffering of the lives of most domesticated cattle, you are losing your second-order desire to want to eat hamburgers—on the contrary, you don't want to eat them—even though you still have the first-order desire to walk over to Five Guys for a burger and fries.

For a long time, I had both the first-order and the second-order desire to commit suicide. If I replayed in my head the Beatles' song "Yer Blues" ("Yes I'm lonely / wanna die"), or the Pink

Floyd song "Goodbye, Cruel World," or daydreamed about the suicides of my heroes Akutagawa, Mishima, Virginia Woolf, Nick Drake, and Sarah Kofman, I tended to think, *Yes, exactly, damn right, it's a good idea to want to get the hell out of this place.* That is, I thought the second-order desire of wanting to want to kill myself was appropriate.

But lately I've come to see that this view is, at least in my own case, mistaken. It's not that my first-order desire to take my life has vanished, any more than your desire to eat a hamburger vanishes once you've decided it's an inappropriate thing to do. But your mental relationship with eating hamburgers has changed. You may well be on the road to being a non-hamburger-eater. And with luck I may be on the road to being a person who doesn't want to kill himself because the philosophical and sometimes unphilosophical arguments on suicide I've learned about have helped me change my daily thinking.

Philosophers spend a lot of time contemplating suicide. The twentieth-century German existentialist Paul-Louis Landsberg, whose book *The Experience of Death and the Moral Problem of Suicide* is one of the best on our subject, correctly observed that "the problem of free choice of death is one of the fundamental problems of all the great moral philosophies." If you are a famous moral philosopher, chances are you have written at some length about why you ought or ought not (be permitted to) kill yourself. Moreover, philosophers like me might worry that only spiritual guides and their contemporary equivalents in trained mental health professionals should approach subjects like suicide, but to our comfort, more than one psychotherapist has observed that, as James Hillman puts it, "neither theology, nor medical science, but a third field, philosophy, comes nearest to formulating the analyst's experiences of death."

In the Western philosophical tradition, the question of whether to kill ourselves arises early. In Plato's dialogue *Phaedo*, which depicts the death by suicide of Socrates, Cebes asks Socrates, who will drink hemlock later that very day: "Why do you say . . . that a man ought not to take his own life, but that the philosopher will be ready to follow the dying?" Which seems a very strange double standard: for the majority of us, suicide is impermissible, but for the philosopher, for someone who is in the know about the meaning of life, it's okay.

For Plato, the question of whether a person may commit suicide has to do with their intention. If the intention is to flee the problems of life or to end irrational suffering—that is, to escape—then suicide is forbidden. But if the intention, as in the case of Socrates, is sound and reasonable—to obey the laws of Athens—then suicide is justified. Does the person considering suicide have a good reason, one that would make sense to the just and sane among us? That is the relevant question for settling whether a suicidal person's intention is defensible.

As I've explored the deaths of famous and relatively well-known philosophers in the modern era, I've found fewer than thirty who died from suicide, and about half of those were suicides prompted by extreme physical illness. Even David Hume, who wrote so brilliantly and sympathetically in defense of a person's moral right to kill herself, when confronted with the suicide of a friend, acted quickly to save him and refused to assist in his death.

The first philosopher we know of who both wrote about suicide and killed himself (we don't actually know whether our melancholy Egyptian author friend went through with his intention) is the Chinese ambassador and poet Qu Yuan (340–278 BC). According to tradition, Qu Yuan wrote his suicide note, a short poem called "Embracing Sand," picked up a large rock, and holding it as a weight, drowned himself in the Miluo River, which runs through today's Hunan Province.

Qu Yuan's reasons for killing himself are reminiscent of our Egyptian author's: he's lonely; he feels unappreciated; the people around him are immoral or fail to understand him; generally speaking, the world is unpleasant and perhaps evil; and eventually he's going to die anyway. He is desperately unhappy and doesn't expect his unhappiness to change. And like our Egyptian author, he sees his unhappiness not as his own failing but as largely a failing of the people around him. Although Qu Yuan was sixty-two years old when he died, to me it reads like a young man's complaint: *I try so hard to be a good person, but how can I suc-ceed or be recognized for my goodness when I am surrounded by such low and vulgar fellows?*

> *Great was the weight I carried, heavy the burdens I bore;*
> *But I sank and stuck fast in the mire and could not get across.*
> *A jewel I wore in my bosom, a gem I clasped in my hand;*
> *But, helpless, I knew no way whereby I could make them seen.*

His feeling of helplessness is relevant. Though he doesn't blame himself for his situation—on the contrary, he sees himself as burdened by the value of his gifts—he admits that he's stuck, powerless. Although some claim that Qu Yuan committed ritual suicide as a form of protest against the corruption of his age, the poem makes it obvious that his was a perfectly ordinary case of killing oneself in despair. And in this way, like our Egyptian author before him and like Robin Williams after him, he feels approachable and familiar. His last poem is a cry for help that goes unanswered.

By far the most famous suicide among philosophers is a quite different and perhaps less sympathetic character, the Roman stoic Seneca. No one else in the history of philosophy has writ-ten so thoroughly and so compellingly in defense of suicide and then died by his own hand, and Seneca did his writing years before he had any reason to suppose he would eventually take his own life. His story is a bit unusual, because while he insisted on the importance of the freedom to take one's own life, in the end he committed suicide under compulsion. He also commit-ted suicide not out of misery—the motive with which I am most concerned—but out of political necessity and, one likes to think, respect for his own philosophical principles.

Seneca was trained in philosophy, and his early career was in politics and law. He was fundamentally a moral philosopher who argued for the virtues of a simple, modest, and balanced life, which emphasized the freedom of the mind from the constraints of ordinary worldly pleasure and pain. His political and philo-sophical views made him unpopular with the emperor Caligula, who considered having him executed, and after Caligula was assassinated, his unpopularity continued. The next emperor, Claudius, banished him to Corsica in 41.

In Corsica, Seneca continued his study of philosophy and wrote two essays collectively referred to as the Consolations. After eight years he returned to Rome, had a very successful political career, and became the tutor of the future emperor Nero. When Claudius was murdered and Nero became emperor, Seneca was catapulted to the very peak of Roman society. He wrote Nero's first speech and has been described as his "fixer." He became enormously wealthy, perhaps as a consequence of the crimes and the favor of his former student; and he was involved in a variety of unattractive intrigues that were part and parcel of Roman politics, including Nero's murder of his mother, Julia Agrippina. Seneca ghost-wrote Nero's letter to the Senate falsely claiming that Agrippina had committed suicide when her plot to kill her son was revealed. The five best and most successful years of Nero's rule were the years Seneca had influence over him. After Seneca retired as one of Nero's chief counselors, the "nine terrible years" began.

By the year 62, Seneca had fallen out of favor with Nero and was likely also unhappy with aristocratic life. He withdrew from politics to his palatial home outside Rome, to write plays and philosophical essays. In 65 he was accused of being involved in a plot to murder Nero. Nero's praetorian guard surrounded his house, and he was briefly interrogated. Seneca denied the charges against him, but he was nevertheless ordered to kill himself. This was considered the desirable alternative to being executed by the soldiers surrounding his home. This notion, that a criminal who occupies a position of social privilege should be given "time to put one's affairs in order" (and "do the right thing" by taking his own life), continued for centuries afterward.

It's a strange and interesting hypocrisy, this idea that killing oneself is more honorable than being executed. Here suicide looks like it's praised as a form of courage, but that's also a bit strange, because it's a suicide that one is brave enough to do only because the alternative is death at someone else's hand. But one finds this view in many different cultures and throughout history: that permitting a doomed person to take their own life, when the alternative is certain death, provides them with a respectable exit.

Seneca wrote extensively about the question of what constituted an honorable suicide.

As soon as there are many events in his life that give him trouble and disturb his peace of mind, he sets himself free. And this privilege is his, not only when the crisis is upon him, but as soon as Fortune seems to be playing him false; then he looks about carefully and sees whether he ought, or ought not, to end his life on that account. He holds that it makes no difference to him whether his taking-off be natural or self-inflicted, whether it comes later or earlier. He does not regard it with fear, as if it were a great loss; for no man can lose very much when but a driblet remains. It is not a question of dying earlier or later, but of dying well or ill. And dying well means escape from the danger of living ill.

Seneca, like so many before and after him, found out that in most cases suicide is actually a lot harder than one thinks. First he cut the arteries in his wrists and punctured his ankles, but the blood kept clotting. He swallowed the hemlock that he had saved aside just in case he should ever need to kill himself (a not uncommon practice for Roman nobility), but though it caused him cramping, nausea, and dizziness, it failed to kill him. Finally, Seneca was taken by his slaves to a hot bath, where, as Tacitus wrote, "the vapor soon overpowered him, and he was committed to the flames." It seems unlikely that "vapor" killed Seneca, and we'll probably never know what finally did him in. He was likely smothered by his servants at his request.

Such tenacity in a suicide attempt might be remarkable if Seneca had not understood very well that a failure to kill himself might result in a much more unpleasant demise at the hands of Nero. For this reason, some thinkers on suicide judge Seneca's death as less dignified than suicide by one who was not compelled. In this way of thinking, Seneca's suicide would have been more dignified if he had done it, say, to protest the immorality of

Nero's rule, or because he felt certain that he could no longer be of any benefit to the people of Rome—that is, to quote his own words, out of fear of "the danger of living ill."

If we have a modern Seneca, it is Jean Améry, who we met in Chapter 2. Like the poet Paul Celan and the writer Primo Levi, Améry survived the Holocaust and imprisonment in Nazi concentration camps, yet died by suicide. (He overdosed on sleeping pills.) He attempted suicide in 1974 but survived. Two years later—and two years before his ultimate death—he broadcast a series of lectures that became a book: *On Suicide: A Discourse on Voluntary Death.*

Améry's book has had a significant influence on this one and took a similar approach. Améry is less interested in the social conditions that might contribute to suicide than in the internal lives of suicidal people. He wrote in a letter that he wanted to consider the subject "from within . . . so that the author completely enters into the closed world of the suicide."

Améry did not examine philosophical arguments for or against suicide. He was interested in the phenomenology of the individual—the experience of the suicidal person—and in what he calls the moment before the leap, that instant when one decides either to go on living or to die. He recognized, as Emily Dickinson did in the poem in Chapter 3, that there is something fundamentally paradoxical about killing oneself. Death, he said, the fact of death, the inevitability of death, is the primal contradiction of life. "Suicides plunge into the abyss of an even deeper contradiction," he insisted, "by not only dying (or preparing to die), but *by de-selfing their self themselves.*"

For Améry, the leap into suicide is neither a sickness nor fundamentally even a reaction to suffering. He was intimately acquainted with extreme suffering, having been tortured by the Nazis. He wrote of that torture, a "slight pressure by the tool-wielding hand is enough to turn the other—along with his head, in which are perhaps stored Kant and Hegel, and all nine symphonies, and *The World as Will and Representation*—into a shrill squealing piglet at slaughter."

Suicide, Améry argues, is the only thing one can do when one is no longer capable of being oneself—by which he means, when the suffering of being oneself is simply unbearable. Any other kind of suffering, including being tortured at the hands of Nazis, one imagines will come to an end. But the suffering of being yourself doesn't end until you put an end to yourself.

Probably because he was writing after making a failed suicide attempt, Améry is powerful when detailing the moments leading up to an attempt. Over several pages, he charts the thinking of the person who has decided to die, noting that as the moment for the act gets closer, the problems of the past get further away: "These things do not establish any further resistance for the subject; it is no longer impelled to cope with them.—And how many minutes are left? But the dice are not yet cast. Maybe ten more minutes that one apportions to oneself. These minutes still let themselves stretch out into a deceptive eternity. Having already chosen to die, one is beset by the sweet enticement of life and its logic right up to the last second."

On Suicide concludes with the view that one should go on living, not because one is obligated to do so, but because "each human being essentially belongs to himself or herself," and while this gives us the right to take our own lives, it also gives us the opportunity to "take hold of myself, *myself*." In other words, taking my life is a way of establishing control over my own particular world—it's my world because I can discard it; but how much more so do I make my world my own by choosing to live? At that point life opens up again, because whatever we have before us is something we've been willing to grant to ourselves. In short, Améry concludes, freedom to live means something much more than freedom to die. Despite his meticulous analysis of the thinking of a suicidal person, *On Suicide* is fundamentally a life-affirming book, which makes its author's suicide two years later that much more troubling.

What Améry insists on perhaps more than any philosopher who wrote about suicide is the importance of freedom when thinking about taking one's own life. In this context, I want to discuss four suicide pacts by prominent intellectuals: those of Heinrich von Kleist and Henriette Vogel, Laura Marx and Paul Lafargue, Stefan and Lotte Zweig, and Arthur and Cynthia Koestler. These strange stories may collectively present a helpful cautionary tale about suicide pacts, which are by their nature coercive, even when the person being coerced is oneself.

When I wrote these pages in the autumn of 2020, we were in another Covid-19 surge, and the news broadcast stories of couples who feared that one or both of them were suffering from the coronavirus—or from trauma caused by the pandemic—made a suicide pact, and so killed themselves together. Suicide pacts and double suicides are, however, extremely uncommon. While no one assumes suicide pacts are a good idea, people get into them anyway, and the internet, unfortunately, facilitates making them and perhaps even increases their appeal to some. (Copycat suicides are on the rise, as are so-called "suicide clusters": when three or more suicides occur at around the same time and place to people who were likely influencing each other. A few hours from where I live, at Truman State University in Kirksville, Missouri, a cluster of five suicides occurred in the span of a few months.)

Suicide pacts between lovers are involved in many of the oldest accounts of suicide. When Seneca was committing suicide, his wife joined him—interestingly and perhaps a bit surprisingly, because his suicide was compelled, and hers was not—though he tried to dissuade her, and she was ultimately unsuccessful. The Japanese term *shinju* refers to "double suicide," usually but not always by lovers whose passion is somehow incompatible with the world they live in, much like the very unlucky, almost accidental double suicide in Shakespeare's *Romeo and Juliet*. The German idea of *Liebestod* ("love death," usually but not always involving suicide) reached its apotheosis in Wagner's opera *Tristan und Isolde*.

For my part, I have on more than one occasion made pacts with people *not* to commit suicide ("I promise I'll call you if I'm thinking about it seriously, and you promise you'll call me"). Just this morning I made one over email with a person who reached out to me about his desire to kill himself. But thankfully I've never made a promise with someone else that committed both of us to dying together. I've always had the good luck to be romantically involved with people who, as far as I can tell (and as they have generally told me), have strong aversions to the idea of killing themselves. That often kept me from being honest with them about my thoughts of self-destruction, but perhaps that wasn't always a bad thing. If I had told the wrong person that I wanted to kill myself, would I still be here to write about it? Certainly, one of my suicide attempts in the not-too-distant past, before I married Aime, was motivated in part by a disgusted lover telling me that I should stop threatening suicide and just kill myself if I was really so certain it was the right thing to do. She was not to blame me making the attempt. And her frustration, irritation, and anger were certainly understandable. But it isn't always a good idea to involve a lover in your desire to end your life—yet I firmly believe people feeling suicidal must reach out to someone, if they are capable of doing so.

To return to the suicide pacts of our philosophers: Heinrich von Kleist (1777–1811) was a well-known young writer and intellectual when he met the terminally ill Henriette Vogel (1780–1811). Their courtship was short, they arranged a love suicide, and both were apparently in good spirits when they went to the banks of Berlin's Kleiner Wannsee to die. Kleist shot Vogel through the heart, then placed the barrel of a second pistol in his mouth and pulled the trigger. The third pistol that he had brought in reserve was unnecessary.

Kleist probably sought out Vogel specifically as a suicide partner because her death was imminent and she was thus unlikely to change her mind, which would strengthen his own resolve. Akutagawa, in one of his own suicide notes, wrote that "Kleist . . . solicited his friends to help him," after suggesting that the way to get past one's fear of suicide was to find a springboard to help oneself commit the act, and that it was "typically a woman who fills the role." Although Kleist and Vogel exchanged love letters, certainly neither of them committed suicide because of their feelings: they seem to have made the pact to facilitate their deaths, and their romantic feelings were likely bound up with that idea. It certainly wasn't a case of either feeling unable to live without the other.

That said, Kleist's letters to Vogel suggest otherwise, seem designed to seduce her, and perhaps reveal a side of his character (and, for that matter, his art) we'd rather not learn about. Here is an example from one of his letters to Vogel in 1810:

> My golden child, my pearl, my precious stone, my
> crown, my queen and empress. You dear darling of
> my heart, my highest and most precious, my all and
> everything, my wife, the baptism of my children, my
> tragic play, my posthumous reputation. Ach! You are
> my second better self, my virtues, my merits, my hope,
> the forgiveness of my sins, my future sanctity, O little
> daughter of heaven, my child of God, my intercessor,
> my guardian angel, my cherubim and seraph, how I love
> you!

In her letters to Kleist, Vogel wrote of her gratitude for the "sublime death" he was providing, and Vogel's case may simply have been one of euthanasia, the reasonable desire for a good death. Kleist's motives are more mysterious, the subject of hundreds of pages of speculation by scholars, though shortly before his death, the thirty-four-year-old wrote to his sister that he was confronting death with "inexpressible serenity."

I've been a fan of Kleist's work for many years and have searched for clues in his writing as to why he killed himself, but without any real results except the fact that death and suicide are recurrent themes with him. At the time of his death, he had financial troubles and had not achieved the fame he'd hoped for—his enormous reputation is almost entirely posthumous—but he was respected by some of the best writers of his time, including Goethe. The night before they died, the staff at the inn where he stayed with Henriette reported that he was in high spirits. As best we can tell, Kleist suffered from what we would now call clinical depression, and perhaps had been for years.

Stefan Zweig—who committed suicide in a love pact with his

wife—rather unsympathetically described Kleist's *Selbstmord* this way: "He climbed into a post-chaise (which had been his only true home during the thirty-four years of his life) and drove to Potsdam, where, beside the Wannsee, he blew out his brains. He was buried by the roadside."

Zweig may have been projecting a bit: though Kleist was an almost constant traveler during his brief adulthood, Zweig admitted that a feeling of homelessness was one of the causes of his own death, writing in his suicide note that he was "exhausted by long years of homeless wandering." That said, Kleist did lead an itinerant life, tried various careers, and lived in many different locations, but he never really settled into anything or anywhere. That may have been both a symptom of his depression and an exacerbating factor. Certainly, other philosophers and writers who argue in defense of suicide frequently mention the feeling of not belonging anywhere.

The case of Paul Lafargue (1842–1911) and his wife Laura Marx (1845–1911, daughter of Karl Marx) is a bit more complicated. Paul and Laura, like Kleist and Vogel, made a suicide pact, but they were both in good health when they died by an injection of cyanide at the ages of sixty-nine and sixty-six respectively. They had been married for forty-three years when they killed themselves.

The reason Lafargue gave for his suicide was the desire for a good death. He wrote in his suicide note (Laura didn't leave one—but one wonders if they composed Lafargue's together):

Healthy in body and mind, I end my life before pitiless old age which has taken from me my pleasures and joys one after another; and which has been stripping me of my physical and mental powers, can paralyse my energy and break my will, making me a burden to myself and to others. For some years I had promised myself not to live beyond 70; and I fixed the exact year for my departure from life.

Although Lenin claimed that they committed suicide because they had "nothing left to give to the movement," Lafargue's nephew pointed out that they had in fact decided on the suicide a decade earlier, and that they proceeded exactly according to plan. Lafargue and Marx had enough money—some of it inherited from the estate of Frederick Engels—to last them until the date of their death, which they apportioned out year by year. When they died, they were penniless. Lafargue emphasized his promise not to live beyond seventy, but oddly, he was apparently comfortable that his wife was only sixty-six. To be fair, he had made that promise to himself, not to her, and she was free to set her own deadline.

When Laura Marx's famous father Karl Marx wrote about suicide, he generally attributed its motives to financial difficulty and other forms of inequity created by the injustices of property ownership. He certainly didn't seem to have in mind the kind of suicide that his daughter and her husband eventually chose (and indeed, he never wrote about those cases). That said, he may have had some influence on the plan: he certainly did not believe that suicide reflected a moral failing of the individual, arguing that when suicide was blameworthy at all, society must bear the blame.

To me, the Lafargue-Marx suicide pact is difficult to understand, and I suspect we don't have all the facts. But like Karl Marx, both were thoroughgoing philosophical materialists— they believed that nothing existed other than matter and motion, and that the meaning of human life consisted in finding happiness and avoiding pain, and helping other human beings to do the same. From this position, it may make sense to find an exit at the point where one has given to life and taken from life as much good as one can reasonably expect. Dean Charles Stanforth (played by Jim Broadbent) makes a wonderful remark in *Indiana Jones and the Kingdom of the Crystal Skull:* "We seem to have reached the age where life stops giving us things and starts taking them away." This kind of suicide was endorsed by many philosophers in antiquity: the free choice of death, rather than old age and sickness imposing the time and manner of death upon one.

One of the reasons this case puzzles me is that as far as we know, they were happy and in good health. Other than their impending financial difficulties (which were to a certain extent self-inflicted, given how they decided to mete out their money), they had every reason to expect more pleasant years to come. But then they may have felt they had taken all from life that it had to give and were frustrated by that fact. The psychotherapist James Hillman wrote that "in older people," suicide may be a response to "a life that no longer nourishes with experiences a still-hungering soul." Alternatively, he says, "there is the sense of having already died. . . . The soul has already left the world through which the body moves like painted cardboard." The suffering that motivates the suicide, in such a case, seems to be almost the absence of suffering. Tired of being shadows in a setting sun, they choose night.

Probably the most famous suicide pact among intellectuals in the past hundred years or so was that of Stefan Zweig (1881–1942) and Lotte Zweig (1908–42). (They are not generally thought of as "philosophers," though as with many of the figures I discuss here, the distinction between writer and philosopher seems a bit silly.) Although we don't know if this is true of Lotte, it's fair to say that Stefan Zweig was obsessed with suicide. On the eightieth anniversary of Zweig's death, the *New Yorker* editor Leo Carey considered the question of why he committed suicide. In a terrific essay, he wrote that "in his work, suicide is everywhere." A lot of Zweig's characters do kill themselves, but unfortunately he doesn't spend much time analyzing suicide. In fiction, suicide tends to be presented as a not unreasonable though obviously undesirable way of ending an otherwise unresolvable difficulty. If life gets too rough, quit. Zweig himself frequently talked about killing himself, asked his first wife Friderike to join him in a suicide pact, and seems to have struggled with depression throughout his life.

During World War II, Zweig moved from Europe to Brazil, where his isolation and depression seem to have increased. His suicide (by overdose of barbiturate) is perhaps not surprising, though again we don't know exactly what precipitated it. More mysterious is why Lotte joined him, as she was only thirty-four years old. In his suicide note, Zweig wrote, "I salute all my friends! May it be granted them yet to see the dawn after the long night! I, all too impatient, go on before."

Certainly 1942 was a dark year in the twentieth century: Hitler's Germany seemed ascendant, and many people despaired for the future. Reading the letters of Stefan and Lotte, Yiyun Li remarks that their lives grow more and more melancholy, and she comes to the conclusion that they lost all hope, both for themselves and for humanity, and "descended into the darkest depression."

The Zweigs had been married for about two and a half years when they died in Petropolis, a German-colonized mountain town about an hour's drive north of Rio. The case is disturbingly akin to that of Kleist: I can't help but think that both men were suicidally inclined all their lives, and the suicide pact was simply an extension, or even an instrument, of that desire. And both women, unlike their partners, were physically ill, which in Vogel's case seems to have been the main reason for her death.

The notice of the Koestlers' deaths, on the front page of the *New York Times* on Friday, March 4, 1983, opens this way:

ARTHUR KOESTLER AND WIFE SUICIDES IN LONDON

Arthur Koestler, an archetype of the activist Central European intellectual who drew on his Communist background for the antitotalitarian novel "Darkness at Noon," was found dead with his wife at their London home yesterday. . . . Mr. Koestler suffered from leukemia and Parkinson's disease but . . . his wife was not known to have had any grave ailment. The police said the deaths appeared to be from an overdose of barbiturate tablets.

Arthur Koestler was seventy-seven; his wife Cynthia was fifty-six. They had been married for eighteen years. Peter Osnos reported in *The Washington Post* about a week later:

IN THE late 1940s, Cynthia Jeffries was 22 and living in Paris when she answered a small newspaper advertisement for temporary secretary, placed by the celebrated author Arthur Koestler. . . .

Eventually they married. Last week Cynthia Koestler was found dead with her husband in their London apartment. Notes made it clear they had committed suicide. Koestler was 77, desperately ill with Parkinson's disease and leukemia. As a longtime advocate of euthanasia, his death had a kind of logic.

But Cynthia Koestler was 56, in good health, a woman who might still have had many full and productive years.

What kind of person was she? Why did she choose this final act?

As the *Post* mentions, the Koestlers were both members of EXIT, the Society for the Right to Die with Dignity. The organization still exists and is one of more than fifty such organizations around the world advocating euthanasia. Koestler even wrote the foreword to one of EXIT's pamphlets, offering practical advice on how best to kill oneself. Given his physical circumstances, his age, his advancing Parkinson's, and his terminal leukemia, his suicide seems relatively straightforward.

But Cynthia's case is hard to explain. Maybe she died for love: her grief at her husband's imminent death was perhaps overwhelming, and she preferred suicide to living without him. But all happily married couples must sooner or later face the prospect of one outliving the other. It makes me think of Gilbert O'Sullivan's song "Alone Again," (a song in which he threatens suicide) when he sings about the death of his father: "And at sixty-five years old / My mother, God rest her soul / Couldn't understand why the only man / She had ever loved had been taken." Nevertheless, though "with a heart so badly broken," she carries on.

About twenty years ago my stepfather Blair died of a rare and unusually aggressive form of leukemia. He was in his seventies and had seemed in excellent health, then one day complained of back pain. He went to the hospital, and during his assessment the staff discovered that he had leukemia and informed him that, without treatment, he would die in a matter of months. They told him that the treatment itself was very risky and could kill him, which it eventually did, within a couple of months of the diagnosis. (If this story sounds a bit like contemporary medicine gone terribly awry, it did to me, too.)

I visited Blair a few days before he died. Hospice had set him up with a hospital bed at home, and a hospice nurse was coming and going in those last few days. What he said to me then was one of the saddest things I've ever heard: "Clancy, I just wanted ten more years."

I wanted to say to him, *Dad, you'll be dead in less than a week. Ten more years?!* Being days from death, and still clinging to the idea that somehow he might hope for another decade—it just broke my heart. He seemed so unprepared for what was about to happen.

But I couldn't very well let him see what I was feeling. Instead, I affectionately squeezed his foot, which was hanging out of the blanket, and said, perhaps dumbly, "Get some rest, Dad."

"Rest?" he replied and frowned at me. "I'm about to get plenty of that."

The hardest part of his death came a couple of days after he died, in the parking lot of the funeral home where he would be cremated. My mom had been in shock ever since his passing, but as we walked toward my car, she suddenly howled and collapsed into my arms, crying as I had never imagined my mother could cry. My family discouraged crying, and I had seen my mother cry only once or twice in my life, and then just a tear or two. She is still recovering from the death of my stepfather today, and I imagine she will go to her own death grieving him.

But this is why the Koestlers' case is so disturbing. I can't imagine my terminally ill stepfather and my mother having a conversation that began with her saying, "Well, I don't know how I will be able to live without you," and my stepfather replying, "You don't have to. The hospice nurse has already told us how much medicine it would take to end my own life"—the nurse had done this in the usual elliptical way that hospice nurses commonly do around the country—"and we have more than enough for both of us. Let's do it together."

To suggest such a thing seems unnatural and unloving. Suppose my mother had argued for it. I'm quite sure my stepfather would have talked her out of it, or at least done his best to talk her out of it. To me, it seems like an act that one beloved persuades the other to drop, not to accept. And yet this is the case *I* am making, as a person who completely understands the fundamental appeal of just putting an end to it all—without facing something as terrible and agonizing as the loss of my partner.

We just don't know in the case of the Koestlers—or really in any of these four cases—whether one lover tried to talk the other out of it. (We do have documents showing Kleist and Vogel talking each other into it, with the enormously gifted Kleist at his most persuasive.) Perhaps in all these love suicides, the partners had a lot of give-and-take before they finally decided to stop arguing and actually do it. "Prove your love to me by dying!" "Prove your love to me by living!" Lovers must have made both demands countless times in the history of suicide.

In one of the great classic Japanese plays on suicide, Chikamatsu Monzaemon's *The Love Suicide at Amjima*, the two lovers Jihei and Koharu are struggling to kill themselves, weeping in each other's arms, and thinking of their families left behind. At the last moment Jihei suddenly grows dizzy and cannot slit Koharu's throat. She tells him, "Be quick. Stay not." And he does it, though it's a slow, painful, and bloody process. Then he hangs himself, saying "*Ichiren takusho*" or, loosely translated, "May we enjoy perpetual bliss together in paradise."

Right up until the moment that he has killed her, both of them are having doubts about whether they should die. But as each of them raises questions, the other offers answers; as each of them hesitates, the other one finds resolve. And then once one of them has died, in this case by decapitation, the murderer is clearly in no position to change his mind about his own suicide. Like Kleist standing over Vogel's body with the smoking pistol in his hand, it's now abundantly clear that he has to keep his promise.

Anyone who is tempted by suicide should examine suicide pacts, because they vividly exemplify the dialectic that a suicidal person engages in with herself, especially a repeat attempter. The person who tries to take her own life knows how difficult it is and tries, like Ulysses binding himself to the mast to resist the sirens (who would lure him to an undesired death), to find ways to bolster her will to self-destruction. She makes promises to herself; she perhaps writes one or more suicide notes; she buys rope or a gun; she sets a date; she does things that feel disastrously irreversible—like deliberately getting drunk, or calling someone to threaten suicide, or breaking ties with loved ones. She argues with herself about living or dying, and like a lover standing over the body of the woman he has killed, she does not want the option of losing the argument, of one part of her mind persuading the other. She wants exactly the opposite of the freedom that Jean Améry insists on for the right to kill oneself. Rather than to kill herself freely, she wants to eliminate the choice to do anything but.

The love pact illustrates what both the Stoics and Jean Améry fail sufficiently to acknowledge in their thinking about suicide: that at least for some cases, killing yourself is not an expression of freedom but the renunciation of it.

In considering Robin Williams and these philosophers who took their own lives, I've tended to argue—or even presuppose—that suicide is a bad idea. But to be fair, the oldest accounts we have of suicide seem to argue in its defense. In many African origin myths, we find the belief that the gods created death itself because human beings found life so difficult that they requested an end to it. Similarly, the ancient Egyptian "Dialogue of a Man with His Soul" seems to take it for granted that the individual has the right to take his own life, and the author seems to incline in suicide's favor.

Before the vilification of suicide during the Christian period in the West, it was often argued by Greek and Roman writers and philosophers that killing oneself could be a calm, sensible choice, a reasonable decision that one might deliberate over and then explain to others, so much so that society itself should provide the means for a person who wants to die to end her own life.

So, for example, the Roman traveler Valerius Maximus wrote of the Massilians (inhabitants of present-day Marseilles, France):

> A poison compounded of hemlock is under public guard in that community, which is given to one who has shown reasons to the Six Hundred, as their senate is called, why death is desirable for him. The enquiry is conducted with firmness tempered by benevolence, not suffering the subject to leave life rashly but providing swift means of death to one who rationally desires a way out. Thus, persons encountering an excess of bad fortune or good (for either might afford reason for ending life, the one lest it continue, the other lest it fail) find a finish to it in an approved departure.

Similarly, some contemporary thinkers on suicide, people on the front lines of the current struggle to reduce suicide today, believe that providing people with the option to kill themselves in a legally, socially sanctioned, and regulated way would not only be humane and morally justifiable but would actually reduce the frequency of suicide and the many harmful consequences that often result from the way we presently handle it.

Philosophical defenses of the right to kill oneself tend to take these forms: (1) arguments in defense of euthanasia when life has become unlivable and will be ending shortly even without the intervention of suicide, what we now often refer to as MAID or medical assistance in dying; (2) arguments that suicide should not be punished by the law, and (3) arguments claiming that the arguments opposing suicide fail.

As for (1), the arguments on medical assistance in dying: I strongly believe that the enlightened healthcare policy of any caring civilization must legally and transparently include thoughtfully regulated medical assistance in dying, but this issue is not where my concerns lie for this book. I teach a class every year that spends some time on medical assistance in dying, and I recommend to the interested reader the work of Margaret Battin, Robert Young, and Peter Singer.

Unfortunately in many cases, especially with the advances in life-prolonging medical technology, the life remaining to someone is nothing but unremitting and intensifying suffering that will soon end in death. In other cases, like my own, the person experiences no serious physical illness or physical suffering—at least not yet—and has every reasonable likelihood of a long life, so long as suicide doesn't intervene. I am here concerned with people like myself who try to or indeed do kill themselves when they have a reasonable, objective expectation that life still had plenty of good things to offer that person and that, barring suicide, he or she would expect to go on living for some time. I and many people to whom I have spoken can look back on a suicide attempt and sincerely say that we're glad we failed. We can say this while at the same time entertaining the thought that suicide in the future may still seem attractive, because we can recognize that our lives, after a failed suicide attempt, have provided us with irreplaceably good things—such as, in my own case, the birth of children who would never have come to be had I succeeded in killing myself—and yet still know that we might find ourselves again in such a place of depression and self-loathing that we once more see suicide as the only escape.

In an interesting middle ground of cases, the person may experience only mild or even no physical suffering, but their mental suffering is severe to unbearable, likely chronic, and while not expecting to die anytime soon—and indeed, that can be part of the problem, because maybe they could endure their suffering a while longer if they knew it would end in the not-too-distant future—they feel certain that the road ahead promises only worsening psychic pain.

So, for example, the last letter and suicide note that Virginia Woolf left her husband Leonard Woolf:

Monk's House, Rodmell, Sussex, Tuesday
[18? March 1941]

Dearest,

I feel certain that I am going mad again: I feel we can't go through another of those terrible times. And I shant recover this time. I begin to hear voices, and can't concentrate. So I am doing what seems the best thing to do. You have given me the greatest possible happiness. You have been in every way all that anyone could be. I don't think two people could have been happier till this terrible disease came. I can't fight it any longer, I know that I am spoiling your life, that without me you could work. And you will I know. You see I can't even write this properly. I can't read. What I want to say is that I owe all the happiness of my life to you. You have been entirely patient with me and incredibly good. I want to say that—everybody knows it. If anybody could have saved me it would have been you. Everything has gone from me but the certainty of your goodness. I can't go on spoiling your life any longer.

I don't think two people could have been happier than we have been.—V.

Woolf had tried to kill herself at least twice before, and she perhaps understood that if she failed this time, she would try again. In her suicide note, she acknowledged what we all should: that mental illness, her "terrible disease," could be just as bad as or indeed worse than physical suffering. We all know this intuitively: which of us doesn't fear the mental deterioration of old age at least as much as a life-ending physical disease? And if we had to choose between a death in great physical pain, while we are still lucid and able to commiserate with and be consoled by our loved ones, or a death in the terrifying loneliness of extreme mental illness, I suspect most of us would choose the physical disease. I certainly would.

But in at least some cases of mental illness, the question of the legitimacy of euthanasia gets rocky, because despite the enormous advances in psychiatry over the past hundred years or so, mental illness is still in many ways mysterious and occurs in a vast variety of forms and gradations. It's hard to know who is a legitimate judge of a person's mental state. In extreme cases, a psychiatrist may be able to say with confidence that a person's mental suffering will never end and will likely only intensify. But such cases are rare. The debate over what level of mental suffering is sufficient to justify euthanasia is particularly acute right now in Belgium and the Netherlands, the two countries in the world where euthanasia can be legally granted on psychiatric grounds.

It's easy to see why the psychiatric justification for suicide is so controversial. It's very hard to assess mental suffering with the confidence that we can assess physical suffering. And although we can predict death as a likely short-term outcome for all kinds of physical ailments, we can't presently do the same with mental struggles. People don't die from their psychiatric conditions—except by suicide or parasuicidal behaviors.

Furthermore, mental suffering creates panic and a desire to escape that manifests as a desire to kill oneself, even though we are nevertheless glad to be alive. When students come to me in great mental suffering and say they are thinking of killing themselves, I usually assume they lack perspective on their mental health and, once they have passed this crisis, will go on to lead lives for which they will mostly be grateful. And that they will look back on their experience and say, *Yes, I'm glad I didn't kill myself.* This is borne out statistically: nine out of ten people who attempt suicide do not die from a later suicide attempt, and many who contemplate suicide don't attempt it. So I might reasonably imagine that I have a privileged perspective on a student's mental health that justifies keeping her alive. The student herself is suffering too much at that moment to have the necessary long-term view. (And naturally, I will encourage her to seek help from a mental health professional and provide her with resources.)

This idea—that the mental pain and panic will pass—is behind the so-called "5150" or seventy-two-hour suicide hold in psychiatric institutions. (These three-day holds are also enforced in hospitals and jails.) It's an old idea, that if we just prevent the suicidal person from killing herself, the dire moment will pass. In Sophocles' *Ajax* (442 BC), Ajax's companions say that if they could delay him from killing himself for "just one day," his mood would likely pass and he would live. In order to do that, they would have to stay and watch him the entire day, which he won't let them do—and he kills himself by falling on his sword. The

Micmac tribe of Indigenous Americans similarly views suicidal people as in a temporary state of crisis, observing that they could "fall occasionally into a melancholy so black and so profound that they become immersed wholly in a cruel despair, and even make attempts upon their own lives." The suicidal person sings sad songs, and it was believed that if someone could stay with them until their singing stopped, to prevent them from actually killing themselves, they were likely to go on living.

But even if we grant that a sympathetic outside observer has a better perspective on the mental health of a suicidal person than the suicidal person does, what are we to make of cases like that of Virginia Woolf, who was afraid of her own mind, or David Foster Wallace, who often insisted that his depression was unbearable? Most of us don't want to turn these people into prisoners, preventing them from doing the one thing that could end their misery. And that is precisely what we tend to do: particularly the chronically suicidal find, as indeed I have in my own life, that to be honest with someone who cares about you is to be whisked off for yet another seventy-two-hour hold, worsening everything else in your life in the meantime.

I won't attempt to sort out all the nuances here, but I do want to insist that if we sometimes countenance medical assistance in dying for cases of great physical suffering, we should extend the same care to cases of great mental suffering. I agree entirely with Andrew Solomon that "it is up to each man to set limits on his own tortures." Yet even a person who survives the most terrible suffering, physical or mental, may later report that she is glad to be alive. Why we treat one person's desire to die as somehow less legitimate than another person's gratitude at being alive is a good question.

As for (2), the arguments that suicide shouldn't be punished by law: these very humane arguments are interesting and continue to be relevant (suicide is still illegal in many countries and is commonly prosecuted in Malaysia and Saudi Arabia), but I won't be directly addressing them. Until very recently, the United States and Europe treated suicide as a crime (and some states in the United States still consider it a crime, though they don't prosecute it) and punished in strange and upsetting ways. A person who made a failed attempt at suicide would be imprisoned or forced to undergo psychiatric treatment, often of some barbaric variety. If they succeeded in committing suicide, the treatment of their body would often be grisly, and debilitating financial punishment would be inflicted on the family left behind. Such measures were generally justified as deterrents, when in fact they likely forced many suicides to be conducted in secret, and many families to hide the real cause of their loved one's death.

For my part, I'm convinced that suicide shouldn't be illegal; I also have doubts about the legitimacy of police forcing themselves into your home because someone reported that you're threatening self-harm (a common practice in the United States and elsewhere). I even worry about the harm that may be done by the mandatory seventy-two-hour hold. The reason I'm not taking up these arguments is that I'm not directly advocating for social reform, even when it comes to banning firearms. (About half of all successful suicide attempts are committed with a handgun, and nearly two-thirds of the gun deaths in the United States are suicides.) Again, in these pages I am trying to talk to the person who has a handgun in her mouth and is asking herself whether to pull the trigger. She is not at that moment particularly interested in the question of whether suicide is or ought to be legal, or in the social and economic causes of suicide. She may however still be reached by arguments about whether she ought to pull the trigger.

Finally, (3), the arguments in defense of suicide that are really arguments against the indefensibility of suicide: philosophers notoriously are much better at showing the weakness of others' positions than at defending their own, and they find many telling flaws in the arguments against suicide (especially the religious ones). I don't think a single argument against suicide can withstand the attacks of David Hume and Arthur Schopenhauer, who both wrote exhaustive and devastating critiques of the anti-suicide position.

But the core of the philosophical arguments defending one's right to take one's own life is always simply that if anything is your own to do with as you please, that thing must be your life. And while it's hard to argue against that idea from the standard

Western individualistic concept of what it is to be human—it's a familiar notion, central to what we think of as human rights—it's also subject to the challenge raised by Aristotle and many later philosophers, which is that our lives depend on people around us. Our lives are fundamentally reciprocal sorts of things. We live from, for, and with each other, and none of us lives truly alone—especially not those of us who have parents or children who are living. So although our lives may well be our own, they are deeply interwoven with others, which might make us wonder whether those people, too, have a stake in us continuing to live. I don't think I could in good conscience tell my wife or my children, "You must go on living for my sake," but I can certainly imagine myself begging them to try. And I know that I feel I've made a mistake when I've tried to take my own life, forgetting that my continuing existence also belonged to them.

7

The Sickness unto Death

Observations from Édouard Levé,
David Foster Wallace, and Nelly Arcan

Three writers recently killed themselves in quick succession: Édouard Levé in 2007, David Foster Wallace in 2008, Nelly Arcan in 2009. Strikingly, both Levé and Arcan had written novels about suicide immediately before their deaths. Levé completed *Suicide*, which concludes with the suicide of its hero, gave it to his editor, and took his own life ten days later; Arcan finished *Exit*, about a failed suicide, then almost immediately hung herself. For his part, David Foster Wallace had been writing about suicide in stories and novels all his adult life, and he attempted suicide at least twice before his death by hanging.

Many other writers have written brilliantly about suicide and then killed themselves, including Sylvia Plath, Ernest Hemingway, and Yukio Mishima: why have I chosen to discuss these three? Part of it is that these writers died when I was an adult, at around my own age (I was born in 1967: Levé was born in 1965, Wallace in 1962, and Arcan in 1973), and when I was myself trying to become a writer, so their deaths impacted me differently than the suicides of writers from before my time. Part of it is that I love their work. But the real reason is that these three writers provide the most detailed and intimate accounts I have found of what it feels like to continue living while frequently or even constantly wanting to kill yourself. In short, these writers superbly capture the phenomenology of the suicidal mind.

They all have particular strengths on the subject. Levé shows us what it is like to no longer want to go on living, to feel that the whole thing, as Albert Camus worried, is more trouble than it's worth; Wallace details all the intimacies of both being determined to kill yourself and at the same time knowing that somehow you must not do it; and Arcan, while painstakingly portraying the nuances of suicidal thinking, is especially good on the psychological life of the failed suicide.

I would like to advise you to skip this chapter if you happen to be feeling suicidal yourself or have been feeling that way recently. As the early psychiatrist Jean-Étienne-Dominique Esquirol wrote, "the reading of works that extol suicide" is itself a likely cause of suicide or at least a catalyst for an attempt by someone who was already feeling so inclined. These writers do not recommend suicide, but as they are all tremendously gifted, they cannot help but give the subject a romantic allure, especially to an impressionable mind.

Let's begin with Levé's *Suicide*. The narrator is writing a memorial to a childhood friend who died by suicide at the age of twenty-five, referring to him only as "you."

In many ways, the nameless hero of *Suicide* seems familiar to me and will be familiar to other suicidal people. Perhaps most intimately, he doesn't expect to be happy but looks for ways to suffer less, and he makes his decisions using this criterion. Though he is often morose, to the people who know him he doesn't seem self-destructive; from the outside looking in, he has plenty to live for, and indeed he acts like a person who enjoys his life.

Levé's hero attends a party with old friends and for a change seems to be genuinely happy. When he leaves the party, his familiar melancholy returns, and we understand that the contrast between how he seemed to his friends and how he appears to himself when alone is part of the suicidal impulse. "Later, none of the guests at the party believed, when they heard what happened, that you were already thinking of suicide then."

The young Søren Kierkegaard remarked in his journals (in one of his very few direct references to suicide in his vast literature on despair), "I have just returned from a party of which I was the life and soul; wit poured from my lips, everyone laughed and admired me, but I went away, and the dash should be as long as the earth's orbit——————————————and wanted to shoot myself." Levé, similarly, is concerned not with an impulsive suicide but with someone who lives with the desire to kill himself, who seems to be merely biding his time or perhaps hardening his resolve, and expects that before long he will in fact take his own life.

Levé's narrator interestingly insists that "your suicide was not preceded by failed attempts." The sentence, which occurs early in the book, stands as its own paragraph, giving it a strange emphasis. One suspects that it matters to the narrator that once his suicidal friend decided to end his life, he was not irresolute, he accomplished it. It contains perhaps a whiff of moral condemnation of those who attempt suicide and fail, or who have to practice a few times before achieving their end.

It is reminiscent of the myth of the macho suicide, represented in American culture by Hemingway. "Real men" don't try and fail; they don't put on a performance of suicide by taking a bunch of pills; when the time is right they go get their shotgun, put both barrels in their mouth, and make a certain end of it. This myth may have done serious harm, as some suicidal American men seem to have accepted the notion of a manly way to kill oneself. As we have observed, suicide has a dramatic aspect; there is the theater of a suicide attempt, but also the drama that insists on a particularly sad understanding of oneself as a self-destructive hero who doesn't fear his own death. (The truth about Hemingway was much more complicated: in his stay at the Mayo Clinic in the last months of his life, he seemed to want to kill himself in all sorts of ways, including perhaps throwing himself into the spinning blades of a small airplane propellor. During his final days, he also often seemed to have every intention of living and was jovial and charming. He was no more or less resolute than any typical suicide, and in the end he probably just had the bad judgment, for a person struggling with depression, to keep a shotgun in the house.)

Macho or not, Levé's suicidal friend is not mysterious to the narrator: he simply wanted to escape his life: "You did not fear death. You stepped in its path, but without really desiring it: how can one desire something one doesn't know? You didn't deny life but affirmed your taste for the unknown, betting that if something existed on the other side, it would be better than here."

Outrageously disingenuous though this may sound when read superficially (He affirmed his taste for the unknown? He killed himself because it sounded like an adventure?), Levé's narrator seems to me to get something exactly right here. The hero did not choose death—as perhaps no one really does, because in some sense it really is impossible meaningfully to choose that about which you know nothing. He chose not-life, which is quite different. He was saying that "life sucks"—a common argument in the literature on suicide—and was willing to make a gamble. Whatever is there, if there is something there, it must be better than this—and if it is nothing, well, even nothing is better than this. The way the narrator puts it, it's as though this suicide is committed not out of hopelessness but out of hope.

About seven or eight months before the Covid-19 pandemic broke out, a screenwriter friend visited me from Los Angeles. He had read an essay of mine about suicide and was interested in why I am suicidal. We drove around Kansas City together, I showed him some of my old stomping grounds, and he was interested in the city generally. As we passed the Nelson-Atkins Museum of Art, heading toward the UMKC campus, he said, "Either you're really happy now, happy to be with Amie and your kids and a very long way from wanting to kill yourself, or you're the best actor I've ever met." I agreed that I was happy, although it's all very fragile, I explained, that Amie could leave me or something else could go wrong in my life, and suddenly I'd be back on the edge.

The point is that even being happy and still wanting to escape from one's life are not at all incompatible. That's not only because one might see one's happiness as an exception to the rule, a pleasant but surely brief surprise. It's also not only because a lot of us seem to have a deeper underlying unhappiness that persists even in cheerful, psychologically stable times. It's also because once you have the habit of thinking you are going to kill yourself, that habit doesn't go away.

Levé's narrator tells us that his friend was destined to kill himself. He felt this way his whole life, and then it came time to stop thinking about it and to do it. He seems to have become impatient with himself, like a person who keeps planning to quit smoking but always waiting another day before throwing away his cigarettes.

One regular correspondent writes to me whenever she really feels like killing herself—I don't know if she's tried during our now four-years-long email acquaintance—and she often says that suicide feels "inevitable" to her. When I push back, she agrees that it's not fated, but I know just what she's talking about: it's the feeling Levé describes, a quality of naturalness to killing oneself that living does not have, an ease of the thought that comes with the thought. Often taking a jog sounds more troublesome, more psychologically difficult or irritating, than killing myself does— despite the fact that I really love jogging (but have never formed the habit).

Levé's narrator doesn't have a clear answer to the question of why his friend wants to kill himself, and he discusses various theories. One is simply biological failure: "You were perhaps a weak link, an accidental evolutionary dead end, a temporary anomaly not destined to burgeon again." That reminds me of a line from the CIA agent who tortures detainees in the movie *Zero Dark Thirty*: "It's cool that you're strong and I respect it, I do," he tells his victim. "But in the end everybody breaks, bro. It's biology."

In an observation recalling our earlier observations about the drive for self-annihilation, the narrator tells his friend, "You directed at yourself a violence that you did not feel toward others." I've often asked my students, "Imagine what your life would be like if you had the same contempt for others that you have for yourself." This to help them to see that others do not have the contempt for them that they may suspect, and also to see, hopefully, that their self-contempt may be unjustified and perhaps even unnecessary. Certainly, we don't judge other people as harshly as we judge ourselves.

It's a motto of self-pity. But we understand feeling sorry for ourselves and wanting other people to feel sorry for us, too. And if we aren't murdering someone else when we kill ourselves, at least we are hurting them because they don't feel sorry enough for us, which might be part of our motivation. "Your mother cried for you when she learned of your death," Levé's narrator says. In this very lean novel, the hero's mother gets a full paragraph of crying over her dead son. She cries and cries and cries: and which one of us, thinking of suicide, hasn't shamefacedly dared to hope for that?

One of the consoling thoughts about dying—and at times, some of the motivation for suicide—is the hope that our mothers, at least, will be inconsolable. This is not just Levé's wish-fulfillment, it is one of the keys to the text. Levé is telling us something about the psychology of the suicidal person, showing us not the world as it is, despite our wishes—one of the ways we often describe the job of the novelist—but the world as it is as dreamed of in the fantasy of the suicidal person. This paragraph, coming very near the end of the novel, is a mockery of the suicide, but it is a melancholy, sympathetic mockery, and also a mockery of himself, the bittersweet self-irony at which the suicidal person excels.

As a six-year-old or even as a teenager, I might have earnestly considered killing myself so that my mother or a girlfriend cried at my funeral. But as a grownup, I can make fun of the fact that I wanted my mother to cry at my funeral and very much still want my mother to cry at my funeral. I can even want to kill myself just so that we can be assured of my mother crying at my funeral, which otherwise is not very likely to happen. "Years later," Levé's narrator says, "there are many, like her, whose tears flow whenever they think of you." Exaggerated, dramatic, and just the sentimental flourish that at least some suicidal people engage in when thinking about ending it all.

William Styron described his preparations for suicide when in terrible depression:

A phenomenon that a number of people have noted while in deep depression is the sense of being accompanied by a second self—a wraithlike observer who, not sharing the dementia of his double, is able to watch with dispassionate curiosity as his companion struggles against the oncoming disaster, or decides to embrace it. There is a theatrical quality about all this, and during the next several days, as I went about stolidly preparing for extinction, I couldn't shake off a sense of melodrama—a melodrama in which I, the victim-to-be of self-murder, was both the solitary actor and lone member of the audience. I had not as yet chosen the mode of my departure, but I knew that step would come next, and soon, as inescapable as nightfall.

Again, we shouldn't suppose that the melodrama is incompatible with the seriousness of the intent. I know this feeling very well. More than once, before or after a suicide attempt, I have looked at myself in the mirror and cried tears over the piteousness of my own situation.

The final paragraph of Levé's book strikes a different tone, in a powerful counterbalance to the teary, self-pitying paragraph that precedes it:

Regrets? You had some for causing the sadness of those who cried for you, for the love they felt for you, and which you had returned. You had some for the solitude in which you left your wife, and for the emptiness your loved ones would experience. But these regrets you felt merely in anticipation. They would disappear along with you: your survivors would be alone in carrying the pain of your death. The selfishness of your suicide displeased you. But, all things considered, the lull of death won out over life's painful commotion.

The honesty of Levé's narrator here—especially given that Levé killed himself not long after writing this sentence—is what stays with me. It's true that the suicide of his narrator's friend is selfish—as indeed many acts of suicide are. In some ways, suicide is the most selfish act one can perform—it is a way of taking something that belongs to many people and making it yours alone. It's burning down a house in which many people live, just because you don't want to live there anymore. There's no point trying to hide from or gloss over the selfishness of suicide.

Levé wants us to see the selfishness of the suicidal person. The novel ends with a long poem, which, we are told, was found in a desk drawer by the wife of the friend who killed himself, after his death. Every line of every stanza (there are 77 stanzas, three lines each) in that concluding poem ends with *me* or contains *my*. *This me me, my my, I I*, is both the suicide's refrain and one reason we are suspicious of the suicide, and perhaps angry with him after the fact. Angry at him if he tried and failed to kill himself, or angry at him if he tried and succeeded. But he might also make us suspicious of people who try to hide from their selfishness. We are right to rebuke the suicide, *You were unforgivably selfish*, which also means "You were so much more selfish than I am." After Mary Karr heard the news of her friend and former lover David Foster Wallace's successful suicide, she wrote, in a brilliant poem about the feelings of those the suicide leaves behind, "Every suicide's an asshole. There is a good reason I am not God, for I would cruelly smite the self-smitten."

But on whose behalf are we self-righteously indignant? And who is feeling sorry for whom now? And who's better off? The dead suicide, who was in too much pain to go on living, or the person left behind, who is in more pain now that their friend is gone?

Unlike Wallace and Arcan, who are full of shame about suicide, Levé suggests that the suicide may even be a hero:

> Your suicide makes the lives of those who outlive you more intense. Should they be threatened by boredom, or should the absurdity of their lives leap out at them from the curve of some cruel mirror, let them remember you, and the pain of existence will seem preferable to the disquietude of no longer being. . . . The joy of simple things appears to them by the light of your sad memory.

One would like to believe that this was possible. It doesn't seem likely, though. When we read the writing of people who've lost friends and other loved ones to suicide, they don't sound as though they feel this way—and speaking as someone who has had both friends and family kill themselves, it has not had that effect on me. More likely this is Levé showing a kind of self-deception that a suicidal person likes to entertain and may use to console himself.

Then again, you typically don't see this interesting idea elsewhere in the literature on suicide. Adrienne Rich, writing about her husband's suicide, described a feeling very much like the one Levé's narrator hopes to leave behind. As a survivor, her husband's death helped her to understand her own life, "which I live now / not as a leap / but a succession of brief, amazing movements." That seems to be something like what Levé's narrator hopes for.

And thinking of those I've loved who killed themselves, I do want to say to them, as Rich said to her dead husband: *Look at what you've missed. Look how you cheated yourself.* But if I believe that much to be true, then I should remember that even in despair, something about life is worth living.

Mostly we wish those people hadn't killed themselves, as in the case of our next phenomenologist of self-destruction, David Foster Wallace. A dear friend of mine was at a literary party in New York when the news swept through the room that Wallace had killed himself just hours before. There was shock, surprise, sadness, in some cases anguish—friends of Wallace's were at the gathering—and perhaps also envy and schadenfreude. "Then it was like an evil whisper went through the crowd," my friend told me. "No one said it, but everyone thought, *He did it for his reputation.* Now his greatness is immortalized, and he never has to write again, or worry about decline."

Now this evil whisper, if my friend was right, says more about the people at the function and perhaps in the literary world in general than it does about Wallace. It's a terrible, unfair thing to think and surely inaccurate: as best we can tell, Wallace was fighting with all his strength not to kill himself until just a few days before the end.

That said, at least one writer killed himself, in part, to secure a position in history. It was in fact a tradition in Japan's modern period. Ryūnosoke Akutagawa, in one of his suicide notes, described the taking of one's life as expressing the "voice of recognition"—for an artist acknowledging the artistic accomplishment and purity of another, and for posterity. This line of thinking is that artists who commit suicide do so, in part, to recognize and salute the artists of the past who killed themselves. By taking his own life, Akutagawa sees himself as signaling his respect for their achievement, their lives and their deaths.

Moreover, since artists are (at least in part) in the business of romanticizing things, a writer who spent so much time writing about it might well have given suicide luster in his own mind. Wallace's longtime friend and former partner Adrienne Miller, told me: "He never outgrew a belief in the myth of the tragic/romantic artist. Most artists, one hopes, evolve from this posture, but it seems that he never did. This had to be part of what killed him."

All his adult life, as best we can tell, Wallace wrestled with the thought of suicide. Some of the most profound and sympathetic observations we have about the mental life of a suicidal person are in his literature, and also some of the best defenses of the act. Perhaps the most famous is a passage from his novel *Infinite Jest*, comparing the suicidal person to someone trapped in a burning building:

> The so-called "psychotically depressed" person who tries to kill herself doesn't do so out of quote "hopelessness" or any abstract conviction that life's assets and debits do not square. And surely not because death seems suddenly appealing. The person in whom Its invisible agony reaches a certain unendurable level will kill herself the same way a trapped person will eventually jump from the window of a burning high-rise. Make no mistake about people who leap from burning windows. Their terror of falling from a great height is still just as great as it would be for you or me standing speculatively at the same window just checking out the view; i.e. the fear of falling remains a constant. The variable here is the other terror, the fire's flames: when the flames get close enough, fall-

ing to death becomes the slightly less terrible of two terrors. It's not desiring the fall; it's terror of the flames. And
yet nobody down on the sidewalk, looking up and yelling "Don't!" and "Hang on!" can understand the jump.
Not really. You'd have to have personally been trapped
and felt flames to really understand a terror way beyond
falling.

Here he is perhaps trying less to excuse the suicide than to
explain the suicidal person's action and perhaps to reply to those
who would accuse the suicide of monstrous selfishness. Yiyun Li
wrote: "People who have not experienced a suicidal urge miss
a crucial point. It is not that one wants to end one's life, but
that the only way to end the pain—that eternal fight against
one's melodrama so that it does not transgress—is to wipe out
the body." She goes on to say, complaining of Thomas Mann's
trivialization of Stefan Zweig's suicide as motivated by the fear
of a sex scandal, but also almost as if in reply to Karr: "I distrust judgments—Mann's, or anyone's—on suicide. They are
judgments on feelings." Sure, the person leaping from a burning
building is doing something selfish, Wallace or Li might tell us,
but it is a selfish thing any of us would do if our suffering were
similar. Even if we can't understand that selfishness, we ought to
be able to sympathize with it, to understand and forgive it.

The problem with the burning building metaphor is that the
person *dies* either way—it's just that one death is less painful than
the other. And it's true that we all die eventually, but the family
and friends of the suicide can reasonably reply, *You didn't have to
die yet. Couldn't you have endured the suffering for us?* One of the
more persuasive arguments made by philosophers against suicide is that the bravest act one can do is choose to live for the
sake of others. And perhaps your loved ones can even find a way
to help with your suffering. Because after all, you weren't always
suffering like that, and you have reason to believe that you may
not always have had to. But it's hard to get past the siren song
of the "the lull of death." When you're dead, yes, the ones left
behind will have things harder, maybe much, much worse than

they do now, and you will have caused that. But they are still in life's painful commotion, and you have exited it.

Wallace made his first suicide attempt about twenty-five years before his death, at his parents' house in Urbana, Illinois, where he grew up. He overdosed on a tranquilizer, then stayed in a psychiatric hospital and underwent a course of ECT treatments for depression. He made one more suicide attempt that we know of for certain—also an overdose—just a few months before hanging himself.

Thinking about suicide started early for Wallace. He was already writing about it as a teenager, and his first known attempt was in his early twenties. He wrestled with depression and the thought of suicide throughout his undergrad years at Amherst, and in 1989, as a graduate student in philosophy at Harvard, he felt close enough to killing himself that he checked himself into a psychiatric hospital.

"I got really worried I was going to kill myself," he reported later. So he walked across campus to Health Services and told a psychiatrist, "Look, there's this issue. I don't feel real safe."

"It was a big deal for me, because I was so embarrassed," Wallace said. "But it was the first time I ever treated myself like I was worth something."

It took real courage to do what Wallace did. The humiliation and shame, of having to tell someone for the first time that he was thinking of hurting himself, were real. It's particularly daunting given that he didn't know—again, particularly the first time—what might happen next, and whether he was going to have any control over the process. *They might lock me up, but for how long, and where?*

They checked him into McLean Hospital, in Belmont, Massachusetts, the same psychiatric hospital where the poet Anne Sexton stayed a year before killing herself in 1974; where the poet and attempted suicide Robert Lowell repeatedly stayed; and where the failed and then successful suicide Sylvia Plath stayed and wrote about so brilliantly in *The Bell Jar*. From there he immediately went to a halfway house, the Granada House in Allston, Massachusetts, which became the model for the Ennet

House Drug and Alcohol Recovery House in his masterpiece *Infinite Jest*.

"When that happens to you," Wallace went on, referring to his near brush with another attempt and subsequent time in the psychiatric hospital, "you get unprecedentedly willing to examine other alternatives for how to live." But whatever the benefits he got at McLean and Granada, they didn't last. A year later, at age twenty-eight, he wrote to his lifelong friend Jonathan Franzen that suicide was "a reasonable if not at this point a desirable option with respect to the whole wretched problem." At a certain point during his love affair with Mary Karr, he rather theatrically (and no doubt wryly) signed his letters "Young Werther," the most famous fictional suicide in Western literature.

In the short story "Planet Trillaphon as it Stands in Relation to a Bad Thing," one of his earliest published meditations on suicide, he wrote:

> You are the sickness yourself. . . . You realize all this . . . when you look at the black hole and it's wearing your face. That's when the Bad Thing just absolutely eats you up, or rather when you just eat yourself up. When you kill yourself. All this business about people committing suicide when they're "severely depressed"; We say, "Holy cow, we must do something to stop them from killing themselves!" That's wrong. Because all these people have, you see, by this time already killed themselves, where it really counts. . . . When they "commit suicide," they're just being orderly.

In a remarkably similar spirit, he wrote much later, in his fundamentally life-affirming 2005 commencement speech to the graduating class at Kenyon College, "It is not the least bit coincidental that adults who commit suicide with firearms almost always shoot themselves in the head. They shoot the terrible master. And the truth is that most of these suicides are actually dead long before they pull the trigger."

This aside strikes a startling note in the midst of a compelling meditation on compassion and gratitude. But it's not an off-note; it's a bit like a comment Akutagawa made to his children in one of his unpublished suicide notes, that life is like a battle. Wallace was not afraid to acknowledge to the graduates that sometimes life would be so hard that they would want to kill themselves, and he's also letting them see—the ones who are really paying attention—that even a wildly successful artist like himself, who has been invited to give them this speech full of wisdom to carry them forward, knows intimately about the desire to kill oneself. Nonetheless, he insists, by being willing to go on offering advice—and the speech is full of good advice, and should be recommended to anyone who has struggled with depression—life should be lived. *It's a battle to have a head like yours, but your existence is worth fighting for.*

Suicide, depression, and the fundamental attractiveness of death are constant themes throughout Wallace's literature. Titles from his first collection of stories include "Death Is Not the End," "The Depressed Person," "Signifying Nothing," "Tri-Stan: I Sold Sissee Nato to Ecko" (references to two famous love and death stories, Tristan and Isolde and Narcissus and Echo), "On his Deathbed . . . ," and "Suicide as a Sort of Present." In *Infinite Jest*, the hero Hal Incandenza's father commits suicide after making the short film from which the novel takes its name. His movie makes you lose all desire, which is an interesting challenge to the Buddhist idea that freedom from desire liberates us from mental suffering. The character of Kate Gompert in the novel is an extremely depressed marijuana addict—sounding very much like the author—who is also a study in suicidal thinking. The "burning building" passage that I mentioned above, defending and explaining the choice of suicide, is from *Infinite Jest*. The hero of his unfinished final novel, *The Pale King*, Fogle, contemplates suicide, overwhelmed by the boredom of his work at the IRS. Lane Dean, Jr., also in *Pale King*, frequently considers suicide.

But out of the many considerations of suicide in his large body of work, two short stories stand out, because they specifically study killing oneself and end with the act. "Suicide as a Sort of Present," which a good friend of Wallace's described to me as "in a way, the key to his whole literature," tells us about a mother who had a bad childhood—"had some very heavy psychic shit laid on her as a little girl"—and who, as a consequence, "loathed herself." In what we might now recognize as a very characteristic description of (at least one familiar type of) the suicidal mind, he goes on: "This mother-to-be knew perfectly well, from an early age, that this constant horrible pressure she felt was an internal pressure. It was not anyone else's fault. Thus, she loathed herself even more. . . . By the time she was grown up, it would be accurate to say that the mother-to-be was having a very hard interior time of it indeed."

The notion of having "a very hard interior time of it" expresses so well what it feels like to suffer mentally, and Wallace takes just a page and a half to get us there, to the crucial point for people who feel they can't go on living. Things outside the mind of this future mother may be more or less okay—they are not incidental, they matter to her—but the crucial point is that her interior world has constantly grown worse, and she has no one to blame but herself. It might help if she had someone else to hold responsible.

And then the mother-to-be becomes a mother. And here the story takes a psychologically improbable but interesting turn: she finds nothing but disappointment in her son. She does not initially loathe the child, she loves him, but she blames herself for anything he does that is misguided or blameworthy. "As he [the child] grew, the mother took all that was imperfect in him deep into herself and bore it all and thus absolved him, redeemed and renewed him, even as she added to her own inner fund of self-loathing."

Now, we do not doubt that the child—who seems to be the author of our story—truly believes that his mother feels this way. And such is the unfortunate situation of constant human misunderstanding and miscommunication that we cannot reproach the child for believing this, or the mother for the fact that her child believes this: our psychological lives are just that hard, and we have trouble understanding the way we are loved no matter how sincere that love may be. Indeed, for the child, who is suicidally inclined, the suspicion that his mother's love for him is in fact a kind of torture he is inflicting upon her becomes one of the sources of his own self-loathing. He sees that she is "at war" with herself because she wants to have loathing for him but cannot bear the thought of being the kind of person who would feel that way about her own child, which worsens her situation. And the contemptible things he does—telling lies, stealing, torturing a cat—are further sources of her self-condemnation, internal battle, and despair.

For his part, his mother becomes "his lone refuge in a world of impossible expectations and merciless judgment and unending psychic shit": precisely the same description of reality that he, earlier in the story, ascribes to her. It all amounts to an accusation of his mother: somehow she wound up making him just as unhappy, self-loathing, and neurotic as she is, somehow she revealed all this misery to him and caused him to feel as she does, and she did so in such a way that it was both his fault and something he was doing to her. Her child accuses her, blames her. And then, the ultimate paragraph, which explains the title:

> So it went, throughout his childhood and adolescence . . . the mother was almost entirely
>
> Filled, deep inside, with loathing: loathing for herself, for the delinquent and unhappy child, for a world of impossible expectations and merciless judgment. She could not, of course, express any of this. And so the son—desperate, as are all children, to repay the perfect love we may expect only of mothers—expressed it all for her.

One hopes that Wallace's mother never read this story (although, based on conversations with friends of his, I expect she did). Now the blaming of her is complete and final—the narrator of the story kills himself—and he does it to repay her perfect love.

Read superficially, the story is shockingly bilious and a bit frightening—could anyone be so bitterly angry at his mother and so self-deceived? But reading it a bit more carefully, we realize that the narrator's mother's psychology is more complicated than the narrator gives her credit for, that the narrator doesn't know what it is like to have children, and that all he can do is imagine that his mother has this enormous self-loathing, suspect himself of increasing it, and so allow himself to blame her for his misery and his suicide. Which is again one more way that she actually does, in his mind, love him—she takes on the guilt for the suicide, which he in the story never even finds the courage to acknowledge taking place.

What Wallace has masterfully done is reveal nothing or next to nothing of the psychology of the narrator's mother, but the devastating misery of his narrator's interior life, who believes that even his mother's love is a function of her own self-loathing and her loathing for him. The person he loves and needs most in the world becomes not just someone he wants to kill in killing himself—as a shallower, Freudian way of thinking about the suicidal mind would have it—but the most compelling reason for his suicide. (Never mind that he is living in a world of "unending psychic shit.") He gets to blame his mother for his situation and his suicide while also telling himself he is doing it out of pure love for her and thus completely excusing himself. And the self-contempt that comes with *that*, with being able to write all that down as a description of his own mental state while feeling suicidal, is the real expression of how deep his mental suffering must go, because what hatred and disgust he must feel for a narrator who feels this way—and yet we have every reason to suppose that he himself is this narrator. The "present" that the narrator is giving his mother is also the "present" that the author Wallace is living every day, or many days.

These downward spirals of self-loathing—"the dark and twisty road," as one person wrestling with the thought of suicide wrote to me—are the real characteristic of so much suicidal thinking. Now that I have children, I can see, sometimes, how grossly unnecessary my own self-accusation and self-laceration are, because I know my children must often suffer just as much (or, though I hope not, more) pain of self-loathing as I ever do, and I can also see how completely undeserved that self-loathing is, and how good (and perfect) they are in their beauty, their struggles, and their insecurities. But then, that must also apply to me, in which case why would I kill myself? Am I so vain that

I imagine I am the only person in the world vile enough to truly deserve to die by his own hand? But again, Wallace's genius is to be able to reveal how such an overweening person may sincerely think as he approaches taking his own life.

I have to try to remind myself, *I don't matter that much. I am not so special. Not even to my own mother.* And then I am relieved of the burden of being me. I can be an ordinary depressed person, who just has to survive, so that I can try to do a little bit to make things slightly better rather than, in killing myself, worse.

The problem of forgetting that one doesn't matter so very much—or being able even to conceive of the idea that one doesn't matter so very much—is the central psychological concern of the story "Good Old Neon." Like so much of Wallace's fiction, "Good Old Neon" is a complex story, and it's a lot longer than "Suicide as a Sort of Present," but we can make some headway on it. The narrator has the same name as the author. At the end of the story, Wallace tells us about the death process of "David Wallace," the hero of the story, which he describes in some detail, because, as he says, "The reality is that dying isn't bad, but it takes forever." In a teaser earlier in the story, he remarks, "I know this part is boring and probably boring you, but it gets a lot more interesting when I get to the part where I kill myself and discover what happens immediately after a person dies." Who is not going to keep reading, with that promise? It's weirdly reassuring, reading it now, to know that even though Wallace did kill himself in the end, at least he didn't pretend to himself that he knew what would happen after death. Obviously, for Wallace the human being, who wrote this story, the mystery of what happened after death was very much a live question.

The story begins with the paradox of wanting to stand out, to seem special, and maybe thereby even to be special—if only especially inauthentic, a uniquely fake person. "My whole life I've been a fraud. I'm not exaggerating. Pretty much all I've ever done all the time is try to create a certain impression of me in other people. Mostly to be liked or admired. It's a little more complicated than that, maybe." He is successful, but he can never feel that the success and recognition are deserved; nor can he take any real pleasure in them. Whenever he achieves any of his goals, "I wouldn't feel much of anything except maybe fear that I wouldn't be able to get it again."

This feeling leads him to what he calls the fraudulence paradox, which, along with suicide, is the theme of the story: "the more time and effort you put into trying to appear impressive or attractive to other people, the less impressive or attractive you felt inside—you were a fraud. And the more of a fraud you felt like, the harder you tried to convey an impressive or likable image of yourself so that other people wouldn't find out what a hollow, fraudulent person you really were."

About this passage, Adrienne Miller comments that the fraudulence paradox was

> one of the many gothic cul-de-sacs of thought he got himself entombed in. David would often say harrowing things to me like "I've never had one honest moment in my life." He'd say that all of his relationships had been fake and that he'd been "performing" in them. I'm sure it's very crude and too simplistic to put it this way, but since he seemed to have this idea he was a kind of con man (another of his favorite terms to describe himself), he believed himself to be unworthy of happiness. I know in my own experience with him, he certainly believed he was undeserving of a functional, emotionally healthy, loving relationship. I remember imploring him once to please try to accept any happiness that came his way, and he said, "Don't you understand? I *can't*." So of course we're not saying anything about David that he didn't understand about himself, or that he didn't think about ten thousand times more deeply than anyone else ever could have.

These days we often refer to this problem as the imposter syndrome, and in the popular and psychological literature on the subject, Wallace's name tends to come up as a prime case because he frequently remarked that he felt like a big phony. Yet we can all agree that he very much deserved his prizes, his fame, and his enormous literary reputation.

But as Miller points out, Wallace puts his particularly dark spin on the imposter syndrome, binding it to an inability to be happy, the emotional expression of a fundamental irreconcilability of himself with himself. "I'd been fraudulent even in my pursuit of ways to achieve genuine uncalculating integrity," he tells us, before giving us the long list of all the various self-help, religious, athletic, and other techniques he used to attempt to escape from his feeling of being a fake. His attempts were obviously paradoxical: one doesn't escape the feeling of not-being-oneself by attempting to change oneself into what-one-is-not. The challenge, as Nietzsche put it in a paradoxical formulation, is rather "How one becomes what one is."

Suppose you are impressed by people, especially other artists and writers, who have despaired and killed themselves because of it. How are you going to live up to their image? By committing suicide yourself. But at the same time you recognize that being impressed by those artists and writers who killed themselves is itself a form of posturing, a fraudulence and inauthenticity, because they killed themselves for reasons of their own—out of sincerely desperate circumstances—not merely in imitation of other artists who killed themselves.

How do you prove to yourself that you aren't a fraud or an imposter who is merely being impressed by other famous suicides of the past? Well, the only way to do that is to actually kill yourself—that is, to show you're not a poser who just thinks suicide is cool because cool people have done it. You're a "real" suicide person, someone who must kill himself. But then you will have killed yourself in an attempt to prove to yourself that you're not an imposter on the basis of the fear of being an imposter in wanting to kill yourself. This vertiginous, paradoxical logic naturally only adds to the misery and feelings of fraudulence of the person bound up in it.

I shouldn't exclude myself here. This entire book could be nothing more than my own posturing at seeming like someone who is trying to escape from his suicidality, or deeper, like someone who is sincerely suicidal despite his many failed attempts, or still worse, like someone who feels that suicide is eluding him and he is trying to find his way further into the possibility of it. And all these may contain layers upon layers of imposture and fraudulence, and I'll never know—though like Wallace's narrator in the story (and like Wallace himself?), there is one way out of the fraudulence: killing myself. But what if that final act is simply the greatest piece of fraudulence yet? And now I've died as a fraud to prove that I wasn't a fraud in the one thing about which I was most fraudulent.

(This may still seem a bit unclear. Let me walk you through the steps. Step one: I want to kill myself. Step two: But why? It might be because my heroes killed themselves. Step three: But that's a bullshit reason to kill yourself, just copying your heroes. Fine to copy them in other things, but pathetic to kill yourself for that reason. Step four: Also, I've failed at suicide, and now other people doubt the sincerity of my wanting to kill myself. They recognize that I'm just doing it because I want to be cool, like my heroes. Step five: But I still want to kill myself and to prove to other people that my desire to die is sincere. Step six: Try again to kill yourself. But step seven: Isn't this insincerity all the way down? Doesn't that leave me killing myself insincerely only to prove that I was sincere? Step eight: Stop waffling. That's the very proof of your insincerity. Just kill yourself and be done with it.)

Wallace's hero recognizes the corner he's painted himself into, commenting, in what may be one of the most devastatingly sad and yet still optimistic lines in the whole history of the literature on suicide, "So cry all you want. I won't tell anybody. But it wouldn't have made you a fraud to change your mind. It would be sad to do it because you think you somehow have to."

He knows this—or is willing to admit it—and yet he doesn't change his mind. The one thing Wallace's hero never tries, unfortunately, is just accepting the fact that he's a fake and admitting to himself that maybe other people are fakes too—some with lesser, some with greater success at fakery than his own—which would be a scary step in the direction of realizing that there was nothing fake or exceptional about his fakery, which would be a second scary step toward admitting that he wasn't really so special or unusual, he was just another human being wrestling with the very ordinary human pressure of trying and failing to live up to his own expectations and the expectations of others. What if he just gave up on those expectations? The narrator never considers it. He doesn't seem capable of it.

Now, Wallace the author is acutely aware of this failing of his narrator. In his commencement speech "This Is Water," he went out of his way to say that the problem of thinking you alone matter and forgetting that others matter at least as much or even more than you do is the central psychological difficulty of existence. In "Good Old Neon," the hero is trying to show us how being addicted to this thought, and the way it twists the course of one's thinking into endless self-referential misery, will lead (paradoxically—the whole story is deliberately full of paradoxes, and includes an explanation of a famous mathematical paradox) to self-destruction. Because Wallace did in fact kill himself six years after publishing this story, we might think that he hadn't been able to see his way out of this problem of self-aggrandizement. But that's not at all the case. He understood very well what his problem was—or what one aspect of his problem was, the aspect he was particularly concerned with in this story—but that didn't mean he could solve the problem. A successful cure doesn't necessarily follow from an accurate diagnosis.

In fact, in the text he offers a solution to his own problem, when the psychiatrist suggests that he try to think of the world and himself in a less clichéd way. The clichés he suffers from, his psychiatrist insists, include the idea that he understands his life and his way of interacting with others in terms of "competitiveness instead of concert." Now, the narrator is not in a position to understand his psychiatrist's advice, having concluded that the man was incapable of helping him: "By this point in the analysis I'd pretty much decided he was an idiot." But this is at the heart of his problem: if he could understand he was required not to see himself as above or beneath others but merely to cooperate side by side with them, the whole necessity of persuading them to see

him in a particular way is abruptly less relevant. If you're collaborating with rather than rivaling against someone, you actually need them to see you as you are rather than trying to bluff
them.

And the psychiatrist's word *concert*: when we are performing
together in a concert, we are still performing—and maybe we
can never escape the performative aspect of being human, and
maybe it is silly or self-destructive to try—but we are performing
with each other, listening to each other, collaborating, working
with each other's strengths and weaknesses, depending on each
other, and acknowledging that what we are doing simply cannot
be done by us alone. This is the truth about our situation: none
of us can exist without the help of the many people around us,
which brings with it a corollary: just as you need others, those
others need you. Now we find ourselves in one of the classic
philosophical arguments against suicide, the argument that
ended Chapter 6, that our lives do not belong to us alone.

Even if our lives don't belong only to us, we like to say that
"everyone dies alone." But even this is false, isn't it? Because
most of us won't be physically alone, other people will be there
with us—with luck, people we love—and even if we are literally alone, all our thoughts of and feelings for the people we
have loved and missed and hurt and cared for will be central
to our dying experience. Our minds are inextricably interwoven
with and fundamentally dependent on the minds of the people
we have known. Even Wallace's self-absorbed narrator, whose
whole problem is his self-absorption, knows that the myth of
the lonely ego, the solitary *I*, is an error: in the moment of his
death by suicide, he acknowledges that he dies "fully aware that
the cliché that you can't ever truly know what's going on inside
someone else is hoary and insipid."

The divide between the inside and the outside of his narrator—as he says, "how impressive and authentically at ease in the
world the guy always seemed, like an actual living person instead
of the dithering, pathetically self-conscious outline or ghost of a
person David Wallace knew himself back then to be"—is familiar
to us by now. It is the feeling of a double-life that not only the suicidally inclined but all of us understand. Ryūnosoke Akutagawa

discusses it in his fiction about suicide. Leo Tolstoy takes it to be fundamental to the way Anna Karenina's psychology unravels before her suicide. Anthony Bourdain was fascinated by "double agents" and "knew all their stories," and it is one of the signature psychological struggles of our own Instagram age.

For Kierkegaard and many other analysts of the self, that feeling of doubling is the nature of the self: we are never what we are, we are always that which considers what we are, and in that consideration consists what we are—another paradoxical, vertiginous sort of operation. Kierkegaard says in one definition of the self, "The self is a relation which relates to its itself, or it is that in the relation that the relation relates itself to its own self; the self is not the relation but that the relation relates itself to its own self." Sort that one out, and you get the prize for smartest kid in the class.

The point is that the search for authenticity is perhaps a life-long pursuit, perhaps a fool's errand, but either way, it's nothing exceptional, even if (as Kierkegaard insisted) it does provoke feelings of terrible anxiety in us. Trying to escape the feeling, or supposing that the feeling is somehow wrong or an indicator of a problem, is what gets this narrator into so much trouble. Learning to live with that feeling is what may have saved him.

The story ends with a page-long sentence that recounts moments from the narrator's past, invoking the old idea that one's whole life flashes before one's eyes at the instant of our passing, trying to capture or "to somehow reconcile what this luminous guy had seemed like on the outside with whatever on the interior must have driven him to kill himself in such a dramatic and doubtless painful way." He is still clinging to this divide between what he seems to be and what he is: he hasn't recognized that the divide and his inability to accept it are both the worst of his problems and quite probably their source. And so the closing line of the story, the end of the long sentence of his life, concludes: "the realer, more sentimental part of him commanding that other part to be silent as if looking it levelly in the eye and saying, almost aloud, 'Not another word.'"

I asked Adrienne Miller how Wallace's suicide affected her. She wrote:

I hope I've become kinder, and maybe more lenient toward people—I now no longer believe that stoic good mental health is the default temperament for many people, and may not even be the default temperament for most people, for example. But I'm still so mad at him. There continues to be a lot of anger. It used to be rage, but the feeling has mellowed into anger. I've found that you hate the person who killed someone you love, but in the case of suicide, the murderer and the victim are the same person. So the love/hate/acceptance/rage circle keeps spinning.

In the case of suicide, the murderer and the victim are the same person. This doubling, this spinning, is what it is like to be a human. It's just that the suicidal person has taken it out further, has tried to end the doubling by enacting the doubling, so to speak.

About ten years before his death, Wallace corresponded with Don DeLillo about his struggles with writing *The Pale King*. He thought he knew what was missing to get his fiction moving forward again, he wrote: "I believe I want adult sanity, which seems to me the only unalloyed form of heroism available today." I like this idea that "adult sanity" is a pure form of heroism. Even really immature sanity might do in a pinch. Because as Miller points out, good mental health is not our default setting. It takes an effort to let myself be a bit saner, rather than always only insisting on the parts that make me feel crazy.

Which brings us to the very particular sort of adult sanity and insanity in the work of the Canadian writer Nelly Arcan and especially her fourth and final novel, *Exit*. Like all her work, *Exit* is heavily autobiographical, but here she imagines a horrible fictional premise, the situation most feared by every would-be suicide: a woman attempts to end her life—in this case, with the help of professional experts—yet the attempt fails so utterly that she is crippled. She is left in the care of her mother, whom she loves and despises. Remarking on her situation, the narrator

Antoinette notes that while she has "finally given myself a valid reason to die" she has, in the process, made the act of suicide "impossible."

The novel is set in an unspecified near future, in which the secretive, exclusive company Paradis, clef en main provides guaranteed suicide to persons whose intent to kill themselves is pure; pure, as in fundamental to who they are, something they can never escape. If the motive is impure in any way, they cannot facilitate the suicide. When, in one of the pre-execution interviews, an employee of Paradis asks Antoinette "Do you want to die?" she shouts, eager to demonstrate her sincerity, "Yes! Yes! Yes! I want to die!"

The lack of clear and identifiable reasons, I would find out later, was part of the prerequisites for being an ideal candidate in the eyes of M. Paradis: a desire to die that was pure, because it was an intrinsic part of your existence. Wanting to kill yourself for the simple reason that you're alive. But above all, being ashamed of not being able to kill yourself and being afraid. Because, in order to have the privilege of dying under the supervision of Paradis, clef en main, you had to be scared by the prospect of staying alive as well as by the fact that you lacked the courage to end your life.

This is the real problem in a nutshell: fear of staying alive and insufficient courage to end your life. It's between these two fears that the would-be suicide oscillates.

The idea of purity is crucial for Arcan's thinking about suicide: she wants to show that succeeding at suicide and living with the relentless desire to kill yourself are two very different things. In the back of her mind is the same frustration and anger that we discussed when talking about failed suicides and "cries for help": that other people suspect the suicidally inclined of an impurity, stain, or blemish in their desire for self-destruction, and that this proves that they didn't really want to die, or don't deserve to be allowed to die, or lack an authenticity about death that is required of the kind of suicide we respect or even endorse.

It is for this reason that Arcan is indispensable reading for failed suicides, and has the kind of adult sanity but also adult insanity I mentioned at the outset. She is so honest and unpretentious about the whole nasty business, and especially about the feelings of cowardice of the suicidal impulse. She never glamorizes suicide, just the opposite: she debases it and anyone who thinks of it, especially herself. Nonetheless she completely understands it and sympathizes with it.

Throughout Arcan's literature, her suicidally inclined heroes express ambivalence about their desire to die. She gets the phenomenology exactly right: she's not afraid to admit the truth that even as one is about to kill oneself, one still doubts, wonders if one is doing the right thing, half-hoping one might yet live, even while desperately needing the suicide to end it all.

Perhaps due to the ultimate impurity of Antoinette's wish to die, the execution fails, and she survives as a paraplegic. The failure itself is hilariously improbable. Arcan chooses the ultimate killing machine for her heroine: a green guillotine, the enormous blade of which will fall on her neck when she pushes a big red button. A guillotine seems like such a good way to kill oneself. The head is severed in an instant. There is no chance of survival, no danger of a bullet skittering through the interior of the skull and leaving you paralyzed or brain-damaged. The blow ought to be so savage and quick as to be next to painless. The neck's vulnerability makes it an attractive place to attack. But the machine fails to cut all the way through; and though her spine is almost severed, Antoinette lives, subsisting almost entirely on vodka and doomed to be cared for by the person she detests most, her own mother.

In the original French, the book is named for the company, *Paradis, Clef en Main*, literally *Paradise, Key in Hand*. The expression *clef en main* is normally translated as "turnkey," as in a "turnkey solution": *We will solve all your problems, your one-stop-shop for paradise*. It also means that one holds the key to paradise in one's hand, a reference to the Stoic argument that the door is always open.

But for Arcan, the door is not always open. "We are a lot stronger than we think," she writes. "Our veins are harder to open, our necks harder to break, than you might imagine." This is the voice of experience speaking. It was what Seneca discovered when he tried to walk through the door that is supposedly so easily entered. Anyone who attempted suicide will tell you the same. She continues: "The body has foreseen the likelihood that we might want to do away with it, to extinguish it. And it has armed itself against that very possibility."

Arcan settled the question for herself on September 24, 2009, when, almost exactly a year after the death of David Foster Wallace, she hung herself in her apartment in Montreal. We don't know if or how many times she had previously attempted suicide, though her work leads us to believe that she had tried before. Certainly, as with Wallace, her desire for suicide and her frustration with the difficulty of taking her own life is a theme throughout her literature. In her debut novel *Whore* (*Putain*) she wrote:

> I did not know that one day it would no longer be possible for me to change my ideas about life and about people. I did not believe that I could announce my death a hundred times without exhausting it, without making it impracticable like these magic tricks that we looked at too closely, I did not think I would continue to believe in it more and terrify myself of its assurance. No, at the beginning of being suicidal, I did not know how much I was telling the truth, how much death was happening hidden behind all my actions.

Here yet again she gets something exactly right about the ambiguity of wishing to kill oneself, confessing the wish to kill oneself, and making a half-hearted attempt to kill oneself. The desire to kill oneself, the expression, and the attempt may all be part, in a perverse way, of trying to escape from the desire to kill yourself—or also, whatever might be the sources of that desire. (The suicidal person may not even be taking herself quite seriously, which is important to Arcan's irony over and even disdain for the idea of a "pure" desire to die that she later discussed in *Exit*.)

Speaking for myself, especially at a certain stage of my life— say from puberty through my mid-twenties—suicide, despite my attempts, was still in some ways a game I was playing. I wanted to believe I could do it, but could I? I would try and fail, but would I try my hardest? I suspected I wouldn't do it successfully, wouldn't actually die and be gone forever, but might I? And while I was playing this game, performing this act for myself of the suicide who didn't really want to die, slowly, slowly, over the course of the decades to come, I became more and more sincerely suicidal. What I might have supposed I was expurgating, I was in fact creating. Behind all my actions, as Arcan wrote, I was inventing my own death.

And how much more might this be true for the writer who was constantly imagining and narrating her own possible suicides in her fiction. Cliché though it is, life does indeed have a tendency to imitate art. In *Folle*, Arcan wrote: "On the day of my fifteenth birthday, I made the decision to kill myself on the day of my thirtieth birthday." And then, a bit later in the book, addressing her rival for the lover who eludes them both (the novel is superficially about two women battling for the love of a man, but more deeply about the war between the two women and how they replay that struggle within themselves):

> As far as you are concerned, I will kill myself to prove you are right, to bow to your superiority, I will also kill myself to silence you and impose respect. No one can attack a dead woman because the dead take their breath away, in front of them, we walk on eggshells. On a wall in my apartment, I stuck a huge nail to hang myself. To hang myself, I will mix alcohol and sedatives and to make sure I don't fall asleep before hanging myself, I will get drunk standing on a chair, I will get drunk with a noose around my neck until I lose consciousness. When death comes, I don't want to be there.

In the end, this is how Arcan did kill herself. Her suicide came at an especially unhappy time in her life. Not long before, she had been interviewed on a television talk show by a male interviewer and an all-male panel, and they openly mocked her for what they took to be her overly sexual appearance, for her low-cut dress and her cleavage, for her past life as a sex worker—this when the subject of the interview was to be her literature. Her humiliation was worsened, as she later wrote, by the demeaning power of the male gaze and her (presumably consequent) obsession with plastic surgery. Even female friends of hers were nasty about the interview and her appearance. She didn't look "bookish"; she didn't look anything like Margaret Atwood or other great female Canadian writers; she was wearing a little black dress, she looked sexy. The unjust implication was that she couldn't play the part of the writer who had outgrown her past as a sex worker and still continue to use her appearance to advance her career by looking attractive on TV. Her shame from this incident, even though she was completely innocent and the only shameful things that took place had been done by others, stayed with her right up until her death, and it seems to have been one of the principal causes of the suicide attempt that killed her. (As a middle-aged white male, I have no idea what Arcan was in fact suffering or how profoundly this incident may have shaped her—I am merely repeating as best I can what she herself expressed about the incident.)

But any reader of her books could see the suicide coming. With both Arcan and Wallace, anyone who reads their work knowing how they died will think, over and over, *Well, it's no surprise that this writer committed suicide.* But unlike Wallace, Arcan shows few if any moments of hope. Her biggest worry about death seems to have been, as the narrator of *Exit* describes it, that perhaps "it wasn't the liberation that was promised."

Here again she is relentlessly honest in a way that few other writers about suicide are. She is willing to grant that, from her perspective, the promise of suicide seems too good to be true. In every culture, we encounter concern that suicide will guarantee a bad afterlife, and in literature, the most famous thinker to fret over it was good old Hamlet. But in the modern period, so many suicidal writers seem to take it for granted that suicide guarantees them escape such as Paradis, clef en main is selling. That's why Arcan makes suicide a service you can purchase from the shady Paradis who runs the operation. Both Arcan and her narrator know that you can't trust a salesman. They know that probably the whole thing is a scam, that she's in for a cheat, a nasty surprise, something worse than the failure of the guillo-tine. And yet Arcan herself was willing to take the risk. She wrote this great novel, which is both an apology for and an indictment of suicide, gave it to her agent, and went home to her lonely Montreal apartment and hung herself with a rope.

So why do I suggest Arcan's writing has a particular adult san-ity, even the kind that Wallace aspired to? For me, her desire for death and her fear of life were authentic, and with a little good luck (rather than the bad luck she had, with that horrible inter-view), they might have saved her. She reads like Yiyun Li, that is, like someone who, in the hard work of thinking and writing about suicide, has overcome any glamorization or self-deception about killing herself. I suppose I cling to this as a form of sanity because it is the same hope I have for myself: that the effort to be as truthful as I can about how I am feeling will keep me alive.

8

The Afterlife, or,
Welcome to the Psych Ward

Once in the faculty cafeteria at Ashoka University, I had a conversation over breakfast with my friend Rita Kothari—one of India's foremost translators of *dalit* (so-called "untouchable" class) literature. I was designing a new class called "How to Be Free and Happy," loosely modeled on Laurie Santos's wildly popular class on happiness at Yale, though with more philosophy mixed in among Santos's well-curated collection of essays in psychology.

"I'm so tired of the word *happiness*," Rita said. "Who expects to be happy? Is it really worth chasing after? I'd much rather hear about a class on unhappiness."

I laughed in agreement, and even though I still taught the course (and my students seemed to like it), I understood what she meant: chasing after happiness is not only a fool's errand but part of the problem. Even peace or rest might be too much to ask of life; come to think of it, I have only the slightest inkling of what a genuine state of peace might be, what true restfulness might look like.

Granted, I definitely know what unhappiness feels like—as we all do—and it's something I would rather avoid. At times unhappiness becomes so acute that it feels unbearable, and those times have unsurprisingly correlated with me at my most suicidal.

After that suicide attempt on New Year's Eve 2008, I was

sober, without a relapse, for two straight years. But 2009 and 2010 proved to be two of the most difficult years of my life, even though I was not drinking (or possibly because I wasn't). I was contending with a depression that was in some ways much worse than even my most desperate childhood depression, because it was compounded by a mixture of psychoactive agents that my doctors were using to try to fix me. I tried to kill myself more than once during that period, though they were the kinds of attempts that I knew I could keep secret if I chickened out or otherwise failed.

So six months into my first year of sobriety, in the summer of 2009, I tried to drown myself. I was on a month-long vacation in Puerto Vallarta with my wife Rebecca, my three daughters, and my mother-in-law. I had lost a fair bit of weight, because most foods disgusted me, and I was living largely on a diet of whole milk yogurt mixed with peanut butter. For some reason, those were the only foods that appealed to me then.

We had rented a house on a cliff above the ocean, in Viejo Vallarta, and at dinnertime I would often walk a half-mile or so to a good restaurant just off the beach to pick up a meal for my family. Sometimes I sat waiting at the bar. The bartender, knowing I didn't drink, always brought me a Diet Coke. I watched surfers come in for the gentle dusk break. I also watched the surfers in the morning, when I would make the same walk down the hill to a café to drink coffee while my family started their morning and I took a couple of hours to try to write. Sometimes I'd stop and sit on the seawall and admire the birds and the surfers.

One night I was especially down, in real psychological pain, and as I watched the sun setting I thought, *I can't continue to do this.* The solution was right there in front of me. I'd swim into the nighttime Pacific as far as I could, and just keep swimming until I drowned. It was a purely selfish thought. I was truly not much use to my family at this time: they tried to include me in things but eyed me nervously, knowing that their formerly happy dad had been replaced by this sad-faced, medicated, often disoriented person who didn't take much pleasure in anything. Nonetheless I understood that I was providing at least some help to my wife in an everyday way with the kids and that I was, at this time, her only source of income. (I had tried to increase my life insurance, but it was prohibitively expensive due to my recent stay in the psychiatric hospital. I have since increased it more than once.)

But the depression I was suffering was excruciatingly painful, and I was certain it would only get worse as the days progressed. And I had a dreadful conviction—an intensely familiar feeling I have fought most of my life—that an unknown personal disaster was imminent, one that would be humiliating, or inexcusable, or at any rate unexcused, and from which I would not recover and for which no one would forgive me. It would be something worse than suicide that only suicide could prevent, but once it happened, not even the act of killing myself could erase it.

That evening after bringing dinner back up to my family, I lied and said I needed more yogurt and peanut butter. Rebecca, knowing something was up, asked if I couldn't wait until morning to get it. I don't know if she was worried that I wasn't going to be back in time to help put the girls to bed, or if she thought I was going out to sneak a drink (I believe she knew how committed I was to not drinking, but she'd been burned before), or if she suspected the truth. Probably she could see I was lying about something but didn't know what it was or why.

It was a dark night. There were no arguments for or against suicide in my mind. I just knew what I wanted to do, and this time I was going to do it. I took the stone steps down to the beach and took off my clothes except for my boxers. I folded them and left them next to my shoes, high on the beach where they wouldn't be swept away, thinking that they would find my clothes. Rebecca would know the truth, but she would tell herself and the girls that I always loved to swim in the ocean at night, which was true, and that I just wasn't a strong swimmer, which was also true. I put my glasses on top of the pile. I am extremely nearsighted—which sounds like a joke, in this context, but I have been since elementary school—and naturally I couldn't use them in the water. *It will make it a bit easier,* I thought, *not being able to see how far out I've swum, and not being able to find my way back, if I try to.*

Like every other time I've tried to commit suicide, I didn't think of leaving a note. What could I say? *I love you. I'm sorry.* They already knew that.

I swam out into the calm night sea. I thought of sharks, as I always do when swimming in the ocean at night. Even on the several occasions when I've brushed against something beneath the black water far from land, and the electricity of real animal fear ran through my body, I've tended to think, *Well, at least there will be a resolution.* I only swim the side-stroke, so I can swim for a long time. I swam, miserably, not enjoying it. The water was cool but not cold. I swam until the beach was far behind me, and I didn't really know which direction I was swimming, only that I was heading away from the lights of Puerto Vallarta, which I could still see like distant fuzzy yellow orbs when I looked back. I swam until I was exhausted.

I knew I needed to swim as far as I could, that this was the only way I would succeed. I swam past the point of not being able to swim anymore. Then when I thought I couldn't take another stroke, when I was gasping a bit and my arms and my legs were aching and I was all out of energy, I tried to sink. I pushed myself under with my arms.

Beneath the water I panicked and came back up. Then I used that jackknife dive they teach you in snorkeling lessons when you bend at the waist until you're at a ninety-degree angle in the water, then you lift your legs directly above you and the weight of them drives you down and you swim into the dark. I swam as deep as I could, down into the ocean, until it was noticeably colder. I started to run out of air. And like every other time I've tried to asphyxiate myself, I panicked again, and scrambled like a terrified animal back to the surface, certain that I wouldn't make it and desperate to breathe. I felt no moment of life affirmation or relief or thought of what a terrible, unforgivable thing I was doing to my children and my wife. I stayed selfish, despairing and ashamed through the whole process. Defeated, hopeless, I swam back to the beach. By the time I got home, my family was asleep. I apologized to Rebecca in the morning, telling her, "I just needed a swim." She was angry but believed me.

But there's also something instructive about this story. The next day Zelly, who was fourteen, and I were swimming in the cove where, the night before, I had stacked my clothing and my glasses. The waves were up a bit, and it wasn't the best beach for swimming during the day, in front of the break, because of the undertow. But Zelly and I were having fun, just the two of us. Then a current took hold of her and started dragging her out.

"Dad!" she shouted. She was crying, panicking, scrambling in the water.

I managed to grab hold of her, and she clung to me, pulling herself up around my shoulders. We swam backward to shore. It took us ten terrifying minutes to reach the sand. Zelly was crying, but okay.

She never would have gone swimming in that rough water in the first place if she hadn't been with me. But I had just saved my child's life. I wasn't proud of myself, but I was immensely relieved. And I told myself, *You know, you have to be there. You never know when they might need you. You in particular. They don't know when they might need you.* I sometimes try to remind myself of that swim the day after I tried and failed to drown, and also sometimes my daughter reminds me of it. (She never knew what happened the night before, and she won't unless she reads this account.)

That was 2009, and as I've mentioned, things got really bad at the beginning of 2011, when I started an affair and returned to drinking. Depression, suicide, and complete confusion and disorientation became everyday things. Hilarity entered my life at this point, a feeling of wantonness and irresponsibility, a way of experiencing things that I felt not just day to day but even hour to hour or minute to minute. I oscillated between irrational exultation and equally irrational desperation. As a reader, you might notice how much my way of looking at the world has changed from how I thought in 2009 (described in Chapter 5) to the way I saw things once I was drinking again and wanted to kill myself every day, as I try to describe here.

And in the story that continues below—the one I started to tell you at the beginning of this book—I had just attempted and failed at suicide yet again and was back, once more, at Research Psychiatric Hospital. It was November 2011, and over the next few months I would go all the way down to the second ring of the seventh circle of hell, where suicides are trapped as trees being torn apart by harpies, before I would start my return to the sunlight.

The psychiatric hospital admission formalities were complete; staffers took me through some hallways and a couple of security doors and showed me to my room. It had two beds, a nightstand by each, two small dressers, a toilet, and a shower. It was like a cheap motel room, only cleaner, unadorned, and without the well-worn hominess that most motel rooms get. I took the bed by the door instead of the one near to the bathroom. In a shared room at a psychiatric hospital, the bed by the door is higher on the social pecking order than the by-the-bathroom bed.

The floor was gray vinyl tile, with two big squares of yellow and one of red in the middle of all the gray. I wondered about the tiler who had installed the floor. Did he miss his home, where maybe there was a tree with yellow and red fruit or flowers, or did he simply want to add a little color to the rooms of the people he knew would be staying here, people he knew would be scared and sad?

A nurse came in, checked my blood pressure and heartbeat, and took a blood sample. This is something they do all night long, for reasons that seem diabolical. Every two hours they wake you up, stick a thick needle into your arm, and take your blood.

"It's almost time for your meds and breakfast. You want to go on and wait with the rest of them."

There were more people in the main entrance area—men and women, younger than me and older. A round receptionist area separated our side from where they kept the dangerously crazy people. That was where they sent you if you really misbehaved. They had honest-to-God padded rooms, I was told, like in the movies, and many different kinds of restraints. Personal

Safety Rooms, they called them. Aldous Huxley couldn't have come up with a name so sinister. I had never been in a Personal Safety Room, and I knew that, if they put me in one, I would go crazy.

People were lining up at one of two portable medication stands—they looked like the tall rolling toolchests you see at Home Depot—and I sat on the floor and waited for the walk to breakfast next to a woman who was being released.

"You going to line up for your medications? That's the best part of the day," she said and smiled at me, a gentle, resigned smile the equivalent of a shoulder shrug.

"I don't think they have my prescriptions yet," I said.

She had red hair and a drawn face. She was too skinny. She didn't ask me why I was being admitted, and I didn't ask her why she was leaving. She told me she was a high school math and science teacher. She said her husband hadn't divorced her yet, but he had moved out and wouldn't let her see the kids.

"Mine hasn't divorced me yet either," I said, "but we've been separated awhile. Sometimes she lets me see the kids, and sometimes she doesn't."

"That's how they do you," she said.

"I guess technically she's my wife, not my ex-wife. But she'll be my ex-wife soon enough. I'm sorry to say. Sorry, I'm talking too much. I'm nervous."

I have always been unspeakably miserable inside psychiatric hospitals. I hate and fear them because of how the staff and psychiatrists control, manipulate, and demean you, and because no good, transparent criteria govern their decisions about whether to keep you in or let you out. But one nice thing about a psychiatric hospital is the other patients. To them, you can mostly truthfully say how you're feeling—and this is hard in ordinary life (though it does occur in AA meetings). You can never truthfully tell your psychiatrist how you're feeling or what you're thinking, because they will use it against you.

But I knew if this patient and I continued to talk about our children for long, we'd both start crying, so I was grateful when she changed the subject.

"Do you want to go outside and smoke? They give out the drugs, and then they let everyone out to smoke. Then it's breakfast. You'll get a smoke break every two hours. You can have the rest of my pack."

"I don't smoke," I said. "But I'll go outside with you. The outside is the only good thing about this place."

"Yeah, I always wonder why nobody climbs the fence," she said.

"Totally. Somebody must have."

"I wanted to go back to Promises, but my insurance only lets you go there once. How many times have you been in here?"

"A few times," I said.

"Yeah, for sure. It's my third time. Actually, looking at you, you look like a Promises guy."

I had never been to Promises, but I understood this was intended as a compliment. Promises is considered to be the swanky place among the Kansas City rehab and mental hospital set.

"What are you doing here, anyway? It's none of my business. Hey, Debbie," she told one of the nurses, "we're going to smoke. If my paperwork comes up, that's where I am. I'll be right back. Don't forget I'm out there! You're going to be too cold without a coat," she said to me. (I was still in nothing but a hospital robe, having somehow lost all my clothes in the process of arriving at the emergency room.) "Here, why don't you just put on my coat, since I've got two sweaters on and my boots."

We stood, and she put her big jade-green parka over my shoulders. She was wearing well-worn, expensive-looking brown leather riding boots. Then we sat back down on the floor.

"Martin? Clancy Martin?" The nurse at the med station was looking around and calling my name.

"Those are your meds," the teacher said. She smiled at me kindly. "You sure don't want to miss those."

"That's me," I said. "I'm Clancy Martin."

"I don't want to have to find you next time," the nurse said. He was a soft-featured man who looked a bit like Barney, the sympathetic psychiatric nurse in *The Silence of the Lambs*.

"I'm sorry."

"I'm just teasing you," he said. "I know it's your first day. What's up with the coat?"

I looked at the science teacher, who was still sitting on the floor about ten feet away.

"It's hers," I said. We both looked at the teacher. She hadn't moved. Barney gave her a smile and a little wave, and she smiled and waved back.

"Rosalind? She's a buddy of mine," he said. "Okay, let's see what we've got here."

There were six of them: my regular antidepressant, an "antidepressant booster," and three new medications that I hadn't taken before. They were also putting me back on lithium, which was not a good drug for me.

I asked Barney what the new medications were for. "What do they do, exactly? I don't need all this medication. I just take Valium and Zoloft. I do need my Valium, though."

"They don't have you down for Valium," Barney said. "I've got Ativan here. It's less addictive."

It had taken me months to get off Ativan, which I had done the year before, using Valium to taper down. Valium is a common taper-down drug for people weaning themselves off benzodiazepines.

For me it has gone (1) booze, and occasionally a little cocaine, speed or weed, 1985–2009; (2) baclofen, Ativan, lithium, Wellbutrin, Zoloft, and two or three others with chemical names, 2009–10; (3) baclofen, Ativan, Zoloft, 2010–11; (4) Valium and Zoloft, 2011–2015; (5) Valium, 2015–December 31, 2016; and (6) pretty much drug-free, 2017 to present. I sometimes still take Valium from an old prescription on plane flights and long taxi drives for nausea. I stored up about 3000 milligrams when I was tapering off for the purpose of using them to kill myself, if necessary.

"I'll take the Ativan. At least until I can get Valium. I have to have it." I was starting to get those little waves of electricity that run through your arms and legs and make your mouth dry when you need your benzo. "What are the others for? I don't want to get started on a bunch of new drugs. It's too much work to get off them."

"You'd better ask your psychiatrist. Let's see who they got you down for. Dr. Ellis. He's all right. You'll like Dr. Ellis."

"That's my doctor," Rosalind told me from the floor. "That's good luck. He doesn't like to keep people in here for more than a few days. He's a pediatrician, and he diagnoses everyone as bipolar and mood disorder. He'll put you on lithium."

"Yeah, they just put me on it. I don't like it. I've taken it before."

"It's harmless, though. I've been taking it for three years now and I don't notice any difference at all."

"You don't notice any difference at all?"

"Exactly." She didn't get my joke, that she was taking a psychiatric drug to adjust her brain chemistry and continued to take it even though it did nothing. She was too happy about leaving to be looking for irony. "It sounds scary, but it just makes you feel more normal. It doesn't have any kick. The ones you should watch out for are the ones that give you a high."

"Yeah," I said. For the past year or so, I'd been trying to avoid the stronger benzos. But during AA meetings, when I was first getting sober, I ate Ativan like they were Altoids. I came to love the flavor. They're a little sweet.

"Klonopin, that's the worst drug I've ever been on," she said. "I'd rather be back addicted to Oxycontin than have to come down off Klonopin again."

"One psychiatrist told me to taper back to three glasses of wine a day and two Klonopin." He was an interesting fellow from Egypt who had his medical practice near my university. He really believed he could slowly wean me off my alcohol addiction, with the right combination of benzos and merlot. "I tried to kill myself after about a month on that regimen."

"I like the sound of that. Come on, let's smoke a cigarette," she said, and laughed. "The principal of my school is coming to get me. He's a good guy. I guess I'll stay tonight at his place."

I raised an eyebrow.

"He's married, though, it's nothing like that. Not that I'm saying I wouldn't. I would. He's very attractive. But married is off-limits. That's what started all this for me. Married men. They're more like heroin than heroin. That's my thing: downers. Watch, I'll be back on dope three months from now. Then in six months I'll be back here."

"Come on, now, Rosie. That's no way to talk," Barney said.

"Yup, downers. That's why I like married guys rather than single ones, I guess." Rosalind gave me the same shrug and smile.

"I'm married," Barney said, and that made me laugh. I hadn't laughed because something was honestly funny in a long time. It was my normal laugh.

I repeated it when we went outside into the yard so Rosalind could smoke: "I'm married." She laughed too.

There were a couple of trees in the yard and a wooden fence, probably twelve feet tall, and a wooden door on the far side of the fence. If you climbed one of the trees, you could probably walk out on a limb and jump over the fence. But you'd have a fifteen-foot drop or so. My ankles broke easily. I had broken both of my wrists and both of my ankles at least once when I was a kid, climbing trees and jumping off our garage into the gravel, plus my elbow at a roller rink. I broke my foot as an adult stepping off a four-foot ledge.

Anyway, it didn't seem like a practical escape plan, climbing the tree and leaping out into whatever was on the other side of that wall. Probably a parking lot for cops.

"I'm getting my feet all wet," I said. My slippers were muddy. I liked watching Rosalind smoke. She hid her cigarette under her hand like it was a secret. I kicked at the snow. It was mostly melted in the wet-paving-stone-and-grass courtyard, but a crust was running against the brick wall of the building. She looked over her shoulder, threw the cigarette into the grass, and lit a second one.

A kid in a black wool hat bent over and picked up Rosalind's half-finished cigarette. I smiled at him. He looked quickly away. He was one of those people in the psychiatric hospital who you try to become friends with but never really connect with for reasons neither of you understands. Mostly other patients give you your space in the psychiatric hospital, though there are exceptions.

"You're lucky you wound up here," Rosalind said to me. "Usually they'd put you in the tower. It's awful up there, like you're stuck in somebody's bad dream. I was up there once for a week before they even knew who my psychiatrist was. They give you your meds and forget about you."

"That's my biggest fear in this place. Being forgotten about."

"If you have lousy insurance, that's where you go. All the homeless wind up there. They don't even separate the violent offenders from the regular ones like us."

I had been up in the tower. It was indeed an awful place. My father had died in a tower like the one we were talking about.

"The tower is the worst," I said. "No. I just woke up in the hospital, and then they brought me over here. But yeah, I spent some time in the tower. Actually, I was up there just a couple of months ago."

Rosalind looked at me with surprise.

The sun was out, and it was warming up a little.

Then the whistle blew, and we went back inside. Rosalind's paperwork was ready, and she gave me a hug before she left. She wrote her email address on a Post-it Note and handed it to me. Then she fished around in a big yellow canvas duffel bag and pulled out a coffee-stained hardback copy of Richard Yates's *Liars in Love*.

"Did you ever read this?"

I shook my head no. I had read it, but I believed she would be happier if she thought she was introducing me to the book. I had almost pretended to be a smoker and taken her cigarettes.

"He spent a lot of time in mental asylums. He was an alcoholic. He was crazy, too, really crazy. So we all have that in common. I didn't know about him, but the last time I was in here someone showed it to me, and it's great. It was still here when I got back, and I was going to steal it because basically it's the only good book we have. The rest is romance novels and Stephen King and the Bible, though we have *The Shining*, which is good, but since you came now I think I should leave it. It's yours if you want it. Nobody here reads. They all just argue about what channel to put the TV on."

"Thank you," I said. "I was hoping I would have a book to read."

I didn't know if anyone would bring me books. During

my first stay at Research, I had Rebecca bring me *The Collected Shakespeare*, for the volume and the variety, and that was a mistake. I must've thought it would make me look cool and smart, but I felt silly reading it in the common room. It was good for going to sleep at night.

"I've read it about thirty times now anyway, and honestly I think it's probably not helping me with my recovery. Dr. Ellis says we should stay away from books that are written by other addicts or about other addicts. He says even literature about recovery can trigger a relapse. But I mean 'Heroin' is my favorite song. Am I never going to listen to Lou Reed again? Really, what does he know?"

"Don't ever read Alvarez's *The Savage God*," I said. "I read it and Styron's *Darkness Visible* in a hotel room downtown a few years ago, and I tried to kill myself about a month later on New Year's Eve."

That was the time I tried to hang myself in the bedroom closet. It was connected to Alvarez because I had been working on a nonfiction book at the time, and my editor, who didn't know I had in the past tried to kill myself, recommended I take Alvarez as a model. I was still a drunk, and one hard day with a blistering hangover I skipped classes, checked myself into a nice hotel downtown, and spent the day in bed reading Alvarez and Styron and drinking myself back onto my feet to come home to Rebecca and our children at five-thirty that afternoon. But the Alvarez (a study of suicidal poets) and the Styron (a study of the depression he suffered when he quit drinking) stayed in my head. While Styron and Alvarez were not romanticizing suicide, they made it seem inevitable.

"Anyway, I wish I was going to get to know you," she said.

"Me too," I said. "I've never had a real friend in one of these places." Which was true.

"Email me if you want when you get out. We always say we're going to email each other, and then we never do. We're not supposed to do that either, really. I dated a guy I met in here. Yup, you guessed it. He was married."

"Okay, Mrs. Maxwell, time to go," the nurse who had Rosalind's paperwork said.

"Okay, time to go," Rosalind said, and hugged me. She was weeping. I felt like I had made a real friend and didn't want to let go of her. She was a mom who couldn't see her kids. We could get an apartment together, just friends, when I got out. We could help each other raise our children. Then she was gone.

Later when I looked for the yellow note with her email address, I discovered I had lost it. That was probably for the best. In just those few minutes, Rosalind and I already understood and forgave too much about each other. As a team, she and I would have been back on her heroin and my Jägermeister in a matter of weeks.

I was trying to be a model citizen, following the routine, going to group, taking my medications, eating all my food. I behaved the way they want you to behave, doing whatever I could to get out as soon as possible.

My other concern was to keep everyone on the outside thinking that I could still function, that I could be a dad, a brother, and a philosophy professor, all the things I knew they could take away from me if they started thinking I was totally crazy. I wasn't crazy, as far as I was concerned, even as far as my doctors were concerned. I was just depressed and extremely anxious. These were things they believed they could medicate away. But to keep everyone on the outside in on the loop, I had to talk to people. Also, if I didn't talk to people outside, I could start to worry that I actually was going crazy.

On the wall near the smaller rec room, there were three phones that we could use almost whenever we wanted—between ten a.m. and eight p.m.—and unlike in jail, a phone was always available.

The phone was important to me. It kept me from growing too claustrophobic. We could call out when we wanted to, but it was a complex system because you had to ask the nurses to turn on the phone, and then as soon as the other person answered, it usually disconnected, and they would have to call you back. Some patients who answered the phone actually tried to find you, but others just said, "I don't see him" or "He's not here" or "Clancy who?" and then hung up. It was hard to get angry at these people—many of us were desperate for any kind word from the real world—but then we were all already so beat up that it was best just to let it go. I never saw the point of losing my temper with another crazy person.

I knew very well that I had only two people I could call: Rebecca (I didn't want my first wife to know, because I felt like she still had a certain respect for me) and Darren (who always told our mom, who told everyone else). Previously I'd called the dean of my college or whoever I happened to be dating at the time.

When you phone from jail, people almost always answer, but curiously, when you phone from a psychiatric hospital, they do not like to take the call. Maybe it's just that I have easier access to the phone in the psychiatric hospital and so wind up calling too many times. In both places, the problem is killing time without losing your mind, without panicking, and the phone can often feel like a lifeline, even for a confirmed phone-talk-hater like me.

I rang my brother Darren and asked him if he could come down from Calgary to get me out.

"I don't know, Clance. It sounds like things are kind of dangerous for you right now. There's an edge in your voice. Have you been having violent thoughts?"

"Come on, Darren, you know me better than that. It sounds like you've been talking to Rebecca." Rebecca was a great believer in keeping me in the psychiatric hospital, for understandable reasons. "I'm not dangerous, Darren. I'm not dangerous to myself or to anyone else. I didn't even exactly try to kill myself. I got drunk, and I got maudlin, and I called my girlfriend"—the person I'd had the affair with that ended my marriage to Rebecca; my brother had met and disliked her—"and then it was like she wanted me to kill myself, so I started making threats, and then I was drunk so I thought I had to act out the threats. It was stupid, yeah, but it wasn't an actual suicide attempt."

This was a lie, but not entirely. If I hadn't been drunk, I wouldn't have taken all that Valium, and if I hadn't taken all that Valium, I might not have tried to cut my wrists in the bathtub. So it certainly wasn't planned. When I went out that night to have a few drinks at the bar, I certainly hadn't expected I was going to end the night in the hospital.

"You were in the emergency room. You are in an asylum. Come on, Clance."

"It's not exactly an asylum," I said. My brother likes these old-fashioned, grandiose words. "I chose to kill myself at some point, sure, but it wasn't deliberate in the rich sense of the word. It was like, spur of the moment. I need to get sober again, but trust me, I have no desire to drink."

I heard the sigh on the other end of the phone. "I know that's not true, Clance."

"Please. I just need to get out of this psych ward before they make me crazy. I need to get off all these medications. I feel like my brain is nothing but chemicals. You don't know what it's like to have this chemical buzzing in your head all day. It's horrible."

There was a long silence on the other end. Then: "Clance, they have you on a seventy-two-hour suicide hold—"

"Stop right there. Please don't say suicide to me right now. I am so sick of the word *suicide*. I am not going to kill myself."

He spoke right over me. "And then they have to release you. As long as you don't do anything else. As I understand it, you just keep your cool for three days, and you'll be out."

"They can renew those holds indefinitely, Darren. There are people who've been in here for six months. Just do me a favor and have your lawyer call. Please. Get your lawyer to call my psychiatrist. He controls the whole thing for me. His name is Dr. Ellis. Or my other psychiatrist. Get them to call Grace Ketterman."

More silence.

"Hello? Darren? Are you there?"

"You know, you really need to try to put things back together with Rebecca, Clance. But listen, bud, I've got a customer. I've gotta—"

"Rebecca is not the solution here. Anyway, she'll never forgive me. What I need, Darren—"

He had hung up.

I remembered the time I hung up on my dad when he called me from the mental hospital. I thought, *So that's what it feels like*. I wasn't angry with my brother, as I was sure my father had been with me. I understood why he'd ended the call without even saying goodbye. I blamed myself, not him. I had no feeling of reproach or betrayal—again, emotions I had been certain, all these years, my father had felt when I did it to him.

It was a feeling of confirmation. Like, even Darren, the one person who always believed in me, had given up. Even he was done with me now, and I got it.

Life in Research was becoming familiar, and I looked at some of the people who had resigned themselves to it, and wondered, *Could I become one of them? Could I go on living, but just do it in here?*

The Fish Bowl was the main recreation room, where we watched TV and played Trivial Pursuit between meals and when we weren't standing outside during the smoke breaks. It got its name because the top half was surrounded by glass, so the nurses and orderlies could keep their eyes on us.

For a few days, I avoided the Fish Bowl because a small group of female patients kept hitting on me. (This happened to me nowhere else, I should add, except Research.) Then one day a woman with yellow hair as fake and dead as a Halloween wig lost her temper after watching how upset I was getting and screamed at a middle-aged woman with glasses—she was harmless, she looked like a philosophy professor—to leave me the fuck alone, and then they mostly stayed away from me.

"Her name's Veronica," a young girl, eighteen or nineteen years old, who was in there for crystal meth addiction and multiple suicide attempts, told me. "I call her Veronica Blonde. She's totally fucked up. Her kids died. Her hair got that way from her ECTs," electroconvulsive therapy, more popularly known as shock treatments. The girl had scars on her neck, wrists, and legs from the places she had slashed herself. She said she had been in Research at least ten times. She was on a ton of Seroquel, and she'd often pass out cold while standing in line for meals in the hallway. Just flop down on the floor in folds and a pile, like a dress falling off a hanger.

"You really cut deeply," I said. "Brave." I showed her my

wrist. My pale scars like chicken scratches didn't compare to hers.

"I always worry I'm gonna cut a tendon and then wake up a freak, with one floppy hand or some shit," she said, laughing. "That would be just my luck. And I think, *No, I'm not going to kill myself, I'm going to call somebody.* But you know how it is. By the time you're so fucked up that you're ready to try, and you really, really want to call someone, then the one person I actually really could call . . ."

"Is the person you can't call, or you'll really have to go through with it," I said. "The person who could save you is the one who has to understand that you aren't bluffing. I know. Because the people you could call are the people who will make consequences for you. The people you could call will make sure that all kinds of things happen that you don't want to happen. And also if you've tried or threatened to try before, the people you could call, you may have called them before, so they may make you feel like now you really have to do it, because you're calling them again. In short, if you call someone, you know you're going to make your situation worse, one way or the other."

"Not to mention," she said, "that when you're the kind of person who's willing to kill herself, that just shows you're so selfish that you don't deserve to live."

"Yeah. That's another one of the paradoxes."

We talked about Hamlet's idea that suicide sounded like a really good sleep, but then who knows? "Nightmares," she said, and I nodded. I told her that I had heard from a failed suicide, a young woman who was like me, a repeat failure, that killing yourself doesn't actually kill you in the way that you think it will. "Most of what you are sticks around, she says. All the bad parts. Killing yourself just gets rid of the good, happy parts."

"I have seen those people," she said. "The stick-arounds. People like us can see them, because we want to be dead. You're right, they are even worse off than we are. Like, actually, if you kill someone else, or you kill yourself, it's the same thing. It's like murder either way. You turn into a murderer. You don't want to be one of them."

"You know I think suicide is like masturbation," she whispered to me once, leaning in close suddenly while we were all standing in line for our meds. "It's like death for masturbators."

The young kid who found my cigarette butt overheard her. "So, like, death is real sex?" he said. "Normal death's like actually having sex?" He was interested in her and was just trying to join the conversation. He wasn't being aggressive.

"Yeah. I guess. Whatever," she said, and looked away from both of us like the conversation had never happened.

Another time, alone in the Fish Bowl watching a game show, she said to me, "It's like a poem, killing yourself. It completely sums up how you feel about life. Who could write a better poem than that?"

I said that I thought poems were really hard to write, and suicide had always been too easy for me.

Many people were in Research for three or even four days before they got to see their psychiatrist. The doctors looked at their chart and prescribed medications based on the case history but didn't actually meet with them until they decided they were good and ready. Nobody could explain any of this to me except other patients. In this way it was exactly like jail. The only reliable information came from the inmates. They were also the only people who looked away from you when they lied. The nurses were like jail guards. They stared you straight in the eyes and said whatever they wanted. It was like they were talking to cartoons instead of humans so the normal rules of communication didn't apply.

"What are you doing here, Clancy?" Dr. Ellis asked me.

He was short and round and very Kansan. He wore an earring in one ear and cheap gray suits and shiny shoes. His short black hair was going gray, though I guessed he was in his late thirties or early forties. He was a very unattractive, lizard-like man. Every word out of his mouth was stupider than the last. But his hands were fine-boned and handsome, and I liked the way he rested them on his desk while we spoke.

"I don't want to be on all these medications. I don't know why you have me on so many drugs. I take seven pills twice a day. I don't need to be on lithium."

"Let's talk about why you're here. You tried to commit suicide, Clancy. You were in your bathtub, and you overdosed on Valium and alcohol and slashed your wrists. How do you feel about waking up and learning that you could be dead?"

"Do you have any clue what you are talking about?"

"Clancy, you have no reason to be angry with me. I'm trying to help you." He picked up a folder on his desk and turned through the pages. He tried to look focused. "It says here you've been doing fine. I'd like to recommend your release this weekend, but not until I'm certain that you're stable. Maybe you'd like to talk about your drinking. Have you had any withdrawal symptoms since you've been here? I notice you're not shaking. Your skin looks bright. Your eyes are clear."

"No, I did not have any withdrawal symptoms when they checked me in, and I don't have any withdrawal symptoms now. I'm not in denial about my drinking. I know I'm an alcoholic. I am open to attending AA meetings, though in the past they haven't helped me much. I've been going to the twelve-step meetings here."

We went back and forth like that until he wore me down, and I said quietly, "Yes. Yes. Yes." He knew what he was doing much better than I did, he understood who was in charge, and so I submitted, which was what everyone has to do. We were going to have weekly office visits after he released me. Then we'd switch to phone consultations if all went well. We'd moderate the drugs as necessary. If I continued to do as well as I had been doing, he'd release me on Sunday or Monday. He recommended I join the AA group that I had in fact previously attended.

"They're very smart people, Clancy. I've never met a stupid alcoholic. Many UMKC professors attend those meetings. I think you'd feel very welcome there."

Thinking of Dr. Ellis, I paced the hallways and stayed in the common areas to read so that the nurses couldn't accuse me of being reclusive, which would get you extra time. I went to the group sessions for the same reason, though you could skip group as much as you liked. We knew this was a chessboard, a movie set, a scary game we all agreed to play, and really therapy wasn't the goal. Recovery wasn't the goal. The goal was just to get you to talk and act like everyone who wasn't presently in a psychiatric hospital, even though no one's really sane outside either, and only some of us can fake it. The goal was to make you pretend to be some made-up idea of ordinary. I wanted to approach the nurses at the station and say, *Let's take five minutes and just be normal.* But I knew better than that.

I once mustered my courage, or was simply foolhardy, and raised this point with Dr. Ellis. "Do you have, like, a form? A list? I'm just asking. How do you decide whether I'm in a better frame of mind?"

"No, Clancy, I don't have a checklist. I do try to assess whether you have accepted the fact that you are struggling. Whether you can see that you have some work to do on yourself."

"Well, but don't you ever worry that we're just telling you what you want to hear?"

"I've been doing this a long time, Clancy. I think I can tell when someone is faking it. Do you feel like you have to fake something in order to show me that you're ready to leave?"

I was a jewelry salesman for years, and like any other salesperson, I specialized in the art of seeming to be what someone needed me to be, of telling people what I knew they wanted to hear. But any child would know better than to answer a question like Dr. Ellis's honestly. It was like he was feeding me the right answers.

"No, please. I just mean that we all have fears we are afraid to express, we all have self-destructive ideas now and then, and it's hard to know, in here, what you can be honest about."

"You can be honest about everything. That's the therapeutic process. Are you having self-destructive thoughts?" The same question the intake nurse had asked me.

"No, no. thank goodness," I lied. "But I do worry they may return, you know, once I'm dealing with my ordinary stresses." More bullshit. "But I guess that's why we continue therapy after

I'm released." I was appalled, listening to myself. Like I could just sit there for hours, repeating clichés from movies about recovery, and his confidence in me would grow and grow.

"Exactly."

I was lying in bed because I was on a new medication and it was too strong. Violent images had been flashing through my mind, but I didn't want to tell Dr. Ellis that because I was sure he would decide I was psychotic and move me to the other ward, the scary ward for serious and dangerous cases. (Even now, when I am feeling suicidal, frightening, violent images flash vividly through my mind and often feel perilously close to the surface of my will. They are at times so terrifying and so real that I hesitate even to write this down.) So I told Dr. Ellis I was having panic attacks and asked for something to calm me. He agreed immediately, but the pills he gave me made it impossible to walk without falling down. Phone messages came in on little slips of paper that gathered on my bedside table.

One night Veronica, the woman with hair turned bright yellow from her electric shock treatments, came and sat at the end of my bed.

"So you're going to stay with us, I guess," she said. "I like it here just fine. I think it's safe here. I'm glad you're staying."

"It doesn't matter to me. I hate to be anywhere," I said. "I don't know why anyone is alive."

"I do," she said, and her eyes grew large and truthful. "Fear."

Another conversation in the Fish Bowl, four of us playing Hearts while the TV blared in the background:

Me: "If you could end it, right now, painlessly, with no fear of the afterlife, no ghastly consequences, and a guarantee that no one would miss you, that they'd be as well off or better off, would you?"

Laughter. Somebody says, "It's a stupid question."

Me: "Why?"

"Because anybody would take that deal. Obviously you'd kill yourself if you could do it like that. Why wouldn't you?"

The young girl who kept passing out from too much Seroquel said quietly, "I think that's basically true. I think the way you described it is right. That's how it is. Except not painless." She looked at her own wrists, which were still bandaged.

General agreement around the card table. I was wondering, *Is it just us, or does everybody feel this way? If everybody feels this way, are we all alive just because we're too scared or too lazy to die? Are we all actually that miserable? Maybe these people in here with me are actually the courageous ones.*

I would like to be able to report that that was my last stay in Research, but it wasn't. I tried to kill myself again and failed. I would like to be able to report that I will never go back, but I dare not.

It has been more than ten years since my last visit there, and more than five years since my last suicide attempt. I have learned, at least, not to get on the phone while trying to kill myself, because of fear of being taken to the psychiatric hospital.

A number of students have written to me after attempting suicide and failing, and I've even had a couple call me from Research. Those are fun calls, in their way, because we can joke about what it's like inside there, and talk and complain in intimate detail about the culture of the place.

I've also visited students at Research, and one visit in particular stays with me. She was one of my brightest—one of my few students ever to really get Kierkegaard—twenty-one years old, charming, popular. She told me that she wasn't sure when they were going to let her out of the hospital. When I went there to see her, I told her that we all needed her, and that she should try to rest. She gave me a baleful, disappointed look, which I deserved. She couldn't believe that I would tell her something so trite. She expected something more from me, a glimpse of genuine understanding.

I've seen her since then. We discussed suicide and our ongoing struggles with it. She'd had a friend kill herself since the last time we'd spoken. "I didn't even know she was having a hard time," she told me.

"I think that happens a lot," I said. "It's hard not to hide it when you're depressed."

She nodded. We were quiet for a minute, drinking tea. Then I asked her what she thought a person should say to someone else who wanted to take her own life.

She said, "Just telling your own story is best. That's what I do."

PART III

THE LONG ROAD BACK

"For here there is no place that does not see you.
You must change your life."

—RAINER MARIA RILKE

9

Relapse Is Part of Recovery

In the past ten years, my life has slowly changed for the better, and lately the thought of suicide has become less and less attractive to me. I would not say that I am the author of that change in my thinking—it's been a consequence mostly of the people around me, and of lots of little things that have happened, and some big things that have happened. I've had good luck. And I have made changes in small, daily sorts of things, and those changes have helped. All this together has combined to alter the structure of my habits and beliefs. But I'll try to explain those events—and my part in them—that may have provided for the possibility of a less suicidal way of thinking.

In some ways, it's been a simple thing, really. My addiction to suicidal thinking, and my gradual liberation from that addiction, have operated almost exactly like my addiction to alcohol. As I became an alcoholic, I increasingly treated drinking as an end in itself: that is, the act of drinking was a good I was pursuing, almost for its own sake. The pleasure and relief that often but not always accompanied drinking was also a benefit, but the truth was, I just really wanted to drink. Similarly, the idea of suicide was initially instrumental to easing the pain of existence, but over time the thing itself became more of a literal goal that I was pursuing. But for some time now I have viewed both drinking and suicidal thinking as a throwback to an older and unnecessary way of understanding myself. And I came to see pursuing them as a kind of relapse.

As with the death of my father at the end of 1997, at the end of 2011 something changed in my life. I destroyed my second marriage that year. I also ended the affair that was one of the main causes of the destruction of that marriage. But the real source of change was that I started to drink again and thus to learn about relapse. Without that experience, I don't expect my thinking about suicide would have changed. (I hasten to add that I'm not a proponent of relapsing—it's just how it worked out for me.)

AA is famous for saying that relapse is part of recovery. Before I was in AA, I thought, as I suspect many people do, that this was just carte blanche for going back to using. *Well, I'm in recovery, but this is just a relapse*—swallow half a beer, snort a line—*and, after all, relapse is part of recovery.* I'm quite sure people sometimes use it for this purpose, but those people are probably going to drink their beer and do their coke quite independently of what they heard at an AA meeting. Once I was in AA, I initially supposed it was just about learning to forgive yourself for backsliding, and not using it as an excuse to give up hope. Like, *Hey, we all fall off our bicycles while learning to ride, the important thing is to get back on.* And that is in fact part of why the slogan is so important.

But now I think of relapse as the opportunity to revise my thinking about alcohol entirely and accepting that I can't will myself to change. Which has let some of the air out of my addiction, because it allowed me to see how long the process of recovery is, that it's not an on/off switch, and that it makes sense to say *I am getting better* even if—or even because—I am not yet well and may never be. It's exactly like dealing with my suicidal thinking: I don't have to stop thinking about it. In fact trying to stop thinking about it might just inflate it. I have to let myself think about it, so that it can get smaller.

If we accept that relapse is part of recovery, then we have to admit that what we mean by sober isn't very clearly defined, there is no oracle of sobriety, and no one, really, can tell an addict whether she or he is sober. And for those of us who know that our families, our livelihoods, and our lives depend on staying sober, whatever that means, not knowing whether you're sober is a terrifying thought.

This observation sheds new light on the meaning of another well-worn AA chestnut: "One day at a time." I'm not sober for nine years, or four years, or since my last relapse: I'm only ever sober today. You know, I'm also only ever alive today. In fact I'm only ever alive right now. I don't know if I'll make it to the end of the day—none of us do, whether we're suicidal or not. Death comes when it pleases.

What does it mean to be sober today? That seems to change from day to day, too. Some days being sober just means not drinking. Other days it means going a whole day and not wanting a drink, despite driving past bars and seeing people drinking at lunch and watching a movie with glamorous people knocking back even more glamorous-looking cocktails and wine.

It also means realizing it's been days or even weeks since I've thought about taking a drink. And then comes another sober day when all day long I want just one (or maybe two? At most three?) cold golden beers in a dark gentle room lit by signs with good music playing and a kind quiet person behind the bar who doesn't want to talk but smiles politely and works without hurry.

My suicidal thinking is just this way. Are there days when I never think of killing myself? I know at the very least that the tone of the thought of suicide changes, it is less urgent, less immediate. Sometimes a few days pass without me noticing any active desire to take my own life. Occasionally, writing this book, I've thought, *But wait, do I still have the right to say these things? Because today I don't feel like killing myself at all.* And I didn't yesterday either. But then I remember a black day can arrive at any moment, and suddenly it's shaking me by the scruff of the neck again.

This is also a bit like the end of a romantic relationship, or the grief after a death. It takes a long time, and there will be turmoil, regret, and regressions along the way. But gradually, over years, your need for that person diminishes. She or he may never be gone altogether from your thoughts, and that is probably a good thing. That person is part of you. But you don't need to talk to her every day anymore, you don't have to lie in bed with her at night, you don't have to try to read her mind or measure her mood. You can have her in your mind without feeling too much hope or fear.

From 2009 to early 2011, I was "sober" without interruption. But that kind of thinking disguised an aggression, a mistaken oppositional reasoning that confirmed my whole death-wish psychology. I want to be quite clear about this. In this way "being sober" was exactly like the desire to kill myself. It's so childish, really: My way or the highway. Sober or drunk. Life the way I like it or no life at all.

I discovered in relapsing that it's much more complicated than that. Relapsing taught me that I wasn't simply a sober person or a drunk, just as I'm neither a person who wants to live nor a person who is trying to kill himself. I don't have to be so on/off, so angry about the whole process. I can be a person who sometimes relapses and drinks and yet is still making progress toward a life that is not dominated (and destroyed) by my desire for alcohol. I can be a person who fantasizes about (and sometimes attempts) suicide and yet is slowly opening his mind to the possibility of just living all his life, including all its suffering, and not trying to escape from it.

This knowledge, if that's what it is, was hard won. To write about it, I have to say a bit more about 2011 and its aftermath, from the perspective of my relapsing, so you can see the process of my accidental self-education.

The first time I learned a little bit about relapse was not during a relapse of mine. A kid, Billy, about twenty years younger than me, got sober the same day I did, on January 1, 2009. Billy was in rehab when I was in rehab, though we weren't in rehab together, and then we wound up in the same meeting and talking a bit after meetings. At this time I was still getting up and leaving meetings every ten minutes or so, often five or six times during a meeting, to "go to the bathroom" and chew up another Ativan.

Billy and I became friends; maybe he looked up to me,

because I was older, a philosophy professor, and drove a nice car, and to innocent eyes I seemed (more or less, from the outside) to have my shit together, despite the fact that, truthfully, I was in much worse shape than he was, since he was getting sober in his twenties and I had waited until middle age. Billy and I had the same sponsor, and Billy was working his program much harder than I was.

A year went by, and I was going to a meeting to celebrate my first year of sobriety. I was still taking bucketsful of medication, seeing a psychiatrist every week, and having trouble looking into the future for more than a few days or so. But I was finally emerging from that sunless, skyless, airless claustrophobia of early sobriety, and I could walk from campus, where I worked, back to my apartment without thinking, *Today I hang myself.*

That day I was not unhappy. I felt, *Yes, I am sober.* I went to the meeting, got my round of applause, and was walking out of the church when someone called my name.

"Hey, Clancy," Billy said. I introduced him to my wife. He was sweeping the church floor, in the main room where we rarely met. I'd been to one or two speaker meetings there.

"Doing some service work? Good for you," I said. I could see that he was struggling. "Everything cool?"

"Yeah," he said. "Well, no, not so much. I got drunk last night. On my one-year anniversary. Can you believe that? Some buddies were going to Tomfooleries"—this was a bar directly opposite the church where we met—"for a friend's birthday, and they invited me along, and I thought, *What the hell, I can have a couple of beers.* And I got really drunk. I mean, nothing bad happened"—he looked at my wife, worrying I suppose what she was thinking—"but yeah so here I am, back to square one. But relapse is part of recovery, right? I'm going to another meeting at eight. I think I'll be at thirty meetings in like ten days or less. I'd like to do ninety meetings in thirty days."

"Can you believe that?" I said to my wife after we left the church and were walking through the parking garage to our car. "He just threw away a year. He seemed totally okay. I mean, a whole year, down the toilet."

"Well, it's not like that year is gone," she said. "He's already back at a meeting. I mean, he had one night. He got drunk. But he's getting right back on the wagon."

"I guess," I said. I felt disappointed, a bit queasy, self-righteous, and judgmental. I didn't think, *If it could happen to him, it can happen to me.* I sincerely thought it would never happen to me. Even though I knew that thinking it would never happen to me is almost a way of making sure that it did happen to me. But I just could not fathom wasting this year that had been too hard, too pricey, too violent ever to repeat. Maybe part of me thought, *It's not that I'm stronger than he is, it's that I'm weaker than he is.*

Fast-forward a couple of years: it's 2011, and I was in an ugly, uncomfortable too-bright little airport bar right next to security at LaGuardia, on my way back to school in Kansas City, texting my boss so that he wouldn't call me on the phone and hear the beer in my voice. I had a noon flight, and officially I was not drinking. Which meant to me: *I'm more or less sober most of the time, but when I'm in New York, I drink.* So the airport was a gray area. I didn't want to arrive in Kansas City drunk, because I had a class to teach that day.

But the problem was that the night before, after the woman I was with got drunk and wouldn't notice, I had sneaked into her kitchen and finished off the bottle of whiskey that she kept in a cabinet above the fridge. So I really needed a beer.

I ordered one of those giant airport Stellas. After drinking it, I felt pretty good, and I ordered another. Then it was like, *Well, I guess I'm going to be drunk, maybe I can sleep on the plane,* and I ordered a third.

On the plane, the flight attendant wouldn't serve me. "I'm sorry sir, you appear to be inebriated."

"It's my Valium," I explained. "It slows my speech. But really I'm fine."

The woman sitting next to me was rigid with fear and disapproval. She stared into her phone. I felt like saying to her, *What, you've never been drunk before?* But I am an old pro at being drunk in public, and I was on my best behavior.

When the flight attendant refused to serve me again, I was very polite. I waited until she was moving the cart back into her station, then hurried to the lavatory. As I passed her, I stole two red wines off the cart. I went into the bathroom.

"Sir? Sir?" She was knocking on the bathroom door. I had the wines in my jacket pocket and nowhere to hide them.

"Just a moment!" I said. "Almost done!"

"Sir, I must insist you come out of the bathroom immediately."

I opened both bottles, drank them as quickly as I could, and dropped them into the garbage. I hoped she wouldn't check the bin.

She was still knocking and demanding I come out. I rinsed my mouth in the sink and looked at myself. I'd spilled red wine on my shirt. It was a dark blue shirt and wasn't too obvious, I thought. I splashed water onto the shirt and my face. I'd just look wet.

When I came out of the bathroom, the air marshal was waiting.

He sat me down in the back and explained that if I left my seat again, they were going to arrest me on landing. I didn't say a word: this was also not my first run-in with an air marshal.

I never made it to school to teach that class. I woke up the next day in the hospital. I had very little memory of anything after a taxi ride from the airport. I had a dark, spotty, dreamlike recollection of a discussion in an office with airport security in Kansas City and them helping me into a taxi—and then a Chuy's in Kansas City, where I was buying people margaritas amid high spirits and happy shouting.

I learned later that I had tried to get into my apartment by struggling with the lock on my neighbors' door, and when they explained my mistake, I was outraged and stormed onto the porch of our building, where I fell down seven or eight stone steps (thus the hospital) and passed out or was knocked unconscious.

My neighbors, who had complained to my landlord about my drunken activities around the apartment building before, did not retrieve me from the stairs and pour me into my apartment.

They called the cops—as they were happy to tell me—who presumably sent the fire department, who presumably took me to St. Luke's.

I looked around, removed an IV, put on my shoes, found my wallet and phone, and sneaked out of the hospital. St. Luke's Hospital is on the edge of Westport, the bar district in midtown Kansas City, and I walked over there to find a bar that was open early. My hangover was crippling, I had a mild concussion, and I needed some help.

Unfortunately, a few hours later and very thoroughly medicated, I ran into some students who were in the class I'd missed the day before, and though they did help me home, they also decided to post the story on Facebook, which led to its own series of unfortunate consequences: my ex-wife learned about it in short order, as did a couple of my colleagues at school.

Sitting in the meeting in my folding chair with its off-balance leg, I was telling myself (1) I wasn't going to drink if I could get through the meeting, and (2) if I could get through the meeting, I could have a drink. It was my turn to speak. With the relief that you will find almost nowhere other than in the company of fellow addicts, I told the truth:

"I got drunk last night. I'm still drunk now." I wasn't telling the whole truth just yet. This wasn't my regular meeting, and these people didn't know my history. "I mean, I first got sober a few years ago, and for the last few months, I've been relapsing almost every week. This is like my fifth time this month getting a one-day chip. And we're not even halfway through the month."

I smiled wanly. A couple of people laughed. Relapse stories are always the most awkward, just as stories of losing your children are the saddest, and stories of mild physical injury or gross embarrassment get a laugh, and stories of losing your job or going to jail get a grim "been there, done that" series of nods.

"The thing is, I can't see my kids except with my ex-wife there, because she doesn't trust me not to drink. So I have to stay sober so that I can see my kids. But I can't bear to be around her without having a drink. And then if I do see them sober, when I leave, the first thing I want to do is go have a beer. And if I don't do it, I tell myself, 'That's one beer you owe yourself. Tomorrow at five you can have that beer.' But by five o'clock today I'll already know where I'm going to have the beer. And there's no point waiting, since I know I'll just have it tomorrow if I don't have it today."

Now I was feeling guilty because I felt like my own logic might be infecting the meeting. But I wasn't telling them anything they hadn't told themselves many times before they heard it from me.

After the meeting, a woman with a cane stopped me. "You know I used to relapse a lot," she said. "Do you know what I did? I just started from scratch. Didn't worry about how long I'd been sober. Now I don't count my days. I don't know how long I've been sober."

"Did you relapse after you started from scratch?" I asked her. She was probably seventy years old, and she could have told me she'd been sober for forty years and I wouldn't have been surprised.

"Sure I did," she said. "I'm more like, glad about all the sober days. Like every day is a new day. I think sobriety is kind of like a marriage. Just don't give up on it."

From 2012 to 2014, my wife Amie was studying at the University of Iowa, and I was still in Kansas City and commuting back and forth. I'd see my daughters in Kansas City and teach my classes and then drive to Iowa City to spend the long weekend with Amie. On the Monday afternoons before I'd drive back to Kansas City, I'd often tell myself that I wasn't going to have a drink when I left. For me, that's the surest sign of treacherous terrain. When I begin saying, *I'm not going to have a drink*, another part of my brain almost always starts saying, *but if I did, this is how and where I might do it.*

So by the time five o'clock came around and it was time to get on the road, I'd already know which frat bar—where none of her friends would ever drink—to stop by on the way out of town, and I had decided on the two beers I was going to have. From there I was on to the next lie, telling myself that I wasn't going to buy a six-pack for the road when I stopped to fill up the car, and then in the QT convenience store telling myself that if I just bought two tallboys instead of a six-pack, I could stretch those until I got home.

During the time Amie lived in Iowa City, I rarely stayed sober for more than a week or two, but I felt like I was heading in the right direction, maybe even almost back on my feet.

And I do think it was important to my long-term recovery that I didn't let go of the idea that I was still kind of sober. In my mind, I had not became a drinker again, and that self-deception was useful.

But whatever had happened the day before on the drive home, the next day, before I taught class, I might go walking to deal with my pre-class nerves, and I might decide to pass by Mike's, my old bar on Troost.

One brisk October day, as I saw the welcoming door standing open, I thought, *Well, I'm really nervous this afternoon, I don't know why. I'll just have one. Or two. I can have two and teach class basically sober, and I'm so jangly today and I really miss Amie, and then I'll have to go right back on the wagon anyway because I'm driving to Iowa City Thursday and it takes twenty-four hours to clean the smell of the booze out of my skin.* (Amie has a very good sense of smell.)

And I did have two and then went to teach a class, but yes, you guessed it, I went back to Mike's afterward and got drunk and woke up late the next morning on top of my bed with my shoes on, covered in ketchup and mustard, which is something that happens to me when I black out: I eat at McDonald's.

But I was still determined not to drink and ready to take it one day at a time.

Then some days the relapse really kicked in, because I started applying the one-at-a-time relapse logic that goes from *a drink tomorrow* to *I won't drink at six* to walking toward the bar district near my old apartment, thinking *I'm not going to have a drink, but if I change my mind, I'll just sit in the back of Kelly's where no one will see me, it's too early for friends of my ex-wife's*—this mattered because custody of my children was contingent on sobriety—to

I know I'm going to have a pint of Guinness at Kelly's but I can still change my mind, I still will change my mind to having that pint.

But then it happened less and less. Why? The usual reasons: wanting to get the stink of drink off me; the general desire to be sober, honest, and trustworthy; self-preservation, happiness, health, inner cleanliness, these sorts of things; sometimes, a meeting, a friend. Probably most important, the fact that every time I relapsed, suicide jumped right to the top of my list of things I needed to do next.

But truthfully, I can no more say why I sometimes chose to not drink than I can specify how I relapsed, or why I got sober in the first place. I've had so many rock-bottoms that selecting one is more or less arbitrary, and like all of us who have been at this shit for a long time, I've heard so many varieties of stories from people about how, when, and why they stopped "drinking and drugging"—and then, often, started again, and stopped again, rinse and repeat—that the notion of "rock bottom" doesn't seem particularly useful to me. It was helpful in my early stages of recovery, because it made me feel, *Well, you know, nowhere to go but up.* But my rock bottom is every time I try to kill myself—which means my "real" rock-bottom would be trying to kill myself and succeeding.

As I write this, it's been six years or more since I've taken a drink. This is my longest stretch without drinking since I was a teenager. Nevertheless many people (maybe especially people in AA) reading this narrative will have concluded, *This guy isn't sober at all, he's just a dry drunk: a guy who still has all the habits and thinking of an addict but just happens not to be drinking.* That's also possible, but I've started to doubt the meaning of the phrase *dry drunk.* (This is sacrilege to real AA old-timers: the concepts of "dry drunk" and "whiteknuckling it" are pretty core to the AA philosophy of recovery.) I have come to think that patterns of addiction are fundamental to ordinary human psychology and that we don't really escape from those patterns so much as moderate them or become more aware of them and so less controlled by them.

For the past three or four years, I no longer think, *I'm not going to have a drink.* I don't have to think about not doing it, because it rarely comes up. My brain seems to have found other things to obsess over. It's like I've lost the habit of *the desire* to drink. As this habit of the desire to drink has subsided, the habit of the desire to kill myself also seems to be subsiding. Not vanishing.

It's not a causal relationship, because the habit of suicidal thinking predated my problems with alcohol. But they are interestingly parallel, and inside my head they have a similar texture. Fundamentally, they both feel like responses to a nameless panic that must have a thousand different sources. And they both feel like knee-jerk reactions that needn't have this stimulus-response structure in my brain. In the case of alcohol, I have learned how to find space between the stimulus and the response, and increasingly the same is true with the urge to kill myself.

My last drinking relapse, my last suicide relapse? I suppose I hope I've had my last relapse in both cases, though it's a tentative hope, maybe even more a request than a hope.

In the case of drinking, I'm much less afraid of relapsing than I used to be, which, perhaps surprisingly, makes beer and wine seem less attractive.

Am I less afraid of attempting suicide than I used to be? Well, there's a difference: I'm not sure I've ever been afraid of committing suicide (while always being afraid of the pain). But I'm less afraid that the thought of suicide will overwhelm me unexpectedly and that I'll follow through on it. Because when the thought of suicide occurs to me now, I don't try to shut it down or swallow it, I try to live with it without acting on it.

Buddhists have a concept called *upaya*, usually translated as "skillful means," and the basic idea is that such truths are useful for as long as you need them, and then at a certain point you don't need them anymore, and you move on to other truths that may or may not cohere with the truths you needed before.

One New Year's Eve, back when I was still drinking, a friend of mine, a jazz critic, came over to my house in Lawrence, Kansas, for a small party. I liked this man a lot—he was in his fifties, then, and I was in my late thirties, and I very much admired him—and like any drunk, I was frustrated that he would never drink with us.

He'd been sober for more than twenty-five years. It was midnight, and we were standing in the kitchen, and again I was cajoling him to have a drink. He said, "You know what? Why not," and he picked up the bottle of wine on the counter. It was a ten-dollar Spanish red with a gaudy label. He looked at it for a few moments, then said, "You know what, Clancy? If I'm going to give up all those years not drinking, I'm going to do it for a wine that's a lot better than this."

I couldn't argue with that, and we went back to the party.

Lately I've been thinking a lot about the advice of that woman with the cane at the AA meeting who told me that she had relapsed plenty of times in her life, and had stopped marking her sober days and her relapses, and had learned to just be glad about the days she was sober. This may be the best advice I've received about sobriety, about the desire to kill myself, and about mental health generally. I notice in this book I have the habit of reporting to myself and to you, my reader, like a kid taking his report card home to Mom: "I haven't had suicidal thoughts in four days." "I haven't tried to kill myself in three years." "I haven't been seriously depressed since January." "I haven't wanted a drink since I don't know when."

There's a prayer I try to read every day that includes the line "May we be happy without hope." I see this as the same wisdom. Part of my problem is counting the days, anticipating forward, regretting backward, filling myself with hopes, fears, and promises. I need to let myself accept the fact that just going forward is what I must do, what I owe to my family and to myself.

But is that morally sufficient? I have five children. Can a person who keeps bringing children into the world and knows himself to be chronically suicidal dare to say such things?

There may be two separate questions here. The first is: what sort of attitude is best for me to stay sober and alive? The second is: what do I owe my family? When I collapse these two questions, perhaps I make it more difficult to maintain the kind of mental health necessary to keep my promises and fulfill my responsibilities.

Which leads me to my next chapter, and how I managed to start to have some trust in my own ability to stay away from alcohol and not try to kill myself.

10

They Fuck You Up / Your Mum and Dad

(PART II)

I've said a lot about my dad, and in a way I've blamed him for my alcoholism and my suicide attempts. But I have five children myself, and three of them were already born when I went through my worst years of drinking and trying to kill myself. So it's time to do a bit of honest accounting of myself as a father. To genuinely work through my failures and successes as a dad would take a book of its own (or several), but one story may illustrate how trying to be a better parent to my children helped me with my slow progress toward a healthier way of thinking.

It started in the early years of my marriage to Amie (we were married in August 2012), after my relapsing was mostly behind me but before my second wife Rebecca (the mother of my daughters Margaret and Portia) could believe that I was really getting and staying sober, and could be trusted to responsibly care for our children.

To be fair to Rebecca, she knew better than anyone how much I wanted to kill myself. She had seen it, and I had told her many, many times, both drunk and sober, about my obsession with suicide. To trust that person with your kids, when he's cheated on you and ended your marriage, when he's been a secret drinker for years and then reveals the fact in a suicide attempt, when he's been an alcoholic for as long as you've known him and then gets sober for two years—as far as you know—before becoming a relapsing drunk again, who again tries to kill himself repeatedly . . . to believe that this guy can responsibly care for the two little people who matter more to you than anything else in the world: well, looking back on it now, as angry as I still sometimes am with her for not letting me see Margaret and Portia, I can at last appreciate where she was coming from. Based on her experience, I was capable of almost anything—and certainly, in her mind, more than capable of placing our daughters in harm's way when I was drunk and suicidal.

This part of the story matters for a number of reasons. It shows how much damage I had done to others, especially my second wife and the two children we had together, with my alcoholism and my suicide attempts. It also reveals how desperately low my everyday life had spiraled. And perhaps it demonstrates, I'd like to believe, that in spite of my disgust with myself and my past, I was still trying to make things better.

What I can see now—and I didn't understand this as it was happening—was that part of what went so wrong in my thirties and forties was that I gave up on myself. I concluded that I was right about all my self-doubt, my self-loathing, and my conviction that I was making the world worse for everyone I loved. I felt like I had the hard evidence. So I acted in such a way that I further confirmed those convictions, and also to punish myself, and also to escape.

But something started to change when Rebecca, who had sole custody of Margaret and Portia, denied visitation. And I realized I had a choice: I could never see my daughters again, or I could find a way to regain her trust.

I would often give up on myself. Those were my most suicidal times. But then sometimes I'd think, *No, you can turn this around. You're not dead yet. Try harder.*

I'd promised Rebecca many times, with all my heart, "I'll never use again." Over and over again I'd pleaded with her: "Let me try to resume my normal life, I won't take another drink. Let me out of the psychiatric hospital, let me live like other human beings, trust me with my own existence: I promise, I don't want to die anymore, I won't attempt suicide."

My words became meaningless. She had no faith in what I

said. "Not that you lied to me, but that I can no longer believe you, has shaken me," Nietzsche remarked. Fair enough. But that you can no longer trust me makes us both pretty shaky.

My need to be believed didn't go away. Especially because—and ultimately only because—she was the mother of two of my children, which meant that in the short term she decided whether and when I was able to spend time with them. Perhaps more important, in the long term, her trust of me, or lack of it, would have an enormous impact on the development of the relationship between my daughters and me. How she saw and felt about me could not help but influence how they saw and felt about me. I knew this from my own experience of my parents' divorce and from being affected by their distrust of each other.

I can't tell you all the lurid details here, but one of the conditions of my current parenting plan with Rebecca, Case no. 1216-FC04987 in the Circuit Court of Jackson County, Missouri, is that I "refrain from the publishing of nonfiction books, nonfiction articles, or any other such nonfiction media that discuss any traumatic episodes that the children have experienced." So I cannot tell you any harrowing stories about drunken irresponsibility or stupidity that my children actually witnessed.

Like many children of alcoholics, Zelly, Margaret, and Portia have experienced traumatic episodes because of my addiction. I was just the other day talking to Portia, who at this writing is fifteen, about whether she and her friends are drinking or doing any drugs, and she told me: "I don't think I'm ever likely to drink, Dad. Because of how drinking was all around me when I was little."

None of these traumatic events were sexual or physically harmful, I would immediately like to add, just to allay your worst fears and maintain some shred of self-respect. The worst damage I have done to my children as a consequence of drinking has been the destruction of what they understood to be their family. Two divorces and three marriages create a lot of emotional havoc. The damage I did while actually drunk was mostly caused by them seeing me in a pitiful state. The damage I did by attempting suicide was done by me creating an atmosphere of fear and chaos. That same turbulent air made me desperate and frightened when my own father was falling apart. Especially with my suicide attempts, I have made my children feel that the world is fundamentally an irrational, unstable, and unsafe place.

Both my divorces were, in their way, suicide attempts, the kind where you are willing to take other people down with you. They were in their way murder-suicides. I imagined, like the suicidal me always does, that by divorcing, I could somehow escape the problems of my marriages and of family life, that I could hit the restart button and begin a new life. Having my children in that new life was absolutely essential to me—but now I'd get to parent them as I saw fit, without all the compromises of parenting together, and in a whole new and better way that I could only begin to imagine. I even had a kind of bardo experience, a between-lives experience, when I first left the house and everything was fluid, in motion, adrift, changing.

That was all bullshit. Which is not to say that no one should ever get divorced or that no good things came from my divorces: most important, four of my children would not exist if I hadn't remarried twice. But it is to acknowledge that my motives for divorce were really the same as my motives for suicide, and my expectations were equally fuzzy, confused, selfish, and stupid.

Zelly, Margaret, and Portia were sixteen, six, and four when everything took a radical turn for the worse both in my second marriage and in my so-called sobriety, and it was not easy on them. As of this writing, in 2022, they're twenty-seven, seventeen, and fifteen, and I know it still isn't.

There is something else I should say here, hard though it is: we now know that one of the most reliable indicators of suicidal thinking and predictors of a suicide attempt later in life is early childhood trauma. One major cause of or contributor to my own suicidal thinking is likely my parents' divorce, the nasty events that led up to it, and the even nastier things that happened after my mother's remarriage. But what have I done to my own daughters? I've put them through a divorce (in Zelly's case, two), I've had them watch all the fights and misery between parents that alcoholism can cause, and I've forced them to endure my subsequent struggle to reassemble the pieces of my own life and theirs, with mixed success. Not only have I likely passed on to them whatever biological factors may increase one's tendency toward anxiety, depression, and suicidal thinking, but I've also created the environment to catalyze that biology. The nature was not in my control, but the nurture (or lack of nurture) certainly was. Owning up to that fact doesn't change it. All I can do now is be watchful of their struggles, be loving when I see that they are in a rough patch (and strive to be keen enough to see it), and hope that they will have enough trust in me to reach out if they ever need to. Maybe I can now help to break the cycle.

My father used to tell me: "Your poor, poor mother, CW. The karma she'll be dealing with from the damage she did to you boys with the divorce. It'll be a thousand lifetimes before she burns through it all. It hurts me even to think of what she will have to suffer."

Yeah, Dad, karma's a bitch.

Trust is a bit like a right: we exchange liberties for protections because we want those protections, and we grant second chances for similarly practical reasons. A mother trusts her child because she doesn't want to have to watch him all the time—she wants some time to herself. An ex-wife trusts an addict ex-husband because she knows her children need both parents—and because she needs some help with the kids.

Let's return again to the dreadful winter of 2011. I had the affair, I started drinking again, and about a year and a half after my wife's and my initial separation, I agreed to give my soon-to-be-ex-wife sole legal and physical custody of our two young daughters. I would be allowed "reasonable" visitation rights, to be determined by her. I had quit drinking, but my soon-to-be-ex-wife had quit believing me. Or perhaps she understood from hard experience that my new sobriety was precarious at best. She needed guarantees, if I was going to visit the girls. She proposed random urine tests.

At first I refused. She shouldn't be allowed to tell me how and when I could see my own children! Though this was precisely what I had agreed to in the divorce decree. And I didn't have time to be driving several times a week to the nearest lab—a place called Quest—which was about twenty minutes away. And I couldn't afford the three to five hundred dollars a month the testing would cost. And anyway, it was none of her business whether I was drinking. All she should care about was whether I was drinking around the kids.

"Then you can't see the girls."

"They need to see their dad. And I need to see them."

"I agree. So get the tests."

Rinse, wash, repeat.

Maybe it wasn't really about the urine tests, my drinking, or even her not-unjustified fear of my attempting suicide while the girls were asleep in my apartment. (After all, I'd tried it at home before—though I don't think I would have tried unless my wife were there with them, for what very little that belief is worth.) Maybe it was about her anger and my capitulation to her demands. But maybe she also understood something I didn't: that I had to learn to trust myself before I could be sober and a decent parent again. To do that, I needed something to lean on. Since there was no magic pill I could take, I needed some other way of guaranteeing my reliability, of bolstering my will. Spending time with my own children was the carrot, but I also needed a stick.

A couple weeks went by without me seeing the kids; I relented. I started driving to Quest two or three times a week for urinalysis, fifty-five dollars a visit. The woman who worked there and owned the place would come into the bathroom with me and watch me take out my penis. Just observing.

"You'd be amazed at how many guys actually want me to watch them peeing," she told me. "Some demand it. If it's all the same to you, I'll just stand to one side and make sure you aren't using a catheter. I've seen every trick in the book."

"I have a bit of trouble peeing with someone watching," I said. "It's not you. It happens to me at urinals, too."

"Yeah, that happens a lot. Performance anxiety." She laughed.

I was standing there with my penis in my fingers and the little plastic cup, waiting.

After my initial resistance, getting tested regularly was strangely liberating. I'd listen happily, eagerly, for the call, which would come a day or two after each test: "Mr. Martin, you tested negative." My not-yet-ex-wife could call anytime she liked to confirm the results. I got to see the girls. They would spend the night in my new apartment, about a mile and a half from the old house, sleeping on hide-a-beds that rolled into the walls like drawers, which they thought was cool. We bought movies and games at Target, went to Science City and the mall. They got two golf-ball-size pet hermit crabs and kept them at my place. The crabs lived in identical clear plastic homes—side by side, so they could look at each other. Me and Hermie and Goldie at 4215 Locust. "As in a plague of locusts," I'd tell people when repeating my address.

After a few months of clean tests, my ex decided the testing was no longer necessary. A month or so later, visiting my girl-friend in New York, I ordered a whiskey while waiting for her at a bar near her office. I had this plan: I would drink only when I wasn't at home in Kansas City. After a few weeks, the plan changed. Now it was: I could drink outside Kansas City and have one or two beers on the plane. Then: Kansas City drinking was okay, but not when I had the girls.

One night Rebecca invited me over for dinner with her and the kids. I was anxious, scared even. It no longer felt natural to be around her and my daughters at the same time. She asked me to pick up a chicken, and on the drive to the grocery store, I was telling myself: *You're not going to have a drink, you're not going to have a drink.* By the time you're telling yourself that, you've already made up your mind. Or rather you're of two minds. Your front mind is saying, *Keep moving, don't look at those shelves, just walk on by.* Your back mind insists, *Listen to that front mind while you buy the booze. Listen to it while you drive with it in the bag. Listen to it all the way until we take a swallow.*

It was our old grocery store, the one where I'd always bought my booze when we were married. I grabbed the chicken; the liquor section was between me and the registers. I looked around furtively to see if anyone I knew might witness my fall. In the liquor section, they didn't have a half-pint of Jägermeister—years of secret drinking had taught me that a mickey would soothe without noticeably intoxicating me—so I bought a twenty-sixer.

Before I went into my ex-wife's house, I stashed it under a bush by the porch. Later, I offered to let the dogs out and had a quick belt or two.

I don't think she noticed I was drinking that night. But I was supposed to take the kids out for dim sum the next day, and I'd brought the bottle with me in my car to tame my hangover. I showed up thinking I felt okay. Rebecca glanced at me, and her face wrinkled with fury and disgust. "You're drunk," she said. Visitation stopped.

She wanted me to get an alcohol monitoring anklet. I wasn't sure that I trusted myself yet, so I went to get the anklet, but I thought, *Well, rather than having them report to her, I'll just give them my phone number, and they can report to me.* A deterrent. It would be like taking the drug Antabuse but without the vomiting if I slipped up.

From the website of the Kansas City branch of Electronic Sentencing Alternative:

> The patented SCRAM ankle bracelet is attached to the user with a durable and tamper-proof strap. It is worn 24/7 by the user for the duration of his or her court-ordered abstinence period. Every half hour, the bracelet captures transdermal alcohol readings by sampling the insensible perspiration collected from the air above the skin. The bracelet stores the data and, at predetermined intervals, transmits it via a wireless radio-frequency (RF) signal to the base station.

The eastern Missouri main office of Electronic Sentencing Alternative is in Blue Springs, about half an hour outside Kansas City. When I pulled into the parking lot of the little strip mall on the frontage road off I-70, I saw a cardboard sign stuck into the grass. WE BUY BROKEN GOLD, it read.

Inside, it looked like a shabby dentist's office. Another fellow was already sitting there in blue jeans and a Kansas City Royals jersey. I took a seat one over from him. The receptionist was on the phone.

"I understand that. I'm sorry, sir. Yes, we can send someone to the jail to attach the bracelet. No, I'm afraid you'll have to pay in advance. No, we can't send the device without the payment. I understand that they won't release you without the anklet." She rolled her eyes. "You can discuss that with your bail officer, sir. I have the number of several bail officers here if you'd like. No, I'm afraid there's nothing I can do." She hung up the phone. "Mr. Reynolds?"

The man in the Royals jersey leaned over to me. "You can beat it if you slip a piece of bologna between the anklet and your skin." Then he stood up. "Yes, that's me," he said, and went in.

When it was my turn, a woman in her midthirties, slender, friendly, but all business—she reminded me of an accountant I'd used back when I was in the jewelry business—told me to take a seat and pull up the leg of my jeans. She used a special tool, a secret custom screwdriver, to attach the device to my leg, while she explained the rules about bathing, exercising, and how the remote monitor worked. For my part, I explained that I was just using this as a deterrent, that it was for my own good. I didn't give her any phone number except my own.

"Is that comfortable? Not too tight?"

"If anything it's a bit loose," I said. "Is it going to slip down my ankle? I have skinny ankles."

She tightened it a bit, and I was on my way.

The experiment failed. After a few weeks, I got drunk with it on my ankle, fell down in a blackout, tried to kill myself by overdosing on Valium, and woke up in the hospital. But I learned something important from this experiment, which was that no device was going to keep me from drinking—or from trying to kill myself. And strangely, this liberated me from the idea that my wife or anyone else could control my behavior by making requirements of me. I realized that quite literally nothing could control me. So it didn't matter what she might ask of me. All that mattered was: Did I want to see my children or not? I did. So it wasn't that she was telling me what I had to do in order to see my own children. Rather, I was willing to do whatever it took so that I could spend time with them. That shift in my thinking was a crucial first step toward becoming something more than a Dino (a dad in name only), something like a real father again.

Barbara Ludlow, my first visitation supervisor, was a kind, soft-voiced, heavyset, very midwestern social worker whose office was in a tall, lonely brown brick building. Most of her work was with sex offenders, and she gave me the impression that for her, I was an easy case. She was especially sympathetic to people struggling with addiction. "I am a food addict," she told me, "so I know how hard it can be."

Barbara Ludlow was also direct. "You owe them an apology," she said, referring to Margaret and Portia, who were sitting with me at her conference table. Trying not to cry, I told my daughters I was sorry. The younger one climbed into my lap and hugged me; the older one, half-laughing, leaned far back in her chair. "You can't drink, Daddy!" she said. It was an admonition but also a request. She laughed as she said it because she was scared to say it to me straight.

I promised them that I never would again.

Barbara took me aside at the end of that visit. "You can't promise them that," she said firmly. It was the only time gentle Barbara spoke sharply to me. "Don't ever make a promise like that again. You don't know that you'll never take another drink. You can promise only that you'll try not to."

During the time the girls and I spent with Barbara Ludlow—one hour once a week—we drew pictures together and ate chocolate mini-doughnuts from the vending machine on the third floor. It often seemed like we'd all forgotten, at least temporarily, how unnatural our situation was. If you focused in tight enough, we seemed like a normal family: safe, happy, morally legitimate.

By the time Barbara announced that we no longer needed her help, I suggested to Rebecca that she had been right all along, and that I was happy to try an electronic alcohol monitor. At the SCRAM office they knew me, and they were happy to take me back. My second anklet went on.

This time around the anklet felt good where it was. It was a comfort to know it was there, proving to myself, my ex-wife, and all the world that I was a good person, an upstanding member of society. In my classes, pacing back and forth as I lectured, I worried that my students would notice the bulge beneath my pant-leg. It buzzed every so often against my anklebone, the medial malleolus, where I was getting a painful blister, and it was audible to me. Could they hear it? Could my students take seriously a philosophy professor—a guy up there talking about morality and the good life—who was in electronic handcuffs? I wanted to show it to them and tell them the story, but I knew the story would get around campus, and soon, with my luck, some parent would call the dean.

"Your corn is ripe today; mine will be so tomorrow," I read from David Hume one day. We were discussing Hume's notion of morality and mutual benefit. " 'Tis profitable for us both," I continued, "that I should labour with you to-day, and that you should aid me to-morrow. I have no kindness for you, and know you have as little for me. I will not, therefore, take any pains on your account; and should I labour with you on my account, in expectation of a return, I know I should be disappointed, and that I should in vain depend upon your gratitude. Here, then, I leave you to labour alone: you treat me in the same manner. The seasons change; and both of us lose our harvests for want of mutual confidence and security."

I finished quoting the passage and looked up at the students. My ankle did not buzz.

I had been wearing the second monitor for about a month, showering with one foot in the tub and one foot on the floor, growing accustomed to teaching and driving with the thing buzzing away, and to the callus that had formed where the blisters used to be, when I got an assignment from a magazine to go to Brazil for a story.

I needed the money, and it was an unusual opportunity to study a particular Tibetan Buddhist practice that fascinated me. There was no way I could wear the anklet through airport security in multiple countries, so I called ESA to ask what to do.

"You can't wear that out of state," the receptionist explained. "You can't just go on vacation with that anklet on. That's not the way this works."

I told her this was a work trip and reminded her that my monitoring was voluntary. She acted as if I were obviously lying to her. "Uh-huh. We can remove it. But we immediately call the court. Just so you know. They'll put out a warrant. It's a same-day thing."

"There's no warrant," I said. "There's no court. I was never arrested. I am doing this as part of a custody arrangement with my ex-wife."

"Uh-huh."

Going away to cover the story was making a big mess with my ex, Rebecca. The conversation with her about removing the anklet hadn't gone well. But in the end it hadn't really mattered, because she admitted that the anklet wasn't reestablishing trust with her anyway. She was convinced that I needed more supervised visitation. "You need coaching on how to be a good dad, Clancy," she'd told me. "Don't think of it as being monitored. Think of it as lessons on how to improve as a parent."

It might surprise the ears of other parents, but this was okay with me. It was, at this point, just one more hurdle being raised by the mother of my children, a person who had legitimate reasons to doubt my capacity to be a sane human being and a capable dad. I was starting to expand my perspective a bit, to see being a father in terms of months and years, rather than just the next upcoming weekend with the girls.

When I showed up at the office to have it removed, their skepticism was almost comical. *Here,* they thought, *is some guy who wants to go on a bender.* But there was no court order, and the only person on the notification list other than me was my ex.

"You know we'll have to call her," they said.

"Yes, of course," I said. "She knows."

Finally, reluctantly, the woman in charge took the anklet off. She looked up at me.

"Now, don't have too much fun," she said.

One of the reasons I abused alcohol was that I wasn't good at dealing with the responsibilities and stresses of being a parent. I seem to be improving lately, maybe. That is, when I'm depressed now, or even just having a bad day, I don't want a drink, and I don't tend to think that killing myself would improve matters for everyone. My mind might very well go straight to self-extermination, but I don't start planning to kill myself or tell myself, *No, I won't kill myself today, but maybe tomorrow.* I don't tend to go down the road of false-belief adjustment that might take me closer to the edge of disaster.

It used to be, when I returned my children to my ex, in that viciously lonely moment of separation, that what I wanted most was a drink. Back in the late 1990s, when I dropped Zelly off with her mom, taking her "home" after a weekend together, the first thing I did was drive to a 7-Eleven and buy a six-pack of Guinness. For twenty years, from 1994 to about 2014, the stress of parenting my children, as much as I love them, made me want to run to the nearest bar. Ashamed though I am to admit it, some days, when I was initially separated from my first wife and then my second, the fact that I didn't have the full-time job of raising my own children was a relief. (When I think of Zelly, Margaret, or Portia reading this, in this book, I don't know what to say, but I hope they'll call me if they want to talk about it.) That relief I felt at times about not being a full-time dad was further proof of something I really didn't want to admit to myself: that signing over full custody of my children to their mother had been another shameful act of fear. By giving up my rights to my children, I was giving myself a get-out-of-jail-free card. The kids were now her responsibility. If I fucked up, if I got drunk or killed myself, well, they had their mom. It was all right there on a legal document.

But I have to say these things if I also want to be able to say, sincerely, this equally true thing: that I want nothing more than to be a good full-time dad who shows his children all the love and care they deserve, and I am trying to be that dad. And this: that during all the time I spent away from them, I missed them and worried about them and felt ashamed that I wasn't with them and wasn't a better father.

When I first met Ronnie Beach, the soft-voiced, redheaded, fifty-four-year-old divorce mediator (and my second supervised visitation monitor), he was climbing out of his Honda with a bag of McDonald's in one hand and a milkshake in the other.

I had resisted Ronnie, because he came into your home, and he was with you every time you were with your kids. To me, it felt creepy, and it seemed to imply even creepier things about me. I thought the girls would also think it was weird, and that it would confuse them. And other people would think it was who-knew-what and probably jump to false conclusions.

"Rebecca, please don't make me do that again. I already did all that with Barbara. She said supervised visitation was unnecessary. She told you there was nothing to worry about."

"It's Ronnie Beach or nothing," she said.

I could accept some supervision, but I wanted a more blended approach. Something like a mix of parenting coaching and maybe urine tests. I called my lawyer. "We can fight it," she said. "It's definitely not something you need to agree to. No judge will require it in your case. But it might take a while before you see your girls."

"How long is a while?"

"I can't say for sure. A few months? If you want to see your kids right away, get Ronnie Beach," she said. "He has an impeccable reputation. You'll like him. He's a very nice guy. It's nothing to be afraid of."

Ronnie was a specialist in court-ordered supervised visitation. He cost a hundred dollars an hour, and we were going to be spending at least a couple of hours a week with him. "I know it sounds expensive," he said on the phone. "But when people tell me that, I ask them, 'How much are you paying your attorney?'"

In his office, the kind of modest, comfortable room one might expect a psychologist to rent out, he assured me that it was not at all unusual for couples to go through a period of supervised visitation without a court order.

"Whether or not a judge is involved, it's about reestablishing trust." Those were more or less the first words out of Ronnie's mouth, and they became my mantra. I couldn't talk my ex into trusting me; I couldn't even "sober" her into trusting me. I had to create the conditions under which she would decide, of her own free will, to trust me again.

"How long do you think this is going to take?" I asked.

"There's no way to know that for sure right now," Ronnie said. He was being very savvy. He knew that if he told me up front that it could be months, even years, I would freak out. "It's incremental. It takes patience. Let's get you spending time with your kids again, and then we'll see where we are."

Despite all my big talk about how I would do anything to see my daughters, I was not happy. Ronnie, I concluded, was going to be my daughters' new dad for the next year, and I was going to be his bumbling sidekick.

Our initial meeting with Ronnie was at Crown Center mall in downtown Kansas City. My daughters and their mom pulled up next to the fountain outside the large glass-fronted building while I waited inside and watched. Ronnie met Margaret and Portia at the car and walked them in.

"Ronnie is going to be hanging out with us today," I said. It still makes me sick to my stomach, writing this years later. "Sound good to you guys?"

They nodded, a bit carefully. They knew that something wasn't 100 percent right, but they were willing to play along. I hadn't told them what role Ronnie was going to be playing in our lives—just that he was going to be keeping us company during our visitation.

We went to Sheridan's Frozen Custard, where I got peanut butter custard, and Ronnie and the girls got Dirt & Worms. We strolled around the mall and shopped, and the girls and I played in the Crayola Store. After a couple of hours, we hugged good-bye, and Ronnie took them back to their mother's car.

The humiliation of this, I can't tell you what it was like. I can't even really imagine it myself anymore. But it was the only way I felt certain I was getting them back.

"On that first day," Ronnie told me later, "I gave you a B plus." He never told me what I'd done wrong. I was disappointed that I didn't make an A, but since I'm laying my cards on the table, I'm probably about a B-plus dad on my best days. I mean, don't get me wrong, I try hard to be a solid A dad. But I expect I'm still too selfish to earn really top grades. (To be totally fair, my wife Amie, my ex-wives, and the three of my children who are old enough to express an opinion all insist that today I have become an excellent and devoted father, and I hope it's true. On good days maybe I get an A-minus, for effort.)

The girls remained cautious around Ronnie. They were quiet and well behaved, always friendly and polite—they liked Ronnie okay—but part of his skill was making himself both ready to hand and unobtrusive. His calm, grandfatherly presence was always nearby, whether he was checking his email, writing in a notebook, or watching a movie with us at home. He'd play Scrabble with us if invited, eat pancakes, and sometimes take me aside to share observations, like "You're giving more attention to X than to Y." He was himself a father. But my daughters never got to know him well enough to let their guard down around him, which was a comfort. It wasn't that I worried they'd like him more than they liked me. But I worried that they might start to see us as co-dads, with Ronnie as Dad Number One and me as Dad Number Two. Maybe I was worried that they'd trust Ronnie more than they trusted me, or that, like their mom, their trust in me would depend on their trust in Ronnie.

Throughout Ronnie's supervision, I did not attempt to kill myself, and though I'm sure I often fantasized about it, this was a relatively stable time, suicide-wise, because I felt I was making moral progress. I saw myself as working hard to get my children back, so I congratulated myself on becoming a better person. Or at least, I seemed less contemptible to myself.

I recently asked one of my closest friends what had made Ronnie special. "I mean, he turned everything around in my relationship with Rebecca," I said, "but what did he *do*?"

"He made things normal again for you guys," she said. "He took what was degenerating into a very unnatural situation and put everything back on solid ground."

That was Ronnie's gift. He didn't just assure my ex that I could be a good dad to our daughters. He also reminded me that I *was* their dad, that I *was supposed to be* their dad, that I *had a right to be* their dad. Naturally, if you'd asked me then, I would have insisted, at every stage of this process, that I had both an obligation and a right to father my own children. But somewhere along the line, I had lost my conviction that this was true. Another ugly truth I shouldn't say, which is probably obvious to you, my reader: at some point in those dark years of 2009 through 2012, I had given up on myself as a father.

One afternoon, after we'd been doing our thing for several months, Ronnie called me and suggested that my ex and I talk about our parenting plan. "I don't think you guys need me at this point," he said. I don't know if the call was prompted by my ex: it may have been, thinking back on it now. At a minimum, it seems likely that he called her before he called me.

He arranged for the three of us—Rebecca, Ronnie, and me—to meet at a local coffee shop, and over the course of a couple of hours we came up with a plan that gave me regular, unsupervised time with the girls.

I walked into that coffee shop as a guy who couldn't see his children without someone else in the room. I walked out an ordinary divorced dad.

"As long as he's willing to agree to alcohol monitoring," Rebecca insisted. "I have to know he's not going to drink."

"That okay with you?" Ronnie asked me. "We'll get you a Sobrietor. When you're with the girls, you'll have to take a blow test every few hours. It's random, but it's not excessive. I've had good luck with them."

"That's fine with me," I said.

After we left the meeting, I called Ronnie. "You're like a wizard," I said. "I would have bet ten thousand dollars before we sat down that there was no way she was going to give me regular, unsupervised time with the kids. I don't know how you did it."

"I got there early on purpose, knowing she would be there early to talk to me. She asked me if she could trust you with the kids. I told her yes." He didn't add, *Don't make a liar out of me.*

At 10:46 a.m. on Christmas morning, my cell phone buzzed. I was at the dining room table wrapping presents. *Sobrietor reminder text: you may send your 11:00 a.m. test now. Do not reply to this text.*

The little blue light on the device flashed: I blew into it for four seconds. It clicked, registering my breath and taking a photo of my face. I waited for sixty seconds. Then my cell phone pinged, *Compliant report successfully sent.*

I kept my Sobrietor in three places in the house: in the butler's pantry by the microwave, upstairs on my bedside table, and in my desk drawer in my office. All three places allowed me to keep it plugged in but out of sight of my children. The Sobrietor was black, about the size of a large, fat billfold—the kind you can keep your checks in—with a replaceable plastic tube that stuck out of one end. Without the plastic tube, it didn't work: if you tried to blow directly into the monitoring hole, your face would be too close for the camera to get an accurate photograph. It was a good idea, I learned, to keep a back stock of plastic tubes—they were easy to lose. I kept a couple in my car and three or four in my desk.

Though I hadn't had a drink in a year, I still got an irrational jolt of pleasure every time that *Compliant report* text came through; it was like seeing an *A* on your report card or a wire transfer in your checking account. Often I'd blow a second time just to get a second confirmation, further proof.

I sent compliant reports from the Four Seasons in St. Louis, on a birthday trip for one of my daughters; from Worlds of Fun, Oceans of Fun, and Schlitterbahn; from gas stations and McDonald's drive-thru lines in Texas, Kansas, and Iowa City; from movie theaters all over Kansas City; from roller rinks, bowling alleys, community pools, and Deanna Rose Children's Farmstead; from the zoo, public parks, Home Depot, Target, Costco, restaurants, and ice cream parlors; from my daughters' elementary school. I shared more pictures of myself on my Sobrietor than I'd ever Instagrammed or Facebooked.

Normally when I used it, I was sitting in a men's room stall, hiding, feeling dirty, like a shoplifter, a criminal, a tearoom trader. I had no guilty pleasure to it, as I had with secret drinking, which also took place in a lot of bathrooms—only shame. Often the report wouldn't transmit, and I'd have to leave the bathroom and step outside to take the test again, in public, as discreetly as I could. People looked at me nervously as I was blowing into an object that resembled a *Star Trek* phaser.

Once at the YMCA pool on Troost Avenue, I was sending a report from the locker room when a young man grabbed my shoulder from behind. I turned around, Sobrietor in hand; the plastic blowing tube was pointing at him, so I pulled it out of the device and tried to put it into my pocket. Then I realized I didn't have a pocket: I was in my swim trunks. So I just stood there.

The young man was wearing a royal blue YMCA polo and khaki shorts. He had short brown hair. I was half-naked with a towel over my shoulder, my middle-aged body pale and saggy.

He frowned at me. He was probably twenty. "Excuse me, sir. What do you think you're doing?" He was trying not to tremble.

"It's a testing device. It's, you know, for alcohol monitoring. You blow in this tube"—I showed him the plastic tube, which now looked obscene—"and it takes your picture. . . ." I trailed off.

"There are no cameras permitted in the locker room, sir," he said, pointing to a sign. "You're gonna have to leave. I don't want to call the police."

I thought, *It's not enough that no one trusts me to stay sober. Now I'm going to be tried as a sex offender.* I make it sound as though I were merely annoyed and feeling sorry for myself; the truth is, I was terrified.

Then suddenly, unexpectedly, perhaps because of my obvious terror, the young guard seemed to understand the situation. His eyes changed; now they were worried, introspective. He looked as though he might have been thinking of someone he knew. He let me put my Sobrietor away in a locker, and I went out to the pool, my towel wrapped tightly around me.

Years ago, when I first stopped drinking, I was talking to a friend about his father's alcoholism. We were in New York at a bar together—I'd been sober about a year—and he was encouraging me to have a pint with him.

"All of you guys, the real alcoholics, start drinking again sooner or later," he said. "It's only a matter of time. You might as well start with me." I was hurt by his cynicism, but I understood where he was coming from. He'd watched his dad climb out of the bottle and fall back in again too many times. He was all out.

And once he'd given up on his dad, I also knew—though I didn't tell him this—that his dad had no longer had much reason to believe in himself. Don't get me wrong: this was not in any way my friend's fault; it was his father's. The addict, especially the addict parent, bears all the responsibility for the destruction of trust. But if you understand that you can't win back someone's trust, you will stop trying. Eventually, you'll give up any hope of trusting even yourself. This is one reason AA works, incidentally: the people in your AA group will go on believing in you no matter how many times you screw up. They teach you, slowly, how to trust yourself again.

By the time I hired Ronnie, I didn't trust Rebecca any more than she trusted me. She didn't trust me with the girls; I didn't trust that she really wanted them to see me. This is how the Sobrietor created some space, some psychological room to move around. It couldn't cure my drinking, any more than it could treat the darkest, most self-destructive parts of my personality. No external constraint, no blood test, Sobrietor, or Antabuse pill, not even a parent supervisor, can ensure sobriety. When all that stands between you and your addiction is someone or something, your desire to satisfy your craving will only increase, and inevitably, you will find some sneaky way around the constraint.

The Sobrietor liberated me from other people's excruciating doubt in me and also my own. I didn't just believe I could do it: it gave me the evidence. No one had to take me at my word that I was sober: it had been demonstrated. It was a fact. I was free to expect trust the way ordinary people do, and that expectation of trust bred more of the same. I was justified and felt self-justified. People could sense that I knew I deserved their trust. The more they gave me, the healthier and stronger I felt. Soon I found myself extending trust to people I had once viewed with wounded suspicion. I even started warily to trust Rebecca. And that air of trust made it easier to breathe. Whenever I did feel like shit was getting bad, I had a newfound confidence that I could handle it. I had done something that was good. I opened my mind to the possibility that I could be a good person.

"The best way to find out if you can trust somebody is to trust them," Hemingway wrote. Most obviously, yourself.

It's been about a decade since I sent my Sobrietor back to John Wells in Topeka. But I still remember the great satisfaction of packing up that black plastic son of a bitch in a padded envelope, then folding the envelope into a FedEx box and overnighting it down south. It wasn't freeing exactly; after all, I'd always been free to do what I wanted. I'd been free to see my children or not to see my children; free to drink or not to drink; free to try to work things out with my ex or to suffer the (yes, sickening) consequences of not finding a solution to visitation; free to exit the whole situation by abandoning everyone and killing myself. But the urine tests, Barbara Ludlow, Ronnie Beach, and the Sobrietor slowly, slowly taught me something: I am not the underground man who will demand his freedom even if it makes him sicker. Freedom is only as good as the range of good choices it provides, and all my good choices involve other people.

Maybe I was afraid of Rebecca. Certainly, part of my motivation was fear of her, and also fear of what my children would think if I failed, and fear of what would happen to my marriage to Amie. Many of my male friends have asked me: "Why didn't you man up and fight her for custody like a normal person? Why did you lie down and let her tell you what to do?" My attorney Amanda Kivett said the same thing. I was a coward, but this way I was a coward who got to see his kids.

Thinking about it in terms of cowardice and courage has long been beside the point. It's been years since my daughters worried about me drinking. When I talk to them about alcohol, they don't seem nervous. Zelly, the eldest, tells me she's proud of me for quitting. Margaret and Portia are sensibly cautious of alcohol—their mother eventually concluded that she had alcohol use disorder and also quit drinking—but they don't think of me as a drinker at all. They will talk about Ronnie if prompted, but they don't have much to say about him. Once in a while, if I'm thinking of him, I'll say, "Remember Ronnie Beach?" And they'll say something like, "Oh yeah, he liked Dirt & Worms," and laugh.

It still makes me sick to my stomach to remember Margaret, leaning back in her chair and saying, half-laughing: "You can't drink, Daddy!" Sometimes when I look at her—she's seventeen as I write this, and will be eighteen soon—I remember that look on her face as a little girl, protesting, hoping that I was listening, trying to tell me the simple truth about what she could see and I hadn't yet understood. *Yes, that's right, honey. I can't drink.*

I sometimes wish there were a Sobrietor for suicide. Not a device or a test that would predict whether you are likely to attempt it, or show your present risk of making an attempt—some people have tried to develop those—but something that could warn you right before you made an attempt. But it'd be a little too easy to outwit such a device: with many methods one might use to kill oneself, by the time they got to the scene, you'd be dead.

One of my closest friends told me recently that his mother had just attempted suicide. She was physically okay, was being transferred to the psychiatric ward, and would soon be on her way to a better facility. I wondered how I would feel if my mom tried to kill herself.

This is quite different than the question of whether my dad killed himself. I do feel responsible for his death and always will.

But that's because I could have liberated him from that psychiatric hospital, as he begged me to do, and I didn't.

But my dad's mental health had been degenerating for a long time, and that was out of my control. My brothers and I had tried so many ways of helping him (admittedly, none of them very wise). If my mom tried to kill herself, I would blame myself in a different way. I wouldn't feel that there was one particular action I should have done that I didn't. I would feel that I had failed to show her how much I loved her, how much I needed her, how much good she had done for me. If she tried to commit suicide, I would blame myself in an emotional and spiritual way. And I wouldn't think it was my fault, I would know it was my fault.

This recognition is what I have to try to synchronize with the desire to kill myself, when it comes. That my children would feel the exact same way I imagine myself (and my friend) feeling, and that they would be profoundly mistaken, but there would be no fixing it, no helping them through it, no recovery. In the past when I tried to kill myself, I ignored the screaming fact of how it would make my children feel (not to mention what it would do to my mom, my brothers, and my spouse).

I'm reminded of that Keanu Reeves line from the movie *Parenthood*: "You need a license to buy a dog, or drive a car. Hell, you need a license to catch a fish! But they'll let any butt-reaming asshole be a father."

Yup, they'll let any butt-reaming asshole be a father. All you can do is keep on trying to do better.

A Good Death?

What if I'd succeeded in killing myself one of those times I've tried? What if I'd gone into a bathroom and hung myself or slashed my wrists in the tub, and it stopped my heart and my brain turned off, and I came back out but forgot—as I always forget, when dreaming, that I'm asleep in bed—and now I was wandering about in some land of the dead, obliviously serving time for a crime against myself and my family that I might never remember?

In the fall of 2020, on a warm morning during some of the worst days of the coronavirus pandemic, I had a big fight with my wife in a coffee shop and went to lick my wounds in the bathroom. When I emerged, I noticed two young women sitting at a table and staring at me with open reproach. I didn't understand until I was on my way out and realized that, after washing my face and my hands in the bathroom, I'd forgotten to put my mask back on. (At this time during the pandemic, in Kansas City, people were wearing masks even when seated at tables in coffee shops, lowering them only when actually drinking or eating.) I stepped outside into the sunlight to walk up the street and saw a white building with a big black sign that read BARDOT, the Tibetan word for the often-nightmarish world between lives. (I googled it later and found it was the name of a business, a "luxury wedding and event space"—a little too apt, given my life.)

Up the sidewalk ahead of me and behind me coming my way were people in masks, and I thought, *Well, if I were watching me in a movie, I'd think, come on, at least now he will figure it out: he's already dead.*

Someone who started a motorcycle behind me was playing Pink Floyd's "Breathe" loudly on the stereo. This song had mattered a lot to me when I was a teenager. The temperature was in the seventies, it was sunny and breezy on that Sunday, September 13, 2020, in downtown Kansas City. I was standing in an empty parking lot, trying to think of where to go next.

I thought, *In the old days, in these circumstances, I'd go get a beer.* But I didn't want a drink. Sometimes, in these circumstances—especially if downtown, as I was—I'd scan the buildings for likely rooftop patios, high and accessible. But I didn't want to kill myself. I wanted to call my wife and make the first move toward ending the fight by telling her I was sorry.

In 2016 a friend who had been emailing me for a few years about his wish to die committed suicide, and I decided to look more closely at death. For all my thinking about killing myself and trying to do it, I had never really gotten intimate with the fact of a dead body or even with people who were dealing with the recent death of a loved one.

I began a kind of death investigation. I attended meetings of a terrific group dedicated to thinking more honestly about death called the Death Café. In these gatherings, which are a bit like AA meetings, people get together and talk openly about their feelings about mortality, both their own and that of the people they love. I hosted a Death Café meeting in Austin, Texas, with my wife Amie and my eldest daughter, Zelly.

But I didn't stop there. I visited several mortuaries and talked with their staffs. I attended a class on how to become a mortician at a community college in Kansas City, and I discussed the death business with the students. I went out to visit a very old woman who, according to her hospice nurse, had officially been dying for several years and could have died at any moment but was just going on living with death at her door.

But after all that, I still hadn't done what I most feared, that I had dreaded for years, and that had kept me from applying to medical school when I was trying to decide between that career and becoming a philosopher: I hadn't participated in the dissection of a cadaver.

It wasn't difficult to arrange. I emailed the dean of the school of medicine at my university—she was a friend of mine—and asked for an introduction to the appropriate professor, Dr. Caroline Rinaldi. Then the two of us talked on the phone: naturally, she wanted to understand my motivations. On the face of it, just asking to dissect a human body was more than a little odd.

"I'm a writer," I told Dr. Rinaldi, "and lately I'm writing about death. So I'm trying to understand it a bit better." I told her that I had always been afraid of dead bodies, and this was a significant reason I hadn't become a doctor. We talked about death for half an hour or so—I explained the other investigations I had conducted and told her about my own personal connection with death through suicidal ideation—and she told me which lab I would be visiting. We set a date.

When I came into the lab, the dead woman was already on the dissecting table. She had a large yellow cardboard tag hanging from her ear: NB-14-514. She was still lying mostly in the thick clear vinyl bag with a knot tied at one end that they delivered her in, and she had an orange and black rope beneath her that would have been tied beneath her arms to hoist and carry her.

Dr. Rinaldi and I said hello. She was a young, enthusiastic, redheaded professor of medicine, not the type you might expect to find dissecting dead humans. We were alone in the gross anatomy dissection room with the corpse of an old woman. I cut a four-inch square into the skin on the back of the hand of this woman of indiscernible race—she was concrete gray—and I tugged at it with a pair of tweezers while I used the scalpel to separate the skin from the fat. The skin had a tendency to tear if I pulled too hard, so I had to make gentle slices beneath in order to peel it away. Her thoracic cavity was open, and I held her heart and her lung and touched her aorta—which was crunchy, a sign of bad diet—and her liver. I was nauseated and dizzy. The dead woman had been shaved but still had traces of hair on her head and her pubic area. She was, I guessed, in her sixties. Her chin was round, and her eyes were bluish-white, and I had the unexpected, tender and frightening impulse to kiss her.

"It's really a privileged club," Dr. Rinaldi said. "What we're doing is so socially unacceptable. It's standard practice in medical school, but most people won't even teach it. The students don't like to talk about it outside the classroom. When I teach it, I explain to my students it's the first patient's body you're entrusted with."

Her entire body was there, and we were cutting it into different pieces. It was just the three of us: me, Dr. Rinaldi, and the old dead woman in UMKC's Cadaver Lab. This was the closest I'd ever been to a dead body. Before this, I suppose, I had seen one made up like a wax figure in a casket for a funeral, and I'd seen wrapped bodies being carried to funeral pyres on the banks of the Ganges. I'd held my father's ashes in the box mailed to me from the crematorium in Florida. But this was a real dead person I was touching.

"When my mom died," Dr. Rinaldi said, while I separated yellow tissue with tweezers, "I understood the concept of the wake. Leaving the body out—I get that now. You went out and visited it for a few days—even if it was a child—and you knew when it was time to bury it, because the body was changing—you could see that she wasn't there anymore. When my own mother died, I wasn't ready to let her go. We are so sterile." By which she meant we don't let ourselves feel the things that we naturally should feel and in fact really are feeling. "We aren't experiencing these things that will allow us to let go. Here try these," she said, and gave me a pair of scissors.

I held the dead woman's hand as I used the small, sewing-sized scissors to separate her veins and tendons from the connective tissue. I pushed the point of the closed scissors into the tissue and then opened them to pull the flesh away. Her nails were long, and her hand felt like, well, a hand—not like a corpse's hand, though her temperature was neutral.

"The hand is one of the most difficult things to dissect," Dr. Rinaldi warned me, a gentle expression in the wrinkles of her eyes. "It's very intimate, very human."

The dead woman didn't smell of anything. But the Cadaver Lab had just been repainted, it was a pale blue-gray, and the smell of paint was strong. Water dripped. I tried to remember those lines from Akutagawa's story "The Life of a Stupid Man": "His friend bent over one corpse, peeling back the skin of its face with a deftly wielded scalpel. An expanse of beautiful yellow fat lay beneath the skin."

I was swallowing too often, and Dr. Rinaldi checked my eyes. "Are you okay? We can stop?"

"No, I'm okay," I lied. I continued to work on the flexor tendon. I looked at the dead woman's quiet face again, her soft round chin, her neck, her flat breasts. When I changed instruments, I rested my scalpel or scissors on her belly.

"At the Cadaver Lab when I was a grad student, there was only one custodian who would go in there. They don't like to come in here either," she said. "I remember one guy told me, 'I'm the only one who will go in there. Because I was in Vietnam.' I always thought that was a bit odd."

I kept looking at the huge opening in the woman's diaphragm where her heart and kidneys rested. Her stomach had been removed. While I worked with the scalpel again—trying to pretend I wasn't about to pass out—I told Caroline the story of Dan Nicolas, who I'd met a few days earlier at an Embalming Theory class in the mortuary science program at Kansas City Community College.

"He was a marine, and one day during a training accident a bunch of his buddies were blown up. 'We had to go pick up the body parts. A lot of the guys had a fear of the dead bodies,' Dan told me, 'But I've never had that. I think being an embalmer, a funeral director, is a way to help a lot of people that most folks just can't do.'"

"Most people won't teach Gross Anatomy either," Dr. Rinaldi told me. "There's a dream a friend of mine had repeatedly, and I've had it, too. You're in the middle of a dissection with your whole class there, and suddenly the cadaver sits up. It's alive. And you don't know if you should kill it or what to do next."

I tugged at the tendon with the tweezers.

"There, now you've got it," she said. "Good work. You've got a second career as a surgeon if you want one. Have you had enough, or . . . ?"

When we left the lab, a painter was talking on his phone. "There's a cadaver in there," Dr. Rinaldi warned him, and he spun on his heel and walked quickly away, down the hall.

Once I was outside, I lay down on my back in the grass with the sun on my skin. I felt like I owed an apology to the dead woman inside, and also that she had told me something I had to remember but was afraid to believe. The voice I had in my head was saying, *It's not so bad to be dead. It's quiet. It's over.*

I was lying in the grass, a little cold in the winter sun, listening to the traffic, worrying about my usual worries: the kids, Amie, money, career. I wasn't sure how real the worries were—or unreal. I wasn't sure I even wanted to be worrying or would rather be looking at my phone, or checking my email, or reading a novel, or making love to my wife. Was I feeling fortunate to be alive? That woman did not have my good luck. What did that mean, to be lucky to be me and alive? I couldn't sort it all out. But I understood that I was still here, living, and she was back inside there, dead.

I thought with clarity, maybe for the first time in my life: *I don't want that. I don't want to be dead.*

Most people, suicidal or not, are not going to undertake this little Virgilian trip into the underworld. And I want to provide some reasons for other people, not just me, to go on living. And that's a very tricky thing to do.

In his essay "Is Life Worth Living?" the great American philosopher and psychologist William James put the difficulty like this: "What I propose is to imagine ourselves reasoning with a fellow-mortal who is on such terms with life that the only comfort left him is to brood on the assurance, 'You may end it when you will.' What reasons can we plead that may render such a brother [or sister] willing to take up the burden again?"

The way you might try to persuade a person not to take a drink isn't quite the right way to go about it. You have to be sneakier than that. You have to talk them around the drinking-thinking until they convince themselves that they don't want the drink. Similarly with suicide. You have to find a way to let them talk until they remind themselves that they actually don't have to do it. An alcoholic has to remind themselves that there's nothing sexy about the whole thing, nothing fun, nothing cool, nothing liberating. For the suicidal person, you might help her remember that she has things to live for, that there is more to life than her present agony.

William Styron wrote, on how to help the depressed and suicidal:

> It is of great importance that those who are suffering a siege, perhaps for the first time, be told—be convinced, rather—that the illness will run its course and that they will pull through. A tough job, this; calling "Chin up!" from the safety of the shore to a drowning person is tantamount to insult, but it has been shown over and over again that if the encouragement is dogged enough—and the support equally committed and passionate—the endangered one can nearly always be saved. Most people in the grip of depression at its ghastliest are for whatever reason, in a state of unrealistic hopelessness, torn by exaggerated ills and fatal threats that bear no resemblance to actuality. It may require on the part of friends, lovers, family, admirers, an almost religious devotion to persuade the sufferers of life's worth, which is so often in conflict with a sense of their own worthlessness, but such devotion has prevented countless suicides.

Styron was writing from his own experience as a depressed and suicidal person, and for people who have friends or loved ones who are depressed or suicidal, his advice is very good. It is also a good reminder for people who are depressed, suicidal or both, that if you can reach out, you should. People will surprise you. If you can call someone, do. Show them that there are people out there who want them to go on living. And you could always remind them that this feeling will pass. Tell them it feels irrefutable and inescapable, but if they can just hang on for another day, their very own mind will bring help.

Probably the most influential American writer on how to prevent suicide was Edwin S. Shneidman. He spent his career working on the problem of how to talk people out of killing themselves. Most immediately, he advised trying to do three simple things: "Reduce the pain; remove the blinders; lighten the pressure—all three, just a little bit." Ideally, a friend or a therapist helps us to do this. But these are also things we can do for ourselves.

REDUCE THE PAIN

The key here is the idea of reduction. You're not trying to eliminate the pain, merely to lessen it. It's okay to baby yourself in those moments. Even something as simple as a cup of tea could help. And never underestimate the power of crying.

The pain is a mental thing—it's fear, it's panic, it's regret, it's anguish, it's heartbreak, it's overwhelming rage, it's shame, it's the unbearable awfulness of being oneself. But it's hard to change thinking from the inside, so the easiest way to reduce that pain is to change something physical. Change rooms, for a start. Change activities. If you've been looking at your phone or your computer, put it away and go outside. Listen to a favorite song on the phone. (American folk music and blues seem to help me, weirdly. Joni Mitchell and Jimi Hendrix are strong medicine.) Eat a few bites of overpriced ice cream. Look at the garden, water it, or pull a few weeds.

If you can text or email or call someone you care about who is not a direct cause of your distress, I believe that can help. Even watching a movie, maybe especially one you know and love, could lessen the pain a little bit. Thinking now about what movies I could have ready to hand the next time I feel like killing myself feels like a healthy exercise. It may sound silly, but as I've often put it to myself: *You're about to commit suicide, it's not like time is an issue, you're about to give all yours away, why not watch a movie first?*

REMOVE THE BLINDERS

By "removing the blinders," Shneidman meant that much of our darkest imagining comes from focusing on a particular aspect of our lives and not seeing our pain in its larger context. The pain creates the blinders, which in turn reinforce it. It's like when you bang your head into something or stub your toe: suddenly all you can think about is that pain. But if you can expand your attention away from the pain, the pain already seems—and is—less important, less compelling.

Andrew Solomon told me that one key to making it through a moment of crisis is remembering that you've been here before and that you survived it and rediscovered joy on the other side (see Appendix I). The crisis therapist Candice Biggins told me she always advises people to stretch their perspective (see also Appendix I). Wearing blinders is a bit like being in a ferocious argument with someone you love: in the flames of rage, you can see only how you are right and the other person is wrong. But it's always more complicated than that—and thinking in rage never solves the problem.

Removing the blinders is not easy. The blinders of my pain restrict my thinking to seconds, or minutes, or maybe hours if I'm lucky. Removing them, these days, means trying to think about people other than myself. Thinking about my children and remembering happy times with them, or thinking about things that seem to be going well in their lives now, helps me to remove the blinders. Thinking about my brothers Darren and Pat, that yes, they're doing okay, they're down in Texas, living their lives, takes the blinders down a little bit. Thinking about happy times with my wife, like hunting around little towns in Cuba so to buy a shovel to plant a peace vase, or lying in bed at night after our son has fallen asleep and watching TV, can help remove the blinders. Sometimes even reflecting on tiny little examples of progress I've made in my life, like learning how to fix a pipe in our basement rather than calling a plumber, can help me remove the blinders.

It's hard to convince yourself that you have felt this way before and that you will feel better again. It can be so hard to believe that you will ever be in less pain than you are right now. If I can try to think about areas of my life or my past that aren't acutely painful and that may even be good and happy, that helps me to remove the blinders a little bit. I'm not as loathsome as I think I am. I even sometimes make people laugh. Sometimes after a good class my students seem fulfilled, and suddenly they love Audre Lorde or Gerard Manley Hopkins or Søren Kierkegaard or Simone de Beauvoir or Rabindranath Tagore. I don't always only project badness into the world, even if I'm feeling bad right now.

LIGHTEN THE PRESSURE

The pressure is the world, everything the world is demanding of you, but also yourself, everything you are requiring of yourself, and your awful, mistaken, but very common and understandable view that you are not okay.

Lightening the pressure may seem insignificant. Sometimes when I am in an absolute panic about work pressure, answering just one email—ideally, one I felt I wasn't up to replying to—suddenly makes it a bit easier to breathe. Sometimes the pressure is feeling like I can't do it all: my job, my marriage, my parenting, driving the kids around, getting out of bed at five a.m. with the baby, writing, keeping up with my friendships, making the bed, folding all that laundry . . . it's just too much. Then I might text a friend I haven't been in touch with for a long time just saying, *What's up?* Or I could go fold a few of the clean clothes heaped on the sofa by the laundry room and put them away (not all of them). Or I might check in with my wife and say, *Holy shit, are you feeling as overwhelmed as I am right now?* And if she isn't, good news, she helps me to remember that we can get through this, and if she is, good news, I'm not in this alone. These are small things but they are lifesaving techniques.

I was talking to a friend about this book recently, and she

asked me what I could say to someone who was thinking about killing herself, and I naturally asked her if she was in this situation. She assured me she was just thinking about the question intellectually. So I asked her a few more questions and then, comforted that she wasn't actually feeling suicidal, told her what I do in fact normally say.

Then I asked her what she would say, and she said, "I don't know. I guess I would ask them why they were wanting to kill themselves. I guess I would say, 'Please don't.'" I liked that response. *Please don't*. Sometimes that might be the best thing a person who is feeling suicidal could hear. *Please don't*.

If you are reading this and contemplating suicide, I want to say, I know how intense your pain is right now. I understand that you feel both that there is no reason to live and that dying would end that pain—or if not end it, at least change it. I know you want solutions. I totally get it. But I want to ask you, as the person writing this book, not to kill yourself. At least not today. The door is always open—so for today, leave it open.

At the end of Yiyun Li's novel *Where Reasons End*, the narrator, a mother, is in dialogue with her dead child who has committed suicide:

"Answers don't fly around like words," I said.
"Questions do, right?" he said.
"Indeed, they do," I said.

We're never going to get all the answers, and maybe we don't have to. We can keep it as simple as getting through the day. Let's not overthink it. We don't have to know so very much about what tomorrow may hold or even about ourselves. Searching for answers may just increase the pressure. Maybe we can lighten things up and just let the questions fly around.

Increasingly, maybe due to getting older, I run into people who are thinking about how to die well. It's the summer of 2020, and we've been in lockdown in Bir, Himachal Pradesh, India, for a few months. I've been having daily AA/NA meetings with my landlord. He is a recovering heroin addict and told me a story about when he was still a daily user of "brown sugar" (heroin that you smoke rather than inject).

"I used to go to the bathroom, smoke a little, and then come back to work," he said. He was sitting opposite me on a brown leather chair at the bar in the kitchen. Behind him was the big window that looks out at the snow-covered tops of the Dauladhar Mountains. "And at some point I came across this book by Friedrich Nietzsche called 'A Good Death.' And I thought to myself, what kind of life would I have to have in order to have a good death? I would need good experiences. Conversations with my family, my friends, sharing people's inner lives. That's not a small thing. And I didn't have that. I would need a totally different life than the one I had. And now, I feel like, that's what I have. Today and yesterday, that's what the day was, when I talked to my wife and my son, and some people I met in the village. I don't want to take anything for granted. I'm not a gratitude person, I don't make gratitude lists. And I know tomorrow could be terrible. I even expect that. But today I feel like, you know, I have that. I don't have to die in awful, ghastly circumstances. I could die a good death."

The story made an impression on me. I do have the choice between dying in fearful, miserable circumstances with nothing but regret and unhappiness behind me—the situation of killing myself—and trying to live long enough so that when I die I feel like I have done what I could to have a happy rather than an unhappy death. Instead of trying only to escape life, I could come to understand it as an opportunity, not one I've already squandered but one I get only by continuing to live. Chögyam Trungpa Rinpoche said, about death: "There is a glory and a humor in it. You don't need to die filled with remorse; you could die happily."

I like the suggestion that by doing nothing more than continuing to live, opportunities for a better death arise. At a minimum, I avoid a death that I know would be lonely and shameful.

At the very moment I am writing these paragraphs, Amie has walked by me on the veranda with Ratna in her arms. Ratna is singing a line from a song in the movie *Cars* (his favorite movie at the moment): "There's a blue sky / waiting, right behind the clouds." I am getting too old and too superstitious to think that this kind of thing is mere coincidence.

Not long after my conversation with the landlord, he and I had a huge argument, over a blanket he no longer wanted us to use, and we moved out of his apartment. The tension of the lockdown had us all on the rack, and our sinews and tendons finally snapped.

Now we are living in the back half of a long garage with three steel shutters in front, painted in bright yellow with Ambuja Concrete advertisements. Across the street is a small lot where a local entrepreneur keeps several large red buses that normally take people to Shimla, Mandi, Palampur.

On the front half of our building are two garage bays with the owner's car and his silver Mahindra SUV; in the third is his small tuck shop, where I go every morning to buy water, cardamom for our tea, honey from his beehives, and staples like onions, potatoes, rice, and beans. This morning I was buying paper napkins, because we had run out of toilet paper, and two bags of toned milk (a mix of buffalo milk and powdered milk), because the guy who brings us a liter of fresh cow's milk every morning had not yet arrived and we were out. I'm getting pretty good at making Indian tea, and we drink it all day long.

I wish things hadn't ended badly with our former landlord. He and I had a lot in common: fathers, former entrepreneurs, addicts. He told me that he spent his whole first year here in Bir wanting to kill himself. The first few times he mentioned it to me, he said he had been "in danger of self-harm." Later, he told me that he "left Delhi to avoid self-harm." Finally, after some days he admitted that the only reason he'd moved up to the mountains was that he otherwise planned to kill himself and so he figured he had nothing to lose, and that for his whole first year here he was plagued with thoughts of suicide, but that also the first peace he'd experienced was up here and that his bouts of suicidal depression were growing less and less frequent. I worry for him that the change of air and scenery—and above all, the change of people, and getting away from the difficulties of his family life and the oppressive effect that the success of his "batchmates from India's second-best business school," about whom he was still constantly complaining—that the effect of these changes would wear off, after a time, and the deeper problems would resurface.

One time my brother Darren was complaining about his present wife Chrystal, and then he said, "You know Heather"— his first wife—"was just the same way as Chrystal. She was just like this." (I'd rather not say what the actual problem was.)

I laughed. "Yeah, me too, three different wives, three different people, exact same problems. Kind of makes me wonder what the problem really is."

"I always used to say that about you—you take perfectly normal women and turn them into demons."

He wasn't getting my point. "I guess it could be that," I said. "But actually, I was thinking that if I keep having the same problem with three very different people, maybe they're not the problem."

This is a cliché observation, but it really did take me three marriages even to start to see that my problems, whatever they were or whoever they involved, were *my* problems. It wasn't that I accepted that I couldn't change the actions, words, thoughts, and feelings of my wife. That may also be true, I don't know. But the point I had to understand was that she wasn't my problem, I was my problem. She may or may not be able to help me with my problems—it depends on the problem. Just as I may or may not be able to help her with hers. But when it comes to my problems, they are not hers or yours or even really ours. (It's very easy to try to avoid responsibility for my problems by making them community property.) They're just my problems. And it's okay to talk about them or whine about them or feel sorry for myself.

Still, making a change may help. Moving out of my landlord's apartment just solved a big problem—he was openly harassing me and had begun to send sexually suggestive and coercive WhatsApp messages to Amie. And this fellow's escape to the mountains reminded me of when I first moved from Dallas to North Carolina, and also when I moved from North Carolina to Austin. In both moves, I worried, *You can't run away from your problems, Clancy. You take your problems with you wherever you go.* And I did take a lot of my problems with me.

But I did leave some of the problems behind, or they were simply a consequence of my needing to be somewhere else. Leaving Texas was the best way I could see to get out of the jewelry business, which was making me miserable, and it worked. If I had stayed in that business, I suspect that sooner or later my gun-in-the-mouth phase would have started up again. I came back to Texas because I missed six-year-old Zelly too much, we had been apart for several months, and I couldn't walk past a playground without feeling sick with guilt and worry and bringing myself to tears. But as soon I was back, we were together every week.

In his autobiography *Ecce Homo*, Nietzsche wrote about finding the right place to live, the right people to be with, the right books to read (spiritual nutrition, he called it), and even the right foods to eat and things to drink. He recommends avoiding coffee, beer, and wine—and notes that they are particularly bad for him, and he must avoid them at all costs. He goes on to include even the weather:

> To the question of nutrition, that of place and climate is of equal importance. No one can live everywhere and anywhere; and he who has great duties to perform, which will require all his strength, may have a very limited choice. The influence of climate on the body, affecting its flourishing or withering, extends so far, that a poor choice of place and climate may not only alienate a person from his goals and opportunities, but prevent him from seeing them at all.

When I first read this in my late teens, I thought, *It can't be like that!* The grand questions of the meaning of my life, my goals and my dreams, can't be matters of the weather and what I eat! But because I loved and revered Nietzsche—and I still love and recommend his work—I read it all metaphorically.

It can and should be read that way. Nietzsche is not talking only about the most ordinary things, he is also talking about how and why we value them at all. But like any master ironist, he also means exactly what he says: it *is* as simple as learning to trust your own body, your own circumstances, your own psychology, your own spirit, as discovering what contributes to your flourishing and what may interfere with it. He extends this to choosing one's friends carefully, and he also mentions exercise, insisting that one can do one's best thinking—as he himself, he says, has always done his best thinking and writing—while moving, ideally hiking out in nature.

I have come to see, in the past eight or nine years, that it is this simple: I have to think of myself like the plants in my garden, which grow or die depending on the sun, the soil, the water, their location, et cetera.

But as a beginning gardener, I can tell you it's not simple at all. It takes a lot of practice, a lot of trial and error, a lot of work, and above all the will to flourish, in order for the process to work. It's easy to care for and love my garden, because every day I can look at it and see new growth and places where it's struggling and I can feel satisfied that the green things are getting bigger and greener and the flowers are blooming, and I can put on my gloves and dig around the soil to try to correct problems and prune and weed. It's much more difficult to exercise that same care with myself, because I don't see the results as quickly or as vividly. Plus my garden doesn't have guilt, shame, or regrets; it doesn't gossip or have other bad habits; it doesn't disappoint people or break promises; it hasn't fucked anything or anyone up.

When I was a drinker, I would sometimes marvel at nondrinkers like my brother Patrick. *Doesn't he get sick of the smell of himself? I wondered. Doesn't he need to turn off his personality? Doesn't he need to escape . . . himself?* I even saw it as a kind of insensitivity as if my own inability to abide Clancy were spiritually admirable. Part of the self-contempt is also self-congratulation.

For me, drinking was, more than anything, getting away

from me. Turning off me. And escaping me was definitely what I missed the most about drinking, and what was most difficult about the first couple of years of living without the tranquilizer of alcohol. Other tranquilizers I took suppressed the feeling of being me—made the smell of myself less pungent—but I was still very much there. But in getting drunk, I could really disappear into a blackout: gone.

But once I was forced to live with myself again—as I had done as a child, before I started drinking—very slowly I learned to resist myself less. Clancy was scaring me less, panicking me less, making me choke less than before, making me less claustrophobic. True, I was just as selfish as ever, but I was losing the habit of trying to escape me.

One of my students said to me recently, "You do everything so slowly!" No one had ever said that to me before. People had always told me to slow down, to be more careful: and to be fair, I still hear that a lot. But I found this complaint—and she was complaining—to be truly encouraging. Maybe I am slowing down a bit.

I recently saw a video of myself playing with my two-year-old son, and I thought, *Jesus, you are so frantic, so spastic, so hysterical. Take a breath! Calm the fuck down!* This was encouraging too, because I'm not sure I would have noticed before. I might have thought, *Well, you're trying to be a good dad, you're trying to play. Look how hard you're working to entertain him!*

And yet I still have fits of panic and despair all the time. And as I said at the outset of this book, very recently I went through an intense—albeit happily quite brief, maybe a month or two—spell of really scary depression. So I can pontificate grandly about gardening and nutrition and living in the right place with the right people, but what I'm also wanting to say is that when I'm angry, or in despair, none of the things I can do ever help very much, if at all. So I can just try not-doing.

Voltaire wrote, "An almost infallible means of saving yourself from the desire of self-destruction is always to have something to do." That is true: staying busy, having a purpose, helps me to avoid dwelling on and exaggerating my problems. Distracting oneself from pain is one way of avoiding pain, and distracting oneself from the thought of suicide may be sufficient to avoiding the suicidal moment, to letting the crisis pass. Focused activity is an excellent distraction. And then if I stay active, my old fortune cookie motto kicks in: "Action brings good luck." Which is also mostly true.

But needing something to do, and needing to do something, can also be the problem. If I'm not-doing, then I'm waiting. And if I wait, if I can learn to let myself wait, something will change. Choosing to wait and sticking with that choice can be precisely the kind of activity that brings the good luck I need. Maybe I can even eventually stop waiting and just . . . be. But that sounds a bit ambitious.

Practically speaking, what does it mean, to think about one's spiritual nutrition, the care and growth of the soul?

Anger provides a helpful example. When I was a kid, I would have violent temper tantrums. I was mostly shy and quiet and even, it's fair to say, emotionally repressed, but at times I would explode. This continued into my twenties, until I started drinking too much, and then I somehow managed to convince myself that I was one of the least angry people I knew, despite the fact that I would sometimes become this nasty, vile, viciously angry person when drunk (or hopelessly maudlin, or disgustingly self-pitying).

But when I met Amie, she pointed out to me, many times over the years, how angry I often am, and then I realized that I had some work to do with the whole anger business, that maybe part of my depression and my suicidality was related to my anger.

Often when I am angry, I want to stay angry. I've noticed I feel similarly when I'm in despair—in both cases, I'm often stubborn about the pain I'm in. In anger I will sometimes consciously say to myself, *I want to go on being angry*, but when I am in despair I never say to myself, *I want to go on feeling desperate*. Still, both kinds of suffering have psychological inertia. When I am experiencing either of them, they are both deeply resistant to reason. I can try to talk myself out of them, but I don't tend to succeed. Also, these emotions frequently go hand in hand. Anger and despair are mixed together, or anger becomes despair, or despair is masking anger.

My brother Darren likes to say: "When you lose your temper, you lose." Amie insists that we are not in control of these emotions, we just have to experience them and be honest about them. She warns me that I hide my anger, and instead of it coming out in fifteen minutes of genuine, authentic rage, I release it slowly in a week of nastiness: little comments, grievances, complaints. Maybe despair is the same way: I'm constantly suppressing a brief wave of real anguish, so it seeps up through the cracks, appearing here, there, and everywhere, for days.

But I don't have to act out of anger or despair. When I was young, I would sometimes hurt my hands when I was angry or frustrated. I would lacerate my fingers or punch a wall or close the door on my knuckles or fingers. As late as age thirty-three, I broke half a dozen bones in my right hand, like a two-year-old having a temper tantrum, punching a brick wall over and over again because of a break-up with a woman. But I don't have to do that. I don't have to try to escape any feeling by doing something.

The Buddha is said to have begun many of his teachings, "Life is suffering." It's always given me trouble, this idea, because I want to reply, *But it's not all suffering. Some of it is happy.*

And when I consider that suffering comes from desire—we suffer when our desires are frustrated, which they seem endlessly to be—I tend to worry that sure, suffering comes from desire, but perhaps I need desire, nevertheless. Then again, maybe it's true that we rely on our desire, yet we needn't necessarily do so. Maybe there's another way.

Anger, despair, desire—these might actually be just three different names for what in the Buddhist tradition are sometimes called the three poisons: hatred, greed, and ignorance. My anger, on this account, is an expression of my hatred for others and for myself. It's my fight instinct. My despair is an expression of my greed, my need to protect my own little territory, my tiny piece of the world, and my feeling that I am incapable of doing it. It's my flight instinct. And my desire is my ignorance—I haven't really thought through what is best for me and mine. But I couldn't have written a novel without the desire to be famous! Wait, was writing that novel the best thing? Wasn't it precisely that novel and its impending publication that led to me hanging by a sheet in my bedroom closet at the end of 2008? What if I had written the novel from some other place rather than the desire to be famous? What about my desire to be rich that led me into the jewelry business? Or my desire to be Mr. Fancy like the Fancy People of the World, which led me to all these boutique hotels and every kind of misconceived waste on luxury meals, clothes, cars, and extravagant habits that are long and happily discarded.

I don't know for sure about any of this. Maybe desires are good things, at least sometimes, and have led to good things. I don't think I would have met Amie unless I had written that first novel. The question is really less about desires than about my willingness to interrogate and investigate them, to question them, to look at them more closely and thoughtfully. To try to honestly ask myself, What does contribute to my flourishing? And what interferes with it? And am I willing to try to do the things that will genuinely help me rather than harm me?

The final scene in Khyentse Norbu's film *The Cup* helps to understand this idea. A group of young monks are sitting with their instructor, who explains that when we go walking barefoot, we often hurt our feet. So what is the solution? Should we cover the world in leather, so we can no longer stub our toe? "No," one of the young monks replies. "We cover our feet."

We cannot cover our lives with leather, and we don't want to. Life is all the experiences that we have, including our emotional experiences, our fears, hopes, desires, and confusions. If we pretend that those things aren't painful—if we are merely the victims of them, if we let them control us, if we don't think about them, if we don't consider them—we are going to continue to stumble and fall. In my case, this may mean returning to drinking, or hanging myself from a cedar beam in the garage office where I am now writing, or both. As long as my feet are naked, I'm going to step on something sharp, I'm going to stub my toe. But I can think about the proper care of my feet. I can cover my feet.

How do I shoe myself? There are lots of ways that I try. Some work better than others. It's an ongoing process. Everyone has to find their own way, because we have different environments, different histories, different vulnerabilities.

Most of the time, like the rest of us, I'm dealing with the more ordinary me, who is not in crisis. I hasten to add that the crises of Nelly Arcan and David Foster Wallace were ongoing and worsening, and in cases like theirs—or if you're feeling that way—psychiatry, and even a psychiatric hospital, often can help. (I am reminded of Wallace's weirdly clairvoyant call to his friend the writer and suicide survivor Donald Antrim to reassure him about the likely benefits of electro-convulsive therapy, just hours after Antrim's psychiatrists had suggested, terrifyingly to Antrim, that ECT might be the only remedy remaining.) Recently a very close friend wrote to tell me that she could no longer trust herself and she was taking an Uber to the emergency room. I knew she was struggling, but I hadn't realized the danger she was in. She was in the psychiatric hospital for a week, and when she came out again, her medications had been adjusted, and she was doing much better. I have great respect for people who can take this kind of care of and responsibility for their own mental health and their own vulnerability. This is exactly what Nietzsche had in mind: recognizing how sensitive and fragile we individual human beings generally are and paying attention accordingly.

But as I write this sentence now, I am feeling pretty good, mostly calm, cautiously optimistic. It's a spring day in Kansas City, birds are singing outside the windows, my children all seem to be okay, the pandemic appears to be somewhat lessening. On the inside, I find my familiar shakiness but also a calm cheer. Life seems like it could be mostly manageable. I ate a small bowl of spaghetti for lunch. I'm drinking a can of sparkling water and thinking about going into the kitchen for an apple. My world, as I am experiencing it in this moment, is something I can handle, even welcome, or investigate.

A famous study of addiction, called the Rat Park experiment, was conducted by Patricia Hadaway, Bruce Alexander, and their colleagues, Canadian psychologists at Simon Fraser University. They put some unlucky rats in small solitary cages, and other lucky rats in large cages with companions, possible sexual partners, exercise equipment, and room both for privacy and play. Both the Unlucky and the Lucky were allowed to drink unlimited quantities of sugared morphine water, at their own discretion. Both the Unlucky and the Lucky rats also had access to regular old boring water.

What happened was, the Unlucky rats drank about nineteen times as much morphine water as the Lucky rats, and the Lucky rats often showed a strong preference for plain old water, even avoiding the morphine water. The researchers tried various combinations of access to the water, and sweetness and strength of the morphine, but the general trend was clear: rats in painful environments as a rule became junkies, while rats in pleasurable environments as a rule did not. So goes the idea of taking a drink, and also the thought of suicide—at least, the thought of suicide as an active option.

Throughout this book I've been developing this idea that I'm addicted to suicidal thinking. That may be another way of saying I'm addicted to Clancy. That is, my addiction to a certain idea of myself and my life (and to hope for escape from the pain, difficulties, failures, and regrets of my life) is the real source of my trouble. What if I don't matter as much as I've supposed? Then my suffering and my fuckups don't matter so much. And maybe then escaping from me or fixing me doesn't matter very much either.

A couple of years ago, when I was in the early stages of writing this book, I would sometimes go to our local grocery store, which is not far from our house and a few minutes' walk from my campus office, to buy a coffee and write. It has a second-floor indoor terrace where people meet friends for lunch. It's not the best coffee shop to write in, but it's not a bad place to work, and there is almost always a free seat with a bit of elbow room and a place to plug in my computer.

One time two friends of mine, a married couple who are also professors, were there working too, and I stopped by to say hello. They asked what I was working on, and I explained a bit about this book, and then I said, "The problem is, I feel like I have to offer some sort of solution to suicide. An editor asked me recently what I do to get through the day, how I keep myself above water." The editor was my friend A. J. Daulerio, who created and runs the excellent recovery website *The Small Bow*. "And I was like, I don't know. Amie, the girls, writing, not drinking, you know. But I can't very well tell people that."

That it could be this simple may seem obvious to you, my reader, but at that time in my thinking about suicide, I still felt like I needed *more* of a reason to live to offer people. Also, I worried, as I still do, that it's all very well and good for me to say *Oh my wife and kids are saving my life*, but that may be exactly the wrong thing to say to some guy who is feeling like putting a gun in his mouth because his wife has just left him and his kids won't talk to him.

"But that's exactly what you should tell people," they both said. "Just tell people what you actually do that keeps you from killing yourself."

These are two people whose opinion I trust. And once I thought about it for a while and thought about what Nietzsche wrote and Andrew Solomon and Yiyun Li, and I realized that yes, that was the thing to do. I changed my environment (including my internal environment) from a solitary cage into a Rat Park. How did I do it? I've hashed out a list:

1. THE TWO DARTS

The existentialist philosopher Paul-Louis Landsberg observed, "What is false is not the struggle against suffering, but the illusion that we can destroy it."

What he means is we're going to suffer, and that's hard. We're even going to struggle against suffering, which can be very unpleasant. Often in the struggling against suffering, we actually make the suffering worse, like a rabbit pulling desperately against a snare. But the really dangerous idea is the notion that we can hope to escape suffering entirely.

Most of us associate the idea of liberating ourselves from suffering with Buddhism. Isn't the whole idea of the Four Noble Truths that we can get out of this mess? (1) There is suffering. (2) Suffering has a cause. (3) There is an end to suffering. (4) There is a path that leads to the end of suffering.

Back in 2015 or 2016, I was teaching a class on the philosophy of mind. We were spending a couple of weeks on the views of the Buddhist philosopher Darmakirti, and two of my best students—both of whom were retired physicians, auditing the class—approached me afterward and told me about a friend of theirs who was the head of a Zen Buddhist center in Colorado. They had told him about the class, and he said, "Be sure to ask him to explain the third noble truth."

To be fair, their friend was having a joke at my expense, as I'm not trained to teach Buddhism—though like most professors, I teach a lot of stuff in my classes that I've had to learn long after graduate school. But mostly I imagine he was playfully setting me up, because the question is so hard. Is there an end to suffering, really? Or was the Buddha using his skillful means as a teacher in order to help us get started along a path that will reveal different aspects of itself as we try to walk it? Wittgenstein famously described his own philosophy as a ladder that, once you had climbed it, you could toss away. The Buddha's teaching here may be a bit like that: there may be some things we should believe for a time that, once we have done the work that we could do only given those beliefs, we will no longer need to believe.

But I'm not an expert in Buddhism, and regardless of the status of the Third Noble Truth and the end of suffering, we can make our own suffering worse or better depending upon how we respond to it. And in this context, I find one teaching of the Buddha's especially helpful, often called "The Two Darts." Here the Buddha explains that we experience suffering (that's the first dart) and then we react to the experience of suffering by making it much worse (the second dart). The fight-or-flight feeling caused by suffering is the real problem. When we suffer, we don't have to freak out, we don't have to feel like something is broken, we don't have to try to fix anything, and we don't have to judge ourselves.

Amie once summarized the simple idea when she said, "The reason I love the First Noble Truth is that suddenly I realized I wasn't the only one. There was nothing I was doing wrong. Everybody suffers just like I do." She sometimes also says that the key to the First Noble Truth is recognizing that "there's no VIP room."

That's definitely part of the solution to the problem of depression and suicidal thinking for me: *Look, Clancy, you're not doing anything wrong when you suffer.* It's not like I am somehow the one person who doesn't get it. I'm not some kind of special fuckup or special fraud (as David Foster Wallace seemed to worry he was); it's not like if only I were a great artist, a Philip Seymour Hoffman or an Audre Lorde, I wouldn't suffer anymore, or if I were a genius at curating my lifestyle like Gwyneth Paltrow, I wouldn't suffer anymore, or if I were a great philosopher like Derek Parfit or Iris Murdoch, I wouldn't suffer anymore, or if I were a billionaire philanthropist like Melinda Gates, I wouldn't suffer anymore, or if I were God descended to earth like Jimi Hendrix, I wouldn't suffer anymore. No matter what, I'm going to suffer, even though my suffering might be different from theirs. (Then again, it might not be so very different, either.)

But I make my own suffering so much worse when I struggle against the suffering, when I suppose it is somehow a sign of something else or has to be turned off or is the cause to panic, to freak out, to attack, or to run away. The worst kind of suffering, the real *I want to kill myself* kind of suffering, is always that second, freaking-out kind. Sometimes it manifests as self-loathing. Sometimes it manifests itself as anxiety or despair. Sometimes it manifests as a terrible claustrophobic panic. But it is the second dart, not the first.

So if I can just tell myself, when I'm struck by the first dart, *Let yourself feel that dart. Don't do anything more about it. Just let that dart stab you.* Then I may very well be a rabbit with his neck caught in a wire snare, but at least I'm not decapitating myself with my scramble against it.

2. FAMILY

I've always admired the old-timers in AA who have literally lost everything. These people, women and men alike, tell the stories of losing their jobs; being left by their partners, by their children, and by their friends; hitting rock bottom and finding themselves abandoned by everyone except their bar buddies or their drug friends. And yet they got sober and stayed that way. And for a lot of these people, their families don't come back, their careers don't come back. And yet they stay sober. To me, this is miraculous, and I have to admit I don't quite understand it. I guess I hope I never do understand, because I suspect there's only one way to really get it, which is to have been through it.

I certainly have lost wives, friends, colleagues, and lovers due to my alcoholism and my time in psychiatric hospitals, and I definitely almost lost my career—and doubtless did irreparable damage to my professional development. And at one time my oldest daughter was so angry with me that she didn't want to talk to me. As I discussed in Chapter 10, I had to win back the right to see Margaret and Portia. That was one of the most difficult things I've ever done. I take a lot of pride in the belief I have about myself—whether it is a complete self-deception or not—that, all things considered, I am mostly a good, kind, and loving dad.

But I have come to see that until quite recently, I always in important ways put my family second. I told myself that I was providing for them by thinking of my work first, but the truth was, I could have reconsidered the way I managed my work and life obligations. Finding that balance is a struggle for everyone, and maybe no one ever gets it exactly right. But the question for me has lately become, *How can I find ways to be with my family more, to put my family more at the center of my attention, to care for my family more?* rather than *How can I keep my family happy enough that they will let me do my work?*

That is, I have been trying to reorder my priorities, at least a little. Even when I feel like my wife is being unkind or unfair to me, or when my kids are driving me crazy, or when I know someone really needs my attention but I'm like *Later, yes, I will try to help, but I really can't right now,* I try to remember that I'm really not making much of a contribution to the world other than to them, and that my emotional, psychological, and spiritual well-being is interwoven with theirs in such a way that helping them and helping me are not really separable things.

Now day in, day out, making that happen, really doing it, is not so easy. When Sartre wrote in *No Exit,* "Hell is other people," I've always thought he meant that the people in our lives make existence tremendously challenging—that no work is as hard as one's family—and also that hell is the place where we burn off our sins, and this is how we truly learn about ourselves, and about the whole messy business of how to live a decent human life.

I have friends who seem to have always understood this. Their families are their fundamental source of strength, without whom they would be hopelessly disoriented. And again, I want to stress, I'm not saying that I'm succeeding at this, but just that my attitude has shifted slightly, and that this modest change in attitude is helping me be a little less freaked out about my place in the world and maybe a little less fragile. I don't have to go at it alone.

3. TRYING TO LEARN TO BE RESILIENT

The French saying "It's the fate of glass to break" is reminiscent of the line from Yukio Mishima's death poem, written immediately before he killed himself: "Falling is the essence of a flower." Both observations make me feel doomed. Like, *You will be here for a while, but don't get used to it. You're the kind of guy who collapses. And since you're that kind of guy, and you haven't done a very good job at handling existence so far, maybe you'd better just end it all now.* And in the way Mishima puts it, suicide sounds awfully romantic.

That on/off thinking, that all or nothing way of considering oneself, that "heroically" self-destructionist approach to life, governed my psychology for many years. It was characteristic of me and my extremely moralistic view of life and the universe. I really thought, for a long, long time, that there was a clear difference between good and bad (or even good and evil), and right and wrong, and that life's project, even though I might not have been very adept at it, was to get myself right. I thoroughly indulged myself in judging others who I thought were importantly getting it wrong.

Speaking of getting it wrong and the pleasure of judging others, you might remember my childhood enthusiasm for Rudyard Kipling (in Chapter 3). Kipling is very much out of fashion now, and for some justifiable reasons. I've taught Kipling in India and discussed his racism and colonialism with my students there. I don't respect his worldview, particularly not the worldview he had toward the end of his life. But he did write some very good things. And by contrast with that "roll to your rifle and blow out your brains" line that I loved so much as a child and teenager, one of the things he wrote that lately sometimes helps me is a line from his much overquoted poem "If—": "If you can meet with Triumph and Disaster / And treat those two impostors just the same."

I try to understand that both victory and defeat are imposters. But doing that means shifting my thinking out of this on/off mode, which is so natural to me and is also very characteristic of my fight-or-flight way of being. Either I'm happy or I'm panicking. Either they love me or they want to be rid of me forever and never cared for me at all. Either I'm a success or I'm a failure. Either I'm good or I'm bad. That way of thinking expresses itself in a particular way of living and processing the experiences of life, which is in my case a dogmatic, know-it-all, stubborn, uncompromising, inflexible, and uncreative approach to the world.

Nelly Arcan wrote this terrific line in *Whore:* "I deserve death for having a stubbornness like a rat, which does not know how to turn back, for this relentlessness of a blind creature which will end up dying because of having gone too far, you will see, I will die because I will not compromise, and too bad for all the healthy and balanced men who will love me and too bad for me especially who will love others, we all end up dying of the discordance of our loves." That discordance of our loves comes down, in my case, to a commitment to incompatibility as a way of being, of seeing my experience as characterized by irreconcilable oppositions, and feeling determined to dig in with them.

Another way of thinking expresses itself in another way of living. It was the old way of thinking that Socrates discussed in Plato's dialogue *Republic*, which comes down to not taking yourself, your beliefs, or your life so terribly seriously. Socrates expressed it in his good-natured irony; today we often call it the virtue of *resilience*.

I had wanted to say something here about the practice of meditation, which I believe has helped me become a little less bivalent in my thinking, a little more ironical, good-humored, and resilient. But these days so many people can teach you about meditation much better than I can, and about a thousand apps can guide you. Even the home exercise equipment we use has meditation options. (I've found Thích Nhất Hạnh's talks on meditation, easily available on YouTube, to be especially helpful.)

So rather than trying to say something about meditation, I want to share a passage about how to be less bivalent in your thinking and living, about how to be resilient. It's edited from a recent talk given by the great meditation master Khyentse Rinpoche:

> I'm suggesting two things here to be resilient: to be creative and to be authentic. I'm talking more about being creative in how to see things. How can we be creative in becoming resilient, when you face the challenge of loneliness, paranoia, anxiety? How do we . . . outwit the anxiety? Here I want to share something very, very simple. And that is simply observing.
>
> Simply be aware of your body, your feelings, your mind. Simply be conscious of your body, your feelings,

your mind. You have a body. You have feelings. You must have a feeling right now. And you have a mind. You have thoughts. And whatever that thought, feeling, mind—be aware of that.

I'm not even talking about being aware of it for hours and hours. I'm talking about—how about something like one minute a day? And when you are aware of your thoughts, your body, your feelings, you are doing this not to judge. If you have some really hideous thoughts or some really heavy emotions, you should not judge them. If a good thought comes, don't get excited. If a bad thought comes, you don't have to brood about it.

I'm sure you are deadly bored and lonely. How about taking this chance, and for the first time, look at your boredom. You know, a great master said, "Boredom is like the dawn. If wisdom is like the sunrise, boredom is like the dawn." If you can appreciate boredom and loneliness, if you can just watch it and observe it, it will lead to wisdom.

And then a lot of stories are written in your head. A lot of daydreaming. A lot of delusion. A lot of fantasies. We never know that those are just illusions, those are just fantasies. In fact, we believe that they are true or they're going to be true. And this is what we call delusion. And when you have that, you are not normal or sober. You are drunk. By simply watching you can pre-empt all of this. I know many of you may think this sounds painfully, ridiculously simple. But this is how it is.

Learning to simply observe also means learning to be more creative, authentic, and resilient.

This is, of course, a form of meditation. It is also supported by more familiar techniques that I practice and recommend, like following your breath.

For me, it means not trying to control things in my life as much as I have attempted to do. It was a major source of my almost violent commitment to on/off, good-versus-bad thinking. It allowed me to feel like I had some control over the world around me, which of course I never did. And so when I tried to control it and it behaved in its inevitably uncontrollable ways, I panicked, and when my panicking hit its worst, I tried to kill myself.

Which reminds me of something that Nancy Bourdain said about her ex-husband Anthony: "Tony . . . was a control freak. He just—he liked control. That was the only thing I have to say about his suicide that makes sense, was the control aspect."

4. EXERCISE

The early psychiatrist Jean-Étienne-Dominique Esquirol wrote: "Suicides, like all [melancholics], think too much. We must either prevent them from thinking, or oblige them to think differently from what they are in the habit of doing. Reasoning effects little; moral commotions are of more service. Celsus advises that individuals who entertain a desire for suicide, should go abroad; and physicians, in all times, have recommended corporeal exercises, gymnastics, riding on horseback, the cultivation of the soil, journeying, etc."

Our culture is so obsessed with the health benefits of regular exercise, and the psychological benefits of exercise are so well documented, that it would be silly of me to recapitulate them here. (That said, most psychiatric facilities today still do not provide patients with opportunities for regular vigorous exercise, or regular exposure to sunlight, the mental health benefits of which are also thoroughly documented. In my many times at psychiatric facilities, the only exercise I ever got was pacing the hallways or doing pushups in my room.)

But we can know that something is good for us and still fail to do it, because of the old philosophical problem that Aristotle discussed so well, *akrasia*, or weakness of will. It has taken me years to develop a regular exercise routine, and I still fall off it if I'm traveling, or feeling overwhelmed with work, or have some other convenient excuse.

Before I took to habitually exercising, I didn't realize that it's not a panacea, it doesn't always work. Sometimes, like when I pushed myself too hard on a bike in hopes that it would help me with a bout of depression, exercise has actually made the depression even worse. I also discovered that running can be better, mood-wise, when I need help, than biking. Which is part of what Nietzsche is trying to teach us: we have to develop the habit of paying very close attention to the tiniest details of what contributes to our psychological well-being and what harms it.

I don't exercise because I want to be fit, or to improve my appearance, or to be healthier and live a long life. Those are all perfectly good reasons to exercise—they just don't happen to be my own. I exercise out of fear of my own brain. I exercise in order to be depressed less, and less often. And mostly it does work.

5. AVOIDING ALCOHOL, DRUGS, ANYTHING LIKE THAT

At a certain point in my slow recovery from my addiction to alcohol, I began to wean myself off the psychiatric medications that I had started taking as part of that process. The hardest one in the end for me (other than alcohol) was benzodiazepine, and it took several years of disciplined, slow reduction of my dosage to finally get off the drug entirely.

But I still kept a huge back stock of Valium in a cabinet, thinking that I might eventually use it as a method of suicide. And I did use it once, and failed to die, and then nevertheless built up a second back stock, with the same vague idea that eventually it might come in handy to augment a suicidal purpose, if not in itself to constitute a sufficient poison.

When Amie and I started traveling regularly to India in the spring of 2017, I took Valium again very occasionally, when I was on a long drive or flight, because I get motion sickness very easily, especially in the back of an Uber in heavy traffic or when I'm on twisty mountain roads, as I often was when traveling in India. Valium is an exceptionally effective treatment for motion sickness, and taking a very small dosage, I didn't seem to notice any other effect.

Eventually, because I was not refilling my back stock, I ran out. I figured it would be easy to replenish if I needed it, but suddenly we were traveling much less, due to the coronavirus, and then not at all, and it was no longer relevant. We were in India during this time, and though the prospect of eventually making a long car journey to an airport to get home bothered me—my motion sickness would be awful—I recognized that I wouldn't be able to get Valium for the trip no matter how much I might want it, so that was that.

In the first week of July 2020, with an itinerary that took us from Dharamshala to Munich to Chicago to Kansas City, we made it home. The next few months were a hard time, as we readjusted to the familiar pressures of our larger family and of work, and that fall, I thought, *I wonder if taking a Valium now and then would help.* So I called my psychiatrist, who said, "You made your last prescription last for years!" and I said, "Yes, well, I haven't really been taking it," and he immediately called the pharmacy, and later that day I picked it up.

And this is what I want to say: these psychiatric medications can be very helpful at times. At one point I don't think I would have survived without pharmacological intervention guided by a medical expert. But right now, as I write this, after having taken it off and on for about a month, I am stopping it again, because I've noticed that since I've been taking it, I've been more depressed. Not when I'm on the drug—it works, the daily anxiety vanishes about fifteen minutes after taking 5 milligrams—but in the other times, when I'm not on it. It reminds me, in a much milder way, of the oscillations of anxiety, depression, and relief I used to experience when drinking.

A couple of weeks ago, a student reached out to ask about benzodiazepines, and after talking with him a bit, I said that I thought he should trust his psychiatrist, who was recommending the drug, among others. Some of the people I love most in the world regularly take a benzodiazepine, and it seems to benefit them in a truly valuable way.

I am not telling this Valium story in order to convince anyone not to take a psychiatric medication—or to make any recommendations about any drug, for that matter. The lesson of my latest experience with Valium is that I have to be very, very sensitive, and very, very cautious when it comes to the question of how psychoactive substances influence not just my immediate feeling but also my overall state of emotional health, my moods, and my attitudes.

You may be thinking, *But all this sounds so joyless! Where's the fun, the adventure, the excitement!?* Some years ago during the course of a long alcoholic relapse, I kept quitting and starting again and quitting again. I was involved with a woman who cared for me, so she went to an Al-Anon meeting to be with others who were struggling with the alcoholics in their lives and trying to help them. When she came out of the meeting, she was shaky, she looked pale, and then she started crying. "What on earth happened?" I said. And she explained that she felt she just couldn't live that way, she couldn't be the caretaker of an addict, it was too much for one person to ask of another. "Those people in there are so unhappy," she told me. And I'm sure many of them were.

There is no joy in addiction, whether it is to alcohol, or Valium, or suicide. And I don't think there's much if any joy in dating someone who is suffering from those addictions.

But I've found a lot more joy out there than I realized was there, as I slowly worked to liberate myself from these addictions. So don't give up. Life is hiding all kinds of joy for you in secret places that you will yet discover if you don't give up.

6. REDUCING MY COST OF LIVING

One more addiction of mine has been trying to live in grand style. It comes down to my misconception that I am somehow special. My dad used to tell me, "You're going to be famous one day, son, your name will be in lights," and I loved it when he said that. I wasn't quite sure I believed him, but I really wanted to believe him, and I three-quarters believed him. When my first novel came out and it got a bit of press, I thought, *Okay, now it's really happening! Dad was right!* My editor wrote me an email that said, playfully echoing the age-old line: "Kid, you're gonna be a star."

In the movie *The Incredibles*, at one point the son, Dash, is riding home with his mom after getting in trouble at school, and his mom is trying to help him work through his rebelliousness. Dash says to his mom that his dad always says that his superpowers are nothing to be ashamed of, that they make him special. His mom sighs and says, "Everyone is special, Dash," to which Dash wittily and sulkily replies, "Which is another way of saying no one is."

I'm not a superhero, I'm not special, except in the way that everyone is special, which is to say that being conscious at all, with all its difficulties, opportunities, and responsibilities, is a pretty interesting business. And accepting that I'm just an ordinary guy with the typical—and yes, very privileged—lifestyle of a white middle-class, middle-aged Canadian male living in the United States means having to live like that guy, not like some imaginary special guy who has all these resources at his command and can fly all over the world or wear expensive clothes or buy an expensive car or stay at luxurious hotels. It means living within the constraints of the profession and budget I actually have. It means, rather than desperately trying to increase my revenue, trying to spend less. It means coming to understand the very old idea, common to philosophers of all cultures, that living within one's means, and trying to live even more modestly than one's means, is a simple, practical way of feeling more satisfied with oneself and one's life.

It's a powerful phrase, "the cost of living." It's like the parable of the two darts. Yes, living is going to come at a cost, but I don't have to inflate it. I can lower the cost of living.

It's hard. I like to buy stuff, I like to make myself feel special by buying things I suppose fancy people buy, for their children, their partners, and themselves. I look at the slideshows of the apartments and the houses in *The New York Times* and think, *Why not me?* But I'm trying to learn to see that this is not me, this is a source of my discontent and confusion, not a way to be healthy and sufficient.

7. TALKING LESS, AND TRYING TO BE MORE HONEST WITH MYSELF AND OTHERS

When I was a child, I had a lot of social anxiety, and whenever I was called upon to speak like the other kids my age—just in ordinary conversation on the playground, or walking down the street together—I could never think of what to say. I became so nervous that my brain seized up. I didn't understand how other people managed it. I was an unpopular kid, and I blamed that fact on my inability to make small talk or jokes, to have witty things to say.

At fifteen, I started in the jewelry business with my older brother Darren, and he eventually put me out on the sales floor. Then I had to learn how to talk to people. How to manipulate people with my speech. How to sell. How to make people like me by talking to them. I studied Dale Carnegie's *How to Win Friends and Influence People*. And in a lot of ways, it worked. Now when I tell people that I am actually an introvert, that I'm still very shy and hate parties and any gathering of more than a few people, that I suffered from crippling social anxiety as a kid, they either don't believe me or think I'm exaggerating.

But maybe because it was unnatural—again, maybe Nietzsche got it right, I was betraying something important about my own natural fit in my own skin—that dark road led me into terrible trouble. Thinking that I could solve my problems through being a smooth talker slowly became one of the most damaging things in my life.

Lately I am trying to learn to talk less and to listen more, and more carefully. (Learning how to listen well is another form of meditation, and I recommend Thích Nhất Hạnh's work on this technique.) I am also trying to tell the truth, when I feel I can speak it, rather than massage my speech into some shape that I suppose will be more pleasing to myself and others.

People don't seem to mind when I talk less. Most of the time when I repeat myself, they heard me the first time and simply politely ignored what I said because it was unkind or ill-considered. So I try not to repeat myself unless someone actually asks me to do so. It's also recently occurred to me that the vast majority of what I say is completely unnecessary and quite possibly unhelpful.

This is very much an ongoing project, and I don't have much that's helpful to say about it. It takes a lot of work, and when I succeed at it, it feels good.

8. HAVING A BIT MORE PATIENCE,
BEING WILLING TO WAIT

I never had much time for the virtue of patience. For years I firmly subscribed to a fortune-cookie belief that I took from a song in the 1967 Pink Floyd album *The Piper at the Gates of Dawn*: "Change returns success / coming and going without error / Action brings good fortune." To be fair, the lyrics depend heavily on the *I Ching*, and "Chapter 24" is a pretty cool philosophical song. But probably the main reason it appealed to me was that it rebuked my natural laziness and procrastination. It also confirmed my deep and ongoing impatience, with myself, with others, and with the world.

Impatience is a trait characteristic of the suicidally inclined. The inability to wait, or the suspicion of waiting, is importantly at the heart of the suicidal impulse. James Hillman wrote that "suicide is the urge for hasty transformation." The musician Alison Mosshart said of her friend Anthony Bourdain, "His impatience was fucking hilarious, entertaining to everybody. When you're a big figure like that, you're allowed to be impatient, because people will make it so you don't have to wait. Any time you do have to wait, your brain explodes."

Here is Dostoevsky on impatience and suicide:

> Very typical is a letter of a girl who took her life into her own hands. . . . This is a snarling, impatient letter: "Do but leave me alone! I am tired, tired! . . . Don't forget to pull off me the new shirt and stockings: on my night table you will find an old shirt and a pair of old stockings. These should be put on me." She did not use the words "take off" but wrote—"pull off"; and so it is in everything: terrible impatience.

Yiyun Li wrote of her own suicide attempts, "You're impatient with yourself, with your work, with others, a friend said to me around this time; you're the most impatient person in the world. Impatience is an impulse to alter or impose. Suicide is a kind of impatience people rarely understand, I replied to the friend, and quoted an Elizabeth Bishop letter in defense." And Édouard Levé added in *Suicide*, "Your impatience deprived you of the art of succeeding by being bored."

I take so much consolation in these observations, because I read them and I start to believe I'm allowed to just be. I don't have to control anything, I don't have to change anything, I don't have to do anything. *Don't worry so much about all that shit. Stop trying to manipulate the future to create some after all probably very amateurishly, childishly conceived goal.*

I'm impatient to become the person I am not, and that is precisely the problem. This whole book may still stink of the garbage of my impatience, my self-accusation, and my anger at myself.

In his masterpiece *The Way of the Bodhisattva*, the Buddhist philosopher Shantideva specifically opposes the virtue of patience (or forbearance, as it is often translated) to the vice of anger. He reminds us that anger may not be in our control, but we do have a choice to cultivate our manner of responding to our anger, whether it is anger with others or with ourselves. Anger at its worst congeals into hatred: and hatred is to be avoided at all costs, again whether it's hatred of another or hatred of oneself. (I regard self-loathing as a principal cause of suicide.) "There is no evil equal to hatred," Shantideva writes, "and no spiritual practice equal to patience. Therefore one should develop patience by various means, with great effort."

If we think about patience the way Shantideva does, we see that suicide is a bit like road rage. No one wants to fly into a fury while driving, and yet many of us do. The ordinary process of piloting a car on the road can suddenly erupt into an episode of wild anger that explodes into violence. I have found myself literally—albeit briefly—*hating* someone else on the highway, without ever having met that person or knowing anything about him or her. And this is just how impatience relates to hatred, and how patience may liberate us from anger. Some trivial incident suddenly fills me with psychic road rage at myself and all of life, and I just want to *kill* . . . myself.

A suicidal friend wrote to me recently, "Thanks for reminding me that we are the problem." I definitely hadn't meant to say that to her. I had meant to say that we have at least one solution, which basically is patience. But I see that as long as I am saying that we have the power to solve the problem, with a certain twist of thinking it contorts into: *Because I am not solving my problem, I am to blame for the problem,* or even *I am the problem.* Which is, come to think of it, why I always distrust many old-timers in AA (even now that, by most standards, I have become one). They always seem somehow to be silently judging me. Especially judging my childish impatience and desire from their viewpoint of long-earned, long-suffering patience and resignation.

From the perspective of *There's something wrong with me,* it's very hard to accept the idea that nothing about me has to change. Or that whatever may change, I simply have to wait and see. That is the only distinction I have to learn, I have to try to cultivate. What if there is no such thing as my territory? What if I have nothing to fight to protect? Then my impatience and my fearfulness start to seem less necessary.

I have responsibilities, and I have to do my best to take care of them. But the future is going to get here whether I try to accelerate it or not. I don't have to try to shove it along. I can just rest. As Lao-Tse says, "Nature never hurries, yet everything is accomplished."

Thinking about patience and procrastination reminds me of some excellent advice Margo Jefferson offered me in an email: "As for the advance of depression and self-destructiveness . . . I try to identify the real life triggers, and talk with/through them. Years ago a recovering alcoholic friend pointed out that AA's One Day at a Time mantra can apply to depression—i.e., one grief/grievance at a time. This helps stave off being completely overwhelmed. I rehearse my usual script—you know, the lines I tell myself, recite them to loosen their believability or at least to recognize them as a ritual. Self-destructiveness is trickier—if it takes the form of a real-life action, I try NOT to act—self-destructive actions are one of the few things procrastination helps with. If need be, I retreat and shut down with comforts at hand. (Easier if you live alone, I admit.) Sometimes I take notes so I can talk it through with my therapist. I have a couple of friends with the same susceptibilities, and sometimes talking—naming the thing to and with them is helpful. Reduces self-excoriation."

9. TRYING TO DO ONE THING AT A TIME, AND TO RELAX INTO ROUTINES

This last technique is related to reducing my cost of living and learning to be patient. Just as it would be silly for me to recommend exercise, it would be a bit silly of me to advise against multitasking, or being on my phone when I am doing things that don't require a phone. I welcome routines I used to rebel against, like doing laundry and folding the clothes every evening, or watching an hour of TV on the computer with Amie at night before going to sleep, or trying to live on a schedule. I used to have an active contempt for schedules and budgets (a budget is really just a financial schedule), because I thought they showed a lack of imagination and because I thought I was too good for such mundane things. Really, probably, I was afraid of them, because I suspected I didn't have the willpower to keep myself on a budget or to keep to a schedule.

And multitasking was for a time a real problem for me. What is a more obvious symptom of a problem with impatience than trying to do different things at once?

I was a waiter throughout college, but I was never a very good one, because I have trouble organizing myself. It takes a lot of self-discipline and patience to be a good waiter. But I always justified my multitasking as the skill of what good waiters call "consolidating": that is, you don't leave the kitchen with just one item, you leave with a full tray; you don't go to the bar for just one beer for just one customer, you make sure you've lined up as many drinks as you reasonably can; you don't come back to the kitchen with just one dirty plate, you bring back everything you have room to carry.

But consolidating doesn't mean doing everything at once.

Just the opposite, in fact: it means focusing on one goal or need, and being willing to wait until you can maximize the effort involved with that goal. It means looking at the big picture rather than responding to the little instantaneous demands that can otherwise pull you in different directions. It means learning to do one thing at a time.

I don't know whether this list will be helpful to anyone else who reads it. As Nietzsche teaches us, we all have our own strengths and weaknesses, and they very much contribute to our psychological well-being or distress.

But having this list has helped me a little. It reminds me that I do in fact have the aspiration to thrive, and that I can do things that take me in the direction of flourishing and away from killing myself.

Let's talk a little bit more about dying. The suicidal person may be in a privileged position with respect to the question of life or death, because she is thinking about it more than other people tend to do. Jean Améry put it this way: "A question, not answered, but almost fearfully posed: don't the suicidal know better?" Not just about life, but also about death.

"I myself *am* in that I *will* die," Heidegger wrote; that is, to be you is to recognize that there will also be not-you. You are confronted with a vast and bewildering array of choices about what to do with yourself, how, and when. Heidegger called this "the consciousness of possibility" (taking the idea from Kierkegaard), which was a German, technical-sounding way of saying that you are free, and that freedom is both difficult and painful. Your acute consciousness of your freedom is intimately tied to your awareness of the fact that, every minute of every day, you are quite literally running toward your own death. You won't always have all these choices. In fact, you have no idea when it might suddenly come to an end—and you might be thinking that the best way to deal with the frightfulness of your freedom is to just hasten your own death. Especially if, like me, you are feeling inadequate to the tasks posed by all the choices you have already made that have created responsibilities, anxieties, and failures that are conditioning your future as you imagine it.

At the very least, the suicidal person is no longer pretending that she is immortal. In desiring death, we may think she is taking her life for granted; but one thing she most certainly is not doing is taking her death for granted. The opposite, much more common case, Heidegger says, is understanding death as something that only happens to "the they": death happens to everyone but you. Furthermore, the way we avoid talking about dying or discuss it purely in abstract terms interferes with our ability to recognize that it is an essential aspect of making sense of our own lives. "Dying, which is essentially and irreplaceably mine, is distorted into a publicly occurring event which the they encounters." This habit is so common and pernicious, Heidegger goes on to argue, that we even "often try to convince the dying person that he will escape death and soon return to the tranquillized everydayness of his world." This is also a sophisticated way of deceiving ourselves about the fact of our own imminent death, of our own "inauthenticity."

Thích Nhất Hạnh argues the same position in *No Death, No Fear*—that the awareness of death should refocus our attention on the experience of life. This standard Buddhist belief is worth remembering, because we really do like to avoid thinking about the fact that we are going to die. Even sometimes when I am longing for death, I still don't want to think about death itself, as much as I want to think about getting out of life.

In one of his few meditations on death, in *The Gay Science*, Nietzsche is characteristically dazzling in his synthesis of these two positions, of the need to focus on life, which also somehow requires us never to forget about death:

> *The Thought of Death.* It gives me a melancholy happiness to live in the midst of this confusion of streets, of necessities, of voices: how much enjoyment, impatience and desire, how much thirsty life and drunkenness of life comes to light here every moment! And yet it will soon be so still for all these shouting, lively, life-loving people!

How everyone's shadow, his gloomy travelling companion stands behind him! It is always as in the last moment
before the departure of an emigrant ship: people have
more than ever to say to one another, the hour presses,
the ocean with its lonely silence waits impatiently behind
all the noise—so greedy, so certain of its prey! And all, all,
suppose that the past has been nothing, or a small matter, that the near future is everything: hence this haste,
this crying, this self-deafening and self-overreaching!
Everyone wants to be foremost in this future—and yet
death and the stillness of death are the only things certain and common to all in this future! How strange that
this sole thing that is certain and common to all, exercises almost no influence on men, and that they are the
furthest from regarding themselves as the brotherhood
of death! It makes me happy to see that men do not want
to think at all of the idea of death! I want to do something to make the idea of life even a hundred times more
worthy of their attention.

Here Nietzsche captures the paradoxical comedy about
our attitude toward death: that despite its certainty, and in fact
because of its certainty, thinking about it ought to force our
attention back onto life. We don't know when death will strike.
But where does that put us? Not brooding about death—don't
worry, one way or another, you'll have that opportunity, however brief it may be—but insisting on life. What we can't do is
fall into the all-too-familiar position of taking life (or death) for
granted, of allowing ourselves to slip into the benumbed world
of procrastination and Facebook and showing our loved ones
that we care about them tomorrow rather than today.

Wouldn't it be nice if the thought of death turned us like
the polar opposite of a magnet away from its partner, as it turns
Nietzsche here, so that all we could think of was the value of life
and championing it?

But the would-be suicide has a different story to tell us. What
she wants is death, and at the very same time, she wants to talk
herself out of it. She does want to believe that there are reasons

to live, even though she can't find them or believe in them. As Albert Camus observed, suicide "is merely confessing that life 'is not worth the trouble.' Living, naturally, is never easy. You continue making the gestures commanded by existence for many reasons, the first of which is habit. Dying voluntarily implies that you have recognized, even instinctively, the ridiculous character of that habit, the absence of any profound reason for living, the insane character of that daily agitation, the uselessness of suffering."

Camus's conclusion, that the very meaninglessness of life ought to provoke us into a mulish defiance toward the rationality of death, is not entirely satisfying. Sure, to go on living is a *fuck you* to a universe that doesn't look like it gives a damn about us, and maybe also a *fuck you* to the people you feel have given up on you, who wish that you would shut up about killing yourself and do it already.

But when Camus insists, "one must imagine Sisyphus happy," we wonder if that happiness may derive from the fact that Sisyphus knows the judgmental gods are watching him, with frustration and grudging respect, push that damn boulder one more time back up the mountainside. As Camus says, "There is no fate that cannot be surmounted by scorn." They can't break him. But since the universe doesn't know that he is telling it to screw itself, and since he is still stuck here suffering, Camus's solution is a bit like an irritable French waiter refusing to quit his job just because he dislikes his customers so much. The customers don't know why he's grumpy, if they notice him at all, so he's punishing . . . who?

But stubbornness is important when it comes to the question of staying alive. Of all the books written by people like me, authors who have wrestled with the threat and the appeal of suicide, one particularly stays with me, in part because of the author's insistence on the merits of being stubborn: Sarah Davys's *A Time and a Time*.

Sarah Davys is a pseudonym: her real name was Rosemary Manning (1911–88), and she was mostly known as a groundbreaking lesbian author and a writer for children. (She also wrote under the pseudonym Mary Voyle.) *A Time and a Time* chronicles her two attempts to commit suicide, among other things, and one reason I'm drawn to the book is that she didn't die by suicide in the end. Like me, she's a writer and an attempter, but her story has a happy ending.

That almost was not the case. Her second attempt, with an overdose of barbiturates, nearly succeeded, and she spent several days unconscious in a hospital bed before waking up. Of the experience, she noted, "I can say nothing about my brief acquaintance with death, for though I must have been very close to his doorway and am a true revenant, I have brought back nothing."

Me too, I want to add. But then I also wonder, *Is that true, Sarah? Have we really brought back nothing because we don't remember the time when we were gone?* She means that she has no wisdom to report from the darkness of her unconsciousness—as close as she came to death, she found no afterlife—but is that even true? Isn't the book part of what she learned from her departure and return?

She goes on: "Nothing was all there was to see. I believe death to be total oblivion, and if I am wrong, then I think I cannot have ventured far enough to know otherwise."

It certainly is possible that she didn't venture far enough to know otherwise. It's also possible that she experienced nothing because she took so many pills that she was too medicated to experience anything, alive or dead. But for her conclusion, I don't think it matters whether there is an afterlife. Either way, she realizes, she's stuck with life. And she finds herself taking a newly deepened interest in the particular life she is living.

"My concern is now entirely with life and how to live it. Quite fortuitously I have been given an opportunity of assessing my life from the fairly unusual angle of having nearly lost it."

This makes sense to me—she is now evaluating her life from a new angle, from a changed perspective. She certainly is not suggesting that she will no longer have any mental struggles, and she is not necessarily affirming her life in response to her near deaths, but she is assessing it differently. Her good luck is this opportunity for revaluation.

Khyentse Rinpoche makes this point when he speaks about resilience. Davys's new emphasis is squarely on the question of how she assesses or evaluates her own life. She is thinking about the simple, basic, practical questions of the significance of her own particular existence rather than pondering the value of life more generally. That makes a big difference for my way of thinking about me.

A Time and a Time begins with the sentence: "I have reached my early fifties despite having made two attempts on my life." She goes on to worry that the reason she is still alive is that "there is a lack of seriousness about me which prevents such attempts being successful." This is another reason I love this book: she's my age, and her self-doubt, her anxiety, is over not being serious enough to kill herself. It should make us laugh at ourselves to think that we suicide attempters aren't as good as the suicide succeeders, and at the very same time to think that we want to kill ourselves out of cowardice in the face of the challenges of life. Are you going to live or are you going to die? Maybe I'm too stubborn to make up my mind one way or the other. *Stop hassling me!*

She adopts a strategy for keeping herself alive: "When I arrived at the summer after I was fifty, and was recovering from my overdose of Luminal, I gave myself three targets . . . : twelve months; another twelve months; and then six months. 'A time and a time and half a time.'" This works as a technique for her, telling herself she doesn't have to live a whole life, it doesn't have to be any grand affair: she just wants to make it another year, even just six months.

She continues: "This is how I seem to have spent much of my life, edging forward step by step, always forcing myself to look down at the abyss between my feet, indeed at times preoccupied with it to the point of falling; at other times foolhardy and willing to take risks which surprise my cautious self, capable of enjoying rapturously the rewards of being alive . . . and privileged to be permitted to exist even on a cliff's edge."

Davys's point here reminds us of the earlier argument by William James, that simply choosing to live expresses breathtaking vigor. When you realize that at any moment you could kill yourself, then every moment you are alive becomes an astonishing triumph. For all of us, this way of looking at it affirms not only the goodness in survival but victory. And she did not kill herself in the end, but died of natural causes at the age of seventy-six.

Earlier I compared my motives for suicide to my motives for divorce, like running away from it all. But it's too easy to think that life is a partner you could leave. It doesn't work like that. I'm not separable from my life. I am my life.

A few months ago I was in the shower thinking about my upcoming birthday. I turned fifty-five this year. For many years I looked forward to my birthdays, as everyone does when young. Then in my late twenties I entered the dreading birthday stage, judging myself for not having completed my Ph.D., for not having made a million dollars, for not having written a novel, and so on. This stage lasted a long time, as the things I had failed to achieve accumulated.

Then there came the stage of both judging myself and actually regretting the fact of getting older: looking older; finding myself less energetic, less quick to rise from the couch; discovering aches and pains I didn't have before; noticing my sex drive decreasing. My math skills and my memory seemed to deteriorate. I thought my modest boldness, my confidence, whatever ease I had in the world, which was not much, was waning.

I am still in this stage, and it will continue until I die. When I tell older friends that I'm feeling old, they smile and say, "Just wait." But what I was thinking about in the shower was *Huh, I'll have lived another year.* Maybe I can take a bird's-eye view and stretch my perspective, maybe I can see a larger narrative, a longer and more complete story, that could end in a good death rather than a bad one.

The hot water felt good on my skin and in my scalp. I stretched my neck back to let it run over my face. It is funny, that despite all my self-destructive desire and effort, I find myself all the way at fifty-five. I can also say, *Good job, Clancy.* Maybe I can do it again. And I have found pleasure in life itself, in just being here, in the world, even though yes, at times, I stand like Davys at the edge of the cliff. Many more times I have felt wholehearted gratitude that I have my family, my profession, and my little home in the world as I understand it.

I did it: another year. Let's see about fifty-six. A time and a time. That goes for you, too. As David Foster Wallace consoles, we can cry all we want, and we can change our minds, and that doesn't make us frauds. Letting myself change my mind may be a step toward a healthier, more realistic authenticity. Maybe slowly I can let this whole suicide thing go. Maybe I'm starting to learn, if not how to live, at least how not to kill myself. Not to get all sentimental on you at the end of the book, but look at us, here we are together, we made it. We don't want to die, just yet.

Acknowledgments

Amie Barrodale, Zelly Martin, Margaret Martin, Portia Martin, Ratna Martin, Kali Martin, Susan Golomb, Denise Oswald, Lisa Lucas, Dan Halpern, Vickie Moody, Pat Barrodale, Darren Martin, Pat Martin, Bill Martin, Alicia Martin, Rebecca Martin, Margaret Link, Joe Link, Matt Link, Tim Culver, Adam Cooper, Andrew Solomon, Candice Biggins, Dese'Rae L. Stage, Drishti Chawla, Reetika Kalita, John Kaag, Mansi Vashisth, Grace Ketterman, A. J. Daulerio, Jonathan Franzen, Daaji, David Benatar, Wayne Vaught, Diane Williams, DJKR, Tashi Colman, Jim Lowery, Margo Jefferson, Peggy Battin, John Draper, Enrico Gnaulati, Lary Wallace, Sydney Harvey, Bruce Bubacz, Gwen Nally, Ben Jasnow, Alex Watson, Rita Kothari, Kranti Saran, Amit Chaudhuri, Sumana Roy, Adrienne Miller, Ellen Rosenbush, David Napier, Hari Haran, Sharon Berry, Tanya T., Rocco Castoro, Carol Hay, Deb Olin Unferth, Blair Moody, Robert C. Solomon, Kathleen M. Higgins, Jim Hankinson, Sanjay Sehgal, Pierre Lamarche, Tatyana Kostochka, Adam Baer, Rafil Kroll-Zaidi, Joe Kloc, the editors of "I'm Still Here" at *Epic* and *Huffington Post*, the editor of "The Drunk's Club" at *Harper's*, the editors of "Big Mother" at *Harper's* and *The Believer*, the editor of "Our Little Tragedy" at *Tricycle*, Daniel Soar, my students, and the many people who have spoken with me in psychiatric institutions or emailed me about their own suicidal thoughts and attempts over the years: thank you.

Appendix I

TOOLS FOR CRISIS

Remember, you don't have to live forever. You just have to get past this moment of panic, and things will get easier. If you truly have to, you can always kill yourself tomorrow. Wait a day.

If you can, call or text a friend or two—you don't have to tell them everything, just reach out, just a *Hi, please text me back,* and if the first doesn't reply, try a couple more.

Consider any of the following:

Go for a walk to someplace less claustrophobic feeling, just to get some fresh air in your lungs. Just stall yourself long enough for a stroll, a glance around.
Visit https://suicide-n-stuff.com/ for some terrific videos and podcasts, or read some of the stories at https://livethroughthis.org/ (These I find are especially helpful.)
Flip through the interviews in Appendix II.
Consult a mental healthcare professional. If you are afraid of a 72-hour hold, discuss that concern with the professional up front.
Turn to Chapter 11 and read whatever grabs you there, perhaps especially my list of nine habits that are helpful to me.
Read this article of mine, which is not long, is hopefully funny, and has helped people (they tell me) make it through to another day: https://highline.huffingtonpost.com/articles/en/life-in-the-psych-ward/
Watch this YouTube video, which really helps me: https://www.youtube.com/watch?v=EMvFZkOg7Dw
If you're in the United States, call the National Suicide Prevention Lifeline at 800-273-8255 or the National Mental Health version of 911 at 988. (Be aware that they may send emergency responders, so if that's not your wish, you'll need to address that with them.)
Visit warmline.org
If you're in the United States, text SAVE to 741741, you'll get a text back in at most a few minutes. They'll assign a person you can chat

live with; it's normally pretty quick, though it can take longer in the middle of the night. I've found the volunteers to be kind (and they too may send emergency responders, so be sure to address that if it isn't what you want).

Attend a meeting of Suicide Anonymous: https://suicideanonymous .net/

Read a few of the stories here: https://www.thesmallbow.com/

Listen to Honor Eastly's podcast, *No Feeling Is Final*, and visit the website: https://www.bigfeels.club/podcast

Watch this excerpt from Thích Nhất Hạnh's interview with Oprah Winfrey: https://www.youtube.com/watch?v=NJ9UtuWfs3U

If someone calls you and sounds like they're suicidal, ask them if they're feeling that way and have them talk to you about it. Listen and stay with that person for as long as you can (on the phone or in person), and be sure to check up on them after the conversation. You might consider reading the excellent article by Jason Cherkis, "The Best Way to Save People from Suicide," which is helpful for people who are struggling with the desire to take their own lives: https://highline.huffingtonpost .com/articles/en/how-to-help-someone-who-is-suicidal/

Here is a compilation of reliable online resources about the prevention of suicide, the treatment of suicidal ideation, and help for those who have lost a loved one to suicide:

American Foundation for Suicide Prevention https://afsp.org/find-support /resources/

National Institute of Mental Health on suicide https://www.nimh.nih .gov/health/topics/suicide-prevention/index.shtml

Society for the Prevention of Teen Suicide http://www.sptsusa.org/

Centers for Disease Control and Prevention on suicide https://www .cdc.gov/violenceprevention/suicide/resources.html

Action Alliance for Suicide Prevention http://actionallianceforsuicide prevention.org/resources

Suicide Prevention Resource Center http://www.sprc.org/

Suicide Awareness Voices of Education https://save.org/

The Trevor Project (focused on LGBTQ mental health) www.thetrevor project.org/

The Ethics of Suicide Digital Archive (a vast compilation of thinking on suicide from great philosophers and other writers throughout history and world culture) https://ethicsofsuicide.lib.utah.edu/

ESPECIALLY FOR YOUNGER PEOPLE AND PARENTS

The crisis resources and strategies I mention above are good for people of all ages. As I have stressed in this book, above all the most important thing is to talk to your friends, if you're a young person in crisis, and, as a medium- to long-term coping strategy, to consider journaling, exercising and perhaps even meditating.

Suicide is now the second highest cause of death among 15-24 year-olds. If you're a parent of a young person who has made an attempt or seems to be at risk, having direct, open, compassionate conversations has been shown by almost every study to be the most effective approach. The best therapeutic practice we know of right now for at-risk youth is Dialectical Behavior Therapy, and a good Dialectical Behavior Therapist is an invaluable resource, but here again the key, as with Cognitive Behavioral Therapy, is starting a conversation with the young person at risk.

I also enthusiastically recommend an ongoing, multipart project from *The New York Times* that explores adolescent mental health:

https://www.nytimes.com/spotlight/inner-pandemic

I have compiled a short list of books that I think are especially well-suited to the needs of younger people and the parents of younger people who may be in crisis.

Brosh, Allie. *Solutions and Other Problems* (New York: Gallery, 2020)
Glasgow, Kathleen. *Girl in Pieces* (New York: Ember, 2018)
McKnew, Donald H. and Cytryn, Leon. *Growing Up Sad: Childhood Depression and Its Treatments* (New York: W. W. Norton & Co., 1998)
Niven, Jennifer. *All The Bright Places* (New York: Ember, 2016)
Sheff, David. *Beautiful Boy* (New York: Mariner, 2009)

Below are some other books that have been especially helpful to me. This list of good books on suicide is by no means exhaustive, but these ones may help with effectively managing suicidal thinking:

Antrim, Donald. *One Friday in April: A Story of Suicide and Survival.* New York: W. W. Norton, 2021.
Chödrön, Pema. *When Things Fall Apart.* Boulder, Colo.: Shambhala, 2016.
Davys, Sarah. *A Time and a Time: An Autobiography.* London: Calder & Boyars, 1971.

Hillman, James. *Suicide and the Soul.* Woodstock, N.Y.: Spring, 1965.

Jamison, Kay Redfield. *Night Falls Fast: Understanding Suicide.* New York: Vintage, 1999.

Joiner, Thomas. *Why People Die by Suicide.* Cambridge, Mass.: Harvard University Press, 2007.

Li, Yiyun. *Dear Friend, From My Life I Write to You in Your Life.* New York: Random House, 2018.

———. *Where Reasons End.* New York: Random House, 2019.

Nhất Hạnh, Thích. *You Are Here.* Boulder, Colo.: Shambhala, 2010.

Rilke, Rainer Maria. *Letters to a Young Poet.* New York: W. W. Norton, 1993.

Rinpoche, Dzongsar Khyentse. *Living Is Dying.* Available at https://www.siddharthasintent.org/assets/Global-Files/Publications/LiDbookv13.pdf.

Shneidman, Edwin S. *The Suicidal Mind.* New York: Oxford University Press, 1996.

Solomon, Andrew. *The Noonday Demon.* New York: Simon & Schuster, 2001.

I think any of these will help. And again, if you are in immediate danger, please call 988, or text 74174, or contact a mental healthcare professional. The rest of us need you to stick around.

Appendix II

IN CASE OF EMERGENCY

Interviews on Staying Alive

A new friend wrote to me not long ago and told me that she had attempted suicide, and that she knew the thoughts might return, but that for the moment she felt firmly rooted in the world. I like that expression, "firmly rooted in the world." It captures more and more how I have come to see the ability to go on living, despite the struggle. We can establish roots, we can find psychological or spiritual nourishment in our everyday lives, we can make a home for ourselves in this weird, confusing mess that is life.

That said, there are times when we feel rootless, when we feel like we are drowning or falling through space, with no safe tether or helping hand we might seize. There are times when we're right on the edge of killing ourselves, or even in the process of planning an attempt. My admittedly ambitious hope for this book is that someone who is thinking about suicide might pick it up and find that she need not act on the thought, or that the urgency of the thought has diminished a bit.

I also hope that the book may help people who are approached by a friend or acquaintance who is feeling suicidal. If someone does reach out to you for help, you should know the six steps recommended by the American Foundation for Suicide Prevention, one of the leading organizations in the world working on the problem of reducing suicide. It's good advice, is proven to help, and I have used it myself to help people. The AFSP principally recommends that we "have an honest conversation" with the person who is feeling suicidal, and

1. Talk to them in private
2. Listen to their story
3. Tell them you care about them
4. Ask directly if they are thinking about suicide

5. Encourage them to seek treatment or contact their doctor or therapist

6. Avoid debating the value of life, minimizing their problems, or giving advice

There is no way for me to do that in a book. And certainly, I am not trying to give you any advice about your life, other than, well, if you are thinking of attempting suicide, don't do it just yet. But what I can do here is share with you some interviews I've conducted with people who are experts on the subject of suicide (who I've sometimes mentioned in the body of the book), and those conversations are below.

In all these interviews my goal was to find advice that would help a person who was actively considering suicide. Maybe glance through them if you are in a desperate place. These people know what they're talking about, and their words can help.

DZONGSAR JAMYANG KHYENTSE RINPOCHE: "THE EXQUISITE TASTE OF MULBERRIES"

It was a cool midsummer morning in 2012, and Amie and I were in the Spiti Valley high in the Himalayas, in India but not too far from the Chinese border. We were hiking up the side of a mountain toward a small Buddhist monastery. We were above the tree line, but we saw moss, scrubby grass, and tiny white, yellow, and blue summer flowers among the gravel, rocks, and dirt.

When we made it to the plateau where the monastery stood, suddenly we could hear a man's voice over a loudspeaker. He was chanting in Tibetan.

"That's Rinpoche's voice," Amie said, and she started walking faster. When at last we got to the temple, we saw him as he was stepping outside the doors, with his retinue of monks. He saw Amie and smiled at her, then looked at me and scowled fiercely.

Dzongsar Jamyang Khyentse Rinpoche, known to his students by the honorific Rinpoche, was born in Bhutan in 1961 and is one of the most respected teachers and scholars of Tibetan Buddhism in the world. Interestingly, he is also a filmmaker, who studied with Bernardo Bertolucci and made an appearance, still a young monk, in Bertolucci's film *The Little Buddha*. I formally became a student of his on August 5, 2012, when I took refuge (the formal procedure of becoming a Buddhist) in Bir, where Rinpoche has one of his teaching centers. On the same day, Rinpoche married Amie and me, while goodhumoredly reminding us that Buddhists do not really have a marriage ceremony.

One of my students once told me, "If you'd fallen in love with a woman at Barnum and Bailey, today you'd be a circus clown," and maybe that's true. Or maybe I just got very lucky that day when I talked to Amie on the phone and persuaded her to come visit me in Kansas City, and then we fell in love and she proposed that we take a trip to Egypt or India. We went to India, and the rest is history.

In Chapter 1, I quoted from Khyentse Rinpoche's book *Living Is Dying* on the problem of the habit of suicide. Here is the full quotation:

> Suicide is a habit we pick up very quickly and is extremely difficult to break. It's a little like being addicted to alcohol and incapable of saying no to a drink. Habit plays a huge role in defining future rebirths. Once you have formed the habit of ending your life when things get tough, you will resort to suicide more and more quickly in your future lives. Buddhists who have studied the teachings on karma and reincarnation should know this.
>
> Of course, this argument will not work if you are not a Buddhist and have no belief in reincarnation. Neither will it work if you think that death is the end of everything.

On other, more literal versions of this view, many Buddhist philosophers claim that committing suicide once means you will commit suicide five hundred times more, either in the bardo, between your earthly lives, or in your future lives.

I find this view very helpful, not just because I am a Buddhist but also because it allows me to think about suicide as less a choice I'm making than a choice I'm *not* making, or not entirely. I have a lot of bad habits, and those habits are things I work to change.

Let's take my habit of looking at the phone when I'm playing with my three-year-old son. We are playing together, having a nice time, using his cars as characters or assembling some Brio train track on the coffee table. He takes a break for a moment to get another car or to bounce on his little trampoline; almost without knowing I'm doing it, I've reached down to my phone on the end table next to the sofa to look at my email or skim *The New York Times*. It's almost like a reflex action unless I set up strategies so that I don't do it, like putting my phone on the charger in a different room or reaching for my phone and then stopping myself and going to join my son.

Similarly, I've realized that for me, suicide is like a knee-jerk reaction that I have to a certain kind of panic. But that means I can set up strategies to avoid it. It means, *Yes, you have this bad habit, Clancy, but it is a habit, it's not a reasonable choice, and like any bad habit, you can change it. Every time you don't try to kill yourself, you're doing a little good thing to break the habit. And anytime you do try to kill yourself, even if it's a half-hearted attempt like duct-taping a laundry bag around your head*—yes, sigh, I have tried this—*you are reinforcing the habit, you are making the habit still worse.*

But as we all know, breaking bad habits is hard. Recently, especially because of the rise of suicides among young people, especially during the pandemic, Rinpoche has been speaking more about suicide.

Q: Rinpoche, can you tell us a bit about your experience with suicide?
A: I have been greatly disturbed by the growing number of suicides, particularly among youth.

Q: Rinpoche, what general advice can you give to someone who is feeling suicidal?
A: I want to remind everyone of a simple truth that we so often forget—how wonderful it is just to see things, and to hear, to smell, to taste, and to feel things. This is called living!

Q: But Rinpoche, there is so much struggle and suffering in life. Mightn't it just be easier to end it all?
A: Of course there is struggle in life. But this life is what we have right now, even when it's not perfect. We don't know what's in the netherworld that we'll encounter after we die. What if we can't see, hear, feel, or taste things there, even though we are conscious of them? We probably won't be able to handle that, because we really don't like uncertainty, and we just don't know what's in that netherworld.

Q: Lots of other people seem to do just fine. Is it unfair that some of us are miserable and others are prospering?
A: While we have this life, we can appreciate the simple things it offers even when matters seem painful and unfair—like seeing your own peers wearing business suits and ties and looking ridiculous driving BMWs and directing internet startups while you roam about, scraping up a few bucks here and there.

Q: What if the pain is just too much? And what about self-loathing and self-contempt?

A: There's a lot you probably won't feel good about, but there are things you can do. And remember that things change. You may go through five years of pain, but the fifteen years after that may be very happy, joyful, and cheerful.

Q: I struggle with the thought of suicide, and so do many people who ask for my advice or help. Is there some specific action we could take to help us with the thought of suicide?

A: I wish some of you could watch an Iranian film called *Taste of Cherry*, in which a man who tried to hang himself from a tree suddenly discovered the wonder and beauty of life when the branch broke, and he savored the exquisite taste of mulberries.

Q: Rinpoche, any final words of wisdom for someone whose suffering is so intense that she feels she can't take another day? Especially a young person?

A: Please don't give up, discover what this life can offer, and appreciate the small but wonderful things in life—like just what you can see, hear, feel, and taste.

DESE'RAE L. STAGE: "ALL IT IS, IS DISTRACTION"

Many people, when they are thinking about suicide, google the subject. They may find Reddit forums discussing suicide and the desire for suicide, or they may find sites that address the various ways of killing oneself. (People are, quite naturally, often looking for the easiest and least painful way of doing it.) They will also find resources they can contact, by phone or email, to help them deal with the crisis, and they may find stories of people who have attempted suicide and lived to tell the tale. I very frequently (and very happily) get emails from people who tell me that they were googling suicide and came across an article of mine on the subject and then changed their minds.

At a certain point, I thought to myself, *But what about all those people who don't read a long article? All those people who might need and be saved by a survivor's account, but aren't going to suffer through thousands of words by a rambling middle-aged white male philosophy professor?* Then I thought, *We need a site or sites that tells the stories of all these survivors, at different lengths, of different ages and from different backgrounds, so that we can reach and help as many people as possible who are at risk.*

Then I found Dese'Rae L. Stage and her wonderful site Live Through This, https://livethroughthis.org/.

Dese'Rae is one of the most prominent contemporary voices in the "lived experience" literature on suicide; that is, the work of people who have attempted suicide and survived to talk about it. Dese'Rae has done the selfless, laborious, painstaking work of reaching out to dozens and dozens of suicide survivors from every possible background and chronicling their stories, in their own words, for just the purpose I was talking about above: that reading the story of someone who has attempted suicide and will tell you about how they got through that makes you—for reasons none of us completely understand—feel better and much less likely to kill yourself, and it reconnects you with others.

Maybe it's because we feel less alone. Maybe it's because see light at the end of the tunnel. Maybe it's because we realize we have nothing to be ashamed of. As Philip Lopate notes, commenting on the benefits of reading literature generally, "It allows us to be more understanding about human frailty, about error, tragic flaws, and therefore, makes us more forgiving, and more self-forgiving."

Recently a graduate student who is helping me with this book—worrying that all this suicide stuff might be getting to her—wrote, "It is actually helping me. I can't remember why I used to want to die. All these people and stories show you that they didn't deserve what was happening to them and nor does anyone else, ever. So, this is giving me actual firsthand experience on why it is important to talk about it. It helps." Naturally, this was a great comfort to me.

Anyway, it works, and one of the best people making it work right now for others is Dese'Rae L. Stage.

Q: How did you come to work on suicide?
A: When did I start this? It's been my whole life. One of the first memories I have is losing a family friend to suicide. I remember asking my mom, "How old was I when this friend died?" And she said, "Maybe two or three." It just registered as this thing that I don't know exactly what it was. I think it might've been the way that people talked about it. My own grandfather specifically, there was very much this feeling of the wife he left behind and his beautiful daughter and he did it in his garage on his weight bench. And that's one of the memories I have. Almost everyone in my family has been

suicidal. Not actively, definitely passively. My grandmother is the queen of the suicide threat. I've seen it manifest in different ways with my uncles to various degrees. My mom too, in recent years. So there's that. And then at fourteen, during the transition from middle school to high school, depression hit me and feeling lonely, feeling misunderstood. I started cutting myself. I started having suicidal thoughts. I stopped sleeping. I've been chronically suicidal my whole life since then.

But I got depressed for the first time when I was fourteen. Suicidal thoughts for the first time. I started cutting myself for nine years.

And actually those urges, even though I stopped cutting myself when I was twenty-three, I would slip once or twice a year up until 2016. So it was another ten years before I realized this really doesn't work for me anymore.

When I was fifteen, I lost my first actual friend to suicide. I found a journal from that time, and I was already suicidal when he died. And I think it must've just scared the shit out of me, you know? It made it really real, and then I tried to kill myself when I was seventeen. I have no memory of it, no recollection at all, but again, found it in a journal. I describe trying to strangle myself with a phone cord. That, that just kept going until I had the suicide attempt that I really recognized as *Oh no, this is what was absolutely happening.* I wanted to die. I wanted to go. And there were other ones leading up to that too, but I don't know. How do you count how many suicide attempts you've had?

Q: When a person is really in crisis but isn't able to reach out to someone, what do you think can be said to that person, if anything?

A: I think it depends on the person. There's no clear answer. And I think that's such a huge part of the problem. We are just trying to stick people into boxes and treat them all the time the same way. And we know that we're all different. I think it comes down to the person. Even the assessments we have that all of these professionals are using has about 50 percent efficacy.

Q: It's frustrating.

A: We have an obsession with trying to predict it. Now they want to see if there's a suicide gene. That's just another way to force me into treatment, right? When that should be a thing that helps. And speaking of treatment, I'm so frustrated by the suicide prevention field having an obsession with making suicide a symptom of mental illness. It's not. But it can be.

Q: It can be. But feeling suicidal doesn't mean you're suffering from mental illness.

A: Or they can coexist. I think that's probably more likely. Most of the time people with diagnoses will have suicidal thoughts. But they aren't the same. It's a response, a response to adversity. I think I've gotten to the point where I just think suicide prevention as a field is killing people. It's not keeping people alive. It's killing people. It's making people think there's something wrong with them. It's putting them in treatment centers where they don't get the help they need, but they may actually be made worse.

I want people to know that all these people that I've interviewed, most of them, they continue to have suicidal thoughts. It's like a cycle. It keeps coming back. That gives me hope to know I can get through this again.

Q: I was talking to Andrew Solomon, and he said something similar that resonated with me. About depression. He said that the thing for me is being able to recognize I've gone through this before, and I'm probably going to go through this again. So I can get through this. It's the same with thinking about suicide. Even when it's very, very close, you know, even when you're really feeling like there's just no other way out. It helps to know that other people feel that way, and they've managed to survive, and it does come back for them.

A: I was literally just talking to my psychiatrist about this. She was like, are you having suicidal thoughts? And I was like, nah, but I know what my triggers are. For me it's usually a relationship issue. If I'm having an argument with my wife and it feels like I'm just so misunderstood, she's never going to understand me. No one will ever understand me. Just feeling misunderstood, feeling like the black sheep. That was what I felt like as a teenager and beyond with my family. For me that feeling of being misunderstood, that being the emotional one is, is hard. So that's a trigger. And if my wife and I are arguing, because I don't really argue with anyone else. I only really make myself vulnerable to her. So when that's happening, that's a big tell. And when I'm feeling like a particularly bad parent, sometimes it'll happen where I'm like, oh, they'd be better off without me 'cause I'm just traumatizing them.

Q: What do you do?
A: First, if I can, I know I need to go to sleep. Usually if it's with my wife, like, either need to take a nap or just go to bed. And even if we wake up the next morning, pissed off at each other, still the suicidal thoughts are gone. Then I have to remind myself of what my self-care list is. I remind myself, *Okay, Dese'Rae, what do you need? What is going to distract you? What is going to bring you some joy?* I had to come to that on my own, had to be very intentional about that and figure out *Okay, what are these things?*

And for me, one of them was going to the movies alone. Also, give yourself a break, number one. And also, if you think you're a bad parent and that's what's driving these thoughts, well killing yourself doesn't make you a bad parent, but it will certainly fucking hurt them.

Q: It's not going to make you a better parent, even though you might feel like it does in that moment.
A: Sometimes you have that like low rumble of like, *Ugh, it'd be better if I wasn't here.* And it lasts about a day or a couple of minutes, just irritating.

Q: I definitely know that low rumble.
A: That's when like the actual self-care list kicks in. So, for example, I have a list of movies that I like that are comforting, and they're kind of sad and whatever. And I just, you know, indulge a little.

Q: Can you give me a couple of examples?
A: *This Is Where I Leave You* is a favorite. *The Perks of Being a Wallflower.* I've watched that movie so many times. *The Family Stone.* That one's good for mommy issues. Or I'll spend time with my dogs.

Q: What else should a person do?
A: Individualized self-care is something that we're absolutely missing. Also, I always get people who are like, "I'm suicidal or my friend's suicidal, and I need to go see somebody, but what do I do? I've had terrible experiences in therapy." I'm like, "What does your therapist specialize in? Have they worked with suicidal people before? Have

they worked with people who hurt themselves? Did you ask them in advance about their policies on hospitalization?" I didn't learn how to do that until I was thirty-two, thirty-three. I had to tell someone the other day, 'cause she was talking about having obsessive suicidal thoughts, which is a version of OCD that I didn't know existed until last year. And it's like, you're not actually suicidal. You're just constantly afraid that you're going to kill yourself. So I explained, "You cannot walk into a therapist's office without knowing where they stand on this, or you will be instantly hospitalized."

Q: You're just going to get hospitalized, before you even leave the office?
A: Right. So, we need to think and talk about how you find a therapist.

Q: Maybe the most significant survival technique that any of us can develop is having a therapeutic relationship with ourselves.
A: This is this education piece. And being able to say, *You know what, I'm going to have to be the one who owns this, this mental situation of mine. And until I own this mental situation of mine, it's going to continue to victimize me.* But at some level you're the one who has to take responsibility for that, because no one is going to do it for you, at least for now.

Q: It's hard to know who else to trust with your mental health. Have you had a good psychiatrist?
A: Yes. One psychiatrist in particular validated me. I said, "I don't want to go on an SSRI because it gives me sexual side effects. It makes me feel like a zombie." And she said, "Sounds like you could be resistant to SSRI." And I said, "Wait, that's allowed? I can just say no thanks? Not for me?" And I also had a bipolar diagnosis at the time, which, turns out, I'm not bipolar. It's ADD. So she made a little list of medications and explained each one, and she was like, "What do you think?" And I was like, "What do you mean?"

Q: That's a good psychiatrist.
A: And she was like, "I mean, I can write you the scripts if you want, and you can go do some research and you can fill it or not. Or we can talk about other options." And I thought, *This is so weird. Just having agency. Having it be a collaboration, able to take responsibility over my own care.*

Q: It's sometimes easier to turn that over to someone else.

A: People don't want to think about their mental health all the time, like fucking obsessed with this. But that's what we need more information about. Here's how you do it. Here's how to think about self-care. Here's a WRAP plan, a wellness recovery action plan. This is how you personalize it. Think about your self-care. Think about your triggers. Write these things down. That's what got me to a place where I was like, *All right, well, it's these movies. It's the dogs. It's going to the movies alone.* It's also like getting a huge Starbucks iced coffee and walking around the Upper East Side. It was very specific to me. That's what made me happy.

Q: Those are real things that can keep a person from killing themselves.

A: All it is, is distraction.

Q: To get past that crisis moment.

A: And here's another thought. How as a society we can do better. I was having this conversation with Jack Jordan recently. He is one of the big clinician researchers around suicide. And we were talking the other day about how physician aid in dying should be legal. You know, the idea of the good death that Peggy Battin talks about. Jack said, "I think it should be legalized." If someone wants to end their life, families should have input. And I'm like, legalize it, introduce a ton of bureaucracy applications. Make it legal, make a center for it. At such a center, they would tell you: If you're in crisis, you'll feel, all right, this is a valid decision that I can make. I can choose to end my life. And I better fill out this application. That's distraction. This is maybe the one time bureaucracy could save lives, because a bunch of paperwork could get a person past the crisis point.

Q: And there is statistical evidence that shows once medical assistance in dying is available . . .

A: Most people don't use it?

Q: The fact that you do have an exit helps you to see that you don't have to take it.

A: I've been thinking about this, this aid in dying thing, and how I think it could save a lot of lives, and like, being able to choose how to go. Even if no one agrees with you, you can say: this is what I'm doing, I'm going, so I would love for you to be there. And then all of a sudden how many fewer people would die scared?

In 2001 when Andrew Solomon's *The Noonday Demon: An Atlas of Depression* was published, I was living in Austin, Texas, with Rebecca, before she became my wife. I had returned to the University of Texas to finish the Ph.D. that I had left incomplete when I joined my brothers in the jewelry business for six long, harrowing years, from 1994 to 2000. The book was immediately recognized as one of the most important works on depression to appear in decades.

When I read the book, I felt like someone else had described my own personal experience. It was a revelation, really: I had read many articles, short stories, memoirs, and books written by other people from the depths of their depression, but for me (and thousands of others), no one had ever before captured so well exactly what it felt like to be depressed. When I asked the great contemporary writer Margo Jefferson about her own struggles with depression, she told me that she, too, first learned to accept and manage her struggle with depression when she read some early work of Solomon's in *The New Yorker*. I'm sure this is true of many people.

Andrew has since become one of the leading champions in the world for people struggling with depression and suicide. His writing in *The New Yorker* and elsewhere, which I can't recommend enthusiastically enough, has also been revolutionary for our contemporary cultural thinking about what it means to have a family. We spoke over Zoom on a warm day in December 2020.

Q: Andrew, when a student or a reader comes to you and says, "I don't think I can keep on going," what do you say to that person?

A: I do have people come to me and say that. I also have people come to me and say that they've been considering suicide and found my work helpful. To quote somebody, I don't remember who, "Suicide is a permanent solution to a temporary problem." I tend to tell people that. And that depression is extremely common and much more common than most people have realized. If you write a book about it, you discover how common it is because everyone you meet talks to you about their depression. It's immensely common but it is in most cases treatable.

I've often said to people that I do believe in a right to suicide in certain cases, when someone has genuinely intractable illness whether physical or mental, but there are many steps between feeling like killing yourself and confirming that you have a genuinely intractable condition and that your life is intolerable. And I say that one of the sad curses in the experience of depression is that while you're in it, it feels permanent. It is difficult to remember that you ever felt better, and it's difficult to believe that you will ever feel better. But the reality is that you have felt better in the past and you are fully capable of feeling better again. And I say there are thousands of treatments out there, and it is very difficult to sort of deal with them, and you respond to this medication or that medication or to EMTR or psychoanalysis or what's available to you, what insurance you have, and there are a million questions that are involved.

But then for most people, ultimately, something can work, and the great mistake is to give up too soon because actually life is rare and precious, and if you can pull yourself out of the depression then there are many good reasons to stay alive.

Q: I sometimes think that being depressed is a little bit like when you're really cold. If it's winter outside and you're really cold, the thought of being warm is just completely inconceivable, you can't imagine it. Maybe you're on a beach somewhere, and it is maybe a little too hot and you think about what it is like to be cold. That's just inconceivable. A question that I really wanted to ask you is, What do you do when you feel it coming on? Or when you worry that it might be coming on?

A: I have a lot of basic behavioral things that I do: I try to regularize my sleep, I try to make sure that I'm eating enough, drinking enough water, and I give up drinking alcohol. I'm not a heavy drinker anyway, but I still give it up. I try to make sure that I exercise, even though I essentially always hated exercising, but I particularly do it when I'm feeling depressed and low. I go to meet my psychopharmacologist to see whether there are any adjustments that can be made to my medication that might make a difference, sometimes there are, sometimes there aren't.

The last episode I had that was considered a very serious episode was three years ago now. It lasted for eight months, I would say. That was eight months where I was feeling really incapacitated and really struggling to get through things. I felt it was very important not to burden my children with it, so I worked very hard at seeming undepressed in my interactions with them. And that actually, though it was stressful, turned out to be helpful.

Q: Could you say a bit more about that?

A: Research shows that if you smile, your mood lifts, that curling the corners of your mouth upward can create the cheer it seems to reflect. Trying to act undepressed for the world when you are in agony is a living hell, but giving in completely to depression feels like drowning. There's a middle path, in which the corners of your psychic grin are not themselves a stress but a redemption.

Q: Yes, that makes sense.

A: But also, I tried to remind myself that I've been through this, and if I was able to get through it before, then I will eventually get through it again. But it was also surprising. I remember in that particular episode, despite having written my book and despite having had various episodes and so on, I remember having dinner with a friend and I said, "Do you feel like . . . ," and I sort of just described what I was feeling as I said to you. And she said, "But I had depression and I felt that way then and you've had depression and felt that way then. But you aren't going to feel that way in the long term."

Q: So she gave you your own advice, and it helped?

A: Exactly. The other thing I do is that I try to cut off contact with the larger social world of New York that I can find fun when I'm feeling more up and to limit myself to a relatively small number of people, but to be very open with that small number of people and say that I am wrestling with this now so that I have their support and their comfort. Part of what I do even when I'm not depressed is to try to put in place structures so that when I am depressed, there will be people who would be confident to give me advice. People I love who can give me reassurance, and people I hire for their wisdom in these areas and to try to have all of that in place and to be very direct when it happens.

Q: Recently a friend was asking me, "What do you think you actually do that is keeping you from committing suicide right now or trying to commit suicide?" I listed these structure kinds of things. The most banal sorts of things: my family, paying bills on time, exercise, and all these like very ordinary simple things. But I worry about teenagers and college-age kids. For a teenager or a college-age kid, everything that you and I might rely upon is less accessible to them. They are not necessarily in a position to put those kinds of structures in place. (On this subject, please also see the resources "For Young People and Parents" in Appendix I.)

A: The worst episodes of depression are your first and your last, because in your first you don't know that you can get through it, and by the time you get to the fourth time that you've been depressed, even if you emotionally feel like, *I'm in a desperate place from which I'll never recover,* intellectually at least you know, *Well, I got through this last time, I'm not sure if I'm up for all these months of it, but I guess I'll get through it again.* But then you get to the point where it happens over and over and over again, what I think of as a Virginia Woolf pain, where you think, *I actually just can't do this anymore,* and that's where I think people tend to commit suicide.

Obviously everyone commits suicide in their last episode of depression because you cannot have any more episodes after you've killed yourself. But I tend to think that the most dangerous stages are that first stage which is what you're talking about with these college students. And also, I mean, I'm less bewildered by it than I was, I'm no less anguished by it, but I don't feel like, *What on earth is happening to me? I don't recognize myself. Who am I?*

That ties into a thing that I've said a lot in the book, which is that I think one of the most important things you can do is to incorporate your depression into your life narrative. When you do that, when you have another depression, you think, *Oh it's this thing and it happened to me five years ago and I guess I got five years that were okay, and now it's happening, and here's how I dealt with it last time.*

A lot of people get depression and then they never want to think about it again once they get out of it because it was so awful, and there's the will to escape, and those are the people who ironically, I think, are the most subject to the horrors of their own depression because it isn't in their life narrative, and when it recurs, as it almost inevitably does, they don't know what to do with it, and they're left completely high and dry.

I guess the first episode thing, it's really tough. I think it's helpful to say that to people and to say to them, "You know, I've had it a bunch of times, many people have had it a bunch of times, it's happening to you for the first time, and it doesn't make any sense, but when you emerge from the worst of it, you'll be able to find some rational ideas to put around."

Q: I can imagine a lot of people responding to that way of thinking about it. Incorporating it into our life narrative: there's a great reassurance in something making sense. In the book you mention that you have this sometimes quieter, sometimes louder suicidal narrative that is running through you. You say you might see a subway train coming and think, *Oh! Maybe I should jump in front of this one.* I wonder if you have any thoughts about dealing with that way of thinking.

A: Well, I mean, there are a few pieces to that. One of them is that I've been in the sometimes burdensome but ultimately fortunate situation of always being aware that if I were to do that, it would be very damaging to other people. For many years I knew it would be very damaging to my father, and now I know it would be very damaging to my husband, especially to my children. Having children raises the guardrail up to the chest level, and I can't just lean over and jump off in the way that at one point I felt like I could. And there have been times certainly when I've felt like, you know, you know you're not allowed to think that anymore.

Even before I had children, I had to have a real conversation with myself and say, *Okay, no, you will be traumatizing people.* But I mean children of people who've committed suicide are traumatized through their whole lives. So for me, if I wanted to think of having children, which I very much did, I thought I had to recognize that in having that wish I was closing down a possibility for myself.

But obviously there are many people who know all that and get to the point of such desperation that it's unbearable to stay alive for another minute. And I don't wish in any way to sound as though I'm passing judgment on those people. It's not that I think it's selfish and irresponsible the way people say. I think it reflects profound despair and also often a distorted way of thinking in which you don't recognize the damage that you will cause, because your mind has shifted to the point where you feel that you're only a burden on everyone.

Q: You might even think you're doing them a favor by eliminating yourself. That's how distorted your thinking can become.

A: But I find it always reassuring to know that the possibility is there. I frequently think, *Okay, if I can get through today, then I can always end it all tomorrow, and I can't commit going through the next six months, but I think I can commit getting through lunchtime tomorrow.* And then at lunchtime tomorrow I think, *I think I can do one more afternoon or one more day or one more week and whatever it is depending upon what my actual state of mind is.*

My mother was diagnosed with cancer when she was fifty-seven and she died when she was fifty-eight, eighteen months later. I'm now fifty-seven, and for a long time I had a magical thinking idea that if my mother has died at this age, then I was going to die at this age, too. I passed that through various kinds of work, but a piece of me keeps me thinking, *What if I only have another year?* And I definitely have got a mix of feelings that it would be a terrible tragedy, I have so much to live for, there's so much I want to do. And thinking, well, that in a way that would be a relief. And that piece of thinking, oh well it would be kind of a relief is the direct opposite of thinking that I have so much to live for. I'm aware that that's a depressive tendency and that having flirted so closely with suicide made me have a very different relationship to the idea of dying. Now if I'm in an airplane and there's terrible turbulence and it feels like we're going to crash, I feel terrified and I don't think *Oh, that would be a relief.* But in the abstract thinking about a crash or a sudden death, I think, *Well, you know, I'll miss everyone, but I'll be done with this, the work of staying alive.* I mean I feel having been where I've been, the work of every day saying *Oh yes, I'm going to be alive today, and I'm going to do my best to remain alive.* You know, it takes a kind of recommitment every day.

Q: One of my favorite observations in your book is that preparing yourself rationally for the thought of suicide can help you when you find yourself confronting the irrational desire to kill yourself.

A: Yes, I mean I think the relationship between one's intellect and one's emotions is so convoluted, and the process of trying to clarify it is so labor intensive. Often a danger is that if you spend a lot of time contemplating suicide, you cease to be afraid of it. And once you're not afraid of it, it's harder to resist. But having said that, if you have thought it through a bunch of times and not done it, and then you have a moment when you think, *Oh you know, I'm thinking about this again. I didn't do it last time. Is there any particular reason to do it this time if I didn't do it last time?* It sort of informs you and you think, *Well, all right, maybe I won't.*

Q: It's analogous to the way you characterize depression. It's like a rational preparation for the passion. You've thought it through first, so you're in a better position to have that appropriate relationship with the emotional response that ultimately will inform the will.

A: My college roommate killed himself ten years ago, eleven years ago, thereabouts. I wrote something about him and his suicide, about the idea of suicide for our college alumni magazine, but it then had quite a lot of circulation, and I finally put it in a collection I organized. But I have so many friends whom I was worried about. Terry was the one I was never worried about, he seemed exuberant and upbeat. After he killed himself, I read through the emails he had sent me over a year or so before he died. We were not inseparably close friends, but he was one I loved and cared about. He lived in Rome, I lived in New York, we didn't see each other all the time. When I read the emails, I thought it was pretty clear from these emails that he was having quite a really rough time. And I wrote back kind of cheerfully, "Oh well, I'm sure you'll get through it," because I just didn't, from the knowledge I had of him, which was clearly much more limited than I realized, I didn't think that there was a lot of danger there, and I was devastated by his death.

I have a painting of him that hangs in my house. He's very present to me a lot of the time. He is in some ways more present to me because of that death than he was when he was alive. And I feel like, not that I could've prevented it, but maybe if I had understood what was going on, I would've been on the next plane to Rome and I would've tried to do whatever I could. And I sometimes think that a lot of people who are outgoing and charming and talkative have a cover over emotions that are more exposed in people whose depression is fully outwardly manifest. And so I think that while in many ways it's much better to have a high-functioning depression to go on doing things that you need to do. Your whole life doesn't fall apart if you can actually continue to function in your professional and family relationships. I think in some ways people who don't fall apart in such obvious ways end up having a harder time because they are neglected or ignored by people, even someone who's written a whole book on depression. It's so hard to be adequately attuned to other people. I feel I was inadequately attuned to what Terry was dealing with.

I recognize that sometimes I'm inadequately attuned to my own vagaries and ups and downs that it's very easy to drift into thinking, *Well, I seem to be okay.* It's easy to forget how around the corner it is, how imminent it is, how terrible it is, and how easily one can end up succumbing to it. And in the same way, back to your wonderful metaphor of being hot or cold, I think in the same way that you can't imagine being hot when you're cold and cold when you're hot, you also can't imagine being suicidal when you aren't and not suicidal when you are. I think it's kind of both things, both kinds of memory that are impossible.

JOHN DRAPER: "YOU HAVE A GIFT"

John Draper is the "suicide helpline guy" in America. If you talk to anyone in the suicide help community for very long, chances are the name John Draper will come up. He has been one of America's leading experts on suicide prevention for about twenty-five years now. He is actively involved in the direction and administration of a number of national crisis hotline networks, including the Disaster Distress Helpline, the U.S. Department of Veterans Affairs' Veterans Crisis Line, and the National Football League's NFL Life Line. He was also the founding director of LifeNet, the crisis hotline that was central to New York's mental health response following the attacks of 9/11. John and I spoke over Zoom on December 4, 2020.

Q: John, you've probably talked to and helped more people who are feeling suicidal than just about anyone else on the planet. What do you say? What do you train people to say?

A: It's not terribly tricky. Be human with them. People tend to think that you have to make them not feel that way. But that's not the best approach. Let them feel the way they're feeling. For every one who dies, there are 280 people who think about it. So you can talk people through this feeling.

Q: How do we best do that?

A: Everybody can do it, first of all. And there are things we can say that therapists and counselors can never say, because they have professional guidelines, insurance, regulations, all that. It's about making a connection, a quality connection. Of course, first you should ask, "Are you thinking about hurting yourself? About suicide?" Research shows us that it doesn't plant the seed, it provides relief, it gives the person permission to talk about it. Explain that you are concerned, you care, you want to talk about it. Then whatever they tell you, just listen, reflect, be curious. Make no judgments. You might let them know that they can get through this.

Ask, "Have you thought about how you're going to kill yourself?" They may say a rope, pills, whatever. Then you could say, "Can I hang on to that for you? I care too much about you. You don't have to be alone with this." It's about scaling helpfulness. What if we just remind the person what it means to show care?

You might also ask that person, "Who else can we trust with this?" Because ideally we can surround the person with people who care, who are watching out for them. And then, maybe most important, after the conversation, follow up. Tell them you're going to check on them. Make a note to yourself so you're sure to do it. Maybe even tell them when you're going to check. And if you can, check regularly, make it a regular thing. It doesn't have to be much. Just check in.

Q: It does seem like a process that a friend or family member is almost in a better position to do than anyone else.

A: Absolutely. There's no question about that. We've taught people that they should just leave it to the professionals, but we need to empower people. We can all do this. And it will take a lot of us doing it, actively doing it, to reduce the crisis that we are facing right now. Because with Covid, I'm afraid things are going to get a lot worse.

Q: What about after a suicide attempt? Is there something one should particularly say?

A: This is particularly important. I tell people, "Now you have a gift. You probably have no idea about that, but you understand this in a way that others don't. You can help others in a way that other people can't." People who have attempted suicide are the real experts on suicidality. The best things I've learned about suicide are the things I've learned from friends of mine who are suicidal.

A problem with suicidal thinking is that we make a mistake in our thinking. We transition from the idea that we are experiencing pain to the idea that we are the pain. You start thinking that the pain would go away if you were gone. That you'd be better, that everyone would be better. But the reality is that the pain doesn't go away. It just gets worse. It becomes a legacy of pain.

Q: Some philosophers argue this idea too, that it doesn't really end the pain but makes it permanent.

A: Exactly. When a person is suicidal, it's not their life that they want to end. It's something in their life that they want to change. If that could change, how would your life be different? That fact, that there could be a difference, that's where the meaning is. Think of all the pain we've been through. That should mean something. That pain is too important to waste it. All the pain that led you to a suicide attempt, or to the thought of a suicide attempt, that could be the climax rather than the denouement. It could be a victory of meaning. There's a book called *The Power of Meaning* by Emily Esfahani Smith. I really recommend that book.

Q: Is there something in particular one might say when a person is, so to speak, right at the edge of the cliff? Suppose someone is feeling that way right now, reading this interview.

A: Look back and ask yourself what got you there, to the cliff's edge. I think you'll see that what feels like one big boulder is actually a pile of rocks. You can take a rock off here and there. And suddenly you realize that you have agency. You have the power to go on living.

CANDICE BIGGINS:
"STRETCH YOUR PERSPECTIVE BEYOND THIS MOMENT"

When talking about suicide and suicide treatment with people here in Kansas City, I asked around about counselors and therapists people respected in the local area. Because I am a white male and there's a lot of white maleness in this book, I was particularly interested to learn about people who might be helping women and other people who weren't like me, people who weren't middle-aged middle-class white males. One name started coming up a lot: Candice Biggins at Rose Brooks.

Rose Brooks is an emergency shelter in Kansas City designed specifically to help people and families who are facing life-threatening abuse—"We not only protect hundreds of adults, children and their pets," they say on the homepage of their website—but also many people who simply can't get quality psychological help anywhere else. Candice is a therapist there. I was warned that "Candice is a very busy, very private person," and that she was unlikely to talk to me. But after a few phone calls and a number of texts, she agreed, and we had this conversation below. Candice wanted me to particularly note that she is speaking not as a representative of Rose Brooks but about her own experience in trying to help people.

Q: If someone comes to you and you can tell that this person has reached a point of panic and despair, where they are considering self-harm or even suicide, what do you do?

A: You can't always tell. And so I think it's important to ask. You really don't know what another person's plan is or what they're thinking. But the only way that you can find out is if you ask the right questions, and it's not just asking, it's also how you ask and when you ask. I think it's important to build a relationship with that person so that they're more likely to give you an honest answer. And relationship building, in my experience, can happen pretty quickly. I mean, in a matter of minutes, really, if you take that not-knowing stance and adopt that active and engaged listening. Ask them about themselves. "What brings you here?" Listen for some of those triggers, and listen for some of those negative thoughts that could be predictors of some suicidal ideation. Ask with the knowledge that it's uncomfortable. I know a lot of people have difficulty with assessing for suicidal ideation because of fear that they're going to impact the relationship in a negative way, or because it's not comfortable. But one of the things I've learned is to accept and lean into the discomfort. It's never comfortable to ask someone those types of questions. It's never comfortable to sit in a space with someone who's in that degree of pain. And so just acknowledge that this isn't going to be comfortable, but it really isn't about your comfort. It's about this person's safety. And so just manage that.

Q: This is about the other person, and being willing to lean into that uncomfortableness.

A: It's helped me to be present with people. Especially when you're younger, and I don't mean in terms of age but in terms of experience, we can be triggered a lot by hearing other people's experiences. But it's so important first of all to have that awareness, and second, to be very intentional on managing that because in that space, it really is about the client. It's not about you. So have that compassion, but work really hard on your own empathy. There's a balance between compassion and empathy. But empathy is really about you. *This is something in me, this is being triggered.* And so you want to manage that so that you have more capacity to have compassion for the person you're working with. To be more present for them so that you can help support them through whatever challenge they're experiencing.

Q: My partner sometimes says that compassion isn't something you can demand. It's something you can only offer to others. Is there anything that you feel like you could say to a person from the pages of a book when they're in a space of despair?

A: One of the things that I do when people are really feeling in that place of despair and hopelessness is, I try to help them stretch their perspective. I can say, "Right now, this is how you're feeling. But when you are able to stretch your perspective and look a little bit beyond your circumstances, you know this feeling will shift, it will change. You've had experience in this space before, and it shifted and it changed." One thing I would recommend is to just try to stretch your perspective beyond this moment. And that can be really difficult, but it can be really helpful if you have someone with you who can support you through that. I know it's not always possible to have someone with you. There are things that you could do to help you to manage this moment so that you can move beyond it.

Q: We need, in those moments, if we can, to stretch our perspective a little bit.

A: And it can be hard. But one thing that I try to do with a person is to normalize that. It doesn't have to be anything huge or profound. It can be a very slight shift because any slight shift is going to change the dynamic. What's just one thing you can do? What's just one thing you can focus on or think about that can shift you out of this moment, however slightly?

Q: What might you say to people, Candice, when they have had a recent suicide attempt and now they are still alive and trying to return to normal life?

A: It depends on the relationship that I have with the person, because sometimes you're working with people that you have an established relationship with and then sometimes you're meeting people through an intake assessment who have a history of suicidal attempts and they may have just been discharged from the hospital. And so it's going to depend on that for one. I would ask them, "What helped you to feel better? What helped you to move beyond that space?" Really fleshing that out. Identify what keeps you connected to life. Helping people to reflect on that. When you ask that question, you find so many different ways that people feel connected, and not in traditional ways that you may think. It can be "Because I love my dogs," or "I really enjoy taking care of my plants." It can be anything. What is it that keeps you connected? Again, perspective stretching. This won't work with younger people, but when you're forty, or thirty, you have life experiences to tap into. You can say, *Hey, I survived this before. I was able to tolerate this before. I can make it through.*

CLANCY-IN-CRISIS

I'm not going to bore you with a Q&A between Clancy and me. But at the end of this appendix, I do want to mention a way I have of trying to talk myself through really awful suicidal moments. This is a technique I have used while concretely preparing to kill myself, and it has worked.

It's a list of ten questions I try to ask myself (made with the help of Edwin S. Shneidman's *The Suicidal Mind*). Some of them have follow-up questions that go along with them. I also often rely on these questions, or variations on them, when someone comes to me to say that they are thinking of suicide.

I don't think the answers to these questions should or do necessarily determine my course of action. But before I kill myself, even if I'm not willing to talk to someone else about it, this is one way I try to talk to myself about it.

1. Is there anything I can do, right now, to feel less panicky, less threatened, less hemmed in? Clancy, could you take a long walk? Clancy, can you do what almost every expert on panic and anxiety says to do, and slow down to take some deep breaths?

2. What am I trying to escape? Clancy, could you be specific? Are there other ways to escape?
3. Do I want to turn off my whole mind? Or just the part that hurts?
4. Is there any other way to alleviate my psychological pain, just a little? For that matter, is my psychological pain unbearable?
5. What is the main frustration that is making me so freaked out? Is that as big as it seems?
6. Is there anything I could hope for? Is there anything I can do to help? To help me?
7. Is there anything I care about?
8. Can you wait until tomorrow to escape? Will you still be able to escape tomorrow?
9. Clancy, have you told someone else that you are planning on killing yourself today? Can you? One last call. Come on, you could do that. Could you please try? At least a text. Okay, you texted. What did they say?
10. Are you here now because of a pattern? Could you be a little less fucking predictable?

When I'm feeling desperate, I try to run through at least a few of these questions, if I can make myself do it, by keeping them in a document here on my computer. I also keep them in the notes section of my phone. When I'm really freaking out, the list seems too long and makes me claustrophobic, so I'll try to make myself read just one question. It helps me to read them out loud.

I should repeat what I've already said before, that as best we can tell from the current literature, reaching out to someone, my question nine, is supposed to be the best way to avoid a suicide attempt. Nevertheless, for me it's near the bottom of the list, because I can almost never do it. This is also why Dese'Rae L. Stage worries that we shouldn't overemphasize reaching out to someone, because we might tend to think, *Okay, I couldn't reach out, that was my last hope, time to shut it down.*

Maybe you are like me and Dese'Rae and you very often can't reach out to someone when you're at your worst. Well, maybe you can do other things (my question one), like Dese'Rae says. You can go to Starbucks and get a Frappuccino like she used to do, or go to McDonald's and get an ice cream cone like I used to do (ninety-nine cents!), or make a cup of tea, or play a song really, really loud. You can distract yourself. You could watch a YouTube video of Prince singing "When Doves Cry." With the camera slowly zooming up to him in the bathtub, and then when he stands and holds out his hand, you'll feel a tiny bit better. You might even be able to smile at your own pain.

About question four, it sounds intimidating, asking myself if my psychological pain is unbearable. But then I almost always realize that yes, it might be really, really bad, it might feel like a suffocating cloud of poison, but it's bearable. It's more my panic about the pain than the pain itself that is creating the problem.

My favorite is number ten. But I'm not really ready for number ten until I've tried a few others. But this one gets to me. I. Am. So. Fucking. Predictable. Could we please try mixing it up a bit, Clancy? There could be nothing more obvious, more unoriginal, more lame, than me killing myself now, after all this.

And who says, after all, that I have to relate to the problem of me in this way? Do I not have the freedom of a little emotional creativity?

Notes

xv   And that's one of the reasons: I will occasionally mention here, but will
not discuss in detail, the special case of medical assistance in dying—
what used to be called euthanasia—which, generally speaking, I support.
Medical assistance in dying is typically provided when a person is in
acute physical pain and death is imminent. The cases that concern me
in this book are not those but rather the many, many cases in which, had
the suicide attempt failed or had the suicidally inclined person changed
her mind, she would later come to prefer to be alive. This is rarely if
ever the situation of someone suffering from a terminal, incurable, and
painful disease and chooses medical assistance in dying.

xvi   There are certain secrets: For people who have had a loved one commit
suicide and are left behind to deal with the anger, confusion, remorse,
and grief, I recommend Yiyun Li's novel *Where Reasons End* as one of
the best. Excellent studies of people who have taken their own lives,
often to the shock of the people who knew them, include Calvin Trillin's
Remembering Denny and A. Alvarez's *The Savage God*, which focuses on
the death of his close friend Sylvia Plath. Psychologists, psychiatrists,
and sociologists have written many books to classify suicidal types, or
to diagnose the psychic and social problems that lead to suicide, or to
help those who work with suicidal people to understand their thinking.
My own favorite is Kay Redfield Jamison's *Night Falls Fast: Understanding Suicide*. One best-selling book tells you how to kill yourself. (Lately,
people tend to turn to the internet for this purpose and to dark websites
that offer instruction and sometimes even encouragement.) But not a lot
of books are intended specifically for the person who is struggling with
the thought of suicide—who has perhaps, like me, struggled with it all
her life—or for those of us who have tried to commit suicide and failed,
maybe repeatedly.

xvi   "I could admit": Anne Sexton, "Suicide Note," *TriQuarterly* 6, no. 79 (1966).

xvii   It's a tough topic: Suicide is taboo to such an extent that other academics have warned me that writing this book would be a "career-killer." I know a very talented young philosopher who has had a terrible time on the job market because she wrote a dissertation on suicide. The subject makes people nervous and uncomfortable. It's probably fortunate that I felt ready to talk about it late in my career rather than when I was getting started. A lot of people have written to me since I began writing this book to tell me about their own suicide attempts, always with a version of the caveat "Please keep this strictly private."

xviii   But suicide is all around: Here are some statistics: on average, every day in the United States there are 130 suicide attempts that result in death. American Indigenous populations—Native American Indian and Native Alaskan—have the highest rate of suicide attempts in the United States, at the truly shocking figure of 25.5 percent in 2019.

Worldwide, Indigenous populations have significantly higher rates of suicide. Suicide is more common among any population that faces discrimination or sustained mental or physical stress, such as LGBTQI persons, especially among the young; refugees and migrants; prisoners; and people in war zones. Lithuania currently has the highest suicide rate in the world. In an argument for living on an island in the Caribbean—as though any of us actually needed to be persuaded—the Bahamas, Barbados, and Antigua seem to have the lowest. Approximately 700,000 people die by suicide every year that we know of, about one every forty seconds of every day—though because of widespread shame and in many countries legal consequences for the family of the suicide, the actual number is no doubt much larger. The World Health Organization's best guess is that for every suicide resulting in death, there are approximately twenty suicide attempts. Worldwide, suicide is the fourth leading cause of death among fifteen-to-nineteen-year-olds.

Even before the coronavirus pandemic, the rates of suicide and suicide attempts were already on the rise, but particularly because of the stresses the pandemic created, what with isolation and lockdowns, they will likely continue to increase significantly in 2023 and beyond. Dr. David Cates, of the University of Nebraska Medical Center, calls it the possible "pandemic within the pandemic." A survey by the Centers for Disease Control and Prevention in August 2020 showed that 11 percent of 5,470 adult U.S. respondents had "seriously considered suicide" over a thirty-day period in the spring of 2020. The last large survey, done in 2018, showed that 4.3 percent had considered suicide in the previous twelve months. That's not quite triple the earlier rate, but it's more than double, which is alarming. "According to surveys of young Americans coming into emergency rooms, rates of suicidal thinking and behavior are up by 25 percent or more from similar periods in 2019," *The New York Times* reported on February 26, 2021. A survey in 2020 showed a slight decline in suicides, to the surprise and relief of many experts, but the numbers spiked in certain segments of the population.

xviii I used to tell: This observation, or a variant of it, is often attributed to Robert Lowell, though I haven't been able to find it in his work. To be honest, I've been saying it for so long, I don't know whether I read it somewhere and stole it from Lowell or we just had the same obvious conviction.

xviii group called Suicide Anonymous: Please visit this website to find a meeting, especially if you're struggling right now: https://suicideanonymous .net/meeting-list.

xix "I realized that everything": Tad Friend, "Jumpers: The Fatal Grandeur of the Golden Gate Bridge," *New Yorker*, October 6, 2003. Twenty-nine people in recent history attempted suicide by leaping from the Golden Gate Bridge and survived; all claim to have "regretted their decision as soon as they jumped." See Ed Newman, "A Lesson from 29 Golden Gate Suicide Attempts," February 20, 2019, https://ennyman.medium .com/a-lesson-from-29-golden-gate-suicide-attempts-a42f4ef3f970.

It's hard to know how much weight to give these accounts: memory is a strange and unreliable thing, particularly when combined with terror. That said, the fact remains that most people who attempt suicide do not subsequently die of the attempt, even when the means they chose— like leaping from the Golden Gate Bridge—were overwhelmingly likely to prove lethal. This suggests that death by suicide is not the inevitable end of the suicidally inclined person, a thesis that I myself strongly believe and have written this book to support.

xix "I've always had": Laurie Woolever, *Bourdain: The Definitive Oral Biography* (New York: HarperCollins, 2021), 421.

xxi the seven-year-old's: Suicide is very rare among children under the age of five, but the CDC reports that in the past decade, their rates of suicide attempts have increased, and suicide is now the eighth leading cause of death in children five to eleven. "Understanding the Characteristics of Suicide in Young Children," National Institute of Mental Health, December 14, 2021, nimh.nih.gov. That statistic is unfortunately probably low because it is easy to confuse a child's suicide with an accidental death. A recent study of children with suicidal thoughts and words found that, contrary to what had been the established doctrine for years, "children expressing suicidal ideation understand what it means to die, and they understand it better than their peers." Laura Hennefield et al., "Changing Conceptions of Death as a Function of Depression Status, Suicidal Ideation, and Media Exposure in Early Childhood," *Journal of the American Academy of Child and Adolescent Psychiatry* 58, no. 3 (2019): 339–49. Very upsettingly, the closer you look at the contemporary psychiatric literature on suicide, the more you find that suicidal thinking and suicide attempts among children are simply not that different than among suicidally inclined adults.

xxi transform my existence: The psychotherapist James Hillman calls this motivation for suicide "the urge for hasty transformation." James Hillman, *Suicide and the Soul* (Woodstock, N.Y.: Spring, 1965), 73.

xxiii alcohol use disorder: Thinking of the contemporary phrase "alcohol use disorder," I am tempted to call my chronic suicidal thinking "death use disorder," with the unhelpful but apt acronym DUD.

I. THE SUICIDAL MIND

5 I don't recommend it: A friend asked me, "Why don't you recommend the book?" Well, it is a book that tells you how best to kill yourself. Especially if you are the sort of person, like me, who often thinks of suicide, I believe it's better not to have that knowledge. Plus, the book, to my mind at least, makes suicide seem weirdly attractive. It seems to suppose that for the suicidal person, the choice is between life (is it happy or too painful?) and infinite peace. But I don't think we can say with confidence that that is the choice, as I try to explain in this book.

6 I believe in ghosts: The Indigenous American Crow Tribe believed that suicides became ghosts. "Lowest on the list of the dead were the suicides and the murderers. Their souls could not enter the 'Other Side Camp,' but roamed the earth as ghosts." William Wildschut, *Crow Indian Medicine Bundles* (New York: Museum of the American Indian, Heye Foundation, 1975), 35. The Navajo may have believed that the ghosts of suicides were more dangerous than other ghosts. One Navajo interviewed on the subject reported that generally people were "more afraid about people who kill self. They [the suicide] mad all time, got mad when start to kill self. When come back already mad." Leland C. Wyman and Betty Thorne, "Notes on Navaho Suicide," *American Anthropologist* 47, no. 2 (1945): 278.

7 "I have always believed": Yiyun Li, *Dear Friend, From My Life I Write to You in Your Life* (New York: Random House, 2018), 54.

7 And the Canadian physician: Dr. Gabor Maté, *In the Realm of Hungry Ghosts: Close Encounters with Addiction* (New York: North Atlantic Books, 2010). Maté is referring to the Tibetan Buddhist belief that alongside the human realm are a variety of other realms, one of which is the realm of hungry ghosts, where creatures tortured by their insatiability reside.

11 "We can only discuss": Johann Wolfgang von Goethe, *The Sorrows of Young Werther,* trans. Victor Lange and Judith Ryan (New York: Suhrkamp, 1988), 71. When Goethe's novella was published in Germany in 1774, it achieved wild popularity and created a slew of copycat suicides, now sometimes known as "the Werther effect."

11 At least since Saint Augustine: For a good catalog of the terrible things done to the bodies and the families of people who killed themselves over the centuries, see Georges Minois, *History of Suicide: Voluntary Death in Western Culture* (Baltimore: Johns Hopkins University Press, 1999).

12 Moreover, any death by suicide: One reason is that we view suicide as shameful. Another is that publicizing a death by suicide, especially if the person is famous or influential, tends to increase the rate of suicide. I discuss this problem of suicide contagion in Chapter 3.

12 "suicide is looked upon": Shelly Kagan, *Death* (New Haven, Conn.: Yale University Press, 2012), 318.

13 For years, it was dogma: Another ridiculous long-standing dogma of psychiatrists about children is that children don't lie until around age six. (This dogma started to change only quite recently and now has been discarded.) As for young children not committing suicide, as recently as 1979 Jean Baechler claimed, in his great classic *Suicides*, that young children do not do it. As noted in the Preface, and towards the end of the book, this unfortunately is not true.

15 Schopenhauer, whose father committed suicide: It might have been an accident, but his family considered it to be a suicide, and he was a depressed, anxious person whose mental struggles worsened with age.

16 "Suicide is a habit": Dzongsar Jamyang Khyentse Rinpoche, *Living Is Dying: How to Prepare for Dying, Death and Beyond* (Boulder, Colo.: Shambhala, 2020), https://www.siddharthasintent.org/assets/Global-Files /Publications/LiDbookv13.pdf.

17 Maybe it was impulsive: See Arielle H. Sheftall, Lindsey Asti, Lisa M. Horowitz, Adrienne Felts, Cynthia A. Fontanella, "Suicide in Elementary School-Aged Children and Early Adolescents," *Pediatrics* (2016) 138 (4): e20160436.

18 "a tendency to collapse": Alfred Adler, "Suicide," in *Superiority and Social Interest: A Collection of Later Writings*, ed. Heinz L. Ansbacher and Rowena R. Ansbacher (Evanston, Ill.: Northwestern University Press, 1964), 248–52.

19 One might say: I like this observation: "the belief in being nothing used to seem to me the most logical way to live." Yiyun Li, *Dear Friend, From My Life I Write to You in Your Life* (New York: Random House, 2018), 67.

23 miserable and abusive events: Childhood trauma is a well-documented source of subsequent suicidal ideation and predictor of suicide attempts. See Peng Xie et al., "Prevalence of Childhood Trauma and Correlations Between Childhood Trauma, Suicidal Ideation, and Social Support In Patients with Depression, Bipolar Disorder, and Schizophrenia in Southern China," *Journal of Affective Disorders* 228 (2018): 41–48; Yong-Chun Bahk et al., "The Relationship Between Childhood Trauma and Suicidal Ideation: Role of Maltreatment and Potential Mediators," *Psychiatry Investigation* 14, no. 1 (2017): 37.

To my mother's credit, my childhood and that of my brothers was much less abusive than that suffered by my stepbrothers and stepsisters, who really had it bad. Obviously these traumatic childhood events were a significant source of my suicidal ideation, though I remember fantasizing about suicide even before the divorce and remarriage. (My mother divorced my father because of his violent physical abuse of her, so that was also a very unhappy home.) But many people have unhappy, abusive childhoods, and though that certainly makes subsequent suicidal thinking and suicide attempts more likely, it is not the whole story of the suicidal mind or an adult's relationship with suicide. I don't know if I would have been a suicidal person had I grown up in a happy home. My suicidal tendencies may well have begun as a consequence of childhood abuse, but the story I'm trying to tell you is the one of how I navigated that terrain as I grew from a suicidal adolescent into a suicidal young man and then a repeat suicide attempter in my thirties and forties.

23   committing suicide: The phrase "commit suicide" has become controversial since Doris Sommer-Rotenburg, "Suicide and Language," *Journal of the Canadian Medical Association* 159, no. 3 (August 1998): 239–40. Sommer-Rotenburg, whose son took his own life, pointed out that "commit" has criminal overtones ("commit a crime") and other pejorative connotations, as in "having someone committed." Here I use a great variety of terms and phrases to refer to the act of ending one's own life, and I mean none of them pejoratively. I want to speak respectfully of anyone who has died in this way, while also arguing that most often the act is an avoidable mistake.

23   My older brother: Darren was for years a classic case of the parasuicidal type, embracing a self-destructive lifestyle that led him both to prison and to many near-misses with death. I'll discuss parasuicides and how they related to more overtly suicidal types in the pages to come.

23   run in families: We don't have definitive evidence on the question of whether a tendency toward suicide may be hereditary, but increasingly the prevailing opinion is that suicidal behavior has a genetic component. An early champion of the view that suicidal tendencies were hereditary—and therefore not the fault of the suicidal person—was the great nineteenth-century French psychiatrist and philosopher Jean-Étienne-Dominique Esquirol (1772–1840). See his *Mental Maladies: A Treatise on Insanity*, trans. E. K. Hunt (Philadelphia: Lea & Blanchard, 1845), 253–317. For a brilliant discussion of recent research on a "suicide gene," see Kay Redfield Jamison, *Night Falls Fast: Understanding Suicide* (New York: Vintage, 2011), 182–212.

23   genetic factors: See Jamison, *Night Falls*, 78–82, 165–73, and 198–200.

23   Ludwig Wittgenstein: The fact that a member of one's own family committed suicide may make it easier to choose to do so. It may implicitly

give one permission to take one's own life, or it may worsen the psychological factors that incline one toward an attempt.

25 "As soon as the terrors": Arthur Schopenhauer, "On Suicide," in *Studies in Pessimism: A Series of Essays,* trans. T. Bailey Saunders (London: Swan Sonnenschein, 1893), 43–50.

26 "At the same time": Jim Lowrey, *Taming Untameable Beings* (New York: Blue Horse, 2015), 202–3.

26 "Rinpoche said that": Ibid., 201.

30 "Stabbing myself": A reader observed that I also claim that I've never been interested in harming myself. I haven't. That's part of what makes these thoughts of self-injury—which seem to come from outer space, almost, they are so alien to me—particularly upsetting. But having obsessive and self-destructive thoughts, including thoughts that run counter to one's desires, is very common in depression and related mental distresses. Several people have told me they suffer from chronic suicidal ideation despite having no desire to die. (I don't suffer from this problem—my suicidal ideation and the desire to die always run hand in hand, and in fact the latter seems to cause the former.)

30 "But the will to fight": The will to fight may be the opposite of hopelessness. But I wonder whether having the strength or courage to go on living even requires hope. I'd like to think that one could be utterly without hope for the future—that one could have no expectations about it—and still choose to go on living. I want to believe this because I suspect the future may well not be better than the past. If my fifty-four years have taught me anything, it's that the future has all kinds of unexpected suffering planned for me. I'm not depressed or in physical pain today, and my children are all well and seem reasonably happy. Today is probably the best it's ever going to get. Should I really be hoping? Or could I rather try to find reasons to live right now, at this very moment, that don't involve expectation of a better or easier tomorrow?

31 "He has failed": Leon Cytryn and Donald McKnew, *Growing Up Sad: Childhood Depression and Its Treatment* (New York: W. W. Norton, 1998), 72. This book is crucial reading for people who worry about children and suicide.

32 "Practically, you should": Dzongsar Jamyang Khyentse Rinpoche, "Vipassana, 11–12 December 2020," lecture, https://www.youtube.com /watch?v=8zTeNjrqXE8.

32 "a deeper type of pain": D. T. Max, *Every Love Story Is a Ghost Story: A Life of David Foster Wallace* (New York: Penguin, 2013), 281.

33 "I have learned to look": Sunita Puri, "We Must Learn to Look at Grief, Even When We Want to Run Away," *New York Times,* February 23, 2022.

2. IS THERE A DEATH DRIVE?

35 Tom Bradford: Throughout this book, some of the names of people in my own life have been changed.

37 "a desire for": In Thích Nhất Hạnh's letter to Martin Luther King, Jr., he explained that the monks who died by self-immolation to protest the Vietnam war were not in fact committing suicide—they had no desire to die. Rather, they were engaged in an especially powerful form of speech and protest. They were not escaping their lives but sacrificing their physical bodies in an act of excruciating pain. In a Christian context, these acts would have been interpreted as martyrdom suicides, which were similarly viewed not as taking or escaping one's life but rather as offering it in the service of a higher good. Thích Nhất Hạnh, *Vietnam: Lotus in a Sea of Fire* (New York: Hill & Wang, 1967), 106–8. See also Thích Nhất Hạnh, *Love in Action: Writings on Nonviolent Social Change* (Berkeley, Calif.: Parallax Press, 1993).

37 three fundamental forms: John M. Koller, *Asian Philosophies*, 7th ed. (New York: Routledge, 2018), 57.

38 fundamental aversion: Having a great fear of death is not incompatible with suffering from the desire for self-annihilation. Part of that suffering may well be the fear that comes with that desire. In fact, many of our desires are accompanied by anxiety, anguish, and fear. Something as simple as the desire to eat a second piece of cake or a fourth slice of pizza may fill some people with terrible self-loathing and panic. That doesn't refute the desire or make it go away.

38 "we have all received": Jean-Jacques Rousseau, *Julie, or the New Heloïse*, in *The Collected Writings of Rousseau*, trans. Philip Steward and Jean Vaché (Hanover, N.H.: University Press of New England, 1997), letters 21 and 22, 6:310–23. In a famous essay on suicide, Rousseau's sometime friend David Hume wrote, "For such is our natural horror of death, that small motives will never be able to reconcile us to it." David Hume, "Of Suicide" (1757), in *Dialogues Concerning Natural Religion*, ed. Richard H. Popkin, 2nd ed. (Indianapolis: Hackett, 1980), 104.

38 "One's wish to die": Yiyun Li, *Dear Friend, From My Life I Write to You in Your Life* (New York: Random House, 2018), 51.

38 "didn't hate death": Jean Améry, *On Suicide: A Discourse on Voluntary Death* (Bloomington: Indiana University Press, 1999), xix.

39 and to death (Thanatos): Many philosophers and psychoanalysts of the twentieth century, including Jacques Lacan and Melanie Klein, have defended and expanded on Freud's notion of the death drive. The contemporary philosopher Slavoj Žižek uses the death drive to explain our rampant consumerism, which seems addictive and destructive both of individual happiness and of the health of the planet.

39 "I made my first suicide": Nelly Arcan, *Exit*, trans. David Scott Hamilton (Vancouver: Anvil Press, 2011), 123.

39 practice before: Although we don't have very good data on the subject, an international review of psychological autopsy studies has estimated that approximately 40 percent of those who die by suicide have made a previous attempt. J. Cavanagh et al., "Psychological Autopsy Studies of Suicide: A Systematic Review," *Psychological Medicine* 33 (2003): 395–405. The people I discuss in this book mostly made multiple attempts before their actual death by suicide. Virginia Woolf, for example, tried at least three times; Anne Sexton tried several times, as did Dorothy Parker and David Foster Wallace.

40 "Practice, practice, practice": Margo Jefferson, *Negroland* (New York: Vintage, 2016), 178.

40 To people who have never wanted to kill themselves, or who wonder why a person like me might try repeatedly and fail—and I've talked to so many people who've tried repeatedly and failed, some of them only a few times, some of them many—I would like to say that irresolution is part of being human, and it may be particularly understandable when it comes to the question of taking one's own life. "You're just being dramatic! Melodramatic!" Of course. Does that make the desire any less real? Does it make it any less threatening?

41 "an urgent and strongly felt": "Cri de coeur" in *The Cambridge Dictionary*, https://dictionary.cambridge.org/us/dictionary/english/cri-de-coeur.

42 This was why Mahatma Gandhi: Gandhi tells an illuminating story in his autobiography: "But we were far from being satisfied with such things as these. Our want of independence began to smart. It was unbearable that we should be unable to do anything without the elders' permission. At last, in sheer disgust, we decided to commit suicide!

"But how were we to do it? From where were we to get the poison? We heard that *Dhatura* seeds were an effective poison. Off we went to the jungle in search of these seeds, and got them. Evening was thought to be the auspicious hour. We went to *Kedarji Mandir*, put ghee in the temple-lamp, had the *darshan* and then looked for a lonely corner. But our courage failed us. Supposing we were not instantly killed? And what was the good of killing ourselves? Why not rather put up with the lack of independence? But we swallowed two or three seeds anyway. We dared not take more. Both of us fought shy of death, and decided to go to *Ramji Mandir* to compose ourselves, and to dismiss the thought of suicide.

"I realized that it was not as easy to commit suicide as to contemplate it. And since then, whenever I have heard of someone threatening to commit suicide, it has had little or no effect on me." Mohandas K. Gandhi, *An Autobiography: The Story of My Experiments with Truth*, trans. Mahadev Desai (Boston: Beacon Press, 1957), 25–28.

42 "All the Valeries": Kees Van Heeringen, *The Neuroscience of Suicidal Behavior* (Cambridge: Cambridge University Press, 2018), xi.

43 Elvita Adams: "Woman Survives Fall at the Empire State," *New York Times*, December 3, 1979.

43 "Few of us can": Sarah Davys, *A Time and a Time: An Autobiography* (London: Calder & Boyars, 1971), 113.

44 Drew Robinson: Jason Duaine Hanh, "Drew Robinson, Who Lost Eye in Suicide Attempt," *People*, May 6, 2021.

45 "One curious paradox": Edwin S. Shneidman, *The Suicidal Mind* (New York: Oxford University Press, 1996), 52. It's not really a paradox for the reasons I strive to illuminate, that we can and do have divided minds about both living and dying, no matter how sincere or desperate a suicide attempt may be.

46 Alvarez didn't know: A. Alvarez, *The Savage God* (New York: W. W. Norton & Co., 1990), 185.

46 "weary of life": Nature "pours forth a profusion of medicinal plants," Pliny the Elder wrote, "and is always producing something for the use of man. We may even suppose, that it is out of compassion to us that she has ordained certain substances to be poisonous, in order that when we are weary of life, hunger, a mode of death the most foreign to the kind disposition of the earth, might not consume us by a slow decay, that precipices might not lacerate our mangled bodies, that the unseemly punishment of the halter may not torture us, by stopping the breath of one who seeks his own destruction, or that we may not seek our death in the ocean, and become food for our graves, or that our bodies may not be gashed by steel. On this account it is that nature has produced a substance which is very easily taken, and by which life is extinguished, the body remaining undefiled and retaining all its blood, and only causing a degree of thirst. And when it is destroyed by this means, neither bird nor beast will touch the body, but he who has perished by his own hands is reserved for the earth." Pliny, "Nature of the Earth," bk. 2, ch. 63 of *Natural History*, trans. John Bostock (1855), at http://www.perseus.tufts.edu/hopper/text?doc=Perseus%3Atext%3A1999.02.0137%3Abook%3D2%3Achapter%3D63.

47 If you're panicking: An expert on suicide at the University of Utah, Dr. Craig Bryan, who studied cases where a suicide was committed with a gun, found that many occurred in fight-or-flight, panic situations. "A third of the firearm suicides in Utah happened during an argument," Dr. Bryan said, in an article about the rise in adult male suicides in relation to the culture of gun ownership. "Two people were having at it. Not necessarily physically violent, but they were yelling. And someone in the moment, almost always a man, basically just says, 'I'm done,' grabs a gun, shoots himself, and he's dead." Stephen Rodrick, "All-American Despair," *Rolling Stone*, May 30, 2019.

48 This might seem strange: I started to write that maybe I was afraid of death but still desired it, which is of course a perfectly natural if acutely uncomfortable mental state. (If you've quit smoking, you both want and fear a cigarette; if you've quit drinking, you both want and fear a glass of wine.) But I don't think that's true. I don't know how I will feel when death eventually comes to take me away. Probably I'm completely confused about how I feel, and when death actually comes and it's out of my control and there's no getting around it, I'll be completely terrified. But even today, in 2022, in a really good head space, when I think about death, I feel not fear but a sense of profound relief. I'm ashamed to feel that way, but it's the truth.

52 "Is it not for us": Sigmund Freud, "Thoughts for the Times on War and Death" (1915), in *The Standard Edition of the Complete Psychological Works of Sigmund Freud*, trans. and ed. James Strachey (London: Hogarth Press, 1947). Volume 14, 299.

53 "Pretty well everyone": Malcolm Muggeridge, "Half in Love with Death," *Guardian*, February 2, 1970.

53 And in fact: On the subject of the similarities between addictive thinking and suicidal thinking, I find the following observation from a lecture given by Khyentse Rinpoche in 2021 especially helpful: "I think suicide is like getting addicted to absinthe. Suicide is an addiction basically, but a very astute addiction. Basically it is an addiction to sort out [the problem of suffering], to fix the problem in a certain way. That's what he or she is thinking isn't it. Actually many animals also commit suicide. But beyond that I think we really need to open Pandora's box to explain this. It is basically and ironically a very vicious form of vanity. And pride. And selfishness, etc. And because it is astute, and profound and strong, this is why I was talking about absinthe. Absinthe is an alcohol that's really strong, right, 80 percent alcohol whatever. So not everybody likes drinking it, but those that get addicted to that, because it's short and strong and decisive so to speak, therefore it can also be very addictive. There's a lot of that, even people who eat chicken curry. There's a certain amount of chili they put. And then they can really get addicted to that astute fast decisive spice. Look at these people who eat chicken curry, they will have a side green chili and onion." Lecture in Taiwan, 2021.

53 Or the poet Robert Lowell: Helen Vendler, the great literary critic who is also an expert on suicidal poets, says of Lowell's last poems that "they acknowledge exhaustion; they expect death." Helen Vendler, "Robert Lowell's Last Days and Last Poems," in *Robert Lowell: A Tribute*, ed. Rolando Anzilotti (Pisa: Nistri-Lischi, 1979), 156–71.

54 "acute mixed drug intoxication": "Philip Seymour Hoffman Died from Drugs Mix," *Sky News*, February 28, 2014; Michael Schwitz, "Hoffman Killed by Toxic Mix of Drugs," *New York Times*, February 28, 2014.

54   "deaths of despair": The term was coined by two famous (and married) economists, Anne Case and Angus Deaton.

54   "Between 1999 and 2017": Atul Gawande, "Why Americans Are Dying From Despair," *New Yorker*, March 16, 2020.

57   "An indirect self-murderer": John Sym, *Life's Preservative Against Self-Killing*, ed. Michael MacDonald (1637; facsimile London: Routledge, 1988).

58   "Maybe consider": Peloton instructor Christine D'Arcole.

3. I CAN ALWAYS JUST KILL MYSELF TOMORROW

60   "Mr. Ripert thought": Dan Halpern, interview by author.

60   into the bathroom: Why the bathroom? We don't know. Maybe it was just that the bathrobe was there, and he made quick work of it all. Probably it was an easier place from which sturdily to suspend a noose. Certainly this explains the frequency of garages and basements for hanging oneself: there are usually wooden beams in such places, often at sufficient height for dangling. Bourdain was six foot four, and finding a high place from which to strangle himself was probably one of the practical worries of his last hour or handful of minutes. Unlike with shooting oneself (supposing one has a gun handy), dying by self-strangulation takes a little time and planning. As the writer Sarah Davys—who tried suicide twice but survived both times—observes in her memoir *A Time and a Time*: "A rope is cheap, but hanging is really a business for experts. There is a great danger that an amateur will not do the job efficiently, and this is a happy issue for no one concerned." But the bathroom, the garage, the basement are also intimate places, where we are allowed or even required to do things that others don't see. Sometimes they're very safe and private places. The bathroom is where we brush our teeth, comb our hair, expose our bodies to ourselves, step on the scale to see what we weigh, shit and piss, and masturbate. It feels like an unnatural place to die, perhaps—we want our loved ones with us when we exit the world—but it's a particularly secure and fitting place to kill oneself. A solitary place where we are accustomed to being alone.

62   "People say I murdered": Hanna Claeson, "The Truth About Anthony Bourdain and Asia Argento's Relationship," Mashed.com, July 11, 2020, https://www.mashed.com/225646/the-truth-about-anthony-bourdain-and-asia-argentos-relationship/.

62   "A friend once remarked": Leo Carey, "The Escape Artist: The Death and Life of Stefan Zweig," *New Yorker*, August 20, 2012.

62   "He had just a weird": Laurie Woolever, *Bourdain: The Definitive Oral Biography* (New York: HarperCollins, 2021), 423.

62   "I don't think he was afraid": We don't know what Morin meant here—afraid of life, or afraid of dying? I think he meant both, actually. Bour-

dain had a fearless quality, and that fearlessness might make his suicide more mysterious, if we think that the suicidal person is killing himself or herself out of fear. But if you're not afraid of life or death, and you've always, as Morin said, kept a metaphorical cyanide pill under your tongue—as I think many suicidal people do—at a certain point you might just fearlessly swallow it.

63   struggle with anxiety: "Sally Freeman: Everyone asks . . . *Which one was the disaster episode?* . . . He kind of had a mental breakdown on that shoot. . . . it was . . . his birthday, and he'd just reached the age that his dad was when he died, and it got dark. He really went into a funk, and he said that he hadn't expected to live beyond that age. . . . We were texting him all night . . . and if he didn't text back, we were gonna break the door in. We were truly worried about him; worried for his health, for his mental state. And there was a day where he just sat in the garden, and he wouldn't film anything. That's when I asked him, 'What's really going on here?' and he talked about his dad. . . . if that was a close friend of mine who had been like that, I would have thought, *Yeah, they probably need some help.*" Woolever, *Bourdain*, 238.

63   And in fact people's resilience: Benedict Carey, "Why Older People Manage to Stay Happier Through the Pandemic," *New York Times*, March 12, 2021.

64   "I believe that suicide": Donald Antrim, "Everywhere and Nowhere: A Journey Through Suicide," *New Yorker*, February 11, 2019.

64   "for some people like me": Nelly Arcan, *Folle* (Montreal: Média Diffusion, 2009). Here the narrator is discussing specifically the question of whether to have an abortion, but for her the case extends to the questions of whether to kill herself and whether life is worth living. This narrator resolves at age fifteen to kill herself at age thirty, and the novel ends with her suicide.

64   "Your weather": I am indebted to my friend the great Aristotle scholar C.D.C. Reeve for this observation, which has helped me and many other depressed people who have come to me for advice. You cannot control the weather. But it really does change, and often more frequently than you think.

64   "It was almost like": Kevin Sampsell, "I'm Jumping Off the Bridge," *Salon*, August 3, 2012.

65   "Andy Spade, her husband": Jonah Engle Bromwich, Vanessa Friedman, and Matthew Schneier, "Kate Spade, Whose Handbags Carried Women into Adulthood, Is Dead at 55," *New York Times*, June 5, 2018.

65   "his California presence": Calvin Trillin, *Remembering Denny* (New York: Farrar, Straus & Giroux, 1993), 95, 8, 216, 94.

66   Some of it is probably: The literature demonstrating this is enormous and well known, but I might mention that splendid book on the vagaries of Western concepts of mental illness and our savagery in dealing

with people suffering from mental distress: Michel Foucault's *Madness and Civilization* (1961). Foucault, who attempted suicide himself, was famously sympathetic to the case of the suicide, even at times recommending it as part of ritual orgies that would end, following the Dionysian tradition, in suicides by many participants.

67 "have already developed": Jean Améry, *On Suicide: A Discourse on Voluntary Death* (Bloomington: Indiana University Press, 1999), 131.

67 For this reason: A 2016 study of 1,490 Minnesotans who had attempted suicide found that 94.6 percent did not die in a subsequent attempt. That said, by far the most relevant factor for predicting a "completed suicide" or death by suicide is a suicide attempt. J. Michael Bostwick et al., "Suicide Attempt as a Risk Factor for Completed Suicide: Even More Lethal Than We Knew," *American Journal of Psychiatry* 173, no. 11 (2016): 1094–1100. Another recent study of people who intended suicide but were prevented found that 7 percent later died by suicide. See Ed Newman, "A Lesson from 29 Golden Gate Suicide Attempts," February 20, 2019, https://ennyman.medium.com/a-lesson-from-29-golden-gate-suicide-attempts-a42f4ef3f970.

68 pesticides and herbicides: In China, approximately half of all deaths by suicide are by pesticide ingestion, and in India, it's nearly 40 percent. Ninety percent of suicide attempts worldwide involve poisoning, but because deadly poisons are relatively hard to get in the United States, the most common way of dying by suicide here is with a gun. In an attempt to reduce suicides, the Israeli Defense Forces stopped letting their soldiers bring their guns home with them over the weekend, and suicides fell by 40 percent. A ban in selective dangerous pesticides in Sri Lanka corresponded with a drop in suicides of nearly 50 percent. See Dylan Matthews, "How Pesticide Bans Can Prevent Tens of Thousands of Suicides a Year," *Vox*, November 15, 2018.

68 guns less accessible: Atul Gawande, "Why Americans Are Dying from Despair," *New Yorker*, March 16, 2020.

68 and in some cases: I am alive today because other people interfered with my attempts to kill myself. That said, I think a person's autonomy in such a basic question as whether she wants to go on living ought to be respected. It may come down to the question: "If her life had been saved, would she subsequently, upon seeing her circumstances differently, been glad her life was saved?" That is the justification given for "5150s" (seventy-two-hour supervised holds, usually in a psychiatric ward but also often in jails) and other kinds of restraints of the failed suicide that have been used for centuries. But there are exceptional cases. Dax Cowart was severely burned in an accident and demanded to be allowed to die, both at the scene of the accident and during his subsequent (torturous) medical treatment for his burns. He lived and went on to have what he frequently described as a good and even enviable

life, but he also always insisted that he should have been allowed to die when he demanded it. Most of us can understand and sympathize with wanting to die rather than endure horrible physical suffering. But these cases become even more complex in places such as Belgium, where legal euthanasia is permitted on the grounds of mental suffering.

68 "Who are you": Douglas Smith, *Rasputin: Faith, Power and the Twilight of the Romanovs* (New York: Picador, 2017), 387.

69 "Me from Myself": Emily Dickinson, "Me from Myself—to Banish—" no. 642, Emily Dickinson Collection, Amherst College Digital Collections, https://acdc.amherst.edu/view/asc:1329214.

69 This is why: Having spent many hours reading suicide notes for this book, I can assure the reader that this is true. Simon Critchley also makes this observation in his excellent book *Notes on Suicide* (New York: Fitzcarraldo, 2020). That suicide notes tend to be letters of apology is also supported by studies. See Kenan Karbeyaz et al., "Analysis of Suicide Notes: An Experience in Eskişehir City," *Archives of Neuropsychiatry* 51, no. 3 (2014): 275–79.

69 four groups: As I and others have remarked, there are many different classifications of suicidal types—so many that one doubts whether the exercise is useful. I do think Baechler's four types are useful for our purposes in this book, because "escapist" nicely summarizes the basic attitude of the suicidal person I hope to address. I also think the recognition that one wants to use suicide to escape can be helpful, because it starts us on the path of asking what it is we are trying to escape, and where we think we are escaping to. It's worth briefly noting here that Baechler and I and many other thinkers on suicide share the view that the act of suicide is helpfully studied from the perspective of the individual's choice. This approach is not in opposition but is complementary to those, like Durkheim and many after him, who believe that the problem of suicide should be addressed at the social level, by analyzing its causes in poverty, addiction, crime, and so on.

70 That said, the escapist: The movie *Harold and Maude* is a particularly nice study of the aggressive motivation for suicide as opposed to other possible motivations. There are two suicidal types in the movie. Harold, a young man, repeatedly enacts grisly suicides for his mother (he is only pretending to commit suicide, but he creates terrifying death scenes), and Maude, a seventy-nine-year-old woman, Harold's friend and eventual lover, a Holocaust survivor, kills herself on her eightieth birthday with a painless drug because she thinks her life is full and complete. Harold's motives for staging acts of suicide are explicitly aggressive against his mother. In a funny exchange, he tells his psychiatrist about his many fake attempts, whereupon his psychiatrist asks him: "Were they all done for your mother's benefit?" Harold replies: "No, I would not say 'benefit.'"

70   But I could: For me, the possibility that suicide was an act of aggression against the people I love seems to have been more plausible in my youth than in later years. As I've aged, I've felt more and more that the people I love are keeping me from death. But I still worry that the desire to kill myself is, in some deep way that I don't properly understand or acknowledge, an expression of anger at other people, a lashing out against the people I love. Certainly, many suicides are interpreted that way, at least in some measure. Following Freud, Menninger argued that suicide is often displaced murder. We want to kill someone else, but we dare not, and so our drive for cruelty turns back on the self. In one of Nietzsche's stories about the creation of human consciousness, the murderous hand becomes a *Selbstmord*, the poetic German word for suicide. (Jean Améry refused to use the word *Selbstmord*, because he thought it morally misleading to think of suicide as in any way analogous to murder.)

70   "There are certain situations": Alfred Adler, "Suicide," in *Superiority and Social Interest: A Collection of Later Writings*, eds. Heinz L. Ansbacher and Rowena R. Ansbacher (Evanston, Ill.: Northwestern University Press, 1964), 248–52.

70   "loss of money": Recent literature from economists on deaths of despair confirms Marx's and Adler's claim that money problems may be among the primary sources of suicide in society. See Atul Gawande, "Why Americans Are Dying from Despair," *New Yorker*, March 16, 2020. The seventeenth-century Manchu district magistrate Huang Liu-Hung (1633–1710) would have agreed with Adler about debt and suicide, writing: "As to men who commit suicide, some suicides are due to dire poverty or suffering from extreme cold and hunger; others are the victims of private or official debts without means to repay. These people are entitled to our compassionate consideration." Huang Liu-Hung, *A Complete Book Concerning Happiness and Benevolence: A Manual for Local Magistrates in Seventeenth-Century China*, ed. and trans. Djang Chu (Tucson: University of Arizona Press, 1984), 319–20, 355–58.

71   "brooding over incurable illness": Dorothea Leighton and Clyde Kluckhohn, *Children of the People; The Navaho Individual and His Development* (Cambridge, Mass.: Harvard University Press, 1947), 111. Very interestingly, the Navajo believe that a person "can end his own life by wishing that he may die. Several times [the interviewer] had Navajo girls or young men tell [him] that a grand-father or a grand-mother was going to die in a short time. When [the interviewer] asked if the grand-parent was ill, the usual response was, 'No, he is the same as usual, but he wants to die and will live only a little while now.' The old person seldom disappointed the expectations of his relatives." This belief makes me wonder if my wish to die has ever been as powerful as I've always believed it to be.

71   "what sets off": Albert Camus, *The Myth of Sisyphus and Other Essays*, trans. Justin O'Brien (1942; New York: Vintage Books, 1955), 3–8, 44–48.

72   "I will find myself": "Buenos Aires," episode of *Parts Unknown*, aired November 2016.

72   Jasmine Waters: Special thanks to Mansi Vashisth for her thorough and sympathetic work on this section. Mansi has been a tremendous research assistant throughout my work on this book, but she was especially valuable on this section.

72   "But how can this": "Black Writer for 'This Is Us' Commits Suicide at Age 39," *Miami Times*, June 17, 2020.

72   "out of four primary": Kamesha Spates and Brittany C. Slatton, "I've Got My Family and My Faith: Black Women and the Suicide Paradox," *Socius: Sociological Research for a Dynamic World* 3 (2017): 1–9.

72   "one white female privilege": Margo Jefferson, *Negroland* (New York: Vintage, 2016), 175.

73   "Survival was the triumph": Margo Jefferson, interview by author, August 5, 2021. Many thanks to Margo Jefferson for her work, her humor, and her kindness.

73   taboo has been used: One particularly interesting example of a taboo being used to discourage suicide was practiced by the Chinese district magistrate Huang Liu-Hung. Alarmed by the increasing numbers of suicides especially among the poorer citizens of the state he was administering, he composed popular rhymes explaining the terrible woes that would afflict people who took their own lives: punishments would be inflicted on their families, and they would suffer torments in the afterlife. "After I had implemented this policy for half a year," he wrote, "the inhabitants of the district began to get my message and the number of suicide cases decreased dramatically. After one year no more cases were reported. Many unnecessary deaths were avoided and I was spared many unpleasant trips [to check on possible suicide cases]." Huang Liu-Hung, *Complete Book Concerning Happiness and Benevolence*, 355–56. See also Jamison, *Night Falls*, 264–89. On taboo and mental illness, see also Foucault, *Madness and Civilization*.

74   "Robin's death hit me": Jas Waters, *Jas Fly*, n.d., "Oh Captain My Captain," "For Anyone That Needs It," at jasfly.tumblr.com/.

75   "anyone can overcome": Jas Waters may be mistaken about this. I don't think "self-work," for example, is a cure for depression, or that anyone can overcome depression, or even that depression is something that we must "overcome." It might even be exactly the wrong way to think about depression—just as "overcoming" boredom is probably not the lesson that boredom is trying to teach us. Depression may be much more like love—that is, incredibly powerful, full of significance, often unbearable, but fundamental to human existence, at least for many of us. This is not

a recommendation of depression (or boredom, or even love for that matter), but the suggestion that it is somehow the enemy or an obstacle to be overcome is unhelpful.

76   a lot of good: Laura Santhanam, "Youth Suicide Rates Are on the Rise in the U.S.," *PBS NewsHour,* October 18, 2019. This article was reported prior to the widely documented mental health crisis among youth worldwide due to the effects of the coronavirus.

76   escalated even higher: Matt Ritchel, " 'It's Life or Death': The Mental Health Crisis Among U.S. Teens," *New York Times,* May 3, 2022.

76   "It's an absolute panic": Niki McGloster, " 'Kidding' Writer Jas Waters on Her Journey to Hollywood and Having a Seat at the Table," *Shadow and Act,* November 20, 2018, shadowandact.com /jas-waters-interview-this-is-us-kidding.

76   Not only are we not helping: Researchers have found that "smart phone access and internet use increased in lockstep with teenage loneliness." Jean M. Twenge, "Worldwide Increases in Adolescent Loneliness," *Journal of Adolescence,* July 20, 2021. See also Jonathan Haidt and Jean M. Twenge, "This Is Our Chance to Pull Teenagers Out of the Smartphone Trap," *New York Times,* July 31, 2021.

76   Many recent studies have documented: For a good general summary of the many negative mental health effects of social media use, see "The Social Dilemma: Social Media and Your Mental Health," McLean Hospital, n.d., https://www.mcleanhospital.org/essential/it-or -not-social-medias-affecting-your-mental-health.

77   And this is without: Statistics on the links between cyberbulling and suicide can be found at "Bullying, Cyberbullying, and Suicide Statistics," Megan Meier Foundation, n.d., https://www.meganmeierfoundation .org/statistics. Tina Meier founded the Megan Meier Foundation in 2007 in memory of her thirteen-year-old daughter Megan Taylor Meier, who took her own life after an adult neighbor pretending to be a boy cyberbullied her on the website MySpace.

78   "the mortification which sometimes": Madame de Staël, *Reflections on Suicide,* in George Combe, *The Constitution of Man, Considered in Relation to External Objects,* Alexandrian ed. (Columbus, Ohio: J. & H. Miller, n.d.), 99–112.

78   "I never got a sense": David Simon, in Woolever, *Bourdain,* 384.

79   "It is in vain that": Johann Wolfgang Goethe, *The Sorrows of Young Werther,* trans. Victor Lange and Judith Ryan (New York: Suhrkamp, 1988), 131.

80   "There are many ways": Yiyun Li, *Dear Friend, From My Life I Write to You in Your Life* (New York: Random House, 2018), 195.

80   Almost every expert: There are a lot of lists of questions, but they tend to be quite similar. A perfectly good one is "Suicide: What to Do When

Someone Is Suicidal," Mayo Clinic, n.d., https://www.mayoclinic.org /diseases-conditions/suicide/in-depth/suicide/art-20044707.

81 but significantly less: About 30 percent of suicides take place in public rather than private spaces. Christabel Owens et al., *Preventing Suicides in Public Places: A Practice Resource* (London: Public Health England, 2015).

81 It's long been a part: Robert I. Simon, "Passive Suicidal Ideation: Still a High-Risk Clinical Scenario," *Current Psychiatry* 13, no. 3 (2014): 13–15.

81 "I didn't know this": Anna Borges, "I Am Not Always Very Attached to Being Alive," *Outline*, April 2, 2019.

81 It's statistically proven: Jamie Ducharme, "How Should the Media Cover Suicides?" *Time*, July 30, 2018.

81 "Do not refer to suicide": "Top 10 Tips for Reporting on Suicide," American Foundation for Suicide Prevention, https://www.datocms -assets.com/12810/1577098744-13763toptennotesreportingonsuicide flyerm1.pdf.

82 "suicide cluster": Seth Abrutyn, Anna S. Mueller, and Melissa Osborne, "Rekeying Cultural Scripts for Youth Suicide," in *Society and Mental Health*, March 29, 2019 at https://journals.sagepub.com/doi/abs/10 .1177/2156869319834063?journalCode=smha.

82 adolescents are: Scott Poland, Richard Lieberman, and Marina Niznik, "Suicide Contagion and Clusters—Part 1: What School Psychologists Should Know," *Communiqué* (National Association of School Psychologists) 47, no. 5 (n.d.): 1, 21–23.

82 suicide is cool: For more on suicide contagion, see D. T. Max's excellent "A Mysterious Suicide Cluster," *New Yorker*, April 19, 2021. Max offers no conclusions about the causes of suicide clusters but looks closely at a recent suicide cluster at Truman State University in my own home state of Missouri. Recalling my earlier remarks about the power of taboo at reducing suicide, one comes away from Max's article feeling that we are much more prone to the suggestion that killing ourselves is a good idea than we probably suppose.

83 discussion of suicide itself: Borges, "Being Alive."

83 "I was ashamed to have": Mark Landler, "Britain Braces for Fallout as Meghan and Harry's Interview Airs," *New York Times*, March 8, 2021.

83 "You don't get to turn it": Benjamin Vanhoose, "Kevin Love Says He Struggles with Suicidal Thoughts on 'Brutal' Days: 'I've Learned to Speak My Truth,'" *People*, November 18, 2020.

84 discussion of the attempt: This is a well-established fact, to which John Draper refers in my conversation with him in Appendix I, "Tools for Crisis." See T. Dazzi et al., "Does Asking About Suicide and Related Behaviours Induce Suicidal Ideation? What Is the Evidence?," *Psychological Medicine* 44, no. 16 (2014): 3361–63.

84 The ripple effects among family: This observation is unfortunately quite

typical: "A fellow officer, Frederick Lee, had a 13-year-old son in nearby Wolf Point who had taken his dad's handgun and shot himself a few weeks prior. Michael Lee was found clutching a keepsake stone that contained a strand of his mother's hair. She had committed suicide two years earlier." Stephen Rodrick, "All American Despair," *Rolling Stone*, May 30, 2019.

84 But the happy statistical fact: Dazzi et al., "Does Asking About Suicide?"

84 "We don't really know": Borges, "Being Alive."

84 "Speaking freely need not": Ibid.

85 mental health difficulties: Silke Bachmann, "Epidemiology of Suicide and the Psychiatric Perspective," *International Journal of Environmental Research and Public Health* 15, no. 7 (2018): 1425. Kees Van Heeringen, who made an extensive review of the recent literature, observed that "hopelessness is a robust predictor of suicidal behavior." See Kees Van Heeringen, *The Neuroscience of Suicidal Behavior* (Cambridge, U.K.: Cambridge University Press, 2018), 97.

86 "I shall never learn": William Styron, "Darkness Visible," *Vanity Fair*, December 1989.

86 "immensely muddled terminology": James Hillman, *Suicide and the Soul* (Woodstock, N.Y.: Spring, 1997), 38–41.

86 entering lions' cages: A particularly disturbing example of this method is detailed in "The Lion Enclosure," *Night Falls*, 154–59. Jamison gives a disturbing, shocking catalog of the many different ways people have attempted to kill themselves. The literature on suicide has many catalogs on bizarre ways people have tried (and succeeded) to kill themselves— almost anything you can think of that might be lethal, no matter how grisly or painful, has been attempted.

86 "suicide is one": James Hillman, *Suicide and the Soul* (Woodstock, N.Y.: Spring, 1965), 41.

88 "There is a doctrine": *Phaedo*, 61B–69E, in *The Dialogues of Plato*, trans. Benjamin Jowett (New York: Random House, 1892), 1920.

88 "from all danger": David Hume, *Of Suicide* (1757), original unpublished manuscript in the National Library of Scotland with corrections in Hume's own hand, text provided by Tom L. Beauchamp. For ease of access, see https://ethicsofsuicide.lib.utah.edu/category/author/david-hume/.

5. DRINKING MYSELF TO DEATH

114 Heavy drinkers and drug users: Those diagnosed as alcohol misusers seem to be at a tenfold risk for suicide. Substance Abuse and Mental Health Services Administration, "Substance Use and Suicide: A Nexus Requiring a Public Health Approach," 2016, https://store.samhsa.gov/sites/default/files/d7/priv/sma16-4935.pdf.

114 A statistic that: N. S. Miller, J. C. Mahler, and M. S. Gold, "Suicide Risk Associated with Drug and Alcohol Dependence," *Journal of Addiction and Addictive Disorders* 10, no. 3 (1991): 49–61.

114 Alcohol is involved: At least 30 percent of male suicide victims in the United States have alcohol in their systems when they kill themselves. In states with higher rates of alcohol abuse, like Wyoming, it is closer to 40 percent. Stephen Rodrick, "All American Despair," *Rolling Stone*, May 30, 2019.

114 more than half of all: Miller, Mahler, and Gold, "Suicide Risk."

114 It's clear that drinking alcohol: An interesting anthropological fact: among the American Indigenous Kaska tribe, suicide almost never occurred, but attempted suicide by drunken men was apparently quite common. The Kaska were very humane in the treatment of men who attempted suicide while drunk. "No punishment or other discrimination is reserved for attempted suicides. The individual is comforted and in the future, while intoxicated, he is watched lest he repeat the attempt." John Joseph Honigmann, *Culture and Ethos of Kaska Society* (New Haven, Conn.: Yale University Press, 1949), 204, 269; and J. J. Honigman, *The Kaska Indians* (New Haven, Conn.: Yale University Press, 1954), 137.

114 It's no secret that alcohol: The ancients often thought that drinking alcohol made you briefly crazy, and that the kind of dementia that might justify suicide was importantly analogous to the craziness of being drunk. So the Stoic philosopher Chrysippus (c. 280–c. 206 BC), when giving his five reasons for the analogy, remarks that the fifth reason for suicide is "dementedness. For just as drunken stupor would break up a party there, so here too can one have oneself depart from life because of dementedness. For being demented is nothing but natural intoxication, and intoxication, nothing but self-induced dementia." In Ioannes ab Arnim, ed., *Stoicorum Veterum Fragmenta*, trans. Yukio Kachi (Stuttgart: B. G. Teubner, 1903), vol. 3, para. 768, pp. 190–91. Something about the anesthesia of alcohol and the blackout of drunkenness reminds me of the desire to die. The style of escape is importantly similar. As the author of the Egyptian "Dialogue of a Man with His Soul" wrote, arguing for suicide, "Death is in my sight today / Like the odor of lotus blossoms, / Like sitting on the bank of drunkenness." "A Dispute Over Suicide," in *Ancient Near Eastern Texts Relating to the Old Testament*, ed. James B. Pritchard, trans. John A. Wilson (Princeton, N.J.: Princeton University Press, 1950), 135.

115 For me, alcohol: Although the data is still emerging, it looks like my case is not isolated. As alcoholics age, as far as we can tell, their risk for suicide increases. K. R. Conner, A. L. Beautrais, and Y. Conwell, "Risk Factors for Suicide and Medically Serious Suicide Attempts Among Alcoholics: Analyses of Canterbury Suicide Project Data," *Journal of Studies on Alcohol and Drugs* 64, no. 4 (2003): 551–54.

115 "a pattern of alcohol use": "Alcohol Use Disorder," Mayo Clinic, n.d., https://www.mayoclinic.org/diseases-conditions/alcohol-use-disorder /symptoms-causes/syc-20369243.

117 We do not yet have: N. K. Syed and M. D. Griffiths, "Nationwide Suicides Due to Alcohol Withdrawal Symptoms During Covid-19 Pandemic," *Journal of Psychiatric Research* 130 (November 2020): 289–91. In India, the press widely reported an unprecedented increase in the number of suicide attempts and suicides because of alcohol withdrawal symptoms.

117 Like every other addict: Perhaps in certain contexts, I could harmlessly take a drink, and no pattern of abuse would immediately resume. I don't know. What I do know is that in the past, when I have taken a drink, often that very same day I would wind up drunk, despite having the most sincere intention to, and conviction that I could, "drink like a normal person." The next morning I would stop drinking again, which seems to be the best solution to the problem of drinking for me.

118 I didn't tell my new friend: Some material from both is included here. See Clancy Martin, "The Drunk's Club: The Cult That Cures," *Harper's*, January 2010.

118 "other treatments might": Austin Frakt and Aaron E. Carroll, "Alcoholics Anonymous vs. Other Approaches: The Evidence Is Now In," *New York Times*, March 11, 2020.

119 "is known in recovery": Recovery Acres Calgary Society, https://www .recoveryacres.org/.

120 He was a better: When I think about it now, I realize that it's much easier to be a good sponsor than to be a good father, because the role of the sponsor is pretty well defined. Basically you're there to call someone else on their bullshit, to help that person when they're struggling, and to remind them of the promises and efforts that come with AA membership and their desire to be sober. It's more like being a good mentor, with all those rewards. But to (try to) be a good parent is an amazingly complex job with no guaranteed rewards, tremendous emotional complexity, and the necessity to face unexpected problems every day. In my experience, it is hard to be a good sponsor; harder still to be a good spouse; and much, much harder than either to be a good parent.

125 overcoming our demons: Thanks to A. J. Daulerio for first pointing out to me the importance and perniciousness of this expression.

129 "Alcohol played a perverse": William Styron, *Darkness Visible: A Memoir of Madness* (New York: Random House, 1990), 33.

133 "It was just like": Al-Anon is the support group for friends and family members of addicts.

136 "A man who is": Dietrich Bonhoeffer, *Ethics: The Last Things and the Thing Before the Last*, ed. Eberhard Bethge (New York: Macmillan, 1965), 155–56.

139 we lie to ourselves: We lie at least as much to ourselves as we do to others, which makes self-knowledge especially tricky. If you are interested in that subject, you might like my book *Love and Lies* (New York: Farrar, Straus & Giroux, 2015), which is a sustained argument against the idea that we can be honest with ourselves, at least in the usual way of thinking about the process. Nietzsche famously argued that we learn to lie to others through lying to ourselves, and that the former is actually much less common than the latter.

142 She takes Adderall: Many AA people would insist that Ronda K. has not achieved sobriety at all but has just replaced one drug with another. But happily AA circles increasingly respect harm reduction rather than total abstinence, and they increasingly acknowledge the possibility that some drugs—recognized pharmaceuticals or otherwise—may help with alcohol use disorder. A particularly nice example is A. J. Daulerio's "The Small Bow" group, which has regular online meetings that are open to all. https://www.thesmallbow.com/.

143 "I actually could please": Bill Wilson, *My First 40 Years: An Autobiography* (New York: Hazelden, 2000), p. 43.

146 He believed this: Dozens of studies are now being conducted to look at the benefits of hallucinogens and other banned substances like MDMA on depression, addiction, suicidal ideation, and other forms of mental suffering. See Kat Eschner, "The Promises and Perils of Psychedelic Health Care," *New York Times*, January 5, 2022. The great nineteenth-century French psychiatrist Esquirol believed that pellagra, a disease caused by vitamin B deficiency, was one of the principal causes of suicidal thinking. For this very reason, in 2012, at the end of a brief relapse, I once spent several hours driving through the streets of Seattle in a desperate search for a sublingual vitamin B supplement with my current-partner-then-girlfriend Amie and her mom, then a research nurse at a Seattle hospital who, on a cellphone call with a neurologist friend of hers who was the world's leading expert on migraines, tried to arrange a vitamin B injection at a local hospital.

148 "clouds just lifted": I owe this expression to my friend C.D.C. Reeve.

148 "I'm on": This particular AA meeting was in 2009. Just twelve years later, in many AA meetings, people are much more open to the use of medication to supplement sobriety. I think a seismic shift is happening in our thinking about sobriety: people are paying more and more attention to the consequences of dependence rather than the fact of dependence or the substance on which one is dependent. We are increasingly asking, Does this help or harm your daily life? Rather than, Shouldn't you be able to live life without this? That said, we may simply be ushering in whole new kinds of addiction with psychospiritual consequences we don't yet anticipate. In 2011 about one in ten adult Americans were taking antidepressants; by 2016, about one in six adults were taking antidepressants.

148 In Oregon the governor: See Ezra Klein, "Can Magic Mushrooms Heal Us?" *New York Times*, March 18, 2021. Probably the tipping point in popular culture for the serious reevaluation of the medical usefulness of psychoactive drugs came with Michael Pollan, *How to Change Your Mind* (New York: Penguin Press, 2018).

152 Adrienne Rich wrote: Adrienne Rich, *On Lies, Secrets, and Silence* (New York, W. W. Norton, 1979), p. 213.

6. PHILOSOPHICAL SUICIDE

156 Williams didn't seem like: Robin Williams, interview by Marc Maron, *WTF with Marc Maron*, April 26, 2010, at 52 minutes.

157 But I didn't stop thinking: Notable philosophers who killed themselves include Johan Robeck (1672–1739), who drowned himself in a river. He is one of the few who both wrote philosophically in defense of suicide and killed himself—Qu Yuan and Seneca are two others. (Robeck was one of Rousseau's principal sources for his views on suicide—he specifically mentioned him in his dialogue on suicide in *Julie*.) The Portuguese philosopher Uriel da Costa (1585–1640) shot himself, as did the depressed and alcoholic Guy Debord (1931–94), of *Society of the Spectacle* fame, and the Missourian philosopher J. Howard Moore (1862–1916). Moore, according to his rather better-known brother-in-law Clarence Darrow, committed suicide in "a temporary fit of insanity." None of these three, however, wrote anything that particularly sheds light on the philosophical question of suicide.

Similarly, the marvelous twentieth-century philosopher Sarah Kofman, who killed herself at the age of sixty on what would have been the 150th birthday of her favorite thinker, Friedrich Nietzsche, offered us no details on her views about suicide. Kofman wrote some of the best work on the German philosopher, who seems to have been an advocate of what he called, in his masterpiece *Thus Spoke Zarathustra*, "voluntary death." He there recommends dying at the right time, and in a manner that celebrates one's life. This certainly does not preclude death by natural causes, but seems to suggest that sometimes one ought to take an active hand in determining the when and the how of life's end.

Another modern philosopher who took his own life is the little-known but influential nineteenth-century Schopenhauerian philosopher Philipp Mainländer (who incidentally made a deep impression on the young Friedrich Nietzsche). Such luminaries as Ryūnosoke Akutagawa (who, like Mainländer, died by suicide at age thirty-five), Emil Cioran, Alfred Kubin, and Jorge Luis Borges were all avid readers of Mainländer's work. Mainländer wrote his masterpiece of pessimism *The Philosophy of Redemption*, and shortly after the publication of the first volume, he hung himself, supposedly while standing on a pile of copies of the book.

Somewhat curiously, Mainländer didn't really discuss philosophical arguments over suicide in greater detail, as he believed that all things longed for death, even God, and that it was through God's suicide that the universe came to exist. (One might wonder how God committed suicide—for Mainländer, choosing to create the universe in all of its misery was God's expression of his need for self-annihilation. This view is not as idiosyncratic as it sounds: the idea that a god's suicide is intimately bound up with our own existence is also found in a number of ancient Central American and African origin myths.) Anticipating the antinatalist movement of our own time (popularized by the character Rust Cohle, played by Matthew McConaughey in the television series *True Detective*), he did claim that human beings would do best, first, to stop reproducing, then to kill ourselves.

The philosopher Cesar Pavese (1908–50), who overdosed with barbiturates, was one of the most famous twentieth-century European intellectuals to take his own life. The Turkish-Uruguayan philosopher Albert Caraco (1919–71) wrote a lot about death but not about suicide and killed himself, apparently over grief at the death of his parents, either by overdose or by hanging (accounts differ). The French philosopher Michel Foucault tried to kill himself at least twice, frequently threatened suicide, and at times imagined (and perhaps recommended) "suicide festivals," though ultimately he died from complications of HIV/AIDS. The Hungarian philosopher Peter Szondi (1929–71) killed himself the same year as Caraco, by drowning himself in the Halensee in Berlin. At the time of his death, Szondi was writing a book on the work of his friend the poet Paul Celan (1920–70), who had drowned himself in the Seine the year before. The chemist, writer, and philosopher Primo Levi (1919–87) died by throwing himself down the stairs at his apartment building in Turin. He had survived the Holocaust, so his suicide was surprising to many, but suicide is not uncommon among the traumatized survivors of concentration camps. Elie Wiesel wrote of Levi's suicide, "Primo Levi died at Auschwitz forty years later." Diego Gambetta, "Primo Levi's Last Moments," *The Boston Review*, June 1, 1999.

157 Suicide was not uncommon: "One has only to read Diogenes Laertius to appreciate that suicide was almost the normal end of all Greek philosophers from Empedocles down to the Hellenistic period." Paul-Louis Landsberg, *The Experience of Death and the Moral Problem of Suicide*, trans. Cynthia Rowland (New York: Philosophical Library, 1953), 65–97. Among many other cases of suicide reported by Diogenes Laertius—who, incidentally, is not generally viewed as the most reliable reporter—is that of Aristotle's student Metrocles (c. 325 BC). This early Cynic philosopher was said to have killed himself by self-suffocation, though he may also have earlier attempted suicide by starvation, supposedly out of shame at farting during a speech he was practicing. Ancient

Greek and especially Roman writers and philosophers tolerated or even praised suicide. See Yoland Grise, *Le suicide dans la Rome antique* (Montreal: Bellarmin/Les Belles lettres, 1982).

157 This is unexpected: Not much empirical work has been done on this subject, but the oft-remarked frequency of suicide as a cause of death among artists and intellectuals seems to be more than merely an expression of the "myth of the tortured artist." A recent statistical study in England concluded that artists were four times as likely to commit suicide, and a larger study in Sweden found that writers were twice as likely to kill themselves. See "Artistic Types Are More Sensitive: Tortured Geniuses Found to be Four Times More Likely to Kill Themselves," *Daily Mail*, March 18, 2017; Lindsay Abrams, "Study: Writers Are Twice as Likely to Commit Suicide," *Atlantic*, October 19, 2012.

158 "you're not working": In his brilliant biography *Robin* (New York: Macmillan, 2018), Dave Itzkoff does a particularly nice job of describing Williams's frustration and even panic, in the couple of years before his death, over his deteriorating ability to do the work he loved. He had dealt with depression and addiction on and off throughout his life, but "to keep working through the pain [was] the one cure-all that had helped him cope with past troubles" (395). This worsening inability was a consequence, as best we can tell, of his worsening neurological condition, though reports of his sparkling comic genius continue right up until the end of his life (394–405).

159 "You've had all this stuff": Many factors contributed to the suicide of Robin Williams in 2014. Most important, he was suffering from Lewy body dementia, which is itself an independent cause of depression and is a terrifying and debilitating disease. That must have led him to consider suicide as a preferable end. Certainly the disease and the terrible mental trauma it produces were major causes of his death. But like Anthony Bourdain, Williams had a complex relationship to the question of suicide. As early as 1992, he was comparing himself to Jerzy Kosinski, who had killed himself the previous spring; see Itzkoff, *Robin*, 274. Suicide was also a theme in his work as an actor. He starred in two of the most popular movies about suicide, *Dead Poets Society* (1989) and *World's Greatest Dad* (2009). Robin Williams was particularly troubled by the problem of suicide in the latter movie. In *What Dreams May Come* (1998) his character journeys from heaven to hell to save his wife, who has died by suicide and so been condemned to damnation. In short, the brilliant riff on suicide he gave us in his 2010 conversation with Marc Maron came from serious thinking about the question of killing oneself.

159 "pursue the happy day": "A Dispute over Suicide," in *Ancient Near Eastern Texts Relating to the Old Testament*, ed. James B. Pritchard, trans. John A. Wilson (Princeton, N.J.: Princeton University Press, 1950).

161 "one never kills": Yiyun Li, *Dear Friend, From My Life I Write to You in*

Your Life (New York: Random House, 2018), 54. The statement is controversial, because, as Li well knows, lots of philosophers do think and argue that one may reason one's way into suicide.

161 "reason is and ought to be": Hume, "Of Suicide."

162 "the only serious": Camus, *Myth of Sisyphus*, 65.

162 "pretty good life": I worry a lot about money and often suppose—especially at night, while falling asleep—that if I had no money troubles, life would be relatively easy. So it's helpful for me to remember that the estate of Robin Williams, at the time of his suicide, was worth somewhere between $50 million and $100 million.

162 The most alluring things: My thanks to Susan Golomb for this terrific observation about the Egyptian poem on suicide.

164 "the more fully": Andrew Solomon, *The Noonday Demon: An Atlas of Depression* (New York: Scribner, 2001), 283.

166 "Now if you suppose": *Apology*, 38C–42A, in *The Dialogues of Plato*, trans. Benjamin Jowett (1892; New York: Random House, 1920), 1:444–53. Many ancients accused Socrates of complicity in his own death and even suggested that his trial and subsequent death sentence were a form of suicide. Friedrich Nietzsche similarly suggested in *Twilight of the Idols* that perhaps Socrates was just exhausted with life and wanted to die.

167 "the problem of free": Paul-Louis Landsberg, *The Experience of Death and the Moral Problem of Suicide*, trans. Cynthia Rowland (New York: Philosophical Library, 1953), 65–97.

167 "neither theology, nor": James Hillman, *Suicide and the Soul* (Woodstock, N.Y.: Spring, 1965), 58.

167 "Why do you say": *Phaedo*, 61B–69E, in *The Dialogues of Plato*, trans. Benjamin Jowett (New York: Random House, 1892), 1920.

168 As I've explored: The philosophers Walter Benjamin (1892–1940) and Arthur Koestler (1905–1983) seem to have committed suicide not from despair but to avoid ghastly impending fates. Benjamin was about to be captured by the Nazis when he overdosed on morphine tablets. Koestler—who had attempted suicide with morphine when fleeing the Nazis, but failed to die—committed suicide with his wife when he felt that a good death would soon be denied to him. Koestler wrote in his suicide note, "My reasons for deciding to put an end to my life are simple and compelling: Parkinson's disease and the slow-killing variety of leukaemia (CCl)." George Mikes, *Arthur Koestler: The Story of a Friendship* (London: David & Charles, 1983), 78–79. Gilles Deleuze (1925–95) leaped from the third-floor window of his Paris apartment to his death, apparently the consequence of both depression and generally deteriorating health. Avoiding a bad death was also the declared motivation of Charlotte Perkins Gilman who, terminally ill, wrote in her suicide note that she "chose chloroform over cancer." *The Diaries of Charlotte Perkins Gilman*, ed. Denise D. Knight (Charlottesville: University Press of

Virginia, 1994), 813. The twentieth-century Australian philosopher of
science David Stove (1927–94) committed suicide after being diagnosed
with esophageal cancer.

168 Even David Hume: In Hume's defense, in his time it was illegal to help
someone commit suicide, as indeed it generally is today. Hume wrote of
the suicide of his friend Maj. Alexander Forbes, "He expressed vast anxiety that he should be obliged to leave his duty, and fear, least his honour
should suffer by it. I endeavored to quiet his mind as much as possible,
and thought I had left him tolerably composed at night; but returning
to his room early next morning, I found him with small remains of life,
wallowing in his own blood, with the arteries of his arm cut asunder.
I immediately sent for a surgeon, got a bandage tied to his arm and
recovered him entirely to his senses and understanding. He lived above
four and twenty hours after, and I had several conversations with him.
Never a man expressed a more steady contempt of life nor more determined philosophical principles, suitable to his exit. He begged of me to
unloosen his bandage and hasten his death, as the last act of friendship I
could show him: but alas! we live not in Greek or Roman times. He told
me, that he knew, he could not live a few days: but if he did, as soon as
he became his own master, he would take a more expeditious method,
which none of his friends could prevent. I die, says he, from a jealousy
of honor, perhaps too delicate; and do you think, if it were possible for
me to live, I would now consent to it, to be a gazing-stock to the fool-
ish world. I am too far advanced to return. And if life was odious to
me before, it must be doubly so at present. He became delirious a few
hours before he died." In J. Y. T. Grieg, ed., *The Letters of David Hume*
(Oxford: Clarendon Press, 1932), letter 53, 1:94–95, 97–98.

168 "Embracing Sand": Filling one's robe or the sleeves of one's robe with
sand in order to facilitate drowning was a method of suicide practiced
in both China and Japan. This was also the method used by Virginia
Woolf, who filled the pockets of her overcoat with stones before drowning herself in the river Ouse. "Embracing sand" is also a reference to the
author's belief in the futility of clinging to life.

169 "Great was the weight": Qu Yuan, from "Huai sha" ("Embracing Sand"),
in *The Songs of the South: An Ancient Chinese Anthology of Poems by Qu
Yuan and Other Poets*, trans. David Hawkes (London: Penguin Books,
1985), 78, 170–72.

170 "fixer": Elizabeth Kolbert, "Such a Stoic," *New Yorker,* January 26, 2015.

170 But one finds: Perhaps the most famous example of honorable suicide
is the Japanese samurai tradition of seppuku, or taking one's own life
because of defeat in battle or to best serve one's lord. So in *The Beginner's Book of Bushido*, for example, a samurai who discovers that his lord
is being served by a bad councilor is instructed in this way: "Therefore
it is best to seize this great rascal of a councillor who is the evil spirit of

the house and either stab him through or cut off his head whichever you prefer, and so put an end to him and his corrupt practices. And then you must straightway commit seppuku [ritual suicide] yourself. Thus there will be no open breach or lawsuit or sentence and your lord's person will not be attainted, so that the whole clan will continue to live in security and there will be no open trouble in the Empire. And one who acts thus is a model samurai who does a deed a hundred-fold better than junshi, for he has the three qualities of loyalty and faith and valour, and will hand down a glorious name to posterity." A. L. Sadler, trans., *The Beginner's Book of Bushido* (Tokyo: Kokusai Bunka Shinkokai, the Society for International Cultural Relations, 1941), 78–79.

171   "As soon as there are": Seneca, *Ad Lucilium Epistulae Morales, Letters 70*, trans. Richard M. Gummere (New York: G. P. Putnam's Sons, 1920), vol. 2, 57–63.

171   First he cut: His wife also tried to kill herself, joining Seneca; but when neither of them managed to bleed enough to die and the pain increased, Seneca asked her to leave the room. She was tended to by their slaves and ultimately recovered.

171   "the vapor soon": Tacitus, *The Annals*, ed. E. H. Blakeney, trans. Arthur Murphy (New York: E. P. Dutton, 1908), 1:498–502. Mary Beard suggested in 2014 that he "suffocated in the steam," but one guesses that either his servants or the combined effects of the loss of blood, the poison, and the accelerating effects of the warm bath actually killed him. See Mary Beard, "How Stoical Was Seneca?" *New York Review of Books*, October 9, 2014.

171   For this reason, some: Jean Améry wrote that freely chosen suicide is quite different from other kinds, such as "letting-oneself-pass-away, as well as from death by martyrdom, including the death of the prophet on Golgotha. Those who lay hands on themselves are fundamentally different from those who surrender to the will of others: with the latter something happens, the former act of their own accord." Jean Améry, *On Suicide: A Discourse on Voluntary Death* (Bloomington: Indiana University Press, 1999), 85. Certainly Seneca understood suicide, generally speaking, as a not unreasonable response to intolerable external events, while Améry was more concerned with suicide motivated by what is internal.

172   the writer Primo Levi: Reasonable minds disagree on whether Levi killed himself. He died by falling down a long set of stairs, and the general conclusion (including that of Elie Wiesel) was that he committed suicide. But some still see it as an accident.

172   "from within": Améry, *On Suicide*, xiii.

172   "Suicides plunge": Ibid., 29; the emphasis is Améry's.

173   "These things do not establish": Ibid., 91.

173   "each human being": Ibid., 101.

174   When I wrote these pages: Six different cases are documented in Mark

D. Griffiths and Mohammed A. Mamun, "COVID-19 Suicidal Behavior Among Couples and Suicide Pacts: Case Study Evidence from Press Reports," *Psychiatry Research* 289 (July 2020): 11310. Our collective experience of the coronavirus epidemic seems to be having a very negative effect on mental health. All the experts to whom I have spoken agree that we should prepare ourselves for a significant increase in the rates of suicide in the years following the pandemic.

174 Suicide pacts and: Love pacts resulting in suicide "represent 0.6–4.0 percent of all suicides, with the vast majority being double suicides." C. Hocaoglue, "Double Suicide Attempt," *Singapore Medical Journal* (February 2009). Though double suicides are very rare, when they do take place, they tend to occur in old, married couples. In India, suicide pacts seem to be on the rise at the moment and sometimes include entire families. "In 2013, 56 cases of family deaths (through suicide pacts) were reported. They involved 108 deaths. In 2019, there were over 70 reported cases involving 180 people with an average of three people per case. This shows an upward trajectory in suicide pacts. Most of the suicide pacts are observed in married couples and family. . . . [in particular the pandemic] led to more loss of jobs, halt in movement from the city of work to hometown due to lockdown leading to uncertainty and sense of hopelessness, and fear of contracting COVID-19 has increased incidences of suicide pacts in couples." Pallavi Pundir, "Why Are More Indians Signing Suicide Pacts? We Asked an Expert," *Vice World News*, December 22, 2020. In part because attempted suicide is a crime in India, it is likely greatly underreported in the country, as it is in many countries where suicide continues to be criminalized.

174 While no one assumes: In a famous case in Japan, an online suicide pact resulted in the death of seven young people, including a fourteen-year-old girl. See Justin McCurry, "Seven Die in Online Suicide Pact in Japan," *Guardian*, March 1, 2005. The rise in these cases is very disturbing. A graduate student of mine at Ashoka University spent a thesis year investigating the dark web and suicide pacts and found a vast variety of websites that discuss and at times recommend suicide, describe suicide techniques, and even help with the arrangement of suicide pacts. (Sanctioned Suicide, one such website, has so far continued to thrive despite justified efforts to shut it down.) These websites have also been used by murderers. In 2017 a serial murderer in Japan used Web-based suicide pacts to lure at least nine victims to their deaths. "Japan Suicide Websites Targeted After 'House of Horrors,'" BBC News, November 10, 2017, https://www.bbc.com/news/world-asia-41941426; and Vanessa Barford, "'Secretive World' of Suicide Websites," BBC News, September 22, 2010, https://www.bbc.com/news/uk-11387910.

174 cluster of five suicides: Max, "Suicide Cluster."

174 Suicide pacts between lovers: In another tradition, partners kill them-

selves after their mate or partner dies of natural causes, which many cultures around the world did (and in some cases still do) consider to be a religious duty. The Hindu practice of *sati*, for example, still occurs in rural communities in India, though it is illegal and is becoming much less common. Among the Aztecs, when a ruler died, his partners were commonly expected to kill themselves, as were his servants, family, retinue, and even extended relatives.

174 "double suicide": Probably the most famous text in this tradition is *Shinju Ten no Amijima* (The Love Suicides at Amijima), by the great Japanese dramatist Chikamatsu Monzaemon (1653–1725). As for *Romeo and Juliet*, the two suicides are irresistibly odd and paradoxical because Romeo kills himself only because he thinks Juliet is dead, and then Juliet kills herself because Romeo has killed himself. Shakespeare spent a lot of time thinking about suicide and is in many ways the greatest thinker on suicide in the English language. There are fourteen suicides in Shakespeare in eight different works, most of them accompanied by splendid psychological insights about self-destruction.

175 yet I firmly believe: Recently the philosopher Peggy Battin pointed out to me that a depressed person could have the good fortune to be partnered with someone who understands the disease and is in a position to help manage it, or the bad luck to be partnered with someone who misunderstands and so potentially exacerbates the condition. In AA it is almost a truism that once you get sober, you won't be able to stay married to the person who you were with as a drunk, and indeed that's been my own case. This enormous subject is beyond the scope of my investigation here, although I do discuss a bit about how my partner and my family relate to my depression, my recovery from alcoholism, and my struggles with suicide in this book.

175 Kleist probably sought out: Vogel J. Sadger, "Heinrich von Kleist" (Wiesbaden: J. F. Bergmann, 1910), 77–79. Sadger suggests that Kleist and perhaps also Vogel had the understandable impulse to die together rather than alone. Sadger, a Freudian psychoanalyst, goes on to relate this to the desire to have sex with each other and with one's mother (and, more simply, just to have company while sleeping). In supporting part of Sadger's account, Ernest Jones quoted Kleist, who wrote to his cousin of the planned dual suicide, "I must confess to you that her grave is dearer to me than the beds of all the empresses of the world."

Jones complicated Sadger's account in his essay "On 'Dying Together': With Special Reference to Heinrich von Kleist's Suicide." Here Jones pointed out that Sadger did not sufficiently emphasize the murderous and necrophiliac aspects of the suicide pact, but pointed out that the love pact style of suicide emphasized "a belief in a world beyond, a region where all hopes that are denied in this life will come true," which belief was intimately bound up with "the idea that death consists in a return to heaven whence we were born, i.e. to the mother's womb." Ernest Jones, *Essays in Applied Psychoanalysis I* (London: Hogarth Press, 1951).

175   "Kleist . . . solicited his friends": In his short story "To a Certain Friend," Akutagawa himself supposedly made a suicide pact with the wife of a friend, which however they did not carry out. See "The Life of a Stupid Man," in *Rashomon and Seventeen Other Stories* (New York: Penguin, 2009), 186–205.

175   facilitate their deaths: In a very good if sometimes scathingly unsympathetic essay on literary love suicides, Patrick Suskind insists that Kleist had been looking for a partner to die with him for months, was frustrated by his cousin's refusal to join him in the pact, and finally settled on someone "sick and depressive and stupid enough to take the part with enthusiasm, the wife of a minor civil servant." Patrick Suskind, "Moths to a Flame," *Guardian*, November 11, 2006.

176   "My golden child": Kleist, in C. H. Charles, *Love Letters of Great Men and Women* (London: Wentworth Press, 2019), 101–102.

176   "inexpressible serenity": As quoted in Sadie Stein, "Final Chapter," *Paris Review Daily*, October 16, 2014, a short, beautifully written account of Kleist and Vogel's dual suicide.

176   I've been a fan: In "Moths," Patrick Suskind, following one trend in the abundant literature on Kleist's death, argued that the case is quite simple: "Kleist . . . was fascinated all his life by suicide, saw suicide pacts as an expression of the utmost intimacy and mutual fidelity, and finally commits suicide in company because he expects the experience to give him what we would describe as the ultimate erotic kick."

176   clinical depression: Kleist's sentence "The truth is that on earth no help was possible for me" is often quoted as evidence of his despair. On this subject and for an interesting discussion of his likely depression as a cause for his suicide, see Jann E. Schlimme, "In Truth Nothing on Earth Could Help Kleist," *Der Nervenartzt* 85, no. 9 (August 2013).

177   "He climbed into": Leo Carey, "The Escape Artist: The Death and Life of Stefan Zweig," *New Yorker*, August 20, 2012.

177   "exhausted by long years": B. Hanrahan, "Death in Exile: Explaining the Suicide of Stefan Zweig," *Handelsblatt*, January 22, 2017.

177   "Healthy in body and mind": B. Mayeras, untitled article, *L'Humanité* 2780 (November 27, 1911), 1.

178   When they died: Paul Sims, "LaFargue Planned Suicide Decade Ago," *New York Times*, December 17, 1911.

178   When Laura Marx's: See Eric A. Plaut and Kevin Anderson, eds., *Marx on Suicide*, trans. Eric A. Plaut, Gabrielle Edgcomb, and Kevin Anderson (Evanston, Ill.: Northwestern University Press, 1999), 45–70.

178   free choice of death: Karl Marx was an enormous influence on both

Laura and Paul. He was philosophically indebted to ancient Greek philosophers, perhaps especially in his thoroughgoing Democritean materialism—that is, his view that the universe was made entirely of matter, that there was no afterlife, and that there was no God or gods. That may have been relevant to the decision that the couple made. Marx was a mentor to both Laura and Paul and made his much-quoted claim that "whatever he was, he wasn't a Marxist" to his son-in-law Paul Lafargue. Engels to Eduard Bernstein, November 2–3, 1882, in Karl Marx and Frederick Engels, *Collected Works* (New York: International Publishers, 1992), 46:356.

179 "in older people": James Hillman, *Suicide and the Soul* (Woodstock, N.Y.: Spring, 1965), 73.

179 Although we don't know: A particularly nice essay both on her own suicidality and on Stefan Zweig's reasons for suicide is Yiyun Li, "Memory is a Melodrama from Which No One Is Exempt," in Li, *Dear Friend, From My Life I Write to You in Your Life* (New York: Random House, 2018).

179 "in his work": Leo Carey, "The Escape Artist: The Death and Life of Stefan Zweig," *New Yorker,* August 20, 2012.

179 More mysterious is: Yiyun Li, "Lotte Zweig's Unalleviated Suffering from Asthma Was Given by Stefan Zweig as One Reason for Her Suicide," in Li, *Dear Friend, From My Life I Write to You in Your Life* (New York: Random House, 2018), 111.

180 "I salute all": Carey, "Escape Artist."

180 "descended into": Li, *Dear Friend,* 76–77.

183 "Be quick": Chikamatsu Monzaemon, *The Love Suicide at Amijima,* trans. Asataro Miyamori (Cambridge, Ont.: Parentheses, 2000), 38.

184 In many African origin: "African Origin Myths: Man Desires Death," in Hans Abrahamsson, *The Origin of Death. Studies in African Mythology* (Uppsala, Sweden: Almqvist & Wiksells Boktryckeri, 1951), 73–77. German and French translated by the author.

185 "A poison compounded": Valerius Maximus, *Memorable Doings and Sayings,* ed. and trans. D. R. Shackleton Bailey (Cambridge, Mass.: Loeb Classical Library, Harvard University Press, 2000), bk. II, 6, alternate English, 167–77.

185 reduce suicide today: See Dese'Rae L. Stage, https://livethroughthis .org/about/. See also my interview with Dese'Rae in Appendix II.

185 euthanasia: Contemporary views on euthanasia have been changing so quickly that lately one lively debate is whether medical professionals have done wrong—morally and even legally—by keeping people alive inappropriately. See Paula Span, "Filing Suit for 'Wrongful Life,'" *New York Times,* January 22, 2021.

185 I teach a class: To learn more about the euthanasia debate, a good place

to start is Robert Young's excellent 2020 entry "Voluntary Euthanasia" in *Stanford Encyclopedia of Philosophy*, https://plato.stanford.edu/entries/euthanasia-voluntary/.

186 "Monk's House, Rodmell, Sussex": Virginia Woolf to Leonard Woolf, March 18(?), 1941, in *Leave the Letters Till We're Dead: The Letters of Virginia Woolf*, ed. Nigel Nicolson (London: Hogarth Press, 1980), 6:481. Woolf was alone when she died: her partner was out of town, and she had been expecting a visit from her friend the poet T. S. Eliot, who had to cancel at the last moment.

188 The debate over what level: A good article on the ethics of euthanasia justified on psychiatric grounds is Mark S. Komrad, "A Psychiatrist Visits Belgium: The Epicenter of Psychiatric Euthanasia," *Psychiatric Times*, June 20, 2018. The debate over euthanasia justified on psychiatric grounds is growing and is the most controversial area of discussion in the ethics of euthanasia.

188 nine out of ten people: Nine out of ten who attempt suicide do not die by suicide at a later date. Only about 7 percent of those who try suicide eventually do die by suicide. About 23 percent try again but go on to live, and the remaining 70 percent don't try again. This leads us to believe what so many people who have tried suicide and failed report (and what people who talk to failed suicides also often report): that a person's suicide attempt may be a crisis rather than an expression of their long-term attitude about the value of their life. See D. Owens, J. Horrocks, and A. House, "Fatal and Non-fatal Repetition of Self-Harm: Systematic Review," *British Journal of Psychiatry* 181 (2002): 193–99.

188 "just one day": Sophocles, *Ajax*, trans. R. C. Trevelyan, in *The Complete Greek Drama*, ed. Whitney J. Oates and Eugene O'Neill, Jr. (New York: Random House, 1938), vol. 1.

189 "fall occasionally into": "The Gaspesians: Suicide, Shame, and Despair," in Chrestien Le Clercq, *New Relation of Gaspesia* (Toronto, Ont.: Champlain Society, 1910), 247–50.

189 I won't attempt to sort: Unsurprisingly, legal euthanasia for people suffering from great mental pain is proving to be even more difficult to implement than euthanasia for physical suffering. See Monica Verhofstadt, Lieve Thienpontand, and Gjalt-Jorn Ygram Peters, "When Unbearable Suffering Incites Psychiatric Patients to Request Euthanasia," *British Journal of Psychiatry* 211, no. 4 (2017): 238–45.

189 "it is up to each man": Solomon, *Noonday Demon*, 283.

189 Yet even a person: The case of Dax Cowart, famous in bioethics discussions of both euthanasia and a patient's right to refuse treatment, is an instructive one. Dax Cowart survived a gas explosion but suffered severe burns over most of his body. At the scene of the accident, he asked his rescuers to let him die. He again refused treatment at the hospital. A psy-

chiatrist evaluated him and decided he was of sound mind to make the decision to suspend the treatment—without which he would die—and yet his health professionals continued treatment, at his mother's request. The treatment was horrifyingly painful, and during sessions he would scream until he passed out. Throughout the treatment, he insisted on being allowed to die, a wish that was not respected. Later in life Dax Cowart insisted both that he was glad to be alive and that he should have been allowed to die as he wished.

190   nearly two-thirds of the gun: CDC, National Center for Injury Prevention and Control, "Web-based Injury Statistics Query and Reporting System (WISQARS) Fatal Injury Reports" for 2012–16 and 2019, https://www.cdc.gov/injury/wisqars/index.html.

7. THE SICKNESS UNTO DEATH: OBSERVATIONS FROM ÉDOUARD LEVÉ, DAVID FOSTER WALLACE, AND NELLY ARCAN

193   "the reading of works": Jean-Étienne-Dominique Esquirol, *Mental Maladies: A Treatise on Insanity*, trans. E. K. Hunt (Philadelphia: Lea & Blanchard, 1845), 253–317. Since almost no book extols suicide, but almost any book that deals with the subject may tend to romanticize it, I want to warn the reader about this fact and of course to include this, my own book, on the list of books to view with caution.

193   "Later, none of the guests": Édouard Levé, *Suicide*, trans. Jan Steyn (Champaign, Ill.: Dalkey Archive Press, 2013), 95. Quotations from Levé are taken from this novel.

193   "I have just returned": Søren Kierkegaard, *Journals*, trans. Clancy Martin, in Robert C. Solomon, *Existentialism* (New York: Oxford University Press, 2005), 7.

194   "your suicide was not": Levé, *Suicide*, 15.

194   suicide has a dramatic: For more on Hemingway, the American myth of the macho suicide, and its contribution to increased rates of death by suicide by American men, using guns, see Stephen Rodrick, "All-American Despair," *Rolling Stone*, May 30, 2019. Rodrick describes suicide among men in western states as an epidemic in part caused by this myth of a macho death.

194   The truth about Hemingway: John Rosengren, "The Last Days of Hemingway at Mayo Clinic," *Minneapolis St. Paul Magazine*, March 1, 2019.

194   "You did not fear death": Levé, *Suicide*, 15–16.

196   "You were perhaps a weak link": Levé's narrator is in some sense correct: it's entirely possible that he had a genetic predisposition toward self-destruction. General scientific consensus holds that suicide runs in families and that genetic transmission of depression and potentially sui-

cidal behavior is significant and identifiable. For a particularly fascinating discussion of the current science, see Jamison, *Night Falls*, chaps. 6 and 7.

More evidence has appeared since Jamison's book. See Ian Sample, "Gene That Raises Suicide Risk Identified," *Guardian*, November 14, 2011. In 2011 Canada's Centre for Addiction and Mental Health confirmed the existence of a specific gene related to suicide, called Brain Derived Neurotrophic Factor (BDNF) gene. The scientists, using previous studies and adding their own, found that those with a methionine variation of the gene had a higher risk of suicide than others with the valine variation. The data came from 3,352 people out of whom 1,202 had a history of suicidal behavior. "About 90 per cent of people who have died by suicide have at least one mental health disorder, the researchers note. Within the studies they reviewed, participants had schizophrenia, depression, bipolar disorder or general mood disorders. In each case, the researchers compared the genotypes of people who had attempted or completed suicide with those who were non-suicidal." The scientists here too added that many other factors apart from the genetics must be considered. Due to this research, they believe it could even be possible to increase BDNF functioning if a low-functioning BDNF variation increased suicide risk. Clement C. Zai et al., "The Brain-Derived Neurotrophic Factor Gene in Suicidal Behavior: A Meta-Analysis," *International Journal of Neuropsychopharmacology* 15, no. 8 (2012): 1037–42.

More research comes from Dr. Douglas Gray, psychiatrist and researcher at the University of Utah School of Medicine. His team examined four variants of a gene that seem to raise the risk of suicide. "Four percent of genes in the genome have current evidence associated with suicide risk," they found. "We have ascertained and studied a unique resource of 43 extended families at high risk for suicide. The design uses the distantly related, high-risk cases to magnify genetic effects, enrich for genetic homogeneity, and minimize shared environmental effects." See Hilary Coon et al., "Genome-Wide Significant Regions in 43 Utah High-Risk Families Implicate Multiple Genes Involved in Risk for Completed Suicide," *Molecular Psychiatry* 25 (2020): 3077–90.

Another study focused on how the genetic variations that may cause suicide attempts overlap with possible genetic or other neurological clues for major depression. The researchers performed a genome-wide association study (GWAS) on European American individuals. "We identified GWS associations near genes involved in anaerobic energy production (LDHB), circadian clock regulation (ARNTL2), and catabolism of tyrosine (FAH). These findings provide evidence of genetic risk factors for suicide attempt severity, providing new information regarding the molecular mechanisms involved." This study suggests that not only successfully performed suicides but suicide attempts or major depression (even where no suicide attempt has made) could be caused by genetic factors. D. F. Levey et al., "Genetic Associations with Suicide Attempt Severity and Genetic Overlap with Major Depression," *Translational Psychiatry* 9, no. 22 (2019). https://www.nature.com/articles /s41398-018-0340-2.

197 "A phenomenon that": William Styron, *Darkness Visible: A Memoir of Madness* (New York: Random House, 1990), 29.

199 "Every suicide's": Mary Karr, "Suicide's Note: An Appendix," *Poetry*, September 2012.

199 "Your suicide makes": Levé, *Suicide*, 25.

200 As a survivor: Adrienne Rich, *Adrienne Rich: Essential Essays* (New York: W. W. Norton, 2018), 151.

201 "He never outgrew": Miller told me Wallace romanticized other suicidal artists generally and was especially fascinated with Ian Curtis; he had "a morbid fascination with Curtis and the myth of the ice block." Curtis, the lead singer of the band Joy Division, died at age twenty-three. According to an urban myth, Curtis committed suicide by standing on an ice block with barbed wire around his neck as a noose. In fact, Curtis hung himself in the kitchen of his apartment with a clothesline. Biographers of Curtis mention, as causes of his suicide, his depression, his epilepsy, and especially the fact that he found himself married to one woman but in love with another. See Adrienne Miller, *In the Land of Men* (New York: Ecco, 2020). D. T. Max, in his biography of Wallace, also discusses the fascination with Curtis.

202 "People who have not": Li, *Dear Friend*, 72.

202 Sure, the person leaping: Reminding me of Wallace's case, Arthur Schopenhauer wrote that "great mental suffering makes us insensible to bodily pain; we despise it; nay, if it should outweigh the other, it distracts our thoughts, and we welcome it as a pause in mental suffering. It is this feeling that makes suicide easy; for the bodily pain that accompanies it loses all significance in the eyes of one who is tortured by an excess of mental suffering. This is especially evident in the case of those who are driven to suicide by some purely morbid and exaggerated ill-humor. No special effort to overcome their feelings is necessary, nor do such people require to be worked up in order to take the step; but as soon as the keeper into whose charge they are given leaves them for a couple of minutes, they quickly bring their life to an end." Schopenhauer, "On Suicide," in *Studies in Pessimism: A Series of Essays*, trans. T. Bailey Saunders (London: Swan Sonnenschein, 1893), 43–50.

204 "You are the sickness": The Buddha used to begin many of his sermons with the observation that "you must think of yourself as one who is sick." Arcan too mentions this feeling of the sickness of the suicidal self, writing in *Whore*, "Ladies and gentlemen, I am sick of this . . . and at the moment I am sick of not being able to name the sickness that I have, and

you will see that I will die because of it." Nelly Arcan, *Putain* (Montreal: Média Diffusion, 2019), 22. I find it comforting that feeling spiritually sick may be not necessarily a symptom of suicidal thinking but an opportunity for spiritual growth. Certainly in the thought of Kierkegaard, for example, despair is a necessary though not a sufficient precondition for coming to know God.

204   "it's wearing your face": David Foster Wallace, *The David Foster Wallace Reader* (Boston: Little, Brown, 2014), 193.

204   "It is not the least": David Foster Wallace, *This Is Water* (Boston: Little, Brown, 2009), 59.

206   "had some very heavy": David Foster Wallace, "Suicide as a Sort of Present," in *Brief Interviews with Hideous Men* (Boston: Little, Brown, 1999), 283–84.

206   "As he [the child]": Ibid., 286.

207   "unending psychic shit": Here our narrator almost quotes the suicidal young soldier-in-training Leonard in Stanley Kubrick's *Full Metal Jacket*, who says, "I am in a world of shit," immediately before shooting himself in the head.

207   "So it went": Ibid.

209   "The reality is": David Foster Wallace, "Good Old Neon," *Oblivion: Stories* (Boston: Little, Brown, 2004), 143.

209   "My whole life": Ibid., 141.

210   "the more time": Ibid., 147.

210   "one of the many": Adrienne Miller to author, June 5, 2021.

215   "double agents": Laurie Woolever, *Bourdain: The Definitive Oral Biography* (New York: HarperCollins, 2021), 24.

215   Kierkegaard says in one: Soren Kierkegaard, *The Sickness unto Death*, trans. Alistair Hannay (trans. modified) (New York: Penguin, 2004), 43.

215   "to somehow reconcile": Wallace, "Good Old Neon," 144.

216   "I hope I've become": Adrienne Miller to author, June 5, 2021.

217   "finally given myself": Nelly Arcan, *Exit*, trans. David Scott Hamilton (Vancouver: Anvil Press, 2011), 29.

217   "Do you want": Ibid., 59.

217   The lack of clear: Arcan, *Exit*, 28.

217   The idea of purity: She also has some other provisos—the company refuses to provide its services to pregnant women, for example. One pregnant client, refused services by the company, subsequently explodes herself and her unborn child with a hand grenade inserted into her vagina. This is classic Arcan: like her life, her work is unhappy and dark, and like one of her influences, Georges Bataille, she often combines violence and sex.

218   "Our veins": Arcan, *Exit*, 123.

219   "I did not know": Arcan, *Putain*, 89.

220 "On the day of my fifteenth": Nelly Arcan, *Folle* (Montreal: Média Diffusion, 2009), 13.

220 "As far as you are": Ibid., 144.

221 "it wasn't the liberation": Arcan, *Exit*, 34–35.

8. THE AFTERLIFE, OR, WELCOME TO THE PSYCH WARD

228 Did he miss: Now it occurs to me that the tiler was just following a pattern mandated by the subcontractor who installed the floors. But at that time anything that seemed like a human touch from outside the walls of the hospital represented the possibility of kindness, happiness, and a better life.

237 When you phone: I have been in jail seven times, usually due to being drunk, though I've also been jailed for other reasons. I wrote about it in Clancy Martin, "Jail Is Where You Don't Want to Be," *Vice*, November 13, 2016.

242 He knew what he: Unfortunately, in my experience, it is difficult and perhaps dangerous to be honest with almost anyone about suicide—except another person who has tried to commit suicide, ideally someone who tried recently. In *Mrs. Dalloway*, writing about her hero Septimus who eventually kills himself, Virginia Woolf put the peril of trying honestly to talk about suicide like this: "But he had talked of killing himself. 'We all have our moments of depression,' said Sir William. Once you fall, Septimus repeated to himself, human nature is on you. Holmes and Bradshaw are on you. They scour the desert. They fly screaming into the wilderness. The rack and the thumbscrew are applied. Human nature is remorseless." Virginia Woolf, *Mrs. Dalloway* (London: Harcourt Brace, 1953), 91–102. This observation that human nature is remorseless, especially with the weak—and a suicidal person like me might be wise to include himself in the class of the weak—ought to give us pause. It's a dark wisdom, a wisdom of fear and depression, but wisdom is there. I think it is so important for suicidal people to reach out for help. But I am sorry to say that I also want to remind those people to reach out with caution and discrimination.

10. THEY FUCK YOU UP / YOUR MUM AND DAD (PART II)

266 early childhood trauma: This is widely documented, but see especially Kees Van Heeringen, *The NeuroScience of Suicidal Behavior* (Cambridge: Cambridge University Press, 2018), 120–45.

273 My second anklet: Here I'd like to thank Ellen Rosenbush and the rest of the team at *Harper's* magazine, who kindly helped to finance my anklet. I tried to write a story about it for *Harper's*, but it never got past the kill

stage, and I am indebted to them for believing in me and paying much of the cost associated with my electronic monitoring.

284 Not a device: See the recent fascinating article Will Stephenson, "The Undiscovered Country: Can Suicide Be Predicted?" *Harper's*, August 2021.

11. A GOOD DEATH?

290 "His friend bent over": *Rashomon*, 190.

291 "What I propose is": William James, "Is Life Worth Living?" in *The Will to Believe and Other Essays in Popular Philosophy* (New York: Longmans, Green, 1896), 32–62.

292 "It is of great importance": William Styron, *Darkness Visible: A Memoir of Madness* (New York: Random House, 1990), 42.

293 "Reduce the pain": Edwin S. Shneidman, *The Suicidal Mind* (New York: Oxford University Press, 1996), 139.

296 "Answers don't fly": Yiyun Li, *Where Reasons End* (New York: Random House, 2019), 170.

297 "And at some point": Nietzsche never wrote any such book. It must have been something collated by an editor out of various works.

297 "There is a glory": Chögyam Trungpa Rinpoche, *Training the Mind* (Boulder, Colo.: Shambhala, 2003), 76.

300 "To the question of nutrition": Friedrich Nietzsche, "Why I Am So Clever," in *Ecce Homo*, my translation.

301 He extends this: See my friend John Kaag's terrific *Hiking with Nietzsche* (New York: Farrar, Straus & Giroux, 2018).

302 "An almost infallible": "Cato: On Suicide, and the Abbe St. Cyran's Book Legitimating Suicide," in *Voltaire's Philosophical Dictionary*, ed. and trans. William F. Fleming (New York: E. R. DuMont, 1901), 3:19–33.

305 I don't think I would: We were first in touch when she emailed me to interview me about the novel. I was in a relationship at that time, but later, when I was single again, I got in touch with her in part because she was the only person I've ever spoken to who understood the importance of the father character in that novel, who was directly based on my own dad.

305 "We cover our feet": Khyentse Norbu is the secular name of Dzongsar Jamyang Khyentse Rinpoche. In this book I have generally shortened his name to Khyentse Rinpoche.

307 rats in painful environments: Patricia Hadaway et al., "The Effect of Housing and Gender on Preference for Morphine-Sucrose Solutions in Rats," *Psychopharmacology* 66, no. 1 (November 1979): 87–91.

308 "What is false": Paul-Louis Landsberg, *The Experience of Death and the Moral Problem of Suicide*, trans. Cynthia Rowland (New York: Philosophical Library, 1953), 79.

313 "I deserve death": Nelly Arcan, *Putain* (Montreal: Média Diffusion, 2019).

316 "Tony . . . was a control freak": Laurie Woolever, *Bourdain: The Definitive Oral Biography* (New York: HarperCollins, 2021), 421.

316 "Suicides, like all": Jean-Étienne-Dominique Esquirol, *Mental Maladies: A Treatise on Insanity*, trans. E. K. Hunt (Philadelphia: Lea & Blanchard, 1845), 253–317.

322 "suicide is the urge": James Hillman, *Suicide and the Soul* (Woodstock, N.Y.: Spring, 1965), 73.

322 "His impatience was fucking": Woolever, *Bourdain*, 240.

322 "Very typical is": Fyodor Dostoevsky, *The Diary of a Writer*, trans. Boris Brasol (New York: Charles Scribner's Sons, 1949), 157–58, 335–38.

323 "You're impatient with": Yiyun Li, *Dear Friend, From My Life I Write to You in Your Life* (New York: Random House, 2018), 112.

323 "Your impatience": Édouard Levé, *Suicide*, trans. Jan Steyn (Champaign, Ill.: Dalkey Archive Press, 2013), 92.

324 "As for the advance": Margo Jefferson, interview by author, August 5, 2021.

326 "A question, not answered": Jean Améry, *On Suicide: A Discourse on Voluntary Death* (Bloomington: Indiana University Press, 1999), 131.

326 "I myself *am*": Martin Heidegger, *Being and Time*, trans Joan Stambaugh (Buffalo: State University of New York Press, 2010), 207.

329 "is merely confessing": Albert Camus, *The Myth of Sisyphus and Other Essays*, trans. Justin O'Brien (1942; New York: Vintage Books, 1955), 93.

330 "I can say nothing": Sarah Davys, *A Time and a Time: An Autobiography* (London: Calder & Boyars, 1971), 13.

330 She goes on: Ibid., 13.

330 "My concern is now": Ibid., 13.

331 "This is how I seem": Ibid., 63–64.

APPENDIX II. IN CASE OF EMERGENCY

343 "Suicide is a habit": Dzongsar Jamyang Khyentse Rinpoche, *Living Is Dying* (Boulder, Colo.: Shambhala, 2020), 184.

343 On other, more literal: Andrew Holocek, *Preparing to Die* (Boulder, Colo.: Snow Lion, 2013), 389n18.

364 It's a list of ten: These questions are indebted to "Ten Commonalities of Suicide," in Edwin S. Shneidman, *The Suicidal Mind* (New York: Oxford University Press, 1996), 131.

Index

A NOTE ABOUT THE AUTHOR

Clancy Martin is the acclaimed author of the novel *How to Sell* as well as numerous books on philosophy. A Guggenheim fellow, his writing has appeared in *The New Yorker*, *New York*, *The Atlantic*, *Harper's*, *Esquire*, *The New Republic*, *Lapham's Quarterly*, *The Believer*, and *The Paris Review*. He is a professor of philosophy at the University of Missouri in Kansas City and Ashoka University in New Delhi. He is the survivor of more than ten suicide attempts and a recovering alcoholic.

A NOTE ON THE TYPE

This book was set in Janson, a typeface long thought to have been made by the Dutchman Anton Janson, who was a practicing type-founder in Leipzig during the years 1668–1687. It has been conclusively demonstrated, however, that these types are actually the work of Nicholas Kis (1650–1702), a Hungarian, who most probably learned his trade from the master Dutch typefounder Dirk Voskens. The type is an excellent example of the influential and sturdy Dutch types that prevailed in England up to the time William Caslon (1692–1766) developed his own incomparable designs from them.

Typeset by Scribe,
Philadelphia, Pennsylvania

Printed and bound by Berryville Graphics,
Berryville, Virginia